GROWING URBAN ECONOMIES

Innovation, Creativity, and Governance in Canadian City-Regions

Even in a globalizing, knowledge-based economy, cities remain engines of growth, innovation, and diversity. Increasingly, they are also active participants in the creation of the social and political conditions necessary to create a thriving community. The Innovation, Creativity, and Governance in Canadian City-Regions series is a focused analysis of how developments at the local and regional level affect these three key determinants of future prosperity. *Growing Urban Economies* summarizes the series's conclusions in a single volume that presents an overview of the evidence and its implications.

A rich and nuanced analysis of the interplay of social, political, and economic factors in thirteen Canadian city-regions, large and small, this collection integrates research focusing on innovation, creativity and talent-retention, and governance in order to understand the distinctive experience of each region. A valuable cross-section of city-region development in a variety of circumstances, *Growing Urban Economies* offers important insights into the ways in which local conditions affect urban economies around the world.

DAVID A. WOLFE is a professor in the Department of Political Science at the University of Toronto Mississauga and co-director of the Innovation Policy Lab at the Munk School of Global Affairs. He was National Coordinator of the Innovation Systems Research Network.

MERIC S. GERTLER is the president of the University of Toronto, the Goldring Chair in Canadian Studies, and a professor in the Department of Geography.

INNOVATION, CREATIVITY, AND GOVERNANCE IN CANADIAN CITY-REGIONS

Series editor: David A. Wolfe

The series on *Innovation, Creativity, and Governance in Canadian City-Regions* presents the research results of a six-year, sixteen-city study of the social dynamics of innovation, creativity, and civic governance in Canadian cities. The first three volumes in the series provide detailed analyses of each of the three research themes carried out across a selection of large, mid-sized, and small Canadian cities, and the fourth one integrates the key findings across all themes for the individual cases.

While the cases covered are primarily Canadian, the volumes present the material in an international and comparative context that addresses ongoing intellectual and policy debates concerning urban economic development and civic governance. As such, the series offers important new insights that contribute to our contemporary understanding of the relationship between urban social dynamics and economic performance.

Growing Urban Economies

Innovation, Creativity, and Governance in Canadian City-Regions

EDITED BY DAVID A. WOLFE
AND MERIC S. GERTLER

UNIVERSITY OF TORONTO PRESS
Toronto Buffalo London

Toronto Buffalo London
www.utppublishing.com

ISBN 978-1-4426-2943-1 (cloth) ISBN 978-1-4426-2944-8 (paper)

Library and Archives Canada Cataloguing in Publication

Growing urban economies : innovation, creativity, and governance in Canadian city-regions / edited by David A. Wolfe and Meric S. Gertler.

(Innovation, creativity, and governance in Canadian city-regions)
Includes bibliographical references.
ISBN 978-1-4426-2943-1 (cloth). – ISBN 978-1-4426-2944-8 (paper)

1. Urban economics – Canada. 2. Community development, Urban – Canada. 3. Regional economics – Canada. I. Wolfe, David A., author, editor II. Gertler, Meric S., editor III. Series: Innovation, creativity, and governance in Canadian city-regions (Toronto, Ont.)

HT127.G76 2016 307.760971 C2015-907875-X

University of Toronto Press acknowledges the financial assistance to its publishing program of the Canada Council for the Arts and the Ontario Arts Council, an agency of the Government of Ontario.

Contents

List of Tables and Figures vii

Foreword to the Series ix

Acknowledgments xv

Part I: Introduction

1 Innovation, Creativity, and Governance in Canadian City-Regions 5
DAVID A. WOLFE AND MERIC S. GERTLER

Part II: The Dynamics of Economic Change in Large Cities

2 Toronto's Fourth Era: An Emerging Cognitive-Cultural Economy 51
DAVID A. WOLFE AND ALLISON BRAMWELL

3 The Revitalization of Montreal: The Significance of Social Innovation as a Pillar for Economic Development 82
DIANE-GABRIELLE TREMBLAY, NORMA M. RANTISI, AND JUAN-LUIS KLEIN

4 Vancouver and the Economy of Culture and Innovation 109
TOM HUTTON AND TREVOR BARNES

5 Moving from Complaisance Revisited: Ottawa Trying Again to Define Its Regional Advantage 139
CAROLINE ANDREW AND DAVID DOLOREUX

6 Innovation from an Oil and Gas Platform: Calgary 157
COOPER H. LANGFORD, BEN LI, AND CAMILLE D. RYAN

Part III: Innovation and Growth in Medium-Sized Cities

7 Innovation in an Industrial City: Economic Transformation in Hamilton 181
PETER WARRIAN AND ALLISON BRAMWELL

8 A City of Two Tales: Innovation, Talent Attraction, and Governance in Canada's Technology Triangle 211
TARA VINODRAI

9 Ordinary City at the Crossroads: London, Ontario 239
NEIL BRADFORD

10 The Social Dynamics of Economic Performance in Halifax 265
JILL L. GRANT

Part IV: Innovation for Survival or Growth in Canada's Small Cities

11 Saskatoon: From Small Town to Global Hub 287
PETER W.B. PHILLIPS AND GRAEME WEBB

12 The Social Dynamics of Economic Performance in the Public-Sector City: Kingston, Ontario 311
BETSY DONALD AND HEATHER HALL

13 Moncton: Innovative or Resilient City? 334
YVES BOURGEOIS

14 The Social Dynamics of Economic Performance in St John's: A Metropolis on the Margins 363
ROB GREENWOOD AND HEATHER HALL

Appendix A: City-Region Profiles 389

Appendix B: Maps 403

Contributors 417

Tables and Figures

Tables

2.1 Key socio-economic and demographic characteristics of the Toronto CMA, 2011 57
4.1 Employment by industry for Greater Vancouver, 1996, 2001, 2006 116
4.2 Experienced labour force by occupations and gender: Vancouver CMA 123
5.1 High-tech and KIBS employment in Ottawa, 2006 144
6.1 Intra- and inter-sectoral knowledge inputs (percentages of knowledge received from originating sectors) 164
7.1 Clusters and employment, Hamilton 2001–6 186
8.1 Key socio-economic and demographic characteristics of the Kitchener CMA, 2006 214
8.2 Industrial clusters in the Kitchener CMA, 2001 and 2006 216
10.1 Halifax population characteristics 267
10.2 Industry characteristics in Halifax, 2006 268
10.3 Industrial clusters in Halifax, 2001 and 2006 268
12.1 Major employers in Kingston, 2015 314
12.2 Socio-economic indicators 315
12.3 PARTEQ statistics, 2009 317
13.1 Key population characteristics, Moncton, and aggregated city sizes, 2011 342
14.1 St John's profile 367

Figures

5.1 High-tech and KIBS employment change in Ottawa, 1971–81, 1981–91, 1991–2001 145

8.1 Growth, size, and industry specialization in the Kitchener CMA, 2001–6 215

Foreword to the Series

Innovating in Urban Economies: Economic Transformation in Canadian City-Regions

Innovation and creative capacity are essential determinants of economic prosperity in a globalizing, knowledge-based economy. Although the process of globalization has led to numerous predictions of the "death of distance," growing evidence suggests that the contemporary global economy make cities more – not less –important as sites of production, distribution, and innovation. Over the past decade, recognition has grown that even the most global of economic activities remain fundamentally rooted in city-regions as critical sites for organizing economic activity. More significantly, the social dynamics of city-regions are crucial in shaping economic outcomes (Gertler 2001).

The interactive and social nature of the innovation process makes city-regions the appropriate scale at which social learning unfolds. Knowledge transfer between highly skilled people happens more easily in cities while talent flows within and between cities is a critical means for the dissemination of innovative ideas. In a country with diverse and strongly differentiated regional economies, relationships between economic actors, organizations, and institutions at the local and regional scale are crucial factors affecting national prosperity. The concentrations of talented people and skilled occupations in urban centres are seen as critical sources of the creative and innovative ideas that generate growth in city-regions. And leading urban regions are no longer prepared to be passive objects at the hands of globalizing forces associated with the spread of information technologies, but are taking control of their own economic future through efforts aimed at the "strategic management" of their own economies (Audretsch 2002). From this perspective, many of the foundations of economic success in a globalizing, knowledge-based economy are the social qualities and properties of urban places.

The chapters in this series report on the research results of a six-year study of the social dynamics of economic performance in Canadian city-regions by members of the Innovation Systems Research Network (ISRN). The ISRN itself was an innovative experiment in knowledge management that came into existence in 1998 through the leadership of the Social Sciences and Humanities Research Council and its partners, the National Research Council and Natural Sciences and Engineering Research Council. The ISRN is a collaborative, multidisciplinary network of university-based researchers analysing how innovation processes unfold in different regions and localities across the country. Since its inception in 1998, the network's research has focused on how the interaction of the major components of the regional innovation system shape innovation and social learning that is critical for Canada's success in the knowledge-based economy. Its primary objectives have been: (1) to understand the process by which regional networks foster the production and circulation of knowledge that is critical to innovation, and (2) to deepen our understanding of the role of public policy in facilitating (or impeding) this process (Holbrook and Wolfe 2005).

The goal of the ISRN's first research program from 2001 to 2005 was to determine the prevalence and success of local industrial clusters across Canada and to analyse how the formation and growth of these clusters contribute to local economic growth and innovative capacity. Underlying this objective was a set of fundamental conceptual questions: How do local assets and relationships between economic actors enable firms – in any industry – to become more innovative? Under what circumstances does "the local" matter, and how important are local sources of knowledge and locally generated institutions (public and private) in strengthening the innovative capabilities of firms and industries? What is the relative importance of non-local actors, relationships, and flows of knowledge in shaping the development trajectories of localized innovation and growth?

The results of that five-year project made a distinctly Canadian contribution to the study of industrial clusters. The international literature on clusters and regional innovation systems recognizes that in a global marketplace, local input factors and inter-firm dynamics are critical to a firm's ability to innovate and thereby gain competitive advantage. But, as noted above, a critical question addressed in the ISRN study concerns the relative importance of local versus non-local factors in cluster performance and the relationship between the two sets of factors. The ISRN case studies provided important insights into these questions. They documented a balance between the relative impact of local and non-local relationships and knowledge flows – in other words, the dynamic tension between the local "buzz" and global "pipelines" that circulate knowledge between clusters (Bathelt, Malmberg, and Maskell 2004). They underlined the sectoral specificity of industrial clusters – clusters in different sectors draw upon different knowledge bases, which influence both innovation within the clusters and the underlying relationship between the cluster and the research infrastructure that supports it. The case studies also highlighted the centrality of a strong, dynamic talent base, or "thick" labour market for the success of most clusters. The ability to draw upon a plentiful supply of labour with the skills required by cluster firms is often the most critical factor that attracts them to, and anchors them in, a specific geographic location (Wolfe 2009a).

Finally, the case studies suggested that some of the most successful clusters have profited from the development of strong social networks at the community level and the emergence of dedicated, community-based organizations. These entities link leaders in the individual clusters to a broader cross-section of the community. They appear to be supported by new institutions of civic governance that identify problems impeding the growth of the cluster and help mobilize support across the community for proposed solutions. The research also found some evidence to suggest that size is a critical variable in the success of civic engagement, with some of the larger, urban centres encountering greater difficulty in achieving effective degrees of mobilization (Wolfe and Nelles 2008).

The results of the first ISRN project led to the overwhelming conclusion that many of the most significant factors that underlay the performance of individual clusters were not specific to the cluster itself. The research thus led to the conclusion that the social characteristics, dynamics, and relationships within the wider city-region are important determinants of economic performance. This led the members of the network to undertake a second Major Collaborative Research Initiative (MCRI) with funding from SSHRC and other partners to investigate the social dynamics of innovation and economic performance, with the city-region as the primary unit of analysis. The second MCRI project from 2006 to 2011 set out to analyse what were believed to be three key determinants of the economic performance at the local level: the broader dynamics of innovation and knowledge flows, the role of creativity and talent, and the contribution made by new forms of civic governance in Canadian city-regions (Wolfe 2009b).

The study involved detailed investigations off all three of these themes – innovation, talent, and governance – in a sample of sixteen large, medium, and small Canadian cities across eight provinces, resulting in more than fifty case studies. Each case was examined using a common research methodology, based primarily on in-depth interviews with key participants in critical sectors in the local economy using common interview guides. The key questions for each theme were largely the same, but were structured to reflect the researchers' detailed knowledge of their own local economy and institutions.

This series of four volumes presents the results of a selection of the case studies conducted under each of themes. The present volume summarizes the complete findings from the six-year research project and integrates the major insights and conclusions published in the three previous volumes of the series. The individual chapters illuminate the contribution that urban size, relative location, the nature of the regional economy, the underlying social and economic dynamics of individual city-regions are making to the trajectory of development in the emerging knowledge-based economy of the twenty-first century. The volume provides a rich and nuanced analysis of how the interplay of the factors that influence innovation, creativity, and governance are influencing the development of the urban landscape across a broad cross-section of Canadian city-regions.

David A. Wolfe, Series editor

References

Audretsch, D.B. 2002. "The innovative advantage of US Cities." *European Planning Studies* 10 (2): 165–76. http://dx.doi.org/10.1080/09654310120114472.

Bathelt, H., A. Malmberg, and P. Maskell. 2004. "Clusters and knowledge: Local buzz, global pipelines and the process of knowledge creation." *Progress in Human Geography* 28 (1): 31–56. http://dx.doi.org/10.1191/0309132504ph469oa.

Gertler, M.S. 2001. "Urban economy and society in Canada: Flows of people, capital and ideas." *Isuma: Canadian Journal of Policy Research* 2 (3): 119–30.

Holbrook, J.A., and D.A. Wolfe. 2005. "The Innovation Systems Research Network: A Canadian experiment in knowledge management." *Science & Public Policy* 32 (2): 109–18.

Wolfe, D.A. 2009a. "Introduction: Embedded clusters in a global economy." *European Planning Studies* 17 (2): 179–87. http://dx.doi.org/10.1080/09654310802553407.

–. 2009b. *21st century cities in Canada: The geography of innovation*. Ottawa: Conference Board of Canada.

Wolfe, D.A., and J. Nelles. 2008. "The role of civic capital and civic associations in cluster policies." In *Handbook of research on innovations and cluster policies*, ed. Charlie Karlsson, 374–92. Cheltenham, UK: Edward Elgar Publishers. http://dx.doi.org/10.4337/9781848445079.00030.

Acknowledgments

A national research project inevitably ends with an army of people and institutions whose contributions merit gratitude. First and foremost, the team acknowledges the vital financial and advisory inputs provided by funding agencies and partners in the research. The primary source of funding for the work came from the Social Sciences and Humanities Research Council of Canada through the Major Collaborative Research Initiatives program #412-2005-1001. Throughout the work SSHRC proved immensely supportive of the team's activities.

In addition we appreciate the support of our research partners: Atlantic Canada Opportunities Agency, Health Technology Exchange, National Research Council, Nova Scotia Economic Development, Ontario Ministries of Economic Development and Trade, Research and Innovation and Economic Development and Innovation, Queen's University, Ryerson University, Simon Fraser University, Statistics Canada, Université Laval, University of Toronto, as well as in-kind support from THECIS in Calgary.

The team's annual meetings (King City, Ontario 2006; Vancouver and Bowen Island 2007; Montreal 2008; Halifax 2009; Toronto 2010) would not have proven productive without the contributions of local organizing groups who helped with logistics, policymakers who participated in the knowledge-exchange opportunities of the policy events, and the local partners mentioned above who provided additional funding.

Several people played pivotal roles in running the research program. This project has been a true partnership from the outset. Without the intellectual guidance and supportive friendship of Meric Gertler, it would not have been possible to see this project through to its successful conclusion. Deborah Huntley, who has been an indispensable member of the team over two major research projects, provided excellent administrative skills that kept the project on time, on track, and on budget. These three key individuals were joined on the project management committee by Charles Davis, Jill Grant, Adam Holbrook, and Réjean Landry. At and between the annual meetings, the team received guidance and oversight from the project's Research Advisory Board: Bjørn Asheim, Susan Christopherson, Susan Clarke, Philip Cooke, Hervey Gibson, Gernot Grabher, Anders Malmberg, Peter Maskell, Kevin Morgan, Claire Nauwelaers, Tod Rutherford, and Allen Scott. Their willingness to freely devote their time to our endeavours is a testament to the collegiality and their dedication to scholarship.

Teams in each of the city-regions studied, coordinated, and conducted the case study work, and many city-region teams involved several junior colleagues and students – too numerous to name – who made invaluable contributions to the work. Many began working on the project as doctoral students, graduated to post-doctoral fellows, and ultimately became colleagues and collaborators.

Without the participation of community members from across the country who donated their time and knowledge to the team in agreeing to sit for interviews or complete surveys, none of this work would be possible. The team sincerely appreciates their willingness to share their wisdom and experience, and hopes that they find the results of the research useful in their efforts to keep their communities vital and progressive.

Final thanks go to Daniel Quinlan and his team at the University of Toronto Press for believing in the importance of bringing this work to a wider audience and for providing assistance along the way to make it possible.

GROWING URBAN ECONOMIES

Innovation, Creativity, and Governance in Canadian City-Regions

PART I

Introduction

1 Innovation, Creativity, and Governance in Canadian City-Regions

DAVID A. WOLFE AND MERIC S. GERTLER

Introduction

The first decade and a half of the twenty-first century has been marked by a profound series of changes in the global economy. Dramatic fluctuations in resource prices, particularly oil, and the continued shift of production to new locations in East Asia and the Global South have been punctuated by the impact of two major recessions. Compounding the problems experienced with the cyclical swings in the economy, the twin forces of globalization and technological change are radically altering the industrial structure of the advanced economies, undermining and transforming industries and eliminating jobs on a wide scale. Many leading regions of the world, including Canada, have struggled to regain the levels of economic performance achieved before 2008. The uncertainty generated by this pace of change, compounded by the cyclical instability caused by the past two recessions, has raised fundamental questions about the future sources of economic growth and employment in the industrial economies and the geography of innovation and production across both industrial and industrializing countries.

The growing interest in the shifting geography of innovation and production has led to a greater interest in the contribution of city-regions to the future dynamism and growth of the economy. Over the course of this period, recognition has grown that even the most global of economic activities remain fundamentally rooted in regions in general, and city-regions in particular, as critical sites for organizing economic activity. In its most simple terms, a city-region is a continuous network of urban communities, whose "boundaries move outward – or halt – only as city economic energy dictates" (Jacobs 1984, 45). More precisely, it can be defined as "the presence of a core city linked by functional ties to a hinterland. The nature of those ties … generally includes a combination of economic, housing market, travel-to-work, marketing, or retail catchment factors" (Rodríguez-Pose 2008, 1027). This renewed focus on the role of city-regions stems from the acknowledgment of both the limits of national and sub-national governments in meeting the challenges that confront twenty-first century economies, as well as of the growing centrality of city-regions as the principal sites for innovation and creativity in generating the ideas, firms, and industries that will create the future sources of economic growth. In effect, the focus is shifting to metropolitan regions out of an increasingly widespread recognition that they are the future drivers of innovation and growth: "Metros dominate because they embody concentration and agglomeration – networks of innovative firms, talented workers, risk-taking entrepreneurs, and supportive institutions and associations that cluster together in metropolitan areas and co-produce economic performance and progress. There is, in essence, no American (or Chinese, or German or Brazilian) economy; rather a national economy is a network of metropolitan "economies" (Katz and Bradley 2013, 1). Despite this growing awareness, the role of the urban region remains profoundly conflicted in twenty-first-century society and politics. There remains a deep reluctance to accord city-regions both the constitutional and political status, as well as the fiscal resources they require to realize this potential. Nonetheless, many city-regions are seizing the initiative to direct their own economic futures by launching new institutional ventures to leverage federal and provincial resources and promote their own futures.

These challenges, concerns, and opportunities provide the motivation for the chapters collected in this volume. Together they represent the summation of a multi-year national study of innovation, creativity, and governance in Canadian city-regions. The project, conceived in 2005 and launched in 2006, set out to investigate the changing role of Canadian city-regions in responding to the challenges of innovation and growth and the extent to which new institutional forms were being adopted at the urban level to respond to these challenges. The project started by recognizing the paradox that, as economic processes move increasingly to a global scale of operation, the centrality of the local has become more important, rather than less. In short, city-regions have become key nodes in the production and flow of ideas (Gertler 2001).

Moreover, we also believed that it is the social character of cities that is responsible for the renewed importance of the local in the global economy. In other words, the foundations of economic success in an increasingly global and competitive world are the social qualities and properties of urban places. This means that the decisions that shape the social character of cities have direct consequences for our overall economic well-being. The interactive and social nature of innovation makes city-regions the appropriate scale at which social learning unfolds. Knowledge transfer between highly skilled people happens more easily in cities. The decisions that shape the social character of urban centres thus have direct consequences for their economic well-being. In a country with diverse and strongly differentiated regional economies, relationships between economic actors, organizations, and institutions at the local and regional scale are crucial factors affecting national prosperity. And leading urban regions are no longer prepared to be passive objects at the hands of globalizing locational forces associated with the spread of information and communication technologies and the knowledge-based economy, but are taking control of their own economic future through efforts aimed at the "strategic management" of their economies. From this perspective, many of the foundations of economic success in a globalizing, knowledge-based economy are the social qualities and properties of urban places.

Globalization and the rapidly increasing pace of innovation pose a dual set of challenges and opportunities for city-regions. Alongside the increased capital flows associated with globalization are people flows that bring large numbers of immigrants predominantly to major urban areas. The success with which an urban region can generate and retain creative activity also depends on its quality of place and community characteristics that promote strong cohesion. The task of responding to these challenges – to compete on the basis of quality of place, quality of life, and innovation, to prevent social polarization and spatial segregation and to accommodate ethnic diversity and cultural pluralism – demands a coherent response from all levels of government, from the national to the local. Yet, increasingly, the city-region is being recognized as an especially important scale at which such strategies must be formulated. Thus, the emerging thesis that guided our research is that the social qualities and dynamics of city-regions constitute the foundations of economic success in the global economy. This chapter provides an overview of the major conceptual frames of reference that guided our collaborative research and contributed to our understanding of these critical local and regional dimensions of innovation.

Although the economic role of cities is increasing in general, not all cities enjoy the same economic prospects. While standard neoclassical theory suggests that initial differences among urban regions should gradually be levelled through the effects of market forces, the evidence points to the opposite result (Venables 2006). As the world economy becomes more globalized, the pressure increases for city-regions to create distinct advantages across a diverse range of sectors and industries. Variations in the ability of cities to create and diffuse new knowledge appear to be important for their long-term growth prospects, as well as their ability to adjust to changing economic conditions. Indeed, as John Montgomery argues, "At the end of the day, there are only a handful of means by which city and urban regional economies can grow. One is the introduction of new production processes and services to create new work and new divisions of labour ... More important than this even is the extension of new technologies to create new products and therefore economic sectors" (Montgomery 2007, 29). This introduces a distinctly Schumpeterian dimension into the analysis of urban economics that underlines the impact of the capacity to innovate. New economy sectors are sustained by the continuous pace of innovation and learning needed to keep abreast of the rapidly moving knowledge frontier in their industries.

The social nature of innovation means that city-regions provide the locale in which the transmission and diffusion of knowledge necessary for innovation occurs. But as Edward Glaeser perceptively notes, "The urban ability to create collaborative brilliance isn't new. For centuries, innovations have spread from person to person across crowded city streets" (Glaeser 2011, 8; Hall 1998). The dense concentration of economic actors in cities offers multiple opportunities for contact, interaction, and exchange of ideas among highly skilled people. Canada's city-regions are not just the dominant sites of economic activity; they are also the leading edges of innovation that will generate the new ideas, new products, and new industries that will drive the economy in the future.

The economic and social characteristics of different cities profoundly influence the life prospects for the residents of those cities. As a result of this difference, it is important to understand how the underlying social and economic characteristics of cities that contribute to their innovative performance, their ability to attract and retain a talented workforce, as well as to fashion the kind of new governance institutions deemed to underlie the metropolitan revolution (Katz and Bradley 2013). It was to answer these questions that the contributors to this volume, in conjunction with other members of the Innovation Systems Research Network, launched this research in 2006. Each of the case studies included in this volume employed a common research methodology based on key interviews with a cross section of local actors in their respective city-region. The research agenda for the project focused on three specific questions:

1. Concerning the *social nature of innovation*, we hypothesized that the economic performance of city-regions depends on the structure (density and diversity) of local networks – in particular, a mix of strong and weak ties, as well as the heterogeneity and diversity of economic actors belonging to these networks.
2. Concerning the *social foundations of talent attraction and retention*, we hypothesized that the economic performance of city-regions depends on a set of characteristics that define quality of place, including cultural dynamism, social diversity, openness and tolerance, social inclusion and cohesion.
3. Concerning *social inclusion and civic engagement*, we hypothesized that the economic performance of city-regions depends on their ability to generate effective new forms of associative governance (including, but not limited to, government). Moreover, in those cases where such new forms of governance have been designed in socially inclusive ways, we were particularly interested in documenting the impact this has on the nature of development strategies pursued by city-regions, as well as the ultimate success of their regional economies.

Dynamics of Innovation and Knowledge Transfer in City-Regions

As noted above, different cities exhibit significantly different growth patterns. Recent conceptual theorizing and empirical research, particularly within the evolutionary economics perspective, underlines the context-specific nature of the way in which cities develop. The innovative performance of both individual firms and agglomerations of firms within city-regions is strongly affected by the way in which capabilities are built up and accumulate within cities over time. As Richard Shearmur has recently argued, "Each locality will evolve in relation to its past trajectory, existing structures and outside pressures, and the extent that the innovation processes also evolve according to evolutionary principles, then these will differ from locality to locality. Thus, for instance, diversity may be a driver of innovation in some contexts, whereas specialization may be in others" (2012, S12). This raises critical questions about the factors that account for these divergent paths of development. A number of hypotheses have been advanced to account for these differences. Traditional explanations of the elements that affect the economic performance of city-regions have been framed in terms of the origins and growth of urban centres, including the position of individual cities within a country's urban system; the impact of city size on urban patterns of innovation; the relative degree of specialization or diversity that characterizes the economic structure of individual cities; and the concentration of talent and human capital in the local labour market, as well as the relative importance of lifestyle amenities and the quality of place in increasing the attractiveness of particular cities (Wolfe and Bramwell 2008).[1]

Key issues in the literature are the relative advantages or disadvantages associated with city size or the degree of urban agglomeration. There is widespread recognition that the largest city-regions enjoy certain advantages as centres of innovation and creativity. Recent surveys of the literature on this question suggest that the doubling of city size can produce a noticeable increase in productivity across a wide range of different city sizes (OECD 2006). The sheer density and concentration of economic players in large cities afford multiple opportunities for contact, interaction, and knowledge circulation (Orlando and Verba 2005). Further research by Enrico Moretti reinforces this point and suggests there is an increasing divergence among the prospects for cities of different sizes in the United States. The underlying cause is the increasingly unequal distribution of human capital levels across urban centres. His research demonstrates that knowledge-related jobs in innovation-based industries tend to create five new additional jobs in other sectors of the local economy, in contrast to new jobs in other sectors that have a much lower multiplier effect (2012, 60). The reason is that knowledge-intensive firms tend to co-locate in response to the advantages created by potential knowledge spillovers and access to a larger labour market. The implication is that urban centres with a higher concentration of jobs in these sectors are likely to grow faster than other cities. This trend is reinforcing the bifurcation of cities between larger ones with greater concentrations of innovation-based and knowledge-related jobs and more traditional manufacturing centres that face increasing difficulty in maintaining their employment base. In the middle may be a few cities that are able to shift their base of economic activity from more traditional activities to knowledge-based ones (Moretti 2012).

Conversely, the alternative case has been made that smaller cities and even non-urban areas reveal significant patterns of innovation, albeit different from those found in larger urban agglomerations. Certain types of innovation require denser and more frequent patterns of interaction than others. The nature of these requirements may influence the willingness of firms to pay the higher land costs and to tolerate congestion associated with being located in larger cities. Firms with lower requirements for intense patterns of interaction, especially those for whom incremental improvements to their products are more important that the introduction of radical innovations, may prefer to be located in smaller urban centres or possibly event outside of cities altogether. The preference for location in larger city-regions may also be more important for firms in newer or emerging industries than those in more established industries, because there is reduced risk associated with the agglomeration effects of larger urban centres. As the cases of the individual cities presented in this volume demonstrate, innovation patterns diverge dramatically in cities of different sizes across the country. In this respect, significantly different types of urban milieus play a role in generating and diffusing innovations (Shearmur 2012, S15). The contributions to this volume help us to understand the nature of those differences and the reasons for them.

A related debate involves the question of how the industrial structure and specific characteristics of urban economies affect innovation and knowledge circulation. The first perspective concerns the advantages that firms derive from locating in cities with firms in similar or different industries, and which type of structure contributes most to industrial innovation and economic growth. This view emphasizes the benefits of specialization for urban growth in similar or closely related industries. It argues that the advantages created by a dense network of suppliers, a deep pool of skilled labour, and the knowledge spillovers that occur among geographically concentrated groups of firms in related industries make the most significant contribution to growth (Krugman 1991). These advantages are associated with a greater degree of specialization in an urban economy; they are derived from forces that lie outside the individual firm, but are embedded in the dense set of relationships among groups of interrelated firms that comprise a cluster within a particular city-region (Porter 1998, 2003).

In contrast, the urban economics literature dating back to Jane Jacobs suggests that the diversity of activity within cities enhances their growth prospect (1969; Glaeser 2000) and innovative capacity (Feldman and Audretsch 1998; Duranton and Puga 2000). The possibility of inter-sectoral knowledge exchange and spillovers arising from this form of economic variety enhances the learning potential for local economic actors. Ideas that are commonplace or widely accepted within a particular sector may have novel value in another. The possibility of cross-fertilization arising from an economic structure with greater variety enhances the potential for the generation of new ideas and innovation within the local economy.

These competing views on the sources of urban economic growth have stimulated a substantial body of academic research that provides some evidence to support both perspectives: that the presence of both specialized *and* diversified urban economies contributes to the overall performance of city-regions, but the two factors may act in different ways in cities of different size. Part of the confusion may arise from the omission of time as a factor in determining whether the economic benefits associated with specialization or diversity exert a more important influence on the economic performance of firms in city-regions. In effect, "the role of externalities varies according to the maturity of the industry. Jacobs externalities predominate in the early stages of the industry life cycle, whereas Marshall externalities enter at a later point, and in the end, specialization will in fact hinder economic growth" (Beaudry and Schiffauerova 2009, 334).

This conclusion is consistent with the view that an industry life cycle perspective helps explain the relative contributions made by specialization and diversification to urban economic growth. The economic benefits associated with a more diversified local economy play different roles in innovation at various stages in the maturity of the industry, while differences in population also affect cities' ability to create and diffuse new knowledge. Duranton and Puga (2000) suggest that firms often develop new products in the diversified, creative environment found in larger urban centres, but as the technology and industry mature, there is a stronger incentive for them to relocate to smaller, more specialized cities in the mass-production phase of the industry's life cycle in order to exploit urban cost advantages. Related findings reveal that levels of innovation are also strongly linked to city size, with R&D, patenting, and major product innovations much more concentrated in large urban areas (Audretsch 2002).

Recognition of the path-dependent trajectories of innovation and technological change has led to a growing understanding within economic geography of the influence of related variety on new trajectories of growth and development. While many industrial activities still occur in identifiable sectors staffed by industry-specific occupations, many of the knowledge-intensive activities associated with new and emerging sectors of the economy are less easily categorized. A whole vein of recent research suggests that regional evolution and growth are affected by the degree to which new industries emerge from the intersections of related industries at the regional level (Boschma and Wenting 2007; van Oort, de Geus, and Dogaru 2015). Diversity matters for innovation, but diversity of a specific kind; relatedness arises in those urban and regional economies where cross-fertilization can occur among industrial sectors that share certain characteristics and have a knowledge base in common. This point is reinforced by the most recent research on economic clustering: "The positive effect of clusters on job creation is driven not by the narrow industries in which employment specialization is already high … It is driven by the related industries within the cluster that are still relatively less developed" (Ketels 2013, 275). The reason is that related variety speeds up lateral absorptive capacity between related sectors within the urban economy and stimulates innovation cross-fertilization via knowledge spillovers. "More related variety means more lateral 'absorptive capacity' from related 'knowledge spillovers'" (Cooke 2014).

The patterns of innovation documented above extend well beyond the manufacturing sector of the economy. As the boundary between traditional sectors of the economy shifts, the distinction between traditional manufacturing and service-oriented activity is blurring. Allen Scott suggests that this blurring in the lines of distinction between the manufacturing and service sectors of the economy, combined with the rapid diffusion of information and communications technologies, is dramatically altering both the locus of the dominant sectors of economic activity and the nature of work in the emerging "cognitive-cultural economy." The core sectors of this new economy can be found in technology-intensive manufacturing, a wide range of knowledge-intensive services, including finance, business and personal services, cultural and entertainment industries, including film, television, digital media, and tourism, and design-based fashion industries, including clothing, jewellery, and furniture (Scott 2007, 1466; 2008).

The industries that form the basis of the emerging cognitive-cultural economy are rapidly displacing the more traditional mass production industries of the post-war era as the driving force of this new economy (Scott 2013). The advance of this new economy both requires and is supported by the formation of a dense occupational layer of professional and quasi-professional workers whose skill requirements are based on the ability to conduct scientific and technological research, and who engage in high-level project management and administration, as well as conception and design, image creation, and entertainment. Most importantly for our analysis, this cognitive cultural economy is concentrated predominantly in major urban areas and leading global city-regions. This concentration is a function of the degree to which advanced producers in these sectors benefit from the increased flexibility and reduced uncertainty associated with co-location and the corresponding degree to which large concentrations of highly skilled workers are simultaneously attracted to the multiple employment opportunities provided by this dense labour market (Scott 2008, 12–13). Thus, the locational choices of the highly skilled concentrations of human capital and the dense concentration of firms in the sectors associated with the cognitive-cultural economy are mutually reinforcing each other in a positive cycle of cumulative causation.

The emphasis on growth driven by the mutually supportive interaction of skilled labour and firm preferences characterizes large metropolitan cities as environments where value chains underlying production, and the associated networks of economic actors, can adapt rapidly because of their efficiency in coordinating and managing the processes that are the basis of innovation and growth. In this sense, cities are acting like giant "Schumpeterian hubs" of innovative activity, or "switchboards which permit the constant creation and reshaping of the chains linking producers, consumers, and different kinds of indirect players of the economy" (Veltz 2004). These emerging areas of cognitive-cultural production tend to be located in, or close to, the central business district and often take advantage of low-cost space available in abandoned industrial warehouses or factories. The conversion of physical spaces associated with the older industrial economy to new uses for the emerging cognitive-cultural economy illustrates the critical way in which the spatial landscape of the inner city is reconfigured in dynamic urban regions (Hutton 2008, 11; Scott 2008).

But the diverse cities in Canada's urban system are participating in the transition to this emerging economy to differing degrees. The economic standing of an individual city and its long-term prospects are influenced by its relative position within the urban system, which is defined by its spatial relations with other cities. The urban system is the organizational dynamic that underlies the economic and human geography of the country. Canada's urban system is distinguished by its relatively large number of smaller cities with only a few large ones, and the substantial differences between those larger cities. The challenge posed by these changes in the Canadian urban system is highlighted in an analysis of trends in the urban system over the past four decades. Pierre Filion notes that the traditional distinction between the core industrial cities and the more distant hinterland cities, referred to as the "heartland-hinterland" distinction, is on the wane. Over this period it has been displaced by a growing differentiation between Canada's largest cities and its medium and smaller-sized ones. Consistent with Moretti's argument above, he postulates that as this disparity continues to grow, the urban system will become more bifurcated, with a growing concentration of population and economic opportunities in the largest cities at the expense of the rest (Filion 2010).

At the same time, those sectors of economic activity concentrated in Canada's largest urban centres are being reconfigured in comparison to small and medium-sized ones. The knowledge inputs, even for Canada's traditional resources industries, are increasingly concentrated in the larger cities while manufacturing activity continues its migration to cities below the one million population mark, consistent with the arguments noted above. "Mid- and low-technology manufacturing is deserting the large metropolitan areas for smaller places where land prices and wages are lower. This industrial exodus ... is the corollary of the concentration of rapidly growing information- and knowledge-rich services in large metropolitan areas" (Bourne et al. 2011, 56). The key challenge posed for the smaller and medium-sized cities is the degree to which they will be able to maintain and expand employment opportunities for their residents, especially as the future of more traditional manufacturing is increasingly challenged. This will depend on the extent to which they are able to leverage their industrial capabilities and knowledge assets to create jobs in the expanding sectors of the economy.

Cities with a diversified economic base are more insulated from the impacts of economic change, while those with a narrower industrial structure are more subject to a life cycle of growth and decline (Brezis and Krugman 1997). Differences in the degree of industrial specialization or diversification may also affect the ability of individual cities to withstand external economic shocks – as the impact of the recent oil price decline on Western Canadian cities reveals. While greater specialization has stimulated the growth of some medium-sized cities, their outlook is tied to the prospects of the specific sectors in which their economy is specialized. The industrial structure of such cities increases the risk that they may become locked into sectors facing a decline in market demand for their products or obsolete technologies that may be supplanted by newer ones. The ability of city-regions to adapt to and absorb rapid changes in technology, and the competitiveness of their industrial mix, are critical to their economic future. Ultimately the source of innovation and economic growth for a city-region rests not just on its relative size, or the degree of specialization or diversification in its industrial structure, but more importantly on its resilience in mobilizing economic assets in the pursuit of a new basis for growth and the governance structures in place to support that resilience. The specific form of adaptation to new forms of economic activity and emerging industries varies considerably across individual cities, but the transition shares the common process of building upon traditional areas of economic concentration by moving into new fields of economic activity through cross-sectoral fertilization and related knowledge diversity.

Talent and Creativity: Spaces of Flows of People, Capital, and Ideas[2]

It is now widely recognized that competitive success in many sectors of the economy rests increasingly on intangible assets, such as knowledge and creativity (Maskell and Malmberg 1999). Accordingly, human capital is understood to be a primary factor shaping the geography of economic activity. Moreover, as noted above, the past two decades have seen the emergence of a knowledge-based, creative, or cognitive-cultural economy, in which creative occupations and sectors are among the most dynamic and propulsive forms of economic activity within city-regions (Scott 2007). For this reason, highly educated and creative workers are acknowledged as a highly localized – yet potentially mobile – resource that city-regions seek to attract and retain.

Moreover, these "regional talent pools of global significance" (Cooke 2005) are viewed as having the potential to attract and embed globally mobile investment, rather than following this capital and the employment-creating capacity it represents. The argument put forth most colourfully by Florida, but also resonating with the work of others during the past decade or so, is that the social characteristics of particular places that make them attractive to talented workers are the critical determinants of local economic growth and prosperity (Florida 2002c; Gertler et al. 2002; Saxenian 2002; Markusen 2006). This work contends that such talent is attracted to and retained by cities, but not just *any* cities. In particular, those places that offer a richness of employment opportunity, a high quality of life, a critical mass of cultural activity and social diversity (in other words, low barriers to entry for newcomers) are said to exert the strongest pull.

Equally noteworthy has been the critical response evoked by this work, which signals fundamental disagreement with the "Florida thesis" on several grounds. Some question the persuasiveness and rigour of the original empirical work, calling into question the claim that particular qualities of place such as coolness, openness, and social diversity exert a causal influence on the flows of talent between city-regions. Others argue that the most important determinants of such flows are more traditional characteristics such as favourable climate and the prior concentration of skilled human capital. Still others contend that the causality runs in the opposite direction: the availability of local employment opportunities and economic growth drive the inter-regional migration of talented workers, not vice versa. More questions focus on the relevance of "Florida factors" in mid-size and smaller city-regions, the kinds of places that have not attracted the same degree of attention from scholars. However, there is growing acceptance, both by Florida and some of his critics, that the emerging economic paradigm is based on a greater bifurcation in the distribution of jobs within the occupational structure of urban centres and the income distribution that flows from that bifurcation. The growing wage and income inequality in large metropolitan regions has become one of the most pressing social and economic issues in the early decades of the twenty-first century.

The seeds of these ideas can be traced to previous research on the migration of skilled talent and human capital theory. Glaeser (2000, 2005b) points to the impact that highly skilled and educated workers have on the economic growth of those city-regions to which they are attracted, demonstrating a strong positive correlation between educational attainment and regional development. He argues further that firms are drawn to places with high concentrations of human capital to gain competitive advantage. Related studies by both Florida (2002c), Berry and Glaeser (2005), and Moretti (2012) further reinforce such findings by showing evidence that regional growth levels are directly affected by high concentrations of talented and skilled individuals. At the heart of these debates is the question regarding how the locational choices of workers intersect with and reinforce those made by firms to contribute to the growth and dynamism of modern cities. This work puts the spotlight once again on an old, but still contentious, question in economic geography: do people follow jobs or do jobs follow people?

There are four complementary streams of thought within this literature to be considered. The first suggests that the geographic distribution of talent is a response to thick labour markets and the availability of diverse and high-quality jobs (Bartel 1979; Carlino and Mills 1987; Blanchard et al. 1992). For example, Shearmur (2007, 2010) indicates that talented workers follow labour opportunities that are available in particular places. Likewise, a study by Houston et al. (2008) determined that job prospects attracted talented workers to Scotland, and in the absence of such professional and employment opportunities, people would not have relocated. Hansen and Niedomysl (2008) provide similar findings that creative-class workers in Sweden moved there primarily for employment reasons rather than other factors.

A second area of research contends that the flow of highly skilled knowledge workers is affected by the distribution of amenities (Roback 1982). Glaeser (2005b) and Glaeser and Gottlieb (2006) argue that a benign climate and urban amenities such as consumer and personal service industries, good public schools, safety from crime, and strong transportation infrastructure appeal to talented workers and consequently affect location decisions and mobility flows. In a similar vein, Clark at al. (2002) claim that the very urban amenities that appeal to tourists, namely restaurants, museums, galleries, and attractive built form, also attract and retain mobile knowledge workers. Lloyd and Clark (2001) and Shapiro (2006) point to the importance of lifestyle, in the form of entertainment, nightlife, and culture, in attracting talent.

Another body of work suggests that the geography of highly skilled talent workers is influenced by the presence of major research universities (Florida 2002c; Berry and Glaeser 2005), a key factor as well in both the production and attraction of human capital. Wolfe and Gertler (2004) show that post-secondary institutions play a pivotal role in the development of industry clusters, which in turn attract mobile knowledge workers to a region. Gertler and Vinodrai (2005) characterize universities as anchors of creativity that build social cohesion in communities, and Florida et al. (2006) suggest that these institutions foster diversity and tolerance. In their study of Waterloo, Ontario, Bramwell, Nelles, and Wolfe (2008) find that quality of life and place characteristics could not account for why firms located in the region; rather they conclude that firms are attracted and anchored by local universities and colleges. Wojan et al. (2007) conclude that university towns often draw artists, and a city's attractiveness to highly artistic individuals is an important indicator of its ability to attract and retain creative workers more broadly. However, the quality of a region's post-secondary institutions alone cannot guarantee that it can hold onto its talent, a reality that is highlighted in work by Florida et al. (2006). In other words, the university is neither a necessary nor sufficient condition for attracting educated and skilled populations to a place, or retaining the ones it produces. While some regions with great universities have large concentrations of talent, others operate as producers and exporters of human capital and skilled talent to other regions.

And finally, an important stream of research contends that the flow of talent between regions is shaped by local levels of tolerance and openness to diversity (in both the social characteristics of the population and the economic structure of the region) (Jacobs 1961; Beckstead and Brown 2003). One body of work has focused on the impact of demographic diversity on economic growth (Ottaviano and Peri 2005). Florida (2002a, 2002b, 2002c) and others (Noland 2005; Florida and Gates 2003) further argue that local cultures of tolerance help create geographic concentrations of talent, higher rates of innovation, and regional development. In other words, the more open a place is to new ideas and new people, the stronger the pull it exerts in the global competition for talent. Florida et al. (2010) suggest that these characteristics of place contribute to economic development by making local resources more productive and efficient, and act through four key mechanisms: low barriers to entry for human capital (see Page 2007; Florida, Mellander, and Stolarick 2008; Mellander and Florida 2011), knowledge spillovers and human capital externalities (Lucas 1988; Markusen and Schrock 2006), signals of openness and meritocracy (Inglehart and Norris 2003; Inglehart and Welzel 2005), and resource mobilization (Florida et al. 2010).

Notwithstanding recent academic debates, the influence of talent-based explanations of urban economic growth has grown in both popular and policy discourse (Bradford 2004; Malanga 2004; Glaeser 2005a; Tremblay 2006; City of Montreal 2007; Conference Board of Canada 2007). It is clear that these ideas have had a significant impact on thinking and public policy in many cities around the world, many of which have adopted creative city strategies (Scott 2006; Wong and Bunnell 2006; Clifton 2008). One thread of policy work deploys creativity indicators (Deller et al. 2001; Beugelsdijk 2007). Another explores the lifestyle propensities of the creative class (Bridge 2006; Danyluk and Ley 2007; McGranahan and Wojan 2007). And yet another focuses on the socio-economic manifestations of creativity that promote innovation and experimentation (Lloyd 2002, 2004; Currid 2006, 2007a, 2007b). While much of this work is U.S.-based, a number of policy studies expand the scope of these concepts to Canada (Schimpf and Sereda 2001; Gertler et al. 2002; Donald and Morrow 2003; Duxbury 2004; Wolfe and Gertler 2004; Rantisi and Leslie 2006; Rantisi, Leslie, and Christopherson 2006; Stolarick and Florida 2006; Sands and Reese 2008; Schimpf 2008; Florida et al. 2010; Lepawsky, Phan, and Greenwood 2010; Grant and Kronstal 2010).

The idea of the creative city in the Canadian context was initially explored by Gertler (2001), who looked at changes in the flow of people, capital, and ideas over time. This work highlights the increasing trend towards income polarization and chronic spaces of exclusion within large Canadian urban centres, phenomena that have the potential to undermine the very social characteristics on which a region's economic prosperity has been based. Donald and Morrow (2003) explore the intersection of Florida's talent model and its implications for broader social and economic policy in Canada. Gertler et al. (2002) were the first to apply the creative city thesis empirically to the Canadian context. Slack, Bourne, and Gertler (2003) emphasized the importance of the city-region to economic and regional development in Ontario, highlighting many of the social and economic challenges faced by the province. Further research reveals that, despite persistent efforts, not all locations in the country will necessarily succeed in the pursuit of talent and amenity-based objectives and that in some cases, communities have encountered significant obstacles in developing deep labour markets. For example, Polèse and Shearmur (2006) find that for the more peripheral regions in Canada, the prospects for sharing in the benefits from inter-regional and international migration are considerably more limited. Many such urban areas are struggling to contend with the loss of home-grown talent to other regions of Canada, as well as the inability to attract and retain well-educated migrants from other regions or countries. Thus the question of city size and relative location remains central to these debates.

Although these recent contributions add significant nuance to theories about talent and urban economic development, a question that is particularly important in the Canadian context remains: what evidence is there that the hypothesized relationships between quality of place and economic performance can also be found in mid-size and smaller urban regions? Moreover, can we expect these factors to produce the same effects in different types of cities and for different kinds of talent? It stands to reason that the relationships that shape the economic vitality and dynamism of city-regions are likely to be articulated differently under locally unique sets of conditions. The spatial diversity within Canada is particularly instructive: cities not only vary in population size, but they are also vastly different in their relative location, economic and demographic structure, and trajectories of change over time.

The findings from our investigation of these dynamics within thirteen Canadian city-regions suggest that the particular characteristics of a place that appeal to these sought-after and often mobile creative workers extend far beyond the usual cultural amenities that are highlighted within much of the prevailing current literature. For example, across all cases, the employees interviewed indicated that their settlement and career location preferences were shaped by "liveability" attributes, including overall affordability, particular environmental or natural qualities, different commuting options, and a sense of personal security. These differences also tended to reflect personal lifestyle and/or family life cycle / life stage dimensions. Moreover, the cases reveal salient differences in how workers in different sectors, occupation types, and at different career and life stages assess the attractiveness of city-regions. For example, people working in cultural industries such as media, fashion, or architecture were drawn to environments (in places like Montreal, Toronto, or Vancouver) that would enable them to interact with people working in the same and complementary fields. On the other hand, creative artists living in smaller or mid-sized cities were attracted to such places because they offered a less competitive, more nurturing environment for the early stages of their careers.

Despite the added nuance and variation that these findings reveal across all city-regions, people continued to cite the availability of employment as the primary consideration shaping their decision of where to live and work. However, while the recent literature frames this question in terms of "jobs versus amenities," the case study findings suggest that it is not simply an immediate job that is at issue. Instead, highly educated and creative workers tend to adopt a longer-term *career* perspective, which includes the possibility to experience a range of employment opportunities and to advance up the career ladder. In other words, a much more dynamic conception of employment, careers, and labour markets is needed to understand the factors that influence the attractiveness of a place for work and residential purposes among highly skilled and creative workers. An important avenue for future research will be to develop a more in-depth understanding of how work opportunities and quality of place characteristics intersect for workers in different sectors of the Canadian economy.

A second question that this project sought to explore was whether there is evidence that this hypothesized relationship between quality of place and economic performance could also be found in mid-sized and smaller urban regions in Canada. In other words, are the arguments made about the importance of cultural dynamism, social diversity, and tolerance and/or openness as enabling conditions for economic prosperity and competitiveness limited to large metropolitan economies? Our findings reveal important variation in the opportunities and challenges associated with the size of the city and the labour market concerns of workers and firms. For example, the larger cities across Canada offer the greatest range of career opportunities for workers in many different sectors. This valued "depth" of the labour market may provide workers with more insulation from job loss because it offers a large number of potential jobs within a field, as well as the opportunity to advance up a career ladder, or to cross over into complementary fields. In comparison, small cities were appreciated for offering a strong sense of community within particular sectors, which also encouraged the development of collaborative and supportive professional cultures within certain fields. Mid-sized cities, by contrast, were situated between the strengths of these two extremes. On one hand, they offer some of the positive aspects of a smaller community and labour market, such as the more accommodating and encouraging professional culture, while also avoiding the challenges and competition inherent in large cities; on the other hand, medium-sized cities also tend to lack the career opportunity and vibrancy available in the large cities, and struggle to retain their talent. These findings reinforce the significance of city size in understanding the dynamics of talent and creativity for the growth prospects of Canadian city-regions. Despite the appeal of a talent-based approach to urban economic growth and development, the uneven distribution of creative occupations and highly skilled labour and the resulting increase in social disparities in some of the most successful city-regions suggests there are inherent limits to this approach to urban growth strategies. The rise of creative cities in North America and Europe is a product of their role as places with the ability to generate a high level of technological innovation and economically useful knowledge.

Governance

The chapters in this volume document the ways in which a range of Canadian cities are adjusting to the transition from the traditional manufacturing and resource industries towards the more knowledge-intensive business services and creative sectors associated with the emerging cognitive-cultural economy. At the same time, this transition poses significant economic challenges; not all cities are equally well situated in the Canadian urban system or vested with the industrial structure or institutional assets needed to facilitate this transition. Cities and regions that remain locked into traditional specializations in mature manufacturing and are unable to capitalize on existing knowledge assets or to mobilize their local endowments of human capital face greater challenges in effecting this transition (Glaeser 2011; Moretti 2012).

At the same time, regions and cities cannot alter their trajectory of development by fiat or an act of political will. Their pattern of development is strongly influenced by the existing industrial structure of the economy, as well as by the broader set of institutions that have supported those sectors. Those sectors in which the urban economy has historically been specialized will constrain its future ability to grow, or create opportunities for new sectors to emerge. The basis on which those sectors emerge is influenced in turn by the capacity of firms and institutions to develop and exploit new sources of knowledge and their existing knowledge infrastructure, as well as the talents and skills of the workforce.

The capacity of individual cities to transform their economies to more knowledge-intensive forms of activity depends not just on the functioning of autonomous market-based processes, but also by their social and political structures (Wolfe 2010). It is important to recognize that these spheres do not act independently of each other. The key issue is how the governance arrangements that affect the trajectory of growth for an urban economy can be influenced most effectively. Future development in city-regions will be driven by the knowledge-intensive innovation and creative and design-based activities associated with the cognitive-cultural dimension of the economy. The chapters collected in this volume illustrate that the fruits of knowledge-intensive economic activity are distributed unequally among cities of different sizes, industrial specialization, and labour markets. Efforts to improve the economic performance of city-regions, therefore, need to pay close attention to the underlying institutions in those city-regions that can support their industrial transformation. Relatively few cities enjoy the more diversified economic base of Vancouver, Montreal, or Toronto, but each has its own institutional assets and capacity for the development of its local economy.

Much work has been devoted to explaining the emergence and growth of dynamic regions based on new technologies, as well as the challenge for older, industrial regions to break free of their locked-in paths of development. However, less attention has focused on the co-evolution of a region's industrial structure and institutional underpinnings. Rather, the path-dependent nature of development in regional economies involves the process by which these interdependent spheres of city-regions co-evolve, as well as the process by which new institutional forms of organization emerge in response to changing economic and environmental conditions. Critical is the ability of firms, industries, and institutions in a city-region to adapt their knowledge base and localized capabilities to the generation and exploitation of new commercially valuable sources of knowledge. The question of how adaptable these institutional ensembles are to changes in the primary industries and technologies of the region's industrial structure lies at the heart of questions of adaptability and resilience. However, the underlying challenge is not simply whether institutional ensembles can adapt to new industries, but whether local civic actors collaborating with municipal and regional governments actively support, encourage, and foster this transition (Swanstrom 2008).

A key to the success of these efforts is to build connections among civic actors and associations in their communities.[3] The exploration of the governance theme in our comparative case studies of Canadian city-regions examines the influence of three interrelated dimensions of local governance and policy development on the strategic response by cities and communities to the economic challenges they face. The first dimension involves governance arrangements at the city-region level – both the administrative structures that govern the city-region and the relative openness of those governmental structures to influence and participation by a broad range of social actors and civic associations within the urban polity. The complexity of economic development challenges requires the active involvement of a broader cross-section of community actors to devise effective policy solutions. The dispersal of power to a broader range of civic actors creates the opportunity for more meaningful dialogue to take place at the city-region level. This is important, because dialogue or discussion is central to the process by which parties come to reinterpret themselves and their relationship to other relevant actors within the urban economy and formulate alternative visions of how the economy can develop. The involvement of this broader range of actors gives them a greater sense of ownership of the strategies adopted and places greater responsibility for the outcome onto those organizations that will be directly affected.

The second dimension concerns the nature of the relations among interests and associations active at the local level. In most cities, influence has traditionally been exercised to a great extent by a local development coalition representing those organizations and actors in the community with the strongest interest in promoting the city's economic development. In recent decades, the role and influence of these coalitions have been contested by a wider range of social and community interests concerned with how the benefits of economic growth are shared among the population of the city at large and the degree of inclusion or exclusion that prevails in local decision-making (Keating 2002). In cities where the contours of the development coalition are successfully expanded, the conditions are laid for the creation of a networked set of collaborative organizations that can contribute to the city's economic development strategy. This, in turn, leads to the presence of higher levels of "civic capital" in the local community, which becomes an invaluable asset in the pursuit of the development strategy (Wolfe 2009).

Regions with strong and dynamic leadership from the civic sector, what Doug Henton and his colleagues term "regional stewards," may prove more successful in working with the public sector to develop new strategies (Henton, Melville, and Parr 2006). Resilient regions are thus ones in which private market forces, a strong and dynamic civic sector, and local governments are capable of adapting to changing economic and environmental circumstances in order to respond to emerging threats and take advantage of emerging opportunities. Local civic associations also help develop new strategies to promote the growth of their local and regional economies and thus contribute to their potential resilience. Regions with a diverse cross-section of civic stakeholders can develop a set of innovative strategies to promote the future economic interests of the region. At the same time, local civic networks that have become excessively ingrown or self-replicating can be the source of an excessive degree of social rigidity that limits the potential for innovative solutions to emerge (Swanstrom 2008; Safford 2009).

The third dimension involves the policy framework adopted to guide urban economic development. The traditional approach to urban economic development, which dates to the 1950s to the 1970s, focused on strategies to attract individual firms to a city-region, frequently by providing low-cost land and services and by offering the targeted firms direct subsidies or tax reductions of an increasingly generous nature. The second approach emerged in the 1980s when a growing number of states and provinces reacted to the industrial restructuring of that decade by focusing their development efforts on building the educational and technological infrastructure that could support the growth of more technologically intensive firms and attract new investments on the basis of their local research capabilities. In the late 1980s, however, regional and local governments began to perceive the limits to this approach. Although the strategy was built on the recognition of a shift from a more industrial to an emerging knowledge-based economy, it relied on the same public sector organizational dynamics to meet policy needs as had been employed in the past. As the focus of economic development policy changed from chasing smokestacks to growing the research infrastructure and stimulating innovation, state and provincial governments created a mix of new policies administered by discrete branches of individual line departments – often with little coordination or integration across programs and minimal involvement from the urban level of government or the local community the policies were targeted at. In response to the perceived weakness of the earlier approaches, a growing number of city-regions have perceived the need to adopt a more coordinated and strategic approach to urban economic development (Ross and Friedman 1990).

The key issue in the governance theme of our case studies was to investigate the extent to which these more coordinated and strategic approaches to urban economic development were emerging in Canadian city-regions. The research conducted for the third theme of our project explored the extent and the ways in which cities were developing more collaborative forms of governance and strategic planning. They probed for indications whether cities were forming broad cross-sectoral coalitions to formulate new local strategies for economic and social development or whether they were locked into more traditional forms of municipal governance and thus failing to seize the opportunity to alter the trajectory of their economic development.

Within the broad framework set out above, our case studies uncovered great variation in how this approach is implemented across the country, but collectively they suggest that there is considerable experimentation in new forms of governance at the urban level. The cases provide some insights into how these new governance models are evolving at the urban level to chart a strategic response to the challenge of economic adjustment. In their analysis of the findings of our studies of urban governance arrangements in Canadian city-regions, Neil Bradford and Allison Bramwell elaborated a typology of the range of governance arrangements and local economic development strategies that captures the emerging configuration of institutional arrangements.[4] The typology organized these arrangements into three main patterns: institutional collaborations that underpin coordinated approaches to economic and social policy; sector-based networks that organize economic and social interests around a specific set of priorities; and more transitory arrangements that convene shifting groups of economic and social actors around specific local projects, but have little lasting effect on the broader governance arrangements in their city-regions.

The first type of arrangement involves more formalized "organizational spaces" that bring together relevant groups of civic actors to articulate a shared vision for the city's economic development and coordinate strategic planning for the design and implementation of that vision. Where effective, collaborative planning assembles key economic and social leaders from the city-region and maintains a professional staff and broad network of volunteers to support both the planning exercises and their implementation. Such collaborations tend to be ambitious governance undertakings, which adopt ambitious goals for their city-regions and propose solutions to a complex set of economic and social problems beyond the capability of any individual actor or association to undertake on their own. While urban size is often seen as a major obstacle in bringing together associational interests, some of the most effective institutional collaborations are found in some of Canada's largest cities. Local municipal or governments play a range of roles in these institutional collaborations, acting as the convener where they have helped assemble the groups or partners in which the leadership was self-organizing.

Sector networks constitute different arrangements where the linkages and degree of coordination between economic and social actors tend to be much weaker or underdeveloped. City-regions characterized by this type of arrangement tend to lack the kind of bridging institutions found in more formalized kinds of institutional collaboration. Often the networks on the economic and social side operate separately from each other but are successful in undertaking major initiatives at the local level to further their respective objectives. What they often lack is the kind of boundary-crossing civic leaders, described by Henton and his colleagues, who have the capacity to organize more integrated initiatives, facilitate dialogue among the diverse range of local interests, and formulate a common agenda for action. In this case, the local government may play the role of a facilitator of the respective networks, assisting in the design or delivery of programs devised by the sector leaders.

The third type of arrangement is characterized as a program partnership, where diverse local interests convene around specific individual projects or programs that are conceived within a specific time frame with well-defined goals and objectives. Such local governance arrangements also take the form of "public-private partnerships" where there is a formal agreement to deliver on specific outcomes. The partnerships may assemble a broader range of economic and social actors than in sector networks, but they are differentiated from the former type of arrangement by their more instrumental and episodic character. Local governments may act as co-investors in these arrangements, with overall responsibility for financial management. The key challenge with this third type of institutional arrangement is whether it is capable of generating a sustained and ongoing form of collaboration to help frame a more institutionalized approach to tackling the city-regions' challenges of economic adjustment.

Within the overall typology of governance approaches that are being developed, several of the cases point to the critical role played by local civic leaders in forging new forms of governance. Key civic leaders often play an instrumental role in focusing attention on local problems and recruiting partners and resources to participate in their collective efforts to formulate an effective policy response at the local level. Overall, the case studies found solid evidence that local civic associations are being formed to identify local issues, formulate new strategies, and tackle the problems. Thus, while virtually all of the case studies present some evidence of institutional innovation underway in Canadian city-regions, the nature and degree of that innovation demonstrates considerable variation. In some cases, local associational interests are relatively well organized and have demonstrated the capacity to collaborate in a sustained institutional capacity, while in others the interests are more fragmented and less well organized, with the extent of collaboration limited to sector networks or specific partnership projects. While novel governance arrangements alone are not sufficient to alter the developmental trajectory of individual city-regions, they do contribute to bringing about change. On the basis of our evidence, the prospects for Canadian city-regions are substantially different, with some of the largest and most diversified urban economies also enjoying greater success in forging new institutional governance mechanisms, while some of our smaller urban centres with more limited resources seem locked into more traditional governance relations with slimmer prospects for formulating innovative or alternative policy responses.

Chapter Overviews

The ensuing chapters in the volume examine how the changing dynamics of innovation, talent attraction and retention, and local governance arrangements are playing out across a range of Canadian cities – large, medium, and small. The cases were selected in order to ensure the representation of different-sized cities in various regions of the country, each with a distinctive industrial structure and areas of economic selection. The following chapters provide a rich set of insights into the way in which the cities that comprise the Canadian urban system are changing in the underlying economic factors described above.

The first section of the book deals with the five case studies of large cities in our research project, those city-regions with a population greater than one million. The first chapter by David Wolfe and Allison Bramwell deals with the emerging cognitive-cultural economy in Toronto's fourth era of post-war growth. Marked by the amalgamation of the previous six cities into the mega-city in 1997 and two subsequent recessions, the economy of the Toronto city-region is rapidly being recast with a dominant focus on higher-end business services, cultural and creative industries, and other design-centred economic activities. At the same time the physical geography of the city has been radically transformed, with the central business district experiencing a more rapid rate of growth than the traditional suburbs and the domination of the city's skyline by a growing number of high-rise towers both for commercial and residential use. Unfortunately, the governance structures of the Toronto city-region have lagged behind the economic and social transformation of the city, leaving serious questions of who speaks for

Toronto and what is the appropriate scale and scope for governance institutions in Canada's largest urban agglomeration.

The Montreal case study, by Diane-Gabrielle Tremblay, Norma Rantisi, and Juan-Luis Klein, depicts a city with a dynamic range of economic activity in a variety of sectors and the most complex and varied set of governance arrangements of any of our cases. Montreal has the most institutionalized form of collaboration of any city-region in Canada, with a formal cluster strategy adopted and implemented at the level of the Montreal Metropolitan Community. At the same time, the unique features of the "Quebec model" provide support for a bottom-up dynamic form of organization, the Community Economic Development Corporations, which provide a strong and inclusive role for civil associations. These organizations play a critical role throughout the city in launching and supporting a number of economic development initiatives. Despite this underlying strength in its governance arrangements, the study finds that the transfer of knowledge across clusters and sectors is more limited, suggesting that the city is not realizing the full potential of its highly diversified economy. The dense network of post-secondary institutions throughout the city and the high level of human capital produced by these institutions, combined with its aesthetic quality of place, means that the city is highly successful in both generating and retaining creative talent. Despite these distinct advantages, the authors suggest that there is still considerable room in Montreal for a better integration of its governance networks to ensure that it reaps the maximum benefit from its socially inclusive institutional structures and its attractive quality of place.

The case study of Vancouver summarized here by Tom Hutton and Trevor Barnes documents the unique features of its urban economy. These features combine elements of a post-staples resource-based commercial centre with an emerging new cultural economy of production and consumption to create an economy configured by diverse specializations and a distinctive set of governance arrangements. While Vancouver has a strong tradition of multi-level governance that effectively incorporates all of the municipalities in the city-region into a high-profile regional government, the researchers find that the city lacks the effective strategic management needed for better coordination and alignment across the region. Despite the lack of an overarching economic policy vision for the region, there is solid evidence of the way the city has managed its transition from a commercial centre for a staples-based economy to a more diverse site for cultural innovation and production, in part by supporting the redevelopment and repurposing of key areas close to the central business district that serve as effective locations for the cultural production to complement the concentration of producer services in the central business district. This confluence of strengths and Vancouver's natural attraction for talent and human capital are helping secure its position as a dynamic centre for the emerging cognitive-cultural economy.

The chapter on Ottawa, by Caroline Andrew and David Doloreux, documents the story of a city in a major state of transition. Long dependent on the primary role of the federal government as the cornerstone of its local economy, Ottawa witnessed a dynamic expansion of its information and communications technology sector from the early 1980s to the mid-2000s. Supported by the research institutions of the federal government and its own post-secondary education institutions, Ottawa developed a strong core of research-intensive business corporations, with correspondingly high levels of professional and highly educated workers in the local labour force and a particular concentration in knowledge-intensive business services. Key civic leaders also emerged who fashioned a unique civic organization that functioned as the centrepiece for local civic governance and worked in close association with the local municipal government. The end of the dot-com boom in the early 2000s, followed by the subsequent collapse or takeover of several of its leading technology-based firms cast the development model into doubt and undermined the effectiveness of its governance institutions. In the past decade, Ottawa has demonstrated considerable innovative capacity in developing new institutional arrangements to deal with a wide variety of social issues in the city-region, but they remain relatively isolated from the dominant organizations on the economic development side and thus qualify as sector networks. As the economy continues to struggle with the challenge of recovering from the loss of a number of its flagship firms and growing the considerable number of new start-ups to replace them, it remains unclear whether the city and its leading civic associations have become convinced of the need for a more coordinated municipal development strategy.

The final study of a large city, Calgary, represents an almost unique case of a city that has been largely dependent on a primary economic sector, oil and gas, as the key driver of its regional economy for the past half century. Despite the widespread perception that this is still the core of its local economy, the Calgary economy has effectively made the transition to a finance and business services centre that specializes in the capabilities to manage the large project requirements of oil and gas exploration and development. The authors of this case study, Cooper Langford, Ben Li, and Cami Ryan, argue that Calgary's strength in a diverse range of service sectors that provide the core of these capabilities qualify the economy as a related knowledge platform that channels knowledge inputs into innovation in its core economic sector. The dynamism of the Calgary economy rests on the talent and creativity of the knowledge workers in these sectors. While key civic and business associations play a critical role in bringing interests together across the Calgary side, they find that real influence rests with a more informal group of civic leaders drawn largely from the industry side of the local economy who play a critical role in driving local initiatives on both the economic and social side of the municipal agenda. While these informal networks do not qualify as institutionalized collaborations, they provide a greater degree of integration on the economic and social agenda than was found in the Ottawa case.

As noted earlier, the challenges facing small and medium-sized cities are distinct from those confronting the largest cities in the country. Yet our case studies reveal substantial degrees of both economic and institutional innovation in some of the country's medium-sized cities as they grapple with the challenge of making the transition out of the core resource and manufacturing sectors that have been the mainstay of their economies into more knowledge-based activities. Peter Warrian and Allison Bramwell's study of Hamilton offers a profile of a city in the midst of just such a transition. The chapter investigates the way in which the local economy is shifting from its traditional role as the lead site for national steel production to a global node in emerging forms of knowledge-intensive steel production. The study also examines the way in which the local strength of the city's post-secondary educational institutions, particularly the McMaster Health Sciences complex, are driving the development of new forms of diagnostic and health services innovation. Surprisingly, they find evidence of interesting cross-sectoral knowledge flows between the local steel sector and medical devices / health services sector, but the linkages are on the demand side of the innovation continuum, rather than the supply side. On the governance side, they find evidence of local sector networks that have grown and evolved over the past decade and a half in response to the social and economic issues the city has faced as the steel industry underwent its fundamental realignment. But the networks are poorly integrated and are aligned around distinctive sets of objectives. In summary, they find that Hamilton possesses the economic diversity, knowledge assets, and local reservoirs of human capital needed to make the transition to a more knowledge-based set of economic activities, but the lack of sustained linkages between its civic networks stands as an obstacle to the initiation of more collaborative, community-wide strategic planning.

Tara Vinodrai's summary of Waterloo challenges some of the predominant conceptions of this dynamic urban centre. The strength of its regional economy is grounded in a broader and more diverse range of manufacturing and service sectors than the strength of its information and communications technology sector suggests. As a consequence, while its success has been driven by the growth of its high-technology firms, it has also faced the challenge of coping with industrial restructuring and manufacturing job loss that has affected other medium-sized cities. One great strength of the regional economy remains its robust institutional architecture that provides strong support for local entrepreneurship and start-ups. However, the University of Waterloo is much less central to this process than in the early period when the high-tech community began to emerge. Its primary role in the region remains as a source of high-quality human capital, particularly in the technology-related fields of engineering and computer science. Graduates of the university provide a steady source of well-trained personnel to maintain the dense and specialized local labour market, which continues to serve as a major source of attraction for investment by leading technology companies in the region. More importantly, through the co-op education program they serve as one of the primary mechanisms for knowledge transfer in the region between the research expertise of the university and the dense network of local firms. However, the appeal of the region as a site for high-quality human capital is not based on many of the traditional factors deemed to be attractive to talent and the creative class. Rather, the employment opportunities seem to constitute the main attractor in retaining talent in the region. One of its great strengths is the dynamism of its local civic associations, but closer inspection reveals weak linkages between the economic and social networks in the region and suggests there remains considerable room to build more inclusive institutionalized collaborations.

Neil Bradford's case study of London, Ontario, provides a fascinating insight into the challenges of an ordinary city grappling with this transition. Since the mid-1990s, London has struggled with overcoming the loss of several of the corporate head offices that were the mainstay of its economy over the second half of the twentieth century and the hollowing out of its branch plant manufacturing economy through a series of recessions. The study reveals that London's innovation profile displays little of the cross-sectoral knowledge flows that are the key to a knowledge-intensive economy and few institutional points of convergence. Furthermore, its position in the national urban system has meant that it has been challenged by the rising status of its key mid-sized competitor in the Waterloo region. The ability to rebound from these losses has been constrained by a number of obstacles endemic to the nature of the ordinary city. First is the conservative and risk-averse business culture forged by the impressive post-war generation of corporate elites in banking and insurance that imposes high barriers to entry on the city's civic leadership. A second issue is the internal fragmentation of its leadership networks with no comprehensive institutional structures emerging to foster a civic dialogue on its longer-term challenges. Complicating its challenge is that the city consistently scores low on most national indices of talent and creativity, and even the presence of one of the country's leading research universities has not proven to be a strong enough asset to build its local pool of human capital. Despite recent efforts to collaborate on local planning, the city faces major attitudinal, organizational, and institutional obstacles. For this reason, Bradford concludes that London is a city in transition and at a crossroads, whose ability to escape its past as an ordinary city remains an open question.

Our case study of Halifax, Nova Scotia, is a story a significantly different from that of the three southern Ontario urban centres. Halifax's predominance in the regional economy is due to its place as a government centre and regional commercial hub for the Atlantic economy. However, the study found little evidence of strong local knowledge circulation between industries or clusters that were investigated. Halifax's economic performance owes more to its traditional sectoral strengths and its growing reputation as a location for creative talent. Despite its relatively small size and the limited diversity in its economic sectors, Halifax score relatively high on indices for talent and creative cities. Jill Grant poses the key question of what factors account for Halifax's ability to attract and retain talented and creative workers. The research suggests that talented and creative young people come to Halifax because of its incipient cognitive-cultural economy, despite some of the more conservative aspects of its dominant local culture. Their decisions about whether to stay in Halifax depend primarily on job availability rather than social diversity or tolerance. The study also finds that Halifax has remained relatively conservative in its governance mechanisms and, despite several efforts at more strategic planning in the past decade, these exercises have been dominated by business interests with little lasting integration of social and cultural interests. While the research reveals some elements of an emerging cognitive-cultural economy, the chapter concludes that local authorities have done little to sustain its long term-development.

The case studies of small cities in this volume tell a different story again. While all the cities share a common size, the differences among them in economic prospects, resilience, governance arrangements, and the extent to which they are transitioning out of the older industrial sectors to newer, knowledge-intensive sectors is striking. An interesting case in this group is the study of Saskatoon by Peter Phillips and Graeme Webb. Well endowed as the regional hub of a strong agricultural and mineral resource economy, Saskatoon has added considerably to its strengths by building on its knowledge assets through the role of its National Research Council labs, the University of Saskatoon, Innovation Place, and most recently the Canadian Light Source. As a consequence, these developments have put Saskatoon squarely on the map as a knowledge hub for canola research and increasingly the work carried out at the Light Source. Despite the diversity of its economic base, the research found little evidence of cross-sectoral knowledge flows, as overall the city demonstrates the more siloed characteristics associated with small and medium-sized places. While Saskatoon enjoys a solid endowment of talented and creative people, quality of place is not its strongest selling point. Finally, in governance, there is clear evidence that the city has benefited immeasurably from the strong presence and contribution of the senior levels of government to its key knowledge assets and the historical contribution of collaborative organizations in the province. Despite this distinct advantage, recent governance efforts remain strongly siloed, and the city displays few signs associated with institutionalized collaborations.

Betsy Donald and Heather Hall's account of the case study in Kingston, Ontario, tells a dramatically different story. As a small-sized public-sector city, it is not one that normally receives much attention in the literature on urban innovation and governance. They argue that public-sector cities like Kingston are closely aligned with ordinary cities like London in their lack of flagship firms or major cluster profiles. The dominance of the public sector in Kingston's urban economy has created an economic geography that is challenging for private sector innovation, as well as the attraction and retention of skilled workers and the creation of novel governance arrangements. Like London, Kingston benefits from the presence of one of the leading research institutions in the province, with an enviable record for spinning out new firms. Yet the city has enjoyed limited success in using this asset to build an entrepreneurial business climate that can stimulate the emergence of new sectors and support the growth of new firms. Recent initiatives by local civic leaders to attract and retain new immigrants to the city show some signs of promise and represent small steps in the right direction. The city is also highly divided in social terms, which makes the task of building more collaborative forms of governance difficult. Overall, the collaborative networks that have been established remain fragile and highly dependent on external funding sources from public agencies. They conclude that despite a few significant successes, the city could face difficult times ahead in building new governance models and charting an alternative trajectory for its economic development.

The final two case studies of Moncton and St John's in Atlantic Canada tell different stories again. Greater Moncton provides an interesting case study of economic resilience as the city has recovered from the major shocks experienced in the 1980s. According to Yves Bourgeois's account, its growth in size is due in large part to interprovincial and internal migration within the province of New Brunswick. Regional economic planning was supported by the local presence of key public institutions, such as federal departments like Fisheries and Oceans and the Atlantic Canada Opportunities Agency, and agencies such as the Canadian Broadcasting Corporation and Société Radio-Canada. These public sector institutions sustained regional income through steady, high-paying jobs and stimulated further employment growth in the economic sectors dependent on population growth. However, the community has not performed as effectively in how it innovates, attracts and retains talent, and aligns regional efforts. In light of the region's isolation from central markets and the limited opportunities to generate innovation from customer and supplier interactions, the region's highly mobile creative workers and professionals play a key role in bringing new ideas into the region and circulating them throughout. If Moncton is to shield itself effectively against future economic shocks, it will need to develop more effective governance strategies to increase productivity and value added through the adoption of technology and worker-training programs. That will require a more consistent long-term outlook and coordinated regional development approach.

The final chapter on St John's, Newfoundland, provides a different perspective again on the issues of innovation, talent attraction and retention, and governance. In this chapter, Rob Greenwood and Heather Hall refer to St John's as a "metropolis on the margins" with a split personality. It shares many of the features found in some of our larger city-regions, due primarily to its status as the provincial capital and largest city in Newfoundland and Labrador. Yet, as the same time, its small size and relative location within the Canadian urban system endows it with many of the characteristics found in more peripheral regions. As a small peripheral city-region on the geographic margins of the country, it faces a serious challenge in innovation, accessing knowledge and research capacity from universities, despite the notable success of some of its clusters, particularly in ocean technology. As a provincial capital, it enjoys certain lifestyle amenities that are more commonly associated with larger city-regions and have attracted and retained skilled labour in the metropolis. However, its most significant challenge arises from its weak and dysfunctional system of governance, which stands as an obstacle to more innovative and collaborative ways of managing the growth potential for the region. Greater attention to this governance deficit is a critical issue for charting a more innovative direction for St John's.

Conclusion

The case studies of Canadian city-regions assembled in this volume present a complex and varied overview of the dynamics of innovation, talent attraction and retention, and governance in Canadian city-regions. Most significantly, they depict the range of variation across the country between cities of different sizes, located in different regions, and with a wide range of economic specializations. Some of the cases of larger city-regions, particularly Toronto, Montreal, and Vancouver, provide evidence of the rapid pace of change underway to a more diversified cognitive-cultural economy and the patterns of cross-sectoral knowledge flows that the comparative literature on urban development and innovation would lead us to expect. Other important examples demonstrate the extent to which the overall dependence of the national economy on resource exploitation is reflected in the industrial structure and economic dynamics of individual city-regions. Those like Calgary, Saskatoon, and St John's enjoy significant economic benefits as a result of their relative specialization in particular resource fields. Calgary stands out within this category for its success in developing a related knowledge platform on the basis of its local expertise in financing and managing the regional oil economy. However, recent developments in the international market raise critical questions about the long-term viability of this strategy, as Calgary has begun to display the lack of resilience inherent in the concentration of talents that converge in support of a single global market. Another cross-section of large and mid-range cities, including Ottawa, Hamilton, Waterloo, and to some degree Halifax, have enjoyed varying degrees of success in making the transition from their more traditional public-sector and manufacturing base to a more knowledge-based economy associated with the development of advanced technologies and related service industries. Our final set of case studies of mostly mid-sized and smaller cities, including London, Kingston, and Moncton, face greater challenges in making this transition as the conventional industries or transportation nodes from which their past success was derived, continue to undergo major restructuring. While each of these has enjoyed some success, the authors of the case studies suggest that major challenges remain. Managing the urban politics of talent attraction and retention and facilitating the transition to more collaborative forms of local governance and more strategic approaches to managing local economic development are key factors in assisting this process.

Policymakers and economic development strategists can draw important lessons from these findings. First, the case studies illustrate that there are indeed different paths and different challenges for city-regions aspiring to participate in the knowledge-based economy. Given the variance in each city-region's characteristics, such as size, relative location, industrial structure, and social and political histories, it is important to tailor strategies for future economic prosperity that build on each community's historical and geographical particularities. In particular, our research demonstrates that there is no single route to success in attracting and maintaining the dense labour market of well-educated and highly skilled workers found in high-growth regions and that city-regions are advised to build on their inherited assets to plan for future sustainable economic growth. The longitudinal, career-based perspective on the factors shaping the mobility of highly educated and creative labour suggests that there are indeed possible opportunities and policy responses that build on one's strengths, rather than imitating generic and possibly inappropriate policy initiatives from elsewhere.

Our research also demonstrates that Canadian city-regions are experiencing significantly different degrees of success in moving to more collaborative forms of local governance and strategic approaches to managing their local economies. The research revealed three different models that can be found in varying degrees across our case studies: institutionalized collaborations, sector networks, and program partnerships. The findings suggest that the prospects for Canadian city-regions are substantially different as a result of their success in forging new institutional governance mechanisms. Less optimistically, some of the greatest challenges are faced in the smaller urban centres that are endowed with more limited resources to begin with and seem locked into more traditional governance relations. These are the urban centres most in need of developing new institutional mechanisms to mobilize their local resources in order to make the transition to a more knowledge-based economy.

A final note underlines the broader significance of our findings for other levels of government. Cities in Canada remain the constitutional responsibility of the provinces, but they have enjoyed radically different degrees of policy visibility at the federal level over the course of the past half century. The fundamental reality is that city-regions are too important as drivers of economic success to be ignored by the senior levels of government, but they lack sufficient fiscal and policy capacity to meet the challenges of growth, development, and talent attraction on their own. In the majority of cases, both the programs and the financing that provide cities with the resources on which they can build new and innovative development strategies come from the federal and provincial governments. This means that senior levels of government must reflect a greater awareness of these issues and align their policy initiatives with urban realities and challenges to ensure that policies to support/promote innovation, economic development, and talent attraction/retention play out at the urban scale in order to secure the economic future of all regions of the country.

Notes

1 The following discussion draws upon the introduction to volume 1 in this series by David Wolfe and the issues are explored in greater depth in that chapter; see Wolfe (2014).

2 The discussion in this section draws extensively on Gertler et al. (2014). We wish to acknowledge the contributions of our co-authors – Katharine Geddie, Carolyn Hatch, and Josephine Rekers.

3 The following section builds on the argument developed in Wolfe (2009).
4 The following discussion draws upon Bradford and Bramwell's introduction to the third volume in this series (Bradford and Bramwell 2014).

References

Audretsch, D.B. 2002. "The innovative advantage of US cities." *European Planning Studies* 10 (2): 165–76. http://dx.doi.org/10.1080/09654310120114472.

Bartel, A.N.P. 1979. "The migration decision: What role does job mobility play?" *American Economic Review* 69: 775–86.

Beaudry, C., and A. Schiffauerova. 2009. "Who's right, Marshall or Jacobs? The localization versus urbanization debate." *Research Policy* 38 (2): 318–37. http://dx.doi.org/10.1016/j.respol.2008.11.010.

Beckstead, D., and M. Brown. 2003. *From Labrador City to Toronto: The industrial diversity of Canadian cities 1992–2002.* http://publications.gc.ca/collections/Collection/Statcan/11-624-M/11-624-MIE2003003.pdf.

Berry, C.R., and E.L. Glaeser. 2005. "The divergence of human capital levels across cities." Working paper 11617. Cambridge, MA: National Bureau of Economic Research. http://www.nber.org/papers/w11617.pdf.

Beugelsdijk, S. 2007. "Entrepreneurial culture, regional innovativeness and economic growth." *Journal of Evolutionary Economics* 17 (2): 187–210. http://dx.doi.org/10.1007/s00191-006-0048-y.

Blanchard, O.J., L.F. Katz, R.E. Hall, and B. Eichengreen. 1992. "Regional evolutions." *Brookings Papers on Economic Activity* 1992 (1): 1–75. http://dx.doi.org/10.2307/2534556.

Boschma, R., and R. Wenting. 2007. "The spatial evolution of the British automobile industry: Does location matter?" *Industrial and Corporate Change* 16 (2): 213–38. http://dx.doi.org/10.1093/icc/dtm004.

Bourne, L.S., C. Brunelle, M. Polese, and J. Simmons. 2011. "Growth and change in the Canadian urban system." In *Canadian urban regions: Trajectories of growth and change*, ed. L.S. Bourne, T. Hutton, R.G. Shearmur, and J. Simmons, 43–80. Toronto: Oxford University Press.

Bradford, N. 2004. "Place matters and multi-level governance: Perspectives on a new urban policy paradigm." *Policy Options* 25 (2): 39–44.

Bradford, N., and A. Bramwell. 2014. "Governing urban economies: Innovation and inclusion in Canadian city-regions." In *Governing urban economies: Innovation and inclusion in Canadian city-regions*, ed. N. Bradford and A. Bramwell, 3–33. Toronto: University of Toronto Press.

Bramwell, A., J. Nelles, and D.A. Wolfe. 2008. "Knowledge, innovation, and institutions: Global and local dimensions of the ICT cluster in Waterloo, Canada." *Regional Studies* 42: 1 (February): 101–16.

Brezis, E.S., and P. Krugman. 1997. "Technology and the life cycle of cities." *Journal of Economic Growth* 2 (4): 369–83. http://dx.doi.org/10.1023/A:1009754704364.

Bridge, G. 2006. "A global gentrifier class?" *Environment & Planning A* 39 (1): 32–46. http://dx.doi.org/10.1068/a38471.

Carlino, G., and E. Mills. 1987. "The determinants of county growth." *Journal of Regional Science* 27 (1): 39–54. http://dx.doi.org/10.1111/j.1467-9787.1987.tb01143.x.

City of Montreal. 2007. *Action Plan 2007–2017: Montreal, Cultural Metropolis.* Montreal: City of Montreal. http://www2.ville.montreal.qc.ca/pls/portal/docs/page/pa0717_en/rep_pa0717/vision.php.

Clark, T.N., R. Lloyd, K.K. Wong, and P. Jain. 2002. "Amenities drive urban growth." *Journal of Urban Affairs* 24 (5): 493–515. http://dx.doi.org/10.1111/1467-9906.00134.

Clifton, N. 2008. "The 'creative class' in the UK: An initial analysis." *Geografiska Annaler: Series B, Human Geography* 90 (1): 63–82. http://dx.doi.org/10.1111/j.1468-0467.2008.00276.x.

Conference Board of Canada. 2007. *City magnets: Benchmarking the attractiveness of Canadian CMAs.* Ottawa: Conference Board of Canada.

Cooke, P. 2005. "Regional innovation, entrepreneurship and talent systems." In "Clusters and Regional Innovation Systems," ed. D. Doloreux and J. Revilla Diez, special issue, *International Journal of Entrepreneurship and Innovation* 7 (2–5): 117–39.

–. 2014. "Related variety, knowledge platforms and the challenge for cities and regions in the global economy." In *Innovating in urban economies: Economic transformation in Canadian city-regions*, ed. David A. Wolfe, 353–67. Toronto: University of Toronto Press.

Currid, E. 2006. "New York as a global creative hub: A competitive analysis of four theories on world cities." *Economic Development Quarterly* 20 (4): 330–50. http://dx.doi.org/10.1177/0891242406292708.

–. 2007a. "How art and culture happen in New York: Implications for urban economic development." *Journal of the American Planning Association* 73 (4): 454–67. http://dx.doi.org/10.1080/01944360708978526.

–. 2007b. *The Warhol economy: How fashion, art and music drive New York City.* Princeton: Princeton University Press.

Danyluk, M., and D. Ley. 2007. "Modalities of the new middle class: Ideology and behaviour in the journey to work from gentrified neighbourhoods in Canada." *Urban Studies* 44 (11): 2195–210. http://dx.doi.org/10.1080/00420980701520277.

Deller, S.C., T.-H. Tsai, D.W. Marcouiller, and D.B.K. English. 2001. "The role of amenities and quality of life in rural economic growth." *American Journal of*

Agricultural Economics 83 (2): 352–65. http://dx.doi.org/10.1111/0002-9092.00161.

Donald, B., and D. Morrow. 2003. *Competing for talent: Implications for social and cultural policy in Canadian city-regions.* Ottawa: Strategic Research and Analysis, Canadian Heritage.

Duranton, G., and D. Puga. 2000. "Diversity and specialisation in cities: Why, where and when does it matter?" *Urban Studies* 37 (3): 533–55. http://dx.doi.org/10.1080/0042098002104.

Duxbury, N. 2004. *Creative cities: Principles and practices.* Canadian Policy Research Networks. http://www.cprn.org/doc.cfm?l=en&doc=1082.

Feldman, M., and D. Audretsch. 1998. "Innovation in cities: Science-based diversity, specialization, and localized competition." *European Economic Review* 43: 409–29.

Filion, P. 2010. "Growth and decline in the Canadian urban system: The impact of emerging economic, policy and demographic trends." *GeoJournal* 75 (6): 517–38. http://dx.doi.org/10.1007/s10708-009-9275-8.

Florida, R. 2002a. "Bohemia and economic geography." *Journal of Economic Geography* 2 (1): 55–71. http://dx.doi.org/10.1093/jeg/2.1.55.

–. 2002b. "The economic geography of talent." *Annals of the Association of American Geographers* 92 (4): 743–55. http://dx.doi.org/10.1111/1467-8306.00314.

–. 2002c. *The rise of the creative class.* New York: Basic Books.

Florida, R., and G. Gates. 2003. "Technology and tolerance: The importance of diversity to high-technology growth." In *The city as an entertainment machine: Research in urban policy*, vol. 9., ed. T.N. Clark, 199–219. Oxford: Elsevier. http://dx.doi.org/10.1016/S1479-3520(03)09007-X.

Florida, R., G. Gates, B. Knudsen, and K. Stolarick. 2006. *The university and the creative economy.* http://www.creativeclass.com/rfcgdb/articles/the%20university%20and%20the%20creative%20economy.pdf.

Florida, R., C. Mellander, and K. Stolarick. 2008. "Inside the black box of regional development: Human capital, the creative class and tolerance." *Journal of Economic Geography* 8 (5): 615–49. http://dx.doi.org/10.1093/jeg/lbn023.

–. 2010. "Talent, technology and tolerance in Canadian regional development." *Canadian Geographer / Le géographe canadien* 54 (3): 277–304. http://dx.doi.org/10.1111/j.1541-0064.2009.00293.x.

Gertler, M.S. 2001. "Urban economy and society in Canada: Flows of people, capital and ideas." *Canadian Journal of Policy Research* 2: 119–30.

Gertler, M.S., R. Florida, G. Gates, and T. Vinodrai. 2002. *Competing on creativity: Placing Ontario's cities in continental context.* Toronto: Institute for Competitiveness and Prosperity, and the Ontario Ministry of Enterprise, Opportunity and Innovation.

Gertler, M.S., K. Geddie, C. Hatch, and J. Rekers. 2014. "Attracting and retaining talent: The evidence from Canada's city-regions." In *Seeking talent for creative cities: The social dynamics of economic innovation*, ed. J. Grant, 3–30. Toronto: University of Toronto Press.

Gertler, M.S., and T. Vinodrai. 2005. "Anchors of creativity: How do public universities create competitive and cohesive communities?" In *Taking public universities seriously*, ed. F. Iacobucci and C. Tuohy, 293–315. Toronto: University of Toronto Press.

Glaeser, E.L. 2000. "The new economics of urban and regional growth." In *The Oxford handbook of economic geography*, ed. G. Clark, M. Gertler, and M. Feldman, 83–98. Oxford: Oxford University Press.

–. 2005a. "Review of Richard Florida's *The rise of the creative class*." *Regional Science and Urban Economics* 35 (5): 593–6. http://dx.doi.org/10.1016/j.regsciurbeco.2005.01.005.

–. 2005b. *Smart growth: Education, skilled workers and the future of cold-weather Cities*. Cambridge, MA: Kennedy School, Harvard University.

–. 2011. *Triumph of the city: How our greatest invention makes us richer, smarter, greener, healthier, and happier*. New York: Penguin.

Glaeser, E.L., and J.D. Gottlieb. 2006. "Urban resurgence and the consumer city." *Urban Studies* 43 (8): 1275–99. http://dx.doi.org/10.1080/00420980600775683.

Grant, J., and K. Kronstal. 2010. "The social dynamics of attracting talent in Halifax." *Canadian Geographer / Le géographe canadien* 54 (3): 347–65. http://dx.doi.org/10.1111/j.1541-0064.2010.00310.x.

Hall, P. 1998. *Cities in civilization*. New York: Pantheon Books.

Hansen, H.K., and T. Niedomysl. 2008. "Migration of the creative class: Evidence from Sweden." *Journal of Economic Geography* 9 (2): 191–206. http://dx.doi.org/10.1093/jeg/lbn046.

Henton, D., J. Melville, and J. Parr. 2006. *Regional stewardship and collaborative governance*. Monograph Series. Denver: Alliance for Regional Stewardship.

Houston, D., A. Findlay, R. Harrison, and C. Mason. 2008. "Will attracting the 'creative class' boost economic growth in old industrial regions? A case study of Scotland." *Geografiska Annaler. Series B, Human Geography* 90 (2): 133–49. http://dx.doi.org/10.1111/j.1468-0467.2008.00283.x.

Hutton, T.A. 2008. *The new economy of the inner city*. London: Routledge.

Inglehart, R., and P. Norris. 2003. *Rising tide*. New York: Cambridge University Press. http://dx.doi.org/10.1017/CBO9780511550362.

Inglehart, R., and C. Welzel. 2005. *Modernization, cultural change and democracy*. New York: Cambridge University Press.

Jacobs, J. 1961. *The death and life of great American cities*. New York: Random House.

–. 1969. *The economy of cities*. New York: Random House.

–. 1984. *Cities and the wealth of nations: Principles of economic life*. New York: Random House.

Katz, B., and J. Bradley. 2013. *The metropolitan revolution: How cities and metros are fixing our broken politics and fragile economy*. Washington, DC: Brookings Institution.

Keating, M. 2002. "Governing cities and regions: Territorial restructuring in a global age." In *Global city-regions: Trends, theory, policy*, ed. A.J. Scott, 371–89. Oxford: Oxford University Press.

Ketels, C. 2013. "Recent research on competitiveness and clusters: What are the implications for regional policy?" *Cambridge Journal of Regions, Economy and Society* 6 (2): 269–84. http://dx.doi.org/10.1093/cjres/rst008.

Krugman, P. 1991. *Geography and trade*. Cambridge, MA: MIT Press.

Lepawsky, J., C. Phan, and R. Greenwood. 2010. "Metropolis on the margins: Talent attraction and retention to the St John's city-region." *Canadian Geographer / Le géographe canadien* 54 (3): 324–46. http://dx.doi.org/10.1111/j.1541-0064.2010.00315.x.

–. 2002. "Neo-bohemia: Art and neighborhood redevelopment in Chicago." *Journal of Urban Affairs* 24 (5): 517–32. http://dx.doi.org/10.1111/1467-9906.00141.

–. 2004. "The neighborhood in cultural production: Material and symbolic resources in the new bohemia." *City & Community* 3 (4): 343–72. http://dx.doi.org/10.1111/j.1535-6841.2004.00092.x.

Lloyd, R., and T.N. Clark. 2001. "The city as an entertainment machine." In *Critical Perspectives on Urban Redevelopment*. Vol. 6 of *Research in Urban Sociology*, ed. F.K. Gatham, 357–78. Oxford: JAI/Elsevier. http://dx.doi.org/10.1016/S1047-0042(01)80014-3.

Lucas, R., Jr. 1988. "On the mechanics of economic development." *Journal of Monetary Economics* 22 (1): 3–42. http://dx.doi.org/10.1016/0304-3932(88)90168-7.

Malanga, S. 2004. "The curse of the creative class." *City Journal* 14 (1): 36–45.

Markusen, A. 2006. "Urban development and the politics of a creative class: Evidence from a study of artists." *Environment & Planning A* 38 (10): 1921–40. http://dx.doi.org/10.1068/a38179.

Markusen, A., and G. Schrock. 2006. "The artistic dividend: Urban artistic specialisation and economic development implications." *Urban Studies* 43 (10): 1661–86. http://dx.doi.org/10.1080/00420980600888478.

Maskell, P., and A. Malmberg. 1999. "Localised learning and industrial competitiveness." *Cambridge Journal of Economics* 23 (2): 167–85. http://dx.doi.org/10.1093/cje/23.2.167.

McGranahan, D., and T. Wojan. 2007. "Recasting the creative class to examine growth processes in rural and urban counties." *Regional Studies* 41 (2): 197–216. http://dx.doi.org/10.1080/00343400600928285.

Mellander, C., and R. Florida. 2011. "Creativity, Talent and Regional Wages in Sweden." *Annals of Regional Science* 46 (3): 637–60.

Montgomery, J. 2007. *The new wealth of cities: City dynamics and the fifth wave.* Aldershot, UK: Ashgate.

Moretti, E. 2012. *The new geography of jobs.* Boston: Houghton Mifflin Harcourt.

Noland, M. 2005. "Popular attitudes, globalization and risk." *International Finance* 8 (2): 199–229. http://dx.doi.org/10.1111/j.1468-2362.2005.00157.x.

OECD. 2006. *Territorial reviews: Competitive cities in the global economy.* Paris: Organisation for Economic Co-operation and Development.

Orlando, M.J., and M. Verba. 2005. *Do only big cities innovate? Technological maturity and the location of innovation.* Federal Reserve Bank of Kansas City Economic Review. Second Quarter.

Ottaviano, G.I.P., and G. Peri. 2005. "Cities and culture." *Journal of Urban Economics* 58 (2): 304–37. http://dx.doi.org/10.1016/j.jue.2005.06.004.

Page, S. 2007. *The difference.* Princeton, NJ: Princeton University Press.

Polèse, M., and R. Shearmur. 2006. "Why some regions will decline: A Canadian case study with thoughts on local development strategies." *Regional Science* 85 (1): 23–46. http://dx.doi.org/10.1111/j.1435-5957.2006.00024.x.

Porter, M.E. 1998. "Clusters and the new economics of competition." *Harvard Business Review* 77 (6): 77–90.

–. 2003. "The economic performance of regions." *Regional Studies* 37 (6 & 7): 549–78.

Rantisi, N.M., and D. Leslie. 2006. "Branding the design metropole: The case of Montréal, Canada." *Area* 38 (4): 364–76. http://dx.doi.org/10.1111/j.1475-4762.2006.00705.x.

Rantisi, N.M., D. Leslie, and S. Christopherson. 2006. "Placing the creative economy: Scale, politics, and the material – the rise of the new 'creative' imperative." *Environment & Planning A* 38 (10): 1789–97. http://dx.doi.org/10.1068/a39210.

Roback, J. 1982. "Wages, rents, and the quality of life." *Journal of Political Economy* 90 (6): 1257–78. http://dx.doi.org/10.1086/261120.

Rodríguez-Pose, A. 2008. "The rise of the 'city-region' concept and its development policy implications." *European Planning Studies* 16 (8): 1025–46. http://dx.doi.org/10.1080/09654310802315567.

Ross, D., and R.E. Friedman. 1990. "The emerging third wave: New economic development strategies in the 1990s." *Entrepreneurial Economy Review* 9 (1): 3–10.

Safford, S. 2009. *Why the Garden Club couldn't save Youngstown: The transformation of the rust belt.* Cambridge, MA: Harvard University Press.

Sands, G., and L.A. Reese. 2008. "Cultivating the creative class: And what about Nanaimo?" *Economic Development Quarterly* 22 (1): 8–23.

Saxenian, A. 2002. *Local and global networks of immigrant professionals in Silicon Valley.* San Francisco: Public Policy Institute of California.

Schimpf, M. 2008. "Creative input: The role of culture occupations in the economy during the 1990s." Culture, Tourism and the Centre for Education Statistics Research Paper 81-595-M no. 064. Ottawa: Statistics Canada.

Schimpf, M., and P. Sereda. 2001. "Towards a geography of culture: Culture occupations across the Canadian urban-rural divide." Culture, Tourism and the Centre for Education Statistics Research Paper 81-595-MIE no. 053. Ottawa: Statistics Canada.

Scott, A.J. 2006. "Creative cities: Conceptual issues and policy questions." *Journal of Urban Affairs* 28 (1): 1–17. http://dx.doi.org/10.1111/j.0735-2166.2006.00256.x.

–. 2007. "Capitalism and urbanization in a new key? The Cognitive-Cultural Dimension." *Social Forces* 85 (4): 1465–82. http://dx.doi.org/10.1353/sof.2007.0078.

–. 2008. *Social economy of the metropolis: Cognitive-cultural capitalism and the global resurgence of cities.* Oxford: Oxford University Press. http://dx.doi.org/10.1093/acprof:oso/9780199549306.001.0001.

–. 2013. "A world in emergence: Notes towards a resynthesis of urban-economic geography for the twenty-first century." In *Reframing regional development: Evolution, innovation and transition*, ed. Philip Cooke, 29–53. London: Routledge.

Shapiro, J.M. 2006. "Smart cities: Quality of life, productivity, and the growth effects of human capital." *Review of Economics and Statistics* 88 (2): 324–35. http://dx.doi.org/10.1162/rest.88.2.324.

Shearmur, R. 2007. "The new knowledge aristocracy: The creative class, mobility and urban growth." *Work Organisation, Labour & Globalisation* 1 (1): 31–47.

–. 2010. "Space, place and innovation: A distance-based approach." *Canadian Geographer* 54 (1): 46–67.

–. 2012. "Are cities the font of innovation? A critical review of the literature on cities and innovation." *Cities* 29 (S2): S9–S18.

Slack, E., L. Bourne, and M.S. Gertler. 2003. "Vibrant cities and city-regions: Responding to emerging challenges – The panel on the role of government." http://munkschool.utoronto.ca/imfg/uploads/141/rp17.pdf.

Stolarick, K., and R. Florida. 2006. "Creativity, connections and innovation: A study of linkages in the Montréal region." *Environment & Planning A* 38 (10): 1799–817. http://dx.doi.org/10.1068/a3874.

Swanstrom, T. 2008. "Regional resilience: A critical examination of the ecological framework." Working Paper 2008-07, Berkeley Institute of Urban and Regional Development. Berkeley: University of California Berkeley.

Tremblay, G. 2006. "Notes for a speech by the mayor of Montreal to the Montreal Real Estate Forum." 29 March, Montreal.

van Oort, F., S. de Geus, and T. Dogaru. 2015. "Related variety and regional economic growth in a cross-section of European urban regions." *European*

Planning Studies 23 (6): 1110–27. http://dx.doi.org/10.1080/09654313.2014.905003.

Veltz, P. 2004. "The resurgent city: Keynote address." Leverhulme International Symposium, London School of Economics, 19–21 April.

Venables, A.J. 2006. *Shifts in economic geography and their causes.* Economic Review, Federal Reserve Bank of St Louis, Fourth Quarter.

Wojan, T.R., D.M. Lambert, and D.A. McGranahan. 2007. "Emoting with their feet: Bohemian attraction to creative milieu." *Journal of Economic Geography* 7 (6): 711–36. http://dx.doi.org/10.1093/jeg/lbm029.

Wolfe, D.A. 2009. *21st century cities in Canada: The geography of innovation.* Ottawa: Conference Board of Canada.

–. 2010. "The strategic management of core cities: Path dependency and economic adjustment in resilient regions." *Cambridge Journal of Regions, Economy and Society* 3 (1): 139–52. http://dx.doi.org/10.1093/cjres/rsp032.

–. 2014. "Introduction to the dynamics of innovation in city-regions." In *Innovating in urban economies: Economic transformation in Canadian city-regions,* ed. David A. Wolfe, 3–32. Toronto: University of Toronto Press.

Wolfe, D.A., and A. Bramwell. 2008. "Innovation, creativity and governance: Social dynamics of economic performance in city-regions." *Innovation: Management, Policy & Practice* 10 (2–3), 170–82.

Wolfe, D.A., and M.S. Gertler. 2004. "Clusters from the inside and out: Local dynamics and global linkages." *Urban Studies* 41 (5–6): 1071–93. http://dx.doi.org/10.1080/00420980410001675832.

Wong, K.W., and T. Bunnell. 2006. "New economy discourse and spaces in Singapore: A case study of one-north." *Environment and Planning A* 38: 69–83.

PART II

The Dynamics of Economic Change in Large Cities

2 Toronto's Fourth Era: An Emerging Cognitive-Cultural Economy

DAVID A. WOLFE AND ALLISON BRAMWELL

Introduction

Toronto's economy is the largest in Canada and the most economically diverse. It differs significantly from the other two large cities – Montreal and Vancouver – in the breadth and diversity of its economic structure and the premier position it occupies in the Canadian urban system. A recent analysis commented that "the Toronto region has become the country's pre-eminent metropolis, its dominant economic engine as well as innovation milieu, as well as its principal gateway to the rest of the world" (Bourne, Britton, and Leslie 2011, 236). Toronto's place in the Canadian urban system is marked by four major eras of growth in the post-war period from its position as the major manufacturing hub in Southern Ontario at the end of the Second World War through to its current position as a centre for higher-order business and financial services as well as research-intensive manufacturing. Since the turn of the millennium, driven by the transition to new economic and social patterns of development, Toronto has entered its fourth era of post-war growth. Demarcated by the growing integration of the urban core within the broader regional economy, this era reflects the emergence of Toronto as a broadly based service economy with a growing concentration in knowledge-intensive business and financial services and the cultural and creative industries (Boston Consulting Group 1995).

The current era of Toronto's economic growth reflects the transition from the old Fordist paradigm of growth that dominated through the first half of the post-war period to what Allen Scott labels a "cognitive-cultural economy." The shift to this new form of production is facilitated by the steady adoption of digital technologies for creating more customized goods through a less routinized organization of production. This transition in urban economies is the product of three convergent trends: the digitization of an ever-larger proportion of the modern economy through the incorporation of information and communication technologies (ICTs), the resulting shift to more modular forms of production systems into a more networked system made possible by the communication and coordination capabilities of ICTs, and finally, the elimination of significant amounts of routine labour, particularly in manufacturing (Scott 2013).

This transition has been marked by the steady decline of manufacturing as a key component of the economic structure of urban agglomerations, largely replaced by the expansion of office and service employment in sectors that rely on higher-level cognitive and cultural labour inputs, an expansion that is increasingly concentrated in the central business districts of larger city regions. At the same time, the boundary between traditional sectors of the economy is shifting as innovation blurs the distinction between traditional manufacturing and service-oriented activity. While many industrial enterprises still occur in identifiable sectors staffed by industry-specific occupations, much of the knowledge-intensive business associated with new and emerging sectors of the economy is less easily categorized. Scott's cognitive-cultural economy paradigm refers to shifts in the nature of economic activity where leading-edge economic growth and innovation are driven by "technology-intensive manufacturing, diverse services, 'fashion-oriented neo-artisanal production,' and cultural products industries" (Scott 2007, 1466).

The dramatic reconfiguration of the economic base and the occupational structure of metropolitan areas is most strikingly evident in urban architecture and the restructuring of downtowns. Redesign of the physical space in central business districts and urban cores is being adapted for use in a growing range of cognitive-cultural activities. Old factories and warehouses are being repurposed for use in a wide range of cultural and design-intensive activities. Increasingly visible and idiosyncratic high-rise office towers are evidence of the dramatic intensification of land use, often reflecting the aesthetic status afforded to an international cadre of star architects, whose unique designs are intended partly to bestow a distinctive character on large urban agglomerations aspiring to "global city" status (Scott 2013, 2014).

Consistent with this transition, the leading sectors in Toronto's fourth-era economy are concentrated in the knowledge- and design-intensive sectors in business and financial services, some core manufacturing sectors, including automotive and computers, the biopharmaceutical and biotechnology sectors, as well as the cultural, creative, and design-intensive sectors that make substantial use of ICTs in a wide range of activities. The sectoral concentrations of Toronto's regional economy increasingly lie in areas that involve higher-order business functions in global services as well as knowledge- and design-intensive activities, drawing on a dense pool of talented and highly skilled labour to drive its continued growth. Given the fact that Toronto has also been a magnet for inward migration, absorbing almost 40 per cent of all immigrants to Canada and with foreign-born residents accounting for 48 per cent of the region's population in the latest census, the steady growth of the local talent pool provides a strong stimulus for the growth of those sectors that comprise Toronto's expanding cognitive-cultural economy (OECD 2010).

However, while the concept of the cognitive-cultural economy focuses on technologies, production processes, and human capital in the knowledge-based economy, it is relatively silent on the institutional dimensions of these social processes. Renewed interest in the role of institutions in regional economic development has yielded theoretical innovations and empirical insights that address this conceptual gap. As outlined in the introduction to this volume, there is growing evidence of a positive relationship between institutional "thickness" and the resilience and adaptive capacity of city-regions; cities with networked civic associations, rich relational environments, and dynamic civic leadership are better poised to adopt coordinated and strategic approaches to urban economic development (Wolfe 2010, 2012; Christopherson, Michie, and Tyler, 2010). It follows that city-regions with these institutional and relational endowments are better positioned to make the transition to cognitive-cultural economy industries.

Using the lens of the cognitive-cultural economy, this chapter analyses patterns of innovation emerging in key knowledge-intensive sectors of the regional economy such as financial services, ICTs, and the creative and cultural industries. It then examines the changing role of talent and creativity in sectors that are linked most directly to the cognitive-cultural economy, including financial services, ICT, creative and cultural industries, fashion and design, and architecture. Finally we conclude with observations about the extent to which governance structures in the region have kept pace with the changing geographic boundaries and shifting industrial and occupational systems in the region. The Toronto Region is moving into a fourth era of cognitive cultural economy with its attendant capacity for innovation, creativity, and talent attraction, but remains encumbered with fragmented and ineffectual second-era governance institutions unable to sustain numerous regional development initiatives. Yet while the region lacks the institutional infrastructure and relational connective tissue to coordinate the strategic efforts of multiple governmental and non-governmental actors, organizations, and agendas across policy sectors and geographical scales, it can claim one of the most successful and innovative civic governance initiatives emerging across the case studies in this volume. The Greater Toronto CivicAction Alliance is a rare example in Canada of an innovative and sustainable cross-sector urban governance initiative (Bramwell and Wolfe 2014; Bramwell and Pierre 2013).

Overview of the Toronto Region Economy

The Toronto region economy is emerging as the pre-eminent example of a cognitive-cultural economy in Canada. As such, it occupies a unique position within the Canadian urban system, marked by the relative size and diversity of its economy across a wide range of industrial sectors. Generating $268 billion in GDP in 2012 and ranking first in economic momentum among Canada's largest cities for two years in a row, the region now accounts for 45 per cent of provincial and 18 per cent of national GDP, and employment growth has recovered well from the global 2008–9 recession (Pennachetti 2014). To better understand Toronto's position as a national leader in the knowledge-based economy, this section offers a brief overview Toronto's trajectory of development through the four eras of post-war growth to the current composition of its industrial structure, the demographic make-up of the population, and employment trends in this complex regional economy.

The first era of Toronto's post-war growth extended from the end of the First World War to the mid-1960s. This was a manufacturing-intensive period in Toronto's development that benefited from the industrial build-up stimulated by the war and the rapid influx of foreign subsidiaries into southern Ontario focused upon the expansion of the aerospace, auto, and telecommunication sectors. Toronto's economy also benefited from the substantial increase in government spending on educational, physical, and social infrastructure associated with the expansion of the post-war welfare state (Boston Consulting Group 1995). This era has also been referred to as the period of planning Fordism (Donald 2002). The second era, from the signing of the Auto Pact Agreement with the United States in 1965 to the negotiation of the comprehensive Free Trade Agreement with the United States in 1988, was marked by an extension and deepening of sectors that had taken hold in the earlier period, strongly augmented by the flight of financial and business services from Montreal to Toronto following the election of the Parti Québécois government in 1976. In this second era, Toronto emerged as the economic capital and corporate headquarters of Canada (Boston Consulting Group 1995; Polèse and Shearmur 2004). In her analysis of the path of Toronto's post-war development, Donald refers to this as the period of "full-swing Fordism" (2002).

The decade following the successful negotiation of the Canada-U.S. Free Trade Agreement and the North American Free Trade Agreement marked a period of dramatic restructuring of the regional economy that was exacerbated by continental integration and the deep cyclical recession from 1990 to 1992. The impact of this restructuring was further compounded by the effects of technological changes that occurred from the mid-1980s onwards, leading to a substantial loss of traditional manufacturing and clerical jobs and increasing income polarization in the city. Through this restructuring, however, industrial sectors such as autos, aerospace, telecommunications, and financial services continued to expand along with the rapid growth of the creative and cultural industries, including film, television, live theatre, music, fashion, design, and publishing (Boston Consulting Group 1995). This period has also been referred to as one of unravelling Fordism (Donald 2002). The phase since the turn of the millennium has been labelled the fourth era in Toronto's post-war development by a study undertaken for the Greater Toronto Area Task Force. In this era, Toronto has extended its lead as the dominant financial and commercial centre in Canada, and has expanded in a growing number of research-intensive manufacturing sectors and knowledge-intensive business services. The position of the city as the dominant centre for the production of cultural and creative content in Canada has also strengthened its attraction for other design-intensive creative sectors with close links to the cultural industries.

Numerous knowledge-intensive, post-industrial economic activities characterize the cognitive-cultural economy emerging in the region, such as information and communications technology (including new media), biomedicine and biotechnology, financial services, fashion and design, aerospace and automotive production, tourism, and the cultural-creative industries. What differentiates the Toronto region most clearly from its closest competitors within the Canadian urban system is its significant lead over both Montreal and Vancouver in financial and higher-order business services, with 28.2 per cent of its labour force in this sector.[1] The Toronto regional economy also achieved above-average performance levels, according to indicators such as employment and population growth.[2] As the data in table 2.1 indicate, the increase in population was one and a half times the national average between 2006 and 2011, employment growth was nearly 50 per cent higher than the national average, and average employment income was almost 20 per cent higher than the national average. It scores well on all the indicators associated with the presence of the creative class, including the proportion of the population with post-secondary education, the percentage in both creative occupations, and science and technology–oriented occupations (table 2.1).

The physical manifestation of Toronto's emergence as a leading cognitive-cultural urban centre is nowhere more visible than in the downtown business core of the city, which has led all other North American cities in the construction of high-rise towers, both residential and commercial. These towers are filled by the firms and occupations associated with the financial service industries and knowledge-intensive business services, the information and communications technology firms that support them, and the design-based activities found throughout the entertainment and creative industries. Recent data from the Toronto Planning Department provides strong evidence that this trend will continue at the same pace over the next decade, based on proposals for new construction that have been approved or are pending approval (Pennachetti 2014). This construction boom, underway for the past decade, is being fed by the stronger population growth in the City of Toronto compared to the Greater Toronto Area (GTA); the downtown core has grown 18 per cent in the last decade, dramatically outstripping growth in the wider city at 4.5 per cent. Toronto clearly benefits from the presence of a highly diversified regional economy, including a strong concentration of creative and cultural industries that is contributing to its development as a "Schumpeterian hub" of innovation and creativity (Wolfe 2009).

Table 2.1. Key socio-economic and demographic characteristics of the Toronto CMA, 2011

Characteristic	Toronto 2011	Canada 2011
Population	5,583,064	33,476,690
Population increase, 2006–11	9.2%	5.9%
Foreign born	47.9%	22.0%
BA or higher	29.9%	20.9%
PhDs per 1000	9.1	7.6
Employment growth	5.8%	3.6%
Unemployment rate	8.6%	7.8%
In creative occupations	37.1%	32.0%
In science tech occupations	8.7%	7.2%
Bohemians per 1,000	20.7	13.9
Number of clusters	12	214
Employment in clusters	55.4%	25.8%
Average full-time employment income	$65,903	$58,129
Income increase, 2006–11	8.5%	13.5%

Source: National Household Survey (2011)

Innovation and Knowledge Flows in Toronto's Emerging Cognitive-Cultural Economy

One of the most notable developments in Toronto over the past two decades has been the marked growth in two major sectors of the regional economy. Particular strengths have emerged in high-end knowledge-intensive business services, especially finance and related industries, and the cultural and creative sector, including media, fashion, and design. The changing nature of innovation in these sectors has been strongly shaped by the widespread adoption and diffusion of ICTs. The progressive digitization of production and services exerts a strong influence over innovation within these sectors, constantly reshaping them in important ways.

The Financial Services–ICT Nexus in the Toronto Region[3]

Toronto has the third largest concentration of financial services employment in North America, after New York and Chicago. According to the Global Financial Centres Index,[4] the Toronto region placed in the top-ten group of financial centres globally in 2011, and in *Cities of Opportunity,* it ranked second after New York City (PwC and the Partnership for New York 2011).[5] Along with the highest concentration of large financial services firms in the country, Toronto is also the headquarters for most of the $700 billion investment management industry and a major pension management hub. Fully 307,963 people were employed in the sector across the Toronto city-region in 2011 (Spencer 2014). An equally dynamic part of the regional economy, the ICT sector employs 161,000 people in 11,500 firms in Toronto alone.[6] Unlike the financial services sector where the firms tend to be large, the vast majority of ICT firms are small and medium-sized enterprises with fewer than fifty employees (City of Toronto 2010).

The growing interconnection between the financial services and the ICT sector in the Toronto region illustrates the blurring of boundaries between economic areas that Scott describes as an important aspect of the cognitive-cultural economy. The financial services industry is one of the largest consumers of ICTs, a pattern that is transforming the region's financial services sector by enabling firms to better meet consumer demand and to increase overall global competitiveness and market share. The finance industry in the Toronto region tends to be more imitative or adaptive than leading edge in its approach to innovation. Financial services firms rely on large and global ICT firms with proven technologies rather than take risks on innovations from smaller and less proven domestic providers. These firms also tend to emphasize reliability, security, profitability, and service quality, focusing on incremental process, product, service, and organizational innovation to support service delivery rather than on radical innovation.

Nonetheless, Toronto has been at the forefront of the IT revolution in financial services introduced across the country over the past two decades. Despite – or perhaps because of – inherent conservatism and risk aversion in financial services, cross-sector combinations of product and process innovations in the financial services–ICT nexus appear to be accelerating. Several important system-wide innovations in the past decade such as the rollout of a national automated teller machine (ATM) system, the establishment of specialized back-office processing facilities, the creation of the debit system Interac, and the effective management of risk, which significantly lessened the impact of the recent financial crisis, not only demonstrate collaboration among Canadian financial institutions, but also illustrate cross-sector innovation in the financial services–ICT nexus. Other recent examples of ICT-driven innovation by Canadian financial institutions include customization of financial products and services for market differentiation, development of new ways of interacting with customers through social media, enhancement of the customer experience in retail banking with attractive banking environments, development of payment methods for smart phones, and business model innovation in online services.

Knowledge flows within the financial services–ICT nexus also involve the outsourcing of expertise and capabilities. The outsourcing of off-the-shelf ICT services and equipment is used extensively by firms with small IT departments; some financial services firms simply do not have the resources to justify internalizing such facilities. In the Toronto region, services are outsourced to national financial institutions by leading international ICT vendors and other large U.S.-based financial enterprises. In addition, financial services firms outsource when they do not have the necessary IT skills themselves and/or if it is less expensive than hiring internally. For instance, an interviewee noted that a major national bank outsources coding if the human resources in another country like India is more affordable than those in Canada.

The importance of client-vendor communication underscores the importance of close geographical proximity for the two sectors in the Toronto region. Because internal and external knowledge flows are critical to innovation in the financial services–ICT nexus, communication is the linchpin to maintaining strong cross-sector relationships. Maintaining a visible physical presence in the Toronto region, especially in the burgeoning central business district, is critical to meeting the needs of financial services firms. Most ICT firms are committed to interacting with their financial services clients every day and have developed strategies for mitigating miscommunication. In interviews, virtually all respondents in the financial services sector reported major benefits to being located in the business hub of Canada along with head offices of many large Canadian corporations, and a variety of industry verticals. Proximity to the financial services sector is also reported as an important advantage for the ICT firms that provide hardware, software, and services. This point was stressed in an interview with a major IT provider who noted that "being close to our customers is core. And that is an advantage to being [downtown] in the GTA … If we had a string that was five or six kilometres long and we drew a circle, other than hitting the lake south of us, we'd probably hit every CEO, CFO, CIO in the financial services industry in Canada, barring a couple of folks up in Montreal and a big insurance company out in Winnipeg, and arguably a few out at the West Coast. But the major ones, we'd hit them all right here" (confidential interview). Small ICT vendors in particular choose to headquarter their operations in Toronto because the critical risk of market acceptance in the local financial services sector is far outweighed by the value of the local talent supply and the proximity advantage that Toronto holds for reaching their key Canadian and U.S. financial services clients.

Other less obvious advantages of co-location include relative cost advantages as a financial services centre, especially when compared to other global financial service capitals such as London and New York, with which it shares the same time zone. From a talent perspective, one respondent observed that "lots of folks that have gone to New York are looking to come home" (confidential interview). The Toronto region is also well endowed with a competitive research infrastructure in the presence of world-class universities and community colleges, an international airport, and a well-developed highway system, although transportation within the Toronto region was mentioned as a hindrance to attracting talent to certain locations throughout the city not accessible by public transit. Thus, innovation, knowledge flows, and locational dynamics all interact in important ways to accelerate cross-sector innovation between financial services and ICT in the Toronto region. The enabling role of ICTs in financial services is expected to gain even more traction as the deployment of mobile platforms and services, and social media is extended.

Media and the Cultural-Creative Economy Nexus in Toronto

Toronto's cultural and creative industries represent a key component of the region's expanding cognitive-cultural economy, sharing close links with, and integration into, the ICT sector.[7] Toronto hosts the principal media agglomeration in English-speaking Canada and the third-largest in North America after New York and Los Angeles. This group contains most of English Canada's major screen production houses, public broadcasters, and many of its private broadcasters. Many Canadian book, magazine, music, and newspaper publishing headquarters are located in Toronto, as are four of the eight principal Canadian media conglomerates. Data from the National Household Survey in 2011 indicate that there were 158,249 people employed in the cultural and creative industries cluster as a whole in the Toronto city-region (Spencer 2014). Practically all of the firms involved in film and television production, either directly or as service providers, are very densely clustered in the greater Toronto region. In fact, many of Ontario's film and television production and post-production firms are clustered in three distinct areas of downtown Toronto: Liberty Village / Queen West, the Distillery District, and Yonge Street north of Bloor (HAL 2009).

Historically Toronto has served as the headquarters for English-speaking Canada's major book, magazine, music, and newspaper publishers, its major media production houses, its major English-language public broadcasters, and many of its private broadcasters. The Toronto media cluster encompasses the country's largest concentration of content producers, specialty broadcasters, and specialized suppliers and supporting institutions such as law firms, post-production services, sound recording studios, media marketing and publicity agencies, financial services, theatrical exhibitors, Internet publishing firms, technical service suppliers, advertising agencies, below-the-line crews and their craft unions, and public and private post-secondary educational programs. Altogether the content layer of the Toronto media cluster (including film and television production, book, magazine, music, and interactive media) employed around 40,000 people and generated about $4.5 billion in revenues in 2007 (Davis 2010).

Most of Toronto's indigenous film and television industry serves the domestic market and is not directly involved in service production, making the Toronto cluster very unlike the organizationally flat "satellite" production centres that mainly provide production services to Hollywood-based entertainment conglomerates and have little indigenous creative production capabilities. Instead, Toronto's media cluster is fully developed with industrial capabilities at every step of the media value chain, from creation to finance to production to marketing and distribution. Toronto's media cluster assets give the Toronto region a far more fully articulated media cluster than any other city in North America, with the exception of the two much larger media clusters in Los Angeles and New York.

The cultural sector affects the broader economy in two principal ways (Frontier Economics 2007). The first is by direct commercialization of cultural products and services. Second, localized spillovers of cultural knowledge into adopter or user sectors induce and enable innovation. Co-location is one indication of likely knowledge spillovers. Toronto's cultural sector displays patterns of co-location among book and magazine publishers, electronic equipment repair firms, broadcasters, recording studios, software publishers, technical and trade schools, specialized design services, independent artists-writers-performers, performing arts organizations, advertising, grant-making services, event promoters, artists' agents, and spectator sports companies (Vinodrai and Gertler 2007), suggesting the existence of largely undocumented knowledge transfers and spillovers among these industries.

In the cognitive-cultural economy, knowledge spills over when technologies developed in the ICT sector are adopted in other sectors, or as when aesthetic attributes developed by one industry are transferred to another (or more properly, are created for customers). The distinction between the cognitive and the cultural attributes becomes blurred when technology in the form of powerful animation and digital effects software enables the creation of photorealistic moving images. Complex cognitive and cultural spillovers occur when a user industry borrows liberally from and contributes to the worlds of technology and visual culture, as well as to related sectors. This is the case in the computer animation and visual effects industry, which in Toronto numbers around a hundred firms, has estimated revenues of $170–200 million, and employs around 2,000 people (Nordicity 2008).

The current technological state of the media industry has given interactive media enormous strategic significance for the Toronto media industry as a whole, since successful transition to a converged media environment is widely regarded as a critically important step in the evolution of the Toronto media cluster. The issue, therefore, is how a screen media innovation system that is path-dependent on the established broadcast industry can create new innovation pathways yielding profitable trans-media properties. We conjecture that firms that develop internal trans-media capabilities are best positioned to discover or invent viable business models for trans-media innovation. However, while the development of trans-media capabilities in the indigenous screen production sector in Toronto is highly dependent on co-located pools of film, television, and interactive media technical, creative, and business labour, Davis (2011) notes that certain non-local factors, notably national broadcast policy, also play a determining role.

Network spillovers occur "where the mere presence of creative businesses in a given place benefits other local firms" (Frontier Economics 2007). The city's most ambitious creative initiatives favour investments in signature cultural buildings, high-profile infrastructure for cultural production and consumption, and major cultural events in the downtown core, seeking network spillovers in the form of attraction of domestic and international talent, investment, high-value-added business activities, high-income local and transient cultural consumers, and domestic gentrifiers. The best documented case of a spillover-intensive cultural district in Toronto is Queen West–Liberty Village, which encompasses art, music, screen media, digital media, and cultural consumption services, and displays the expected gentrification effects (Catungal, Leslie, and Hii 2009; Matheson 2004; Sharpe et al. 2004).

In summary, both the financial services and media sectors represent critical components of Toronto's expanding cognitive-cultural economy, illustrating the numerous ways in which innovation flows within large urban agglomerations occur across traditional sectoral boundaries or dividing lines. The accelerating digital revolution continues to transform the nature of both product and process innovations in these sectors. The resulting confluence of economic forces is rapidly transforming the economic geography of larger urban agglomerations and has contributed in no small measure to the tremendous dynamism experienced in Toronto over the past decade and a half.

Talent and Creativity in the Toronto Region

The transformation of large metropolitan economies from the post-war Fordist model to the cognitive-cultural economy has been accompanied by a gradual shift in employment structures away from occupations associated with traditional manufacturing industries towards knowledge-intensive occupations requiring high levels of education and specialized skills. As manufacturing has declined in the urban cores of large metropolitan cities and regions, the industrial occupations that populated these traditional sectors have also declined as a proportion of the urban labour force. In its place, there has been a dramatic expansion of those occupational components of the labour force associated with Florida's definition of the creative class or what Reich has previously labelled "symbolic analysts" (1992). These include professional, technical, and design-intensive occupations that predominate in the sectors associated with cognitive-cultural activities and, according to Scott, "deploy high-level cognitive and cultural skills, such as deductive reasoning capacities, technical insight, leadership, cultural awareness and visual imagination – in other words, more or less creative capacities – in the workplace" (Scott 2014, 570).

The progressive shift of a growing proportion of the economic activities in large metropolitan cities and regions involves the steady expansion of interrelated clusters of economic activity involving technology-based, knowledge-intensive service and cultural production. It is in the labour markets and the specific occupational categories associated with these productive activities that much of the creative energy of the modern urban, post-Fordist economy can be found. As the industrial structure of the Toronto city-region has progressively made the shift towards a cognitive-cultural economy in the fourth era, the occupational composition of the labour force has been transformed along the lines described above.

Talent in Toronto's Finance-ICT Nexus

As documented in table 2.1 above, employment in the financial and business services sectors constitutes a substantial proportion of Toronto's labour force, which tends to be overwhelmingly concentrated in the growing number of high-rise towers that mark the skyline of the downtown business core. The group draws its strength in good measure from the expansive talent pool developed and supported by world-class educational and training institutions within the region, and from mobility with the local, national, and global industries. It was not uncommon in the interviews for this sector to hear stories of highly qualified talent moving back and forth between Toronto and other financial centres in North America, especially New York, as well as moving in and out of the financial services "vertical" in other industry sectors, such as ICT. This concentration of highly qualified personnel affords the region a formidable competitive edge. A key feature in both sectors was the large and diverse population base in the region, which is being replenished with a steady stream of highly skilled and educated immigrants.

The co-location of financial services and ICT firms has a substantial impact on labour market dynamics in the GTA, which has attracted an impressive array of talent seeking employment in the financial services and ICT sectors in recent years. Firms in these areas recruit human capital in a number of different ways. Internships and cooperative education programs attract young, highly educated workers and facilitate the development of specialized local expertise. In turn, financial services and ICT firms are supplied with a pool of potential contract or full-time hires, which for some firms could mitigate the desire to move development and testing offshore.

Employers from the financial services and ICT sectors face the constant challenge of finding skilled employees who best suit the firm's skill requirements. Firms target well-educated, highly trained personnel with advanced knowledge of the industry. It was discovered that some ICT employers in particular were comfortable hiring staff who were technologically skilled but had a limited knowledge of the financial services industry and wealth management, whereas other ICT employers placed a premium on the ability of the employee to speak the financial services client's language.

However, while the Toronto region provides considerable attractions for recruiting and developing talent, financial services and ICT firms in the region encounter challenges in attracting and retaining staff as a result of rigorous competition between firms in acquiring highly qualified personnel with specialized skills. Some companies are unable to offer more competitive pay scales or to convince potential candidates that they are as innovative as their competitors.

The continued growth of the finance and ICT sectors in the Toronto region confirms the interdependence of the jobs and talent relationship. It is the concentration of financial services and ICT firms in the region that creates numerous employment opportunities for skilled workers interested in pursuing a career in these industries. At the same time, however, the presence of a dense labour market in the region makes Toronto a desirable location within which to recruit highly qualified talent, both for firms located inside and outside the region. The challenge is whether the smaller and more marginal firms in both sectors will be able to compete successfully with the employment opportunities offered by the larger firms and how this will affect the dynamism of the sector.

Attracting and Retaining Talent in the Design and Fashion Industries

The case of talent in the fashion and design industries tells a story slightly different from that in financial and business services. Although Toronto ranks as the second-largest centre for the production of fashion in Canada, it falls well behind the leading North American fashion centres of Montreal, New York, and Los Angeles. Nonetheless, Toronto has a more than 550 apparel manufacturers that employ over 50,000 people. It is more difficult to determine the precise number of fashion designers in the city, but one study estimated the number at almost 2,700 (Leslie and Brail 2011, 2904).

The majority of Canadian-born designers working in the Toronto industry were drawn to it by a combination of educational and labour market opportunities. A significant portion came to Toronto to study in the region's diverse range of post-secondary educational institutions and decided to stay because of the work opportunities that the region afforded. The city also has a small but significant proportion of designers who came from other countries, but in their case the factors that attracted them to the region are more personal or general, such as following a family member who has already moved to the region or being attracted by the general characteristics of tolerance and cultural diversity that they perceive in Canada (and Toronto). Few of the foreign-born designers interviewed for the study moved to Toronto because of its reputation as a centre of fashion design; but the general economic prospects that provided opportunities to pursue their careers and the overall quality of life were important factors for staying in Toronto once they arrived (Leslie and Brail 2011).

However, in fashion and design, it is not just the strong concentration of employment opportunities in the regional economy that attracts people to work in the sector, but rather the broader "qualities of place" – including diversity, tolerance, and cultural dynamism – that characterize Toronto as a desirable city in which to live (Leslie and Brail 2011). A critical factor influencing the way in which designers pursue their craft is the inspiration they draw from the broader cultural and social milieu of the city. An overwhelming proportion of the designers interviewed indicated that Toronto's rich cultural diversity was an important source of inspiration for their work. The established multicultural networks in the city assist newcomers to integrate more effectively into the city. The strong multicultural communities that comprise Toronto's rich and diverse social fabric also provide built-in customers and markets for some of the designers, allowing them to produce for a more sophisticated clientele than they would encounter in a city with a narrower social base (Leslie and Brail 2011).

An underappreciated but highly significant factor in attracting and retaining talent for the fashion industry in Toronto is the city's status as a major hub for other leading creative industries, including film, theatre, dance, food, architecture, interior design, and music. These related industries generate a wide range of synergies that contribute to the overall attractiveness of Toronto as a city for design work. They simultaneously provide a wealth of experience in different styles that can be consumed across a range of activities, but also generate a broad array of artistic influences and experiences for designers to draw upon. Fashion designers in Toronto reported how important it was to be located in a city with a large live theatre sector, as well as dance and film production, where they could realize their passion for design by creating the more elaborate costumes needed by actors in these productions. The presence of a strong and dynamic theatre sector in the city also provides the fashion industry with a range of talented seamstresses with experience in producing costumes for the highly demanding conditions of the theatre industry. At the same time, the broader cultural industries in the city – film, television, theatre, art, and music – all contribute to building a larger target market for the sophisticated products of Toronto's fashion and apparel industry. The increasing prominence of some of Toronto's internationally recognized cultural events, such as the International Film Festival and Luminato further help to build the market for fashion in the city (Leslie and Brail 2011).

The positive spillovers between the fashion and cultural industries closely parallels a phenomenon observed from other interviews in a related study among editors, publishers, and writers in the magazine-publishing sector who noted that it was essential for them to be located in a large city with a vibrant dance, literary, or fashion scene (Leslie and Brail 2011). The cross-sectoral fertilization that Jane Jacobs viewed as central to innovation and urban growth clearly seems to flourish in the cultural and creative sectors concentrated in our larger cities. At the same time, labour mobility across sector/cluster boundaries is considerably more prevalent for firms in Toronto's fashion industry, whose owners and designers report working regularly in related sectors such as theatre, film, TV, and dance, as well as hiring workers who have experience in these industries. This phenomenon provides an opportunity for these firms to enrich their design skills and experience by working on projects that are more demanding technically and offer greater scope for creativity.

While often overlooked as part of the cultural and creative sector in the urban economy, a substantial cluster of architectural firms represents a design-intensive industry displaying many of the features associated with the "cognitive-cultural economy." There are 3,960 architects in the Toronto region spread across 608 registered practices and representing almost 30 per cent of architects in Canada. Only Vancouver has a higher relative concentration of architects than Toronto, and only by a slight margin. Architects are very highly educated, with 85 per cent holding a university degree and 21 per cent with a master's degree or higher. Architecture as a profession is highly reflective of the diverse and multicultural character of Toronto's demographic and social make-up, with 44 per cent of people in the sector born outside the country (Gertler and Geddie 2008). The accelerated growth of population in Toronto's downtown business core has fed the dramatic growth in both residential and commercial high-rise construction noted above. The construction boom has been marked in recent years by the dramatic increase in the sophisticated and innovative designs incorporated in some of Toronto's current and proposed towers, as well as in the wave of construction of new cultural buildings in the first decade of the millennium.

While the three sectors surveyed in the study of Toronto's emerging cognitive and cultural economy differ in a variety of significant ways, they share certain features. Employment in the sector is bolstered by the strong infrastructure of post-secondary educational and training institutions in the Toronto region, which serve as an initial draw for creative talent from across the country and sometimes around the world. Once they are here, the diverse range of employment opportunities provided by the density of the labour market across all sectors surveyed helps retain workers in the region, further confirming the importance of thick labour markets and the mutually reinforcing spiral of interdependence between jobs and talent. In Toronto, these factors are strongly reinforced by the city's distinct characteristics as a diverse multicultural centre with reputation for tolerance and openness to immigration.

Finally and perhaps most significantly, we found strong evidence that the breadth and diversity of Toronto's expanding cognitive-cultural economy provides a wide range of opportunities for cross-sectoral spillovers and fertilization among the industries studied. For example, the rapid growth of the financial and business services sectors spurs the further expansion of the high-rise building boom in the downtown business core, and the cultural sector provides opportunities for Toronto's leading architectural firms to practise their craft. The synergies and spillovers among the fashion, design, theatre, magazine, and even food industries all contribute to an artistic and cultural milieu in which Toronto's fashion designers thrive. The burgeoning size and relative stability of Toronto's financial services industries creates a steady market and demand for the products and the services of the region's ICT industry, while some of the bespoke software products generated in the industry provide important means for financial services to expand the range of products they offer, contributing to the further growth in the sector and creating greater employment opportunities. In short, the synergies and positive spillovers across the range firms in the city's cognitive-cultural economy are critical to Toronto's long-term vitality and growth.

Governance Gaps in Toronto's Cognitive-Cultural Economy

Clearly, the Toronto region has benefited substantially from the transition to a knowledge-intensive cognitive-cultural economy. However, not only are these developments unlikely to proceed unabated without strategic intervention, but balancing economic growth with social inclusion for those less able to participate in these knowledge-intensive activities requires concerted policy attention. Conventional studies of urban politics and governance focus on how coalitions of local governmental and societal interests shape policy decisions and resource allocation in the city-region (see, for example, Stone 1989, 2005; Pierre 2011; DiGaetano and Strom 2003), and a large economic geography literature examines how regional institutions shape the locational decisions of firms (Storper 2013; Rodríguez-Pose 2013). Operating at the intersection of these disciplines, more recent work draws important conceptual links between the two, emphasizing important interaction between urban political processes, the economic decisions of firms, and the methods by which key actors collaborate to develop and sustain regional economic development (Storper 2013; Gertler 2010). Relatively under-studied, this remains a central empirical question for Canadian city-regions in general, and for the Toronto region in particular (Bradford and Bramwell 2014).

Characterizing governance processes is especially challenging in a city-region as vast and diverse as Toronto. As the fourth-largest metropolitan economy in North America and one of the continent's fastest growing mega-regions, the Toronto region's sheer size and economic dynamism affords it significant social, cultural, and economic advantages. Yet the region also grapples with multiple and complex inter-connected policy challenges such as economic restructuring, changing local labour markets, high levels of immigration and ethno-cultural change, affordability, social polarization, growing concentrations of poverty, and dysfunctional regional transit systems, all of which threaten to compromise both regional economic dynamism and social equity (Bourne, Britton, and Leslie 2011; see also Hulchanski 2007).

Following on the discussion of innovation, knowledge flows, talent and creativity, and the emergence of hybrid industrial activities, this section examines the evolution of social and economic dynamics over the past decade and emerging forms of governance in a time of major challenge and change for the city-region.[8] Examining recent efforts to forge more integrated and collaborative development strategies, we find that regional networks and voluntary governance mechanisms in the Toronto city-region are generally weak and disconnected. Somewhat unexpectedly, we also find evidence of a durable multi-sector coalition – the Greater Toronto CivicAction Alliance – that integrates social, economic, and cultural dimensions of city-region development. However, while the CivicAction Alliance represents innovative and high-performing regional governance driven and sustained by influential and engaged civic leaders, it lacks meaningful linkages with elected municipal leaders and has been unable to leverage sustained policy support commensurate with Toronto's unique position in the national economy.

Challenges of Scale, Scope, and Governance in the GTA

The Greater Toronto Area (GTA) lacks key institutional supports and administrative structures to coordinate regional social and economic development strategies. On a spatial basis, the lack of a single administrative structure to represent the Toronto region, which is governed by the upper-tier City of Toronto and surrounded by the four other upper-tier municipalities of Halton, Peel, York, and Dufferin and twenty-four lower-tier municipalities, is reflected in the competing range of definitions of what geographies it constitutes – the Greater Toronto Area (GTA), the Greater Toronto Area and Hamilton (GTAH), or the Greater Golden Horseshoe (GGH).[9] Scholars also underscore the problems caused by the forced amalgamation of the former Municipality of Metropolitan Toronto or "Metro Toronto" into the City of Toronto by the Ontario government in 1998, which had a questionable impact on increased efficiencies in service delivery and did little to address problems of metropolitan governance for the GTA (Sancton 2005; Boudreau, Keil, and Young 2009).[10]

Weak inter-municipal cooperation has impeded efforts to coordinate infrastructure and transit and to reduce poverty and social exclusion on a regional basis (Bourne 2001; Stren et al. 2010). From a governance perspective, the "almost dysfunctional" structure of municipal government coupled with a lack of "consensus on the identity of the city or the region" makes it "difficult to construct a single narrative that does justice to the highly varied and distinctive local economies, cultures, and landscapes" that make up the Toronto region. The result is an urban powerhouse struggling to implement "political initiatives and strategic planning for economic development and innovation at the regional scale" (Bourne et al. 2011, 237, 241).[11]

Scalar challenges are not the only obstacles to collaborative governance in the GTA. Coalitions form to advance a variety of policy agendas, but their sustained impact requires some degree of coordination and consolidation. A wide array of organizations represents both the economic and social development sectors at the municipal and regional levels in Toronto, but neither has well-developed internal networks. Echoing many descriptions of how different networks interact in the region, one person described Toronto as "a city with weak networks [that] don't hang together well ... It doesn't feel like a city that ... finds a way of having a common goal [that] everyone can contribute to and move towards" (confidential interview). Social equity groups and service-delivery organizations have informal "tables" for information-sharing and small one-off projects but lack "one major network" or single table around which all key organizations gather to coordinate strategic approaches to social welfare in the city.[12] Economic development is similarly fragmented, and successive municipal attempts to implement strategic plans have lacked the civic leadership and broad support from the business community to gain sufficient traction, underscoring the general impression that "the economic development field [in Toronto] is strewn with the bodies of failed initiatives" (confidential interview).[13]

Prior to the early 2000s, these weakly organized social and economic development networks, coupled with an absence of boundary-spanning civic leadership, historically exacerbated structural impediments to coalition-building at municipal and regional levels in the GTA. More recently, some of these governance gaps have been addressed by the Greater Toronto CivicAction Alliance. Arising out of a one-day event held in June 2002, the inaugural Toronto City Summit brought together a diverse and representative group of leaders to identify the region's strengths and challenges and to frame an agenda to respond to them. Following the successful conclusion of the summit, a coalition of more than forty civic leaders from the private, labour, voluntary, and public sectors came together to form the Toronto City Summit Alliance (TCSA), which was later renamed the Greater Toronto CivicAction Alliance (CivicAction for short) to reflect its regional scope. The resulting plan, "Enough Talk: An Action Plan for the Toronto Region," released in April 2003, set out a broad agenda for change in a number of areas including physical infrastructure, tourism, research infrastructure, education and training, immigration, and social services that has guided its strategic activity ever since.

Since its formation in 2003, CivicAction has operated on the principle of building a collective vision for future directions in the city, building a common agenda for action, and subsequently developing and launching new programs in these strategic areas. Playing the role of convenor and catalyst, CivicAction has been "very conscious about not replacing or substituting for the work that everybody else is doing but to try and bring more resources to them and support them or connect them with other people" (confidential interview). With the basis for its activity clearly set out in the "Enough Talk" report, subsequent work has been supported by a series of working groups in areas including the economy, infrastructure, financing municipal and regional services, and education.[14]

In boundary-spanning activity, CivicAction links up the most networks and is often the only organization with which more focused business, arts and culture, or social networks will have regular contact beyond their own smaller networks. Members of many networks and organizations interviewed reported some affiliation. Its agenda has included a wide range of economic, social, and cultural initiatives including the Toronto Region Research Alliance, the Toronto Region Immigrant Employment Council, the Modernizing Income Security for Working Aged Adults Task Force, the Strong Neighbourhoods Task Force, Greening Greater Toronto, DiverseCity, and Luminato, a yearly arts festival.

Thus, the Greater Toronto CivicAction Alliance can be said to have gone a long way towards filling the civic governance gap in the city, and with its renaming to reflect its regional focus, perhaps in the region as a whole. It can take credit for providing previously lacking visionary civic leadership, encouraging boundary-spanning and networking across social, cultural, and economic development agendas, overseeing the implementation of innovative projects, and attracting policy attention for critical local and regional issues. Not only has this inclusive civic coalition been sustained over time, it has made tangible and durable contributions to addressing social and economic development challenges in Toronto. At the same time, however, major governance challenges remain. The Toronto region continues to struggle with weak municipal policy capacity, a perceived lack of concerted and visionary leadership, and strained multi-level governance relations.

Recent approaches to economic resilience in city-regions suggest that the most adaptable and agile places have supportive strategic governance institutions that are underpinned by high levels of civic and political leadership (Wolfe 2010; Safford 2009; Storper 2013). While little is known about power relations between elected municipal politicians and civic leaders, particularly in Canadian cities, our research suggests that these relationships may not be as straightforward or harmonious as might be assumed. Many interview respondents mentioned the absence of "vision and leadership to mobilize things," the "lack of unifying ideas," and the dearth of elected politicians willing to "step up to the plate" with "an emerging agenda around which they could build a coalition and a consensus" in Toronto. There was a strong sense that before the CivicAction Alliance was established, Toronto suffered from a distinct lack of political "champions" willing to articulate and drive a visionary agenda forward (confidential interviews). While David Pecaut, its inaugural chair, was most often referred to as the civic leader who was most committed, effective, and visible in championing the interests of Toronto and the work of the TCSA, there was little evidence that the mayor of Toronto or senior municipal staff at the time sought to build linkages with the original TCSA, leaving the potential for productive linkages between the city-region's political and civic leadership untapped.

In summary, this evidence of a durable cross-boundary coalition operating in the Toronto region suggests that explanations of urban governance dynamics in Canadian cities need to be expanded to account for the emergence of novel forms of state-society relations (Tindal and Tindal 2009; Bradford and Bramwell 2014). At the same time, however, further systematic research is required to better understand the barriers to collaborative governance in Canadian cities. Major governance challenges remain, and the Toronto region continues to struggle with weak municipal policy capacity, a perceived lack of concerted and visionary leadership, and until very recently, the absence of productive linkages between civic and political leaders. John Tory, a founding member of CivicAction and its most recent chair (taking over in 2010 after David Pecaut's untimely death) was elected mayor of Toronto in 2014, opening an interesting window of opportunity to align civic and political interests, at least at the municipal scale.

Conclusion

The past two decades have been a period of unusual economic challenge for Canadian cities, as even the economically strongest of them have undergone three major recessions and experienced dramatic fluctuations in the price of resource commodities. The Great Recession of the late 2000s posed a particular challenge for the Toronto region, Canada's largest and most diversified urban economy. Demarcated by the amalgamation of the municipal government into a unified structure in 1998 and the rapid growth of the Greater Toronto Area, the past two decades have witnessed the gradual emergence of Toronto as a leading cognitive-cultural economy. The Toronto region economy is marked by a continuing shift from its traditional strengths in the manufacturing sector to an increasing range of service activities, which can be seen in the dense concentration of both ICT and financial services in the regional economy and the growing linkages between the two sectors.

Toronto's emergence as a cognitive-cultural economy is also marked by the continued prominence of the cultural and creative sector in the region's economy. Toronto has long served as the cultural capital of English Canada and is home to a dense network of firms in the traditional cultural industries, as well as the burgeoning digital media industry. Toronto's diverse cultural, creative, and knowledge-based industries generate extraordinary potential for knowledge and innovation spillovers within the cultural and media cluster. In particular, creative industries, business services, and information and communication technology are notable as three sectors of specializations that are also leading in growth. Resilient cities are ones where existing industries may provide the essential building blocks for the emergence of a new innovative industry because the skills and talents that have accumulated over time in the city may furnish critical inputs needed by the emerging industry, as has often been the case with the digital media industry. This is currently the case with the convergence of the cultural and media industries, where all subsectors of the media industry are being affected by convergence. The boundaries are blurring among the older media subsectors as both the content and methods of delivery are being digitized, and digital media is emerging as one of the high-growth sectors in the industry.

The expansion of the cognitive and cultural sectors of the regional economy is simultaneously stimulating the growth of demand for highly skilled and creative talent in key occupational categories and making the city a more attractive location for creative talent. The dense labour market in the Toronto regional economy is the most important factor for attracting and retaining talent in the area. Employment opportunities across a wide range of firms provide prospective employees with a potential degree of choice not available in many other local labour markets. This varies substantially across the industries surveyed, ranging from financial services to ICT, the cultural and creative sector, fashion design and architecture. For the industry segments that comprise the cultural, creative, and design sectors, the most important factors are the overall quality of life in the city, but more specifically the dense interaction that is possible across many of these sectors within the city-region.

While civic governance in the City of Toronto has made significant progress over the past decade through the leadership of the CivicAction Alliance, its impact has been limited by a lack of coordination with elected municipal governments in the city, as well as by ongoing intra-regional competition. There is no shortage of entrepreneurial civic leadership or organizational presence in the city, but the past lack of coordination with the city's governance mechanisms signifies the inability of the megacity to forge a cohesive development coalition since amalgamation in 1998. This weakness is even more apparent in broader governance at the city-region level. Thus the Toronto city-region remains characterized by a fragmentation of scales and scopes in which the regional dimension is often contested. The adoption of a more cohesive planning approach to a wide range of issues in the Toronto city-region is hampered by the puzzling contradiction of relatively strong civic capital at the local or city level that has not translated into a cohesive coalition across the region as a whole. This limitation is compounded by the weak links at the level of the city-region, the absence of administrative structures that correspond to the economic boundaries of the region. In this context, linking the innovative, social entrepreneurial local grass roots organizations that are springing up across the region could provide a potential source for the emergence of more effective governance mechanisms appropriate to the emerging cognitive-cultural economy for the region as a whole.

Notes

1 The next largest concentration of financial services in Canada is in Montreal, with 22.6 per cent of its labour force in the sector (Wolfe 2009).

2 Between the 2006 and 2011 census, total population grew by 6 per cent, down slightly from the growth rate of more than 9 per cent that occurred between 2001 and 2006. Employment growth also slowed somewhat to 3.6 per cent between 2006 and 2011, and average employment income increased by 13.5 per cent.

3 The following section draws upon Wolfe et al. 2011.

4 The Global Financial Centres Index (GFCI) was first produced by the Z/Yen Group in March 2007, following another research project into city competitiveness undertaken in 2005. The aim of the GFCI is to examine the major financial centres globally in terms of competitiveness. For more information, see Yeandle (2011).
5 The Cities of Opportunity study analyses and ranks how twenty-six global centres of finance, business, and culture perform across ten key indicators. In the fourth edition, New York leads the report, but is followed closely in the top five by Toronto, San Francisco, Stockholm, and Sydney – cities more notable for quality of life and balance than global business dominance. See Yeandle (2011, 14, 20, 23, 47).
6 It is noteworthy that an even larger component of employment in the sector is located in the Greater Toronto Area or Toronto CMA, particularly in Markham, which has its own concentration of ICT firms, including one of IBM's global R&D centres.
7 This section draws upon Davis and Mills (2014).
8 The material for this section is based on sixty-five key informant interviews conducted across the economic, social, and cultural sectors in Toronto, as well as participant observation by the authors at key events in the region.
9 According to the OECD's most recent survey, if the definition of the Toronto region is extended to the GGH, then it subsumes 110 municipal governments.
10 In 1998 the Ontario government rejected the recommendation of the Task Force on the Greater Toronto Area to establish a regional level of government that would correspond more appropriately with the economic boundaries of the Greater Toronto Area and, instead, created the current City of Toronto, which covers only a small portion of the rapidly growing regional economy that comprises not only the CMA, but a much greater area as well. In addition, the upper-tier governments of Halton, Peel, York, and Durham each have elected chairs and responsibilities for economic development and regional planning.
11 On this point, several key agencies established at the time of amalgamation to deal with region-wide issues have met with varying success; the Greater Toronto Marketing Alliance lacks buy-in from surrounding municipalities, and the regional transportation agency Metrolinx has had limited effectiveness in forging a region-wide consensus on the future of regional transit (Wolfe and Nelles 2009).
12 The United Way of Greater Toronto, the City of Toronto, and the Toronto City Summit Alliance collaborated on the Strong Neighbourhoods Task

Force whose final report formed the basis for the adoption of the Strong Neighbourhoods Strategy by city council in October 2005, an ongoing joint initiative targeted at thirteen distressed neighbourhoods across the city. However, this initiative has also recently experienced challenges to maintain funding, coordination, and momentum (see Horak and Moore 2015).

13 For instance, some key municipalities in the region, including the cities of Toronto and Mississauga, have opted to mount their own foreign trade missions without the participation of the GTMA, while the City of Toronto has recently created a new agency, Invest Toronto, which overlaps with the GTMA's mandate.

14 In addition, subgroups have often formed out of existing working groups to tackle specific issues.

References

Boston Consulting Group. 1995. "The fourth era: The economic challenges facing the GTA." Study prepared for the GTA Task Force, Toronto.

Boudreau, J.-A., R. Keil, and D. Young. 2009. *Changing Toronto: Governing neoliberalism*. Toronto: University of Toronto Press.

Bourne, Larry. 2001. "Designing a metropolitan region: The lessons and lost opportunities of the Toronto experience." In *The challenge of urban government: Policies and practices*, ed. M. Freire and R. Stren, 27–46. Washington, DC: World Bank Institute.

Bourne, Larry, John Britton, and Deborah Leslie. 2011. "The Greater Toronto Region: The challenges of economic restructuring, social diversity, and globalization." In *Canadian urban regions: Trajectories of growth and change*, ed. Larry S. Bourne et al., 236–68. Toronto: Oxford University Press.

Bradford, Neil, and Allison Bramwell, eds. 2014. *Governing urban economies: Innovation and inclusion in Canadian cities*. Toronto: University of Toronto Press.

Bramwell, Allison, and Jon Pierre. 2013. "Collaborative cities: A new mode of urban governance?" Paper presented at the American Political Science Association Annual Meeting, Chicago, IL.

Bramwell, Allison, and David A. Wolfe. 2014. "Dimensions of governance in the megacity: Scale, scope, and coalitions in Toronto." In *Governing urban economies: Innovation and inclusion in Canadian cities*, ed. Neil Bradford and Allison Bramwell, 58–87. Toronto: University of Toronto Press.

Catungal, John Paul, Deborah Leslie, and Yvonne Hii. 2009. "Geographies of displacement in the creative city: The case of Liberty Village, Toronto." *Urban Studies* 46 (5–6): 1095–114. http://dx.doi.org/10.1177/0042098009103856.

Christopherson, Susan, Jonathan Michie, and Peter Tyler. 2010. "Regional resilience: Theoretical and empirical perspectives." *Cambridge Journal of Regions, Economy and Society* 3 (1): 3–10. http://dx.doi.org/10.1093/cjres/rsq004.

City of Toronto. 2010. *Canada's high tech hub: Toronto*. Toronto: City of Toronto.

Davis, Charles H. 2010. "New firms in the screen-based media industry: Startups, self-employment, and standing reserve." In *Managing media work*, ed. M. Deuze, 165–78. Sage: Thousand Oaks.

–. 2011. "The Toronto media cluster: Between culture and commerce." In *Media clusters across the globe: Developing, expanding, and reinvigorating content capabilities*, ed. Charlie Karlsson and Robert Picard, 223–50. Cheltenham, UK: Edward Elgar. http://dx.doi.org/10.4337/9780857932693.00019.

Davis, Charles H., and Nicholas Mills. 2014. "Innovation and Toronto's cognitive-cultural economy." In *Innovating in urban economies: Economic transformation in Canadian city-regions*, ed. David A. Wolfe, 59–91. Toronto: University of Toronto Press.

DiGaetano, A., and E. Strom. 2003. "Comparative urban governance: An integrated approach." *Urban Affairs Review* 38 (3): 356–95. http://dx.doi.org/10.1177/1078087402238806.

Donald, Betsy. 2002. "Spinning Toronto's golden age: The making of a 'city that worked.'" *Environment & Planning A* 34 (12): 2127–54. http://dx.doi.org/10.1068/a34111.

Frontier Economics. 2007. *Creative industry spillovers: Understanding their impact on the wider economy*. London: Frontier Economics Ltd.

Gertler, Meric. 2010. "Rules of the game: The place of institutions in regional economic change." *Regional Studies* 44 (1): 1–15. http://dx.doi.org/10.1080/00343400903389979.

Gertler, Meric S., and Kate Geddie. 2008. "Architectural knowledge: Reflexive dynamics between place and design." Paper presented to the Annual Meeting of the Association of American Geographers, Boston, MA. 18 April.

HAL. 2009. "Ontario's creative cluster study." Unpublished report prepared for the Ontario Ministry of Culture. Ottawa: Hicklings Arthurs Lowe.

Horak, M., and A. Moore. 2015. "Policy shift without institutional change: The precarious place of neighborhood revitalization in Toronto." In *Urban neighborhoods in a new era: Revitalization politics in the postindustrial city*, ed. C. Stone and R. Stoker, 182–208. Chicago: University of Chicago Press.

Hulchanski, David. 2007. *The three cities within Toronto: Income polarization among Toronto's neighbourhoods 1970–2005*. Centre for Urban and Community Studies Research Bulletin 41.

Leslie, Deborah, and Shauna Brail. 2011. "The productive role of 'Quality of place': A case study of fashion designers in Toronto." *Environment & Planning A* 43 (12): 2900–17. http://dx.doi.org/10.1068/a43473.

Matheson, Sarah A. 2004. "Projecting placelessness: Industrial television and the 'authentic' Canadian city." In *Contracting out Hollywood: Runaway productions and foreign location shooting*, ed. Greg Elmer and Michael Gasher, 117–39. Lanham, MD: Rowan and Littlefield.

Nordicity. 2008. *Economic profile of the Ontario computer animation and visual effects industry*. Toronto: Nordicity, for Computer Animation Studios of Ontario.

Organisation for Economic Co-operation and Development. 2010. *OECD territorial reviews: Toronto, Canada*. Paris: OECD.

Pennachetti, Joseph. 2014. "Toronto: Looking forward 2014–2018, reinvesting for the future." Institute on Municipal Finance and Governance 3rd Annual City Manager's Address, University of Toronto, 13 May.

Pierre, Jon. 2011. *The politics of urban governance*. Basingstoke, UK: Palgrave.

Polèse, Mario, and Richard Shearmur. 2004. "Culture, language, and the location of high-order service functions: The case of Montreal and Toronto." *Economic Geography* 80 (4): 329–50. http://dx.doi.org/10.1111/j.1944-8287.2004.tb00241.x.

PwC and the Partnership for New York. 2011. *Cities of opportunity, 2011*, 4th ed. http://www.pwc.com/gx/en/industries/government-public-services/public-sector-research-centre/global/cities-of-opportunity-2011.html.

Reich, Robert B. 1992. *The work of nations: Preparing ourselves for 21st-century capitalism*. New York: Vintage Books.

Rodríguez-Pose, A. 2013. "Do institutions matter for regional development?" *Regional Studies* 47 (7): 1034–47. http://dx.doi.org/10.1080/00343404.2012.748978.

Safford, Sean. 2009. *Why the Garden Club couldn't save Youngstown: The transformation of the rust belt*. Cambridge, MA: Harvard University Press.

Sancton, A. 2005. "The governance of metropolitan areas in Canada." *Public Administration and Development* 25 (4): 317–27. http://dx.doi.org/10.1002/pad.386.

Scott, Allen J. 2007. "Capitalism and urbanization in a new key? The cognitive-cultural dimension." *Social Forces* 85 (4): 1465–82. http://dx.doi.org/10.1353/sof.2007.0078.

–. 2013. "A world in emergence: Notes towards a resynthesis of urban economic geography for the twenty-first century." In *Re-framing regional development: Evolution, innovation and transition*, ed. Philip Cooke, 29–53. Oxfordshire, UK: Routledge.

–. 2014. "Beyond the creative city: Cognitive-cultural capitalism and the new urbanism." *Regional Studies* 48 (4): 565–78. http://dx.doi.org/10.1080/00343404.2014.891010.

Sharpe, Dean, Tim Jones, Tony Lea, Ken Jones, and Sue Harvey. 2004. *Critique and consolidation of research on spillover effects of investments in cultural facilities*. Report prepared for Heritage Canada. Toronto: Artscape and Ryerson University.

Spencer, Gregory M. 2014. *Cluster atlas of Canada*. Toronto: Innovation Policy Lab, Munk School of Global Affairs.

Stone, Clarence. 1989. *Regime politics: Governing Atlanta 1946–1988*. Lawrence, KS: University Press of Kansas.

–. 2005. "Looking back to look forward: Reflections on urban regime analysis." *Urban Affairs Review* 40 (3): 309–41. http://dx.doi.org/10.1177/1078087404270646.

Storper, Michael. 2013. *Keys to the city: How economics, institutions, social interaction and politics shape development*. Princeton: Princeton University Press.

Stren, R., E. Rae, F. Cunningham, L. Feldman, G. Eidelman, A. Moore, A. Sancton, A. Sorenson, and M. Valverde. 2010. *The governance of Toronto: Challenges of size and complexity*. Toronto: Cities Centre.

Tindal, C.R., and S.N. Tindal. 2009. *Local government in Canada*, 7th ed. Toronto: Nelson Canada.

Vinodrai, Tara, and Meric S. Gertler. 2007. "Measuring the creative economy: The structure and economic performance of Ontario's creative, cultural and new media clusters." Unpublished report prepared for the Ontario Ministry of Culture.

Wolfe, David A. 2009. *21st century cities in Canada: The geography of innovation*. Ottawa: Conference Board of Canada.

–. 2010. "The strategic management of core cities: Path dependence and economic adjustment in resilient regions." *Cambridge Journal of Regions, Economy and Society* 3 (1): 139–52. http://dx.doi.org/10.1093/cjres/rsp032.

–. 2012. "Civic governance, social learning and the strategic management of city-regions." In *Creating competitiveness: Entrepreneurship and innovation policies for growth*, ed. David B. Audretsch and Mary L. Walshok, 6–25. Cheltenham, UK: Edward Elgar. http://dx.doi.org/10.4337/9781781954058.00006.

Wolfe, David A., Charles H. Davis, Nicola Hepburn, Nicholas Mills, and Gale Moore. 2011. "Innovation and knowledge flows in the financial services and ICT sectors of the Toronto region." Prepared for the Ontario Ministry of Research and Innovation, the Toronto Region Research Alliance, and the City of Toronto, Munk School of Global Affairs, Toronto.

Wolfe, David A., and Jen Nelles. 2009. "Strategic management of urban economies and the scope for intermunicipal cooperation: Alternative approaches to local and regional development." Ontario in the Creative Age Working Paper Series. Toronto: Martin Prosperity Institute.

Yeandle, Mark. 2011. "The Global Financial Centres Index 10." http://www.zyen.com/PDF/GFCI%2010.pdf.

3 The Revitalization of Montreal: The Significance of Social Innovation as a Pillar for Economic Development

DIANE-GABRIELLE TREMBLAY,
NORMA M. RANTISI, AND JUAN-LUIS KLEIN

The Montreal metropolitan region is in transition to the new knowledge-based economy (Tremblay, Klein, and Fontan 2009; Tremblay and Rolland 2003; Shearmur and Rantisi 2011) and, economically speaking, performed rather well over the course of the last crisis (2008–10) in comparison with other Canadian and North American regions. Representatives of the business community and the main private and government institutions shifted their focus to the development of high-technology businesses, in the wake of the 1985 federal task force chaired by Laurent Picard. Based on the deliberations of its sixteen institutional leaders from Montreal, it produced what is known as the Picard Report (Klein et al. 2005), which became a reference point on Montreal's economic reconversion. The report proposed a strategy that encourages private leadership, internationalization, and the development of high-technology sectors (telecommunications, aerospace, bio-pharmaceuticals, information technologies, and microelectronics). These objectives were to be implemented at the metropolitan level (Tremblay and Van Schendel 2004).

The transition to this new economy occurred quite naturally in some suburbs that successfully developed high technology-oriented strategies, as they specialized in high-value-added sectors such as aeronautics, aerospace, pharmaceuticals and multimedia (Klein, Tremblay, and Fontan 2003; Tremblay et al. 2003; Tremblay and Rousseau 2006; Hassen, Klein, and Tremblay 2011). However, the inner part of the city, especially the city's first industrial areas on the periphery of the central business district, were hard hit by this change (Fontan, Klein, and Tremblay 2005). The industrial function that was once the basis of the local economy gradually relocated elsewhere, with severe effects. Beginning in the 1950s and intensifying in the 1970s, the relocation of the industrial sector from these areas triggered all of the problems associated with social and urban restructuring: unemployment, low incomes, and population loss.

An alternative strategy proposed by the community was developed by social organizations rooted in these marginalized districts, those put at risk by industrial restructuring. These districts mobilized around the community leaders to defend their assets and develop strategies that are adapted to new economic conditions and respect the interests of the local population (Fontan, Klein, and Lévesque 2003; Klein, Tremblay, and Bussières 2010). The main results of this mobilization can be seen in what is described by the actors as a "community economic development" strategy and in the creation of Montreal's community economic development corporations (CEDCs) (Fontan 1991; Hamel 1991).

These two strategies represent two distinct approaches to promoting Montreal's economic revitalization. On the one hand, Montreal's economy has moved in the direction of knowledge and innovation, and on the other, local actors and grassroots organizations have become important economic stakeholders in the transformation of the older manufacturing districts. Therefore, converging strategic orientations are taking shape. In economic development, clusters in Montreal's strongest business sectors (including aeronautics, biopharmaceutics, IT, film) are forming, thanks to the drive of the Montreal metropolitan community (MMC), private businesses, and provincial and municipal government. The choice of culture as a major pillar for metropolitan development is also influenced by Culture Montréal, a lobby organization promoting culture as a base for the development of Montreal, and cultural entrepreneurs. This is demonstrated in prestige projects such as the Quartier des spectacles, the designation of Montreal as a city of design by UNESCO, as well as by initiatives of social diversification for disadvantaged neighbourhoods, such as Tohu in the Saint-Michel borough, stimulated by the Cirque du Soleil (Pilati and Tremblay 2008) or the development of design and cultural activities in the Mile-End neighbourhood (Leslie and Rantisi 2006; Rantisi and Leslie 2010; Klein, Tremblay, and Bussières 2010). Concurrently, union and social economy organizations are trying to answer the crisis of the Fordist manufacturing industry and the resulting socio-economic conditions.

"Small, big city" is a label that captures the set of qualities that makes Montreal an appealing place to live and work (Rantisi 2009b) and thus has helped it survive a series of economic crises in the 1980s, 1990s, and again in 2008–10. This characterization of the city reflects the fact that Montreal was committed to devising new technology-oriented strategies but was still concerned with quality of life and social cohesion. This continued emphasis on quality of life (ranging from cultural diversity to the cost of living) has been instrumental for integrating a diverse set of socio-economic actors. While "creative" workers are lured primarily by the availability of work opportunities, quality-of-life attributes contribute to the liveability of the city as well as the development of social networks that facilitate knowledge exchange and the generation of new ideas. Therefore, Montreal is the scene of a broad array of innovations, from technological and productive (Klein et al. 2005) to social (Fontan, Klein, and Tremblay 2005; Tremblay, Klein, and Fontan 2009).

In general terms, social innovation concerns the implementation of new social and institutional arrangements, new forms of resource mobilization, new answers to problems for which available solutions have proven inadequate, or new social aspirations (e.g., autonomy and empowerment). They mobilize tangible and intangible resources in a new way (Klein and Harrisson 2007; Moulaert et al. 2013; Klein, Laville, and Moulaert 2014). In Quebec and Montreal, the work on social innovation began towards the end of the 1980s and is strongly inscribed in the theorization of an alternative economy. Such a theorization focused on the associative dynamics that are the basis of Quebec's distinctive socio-institutional structures that characterize "the Quebec model" (Klein et al. 2009). Industrial development, urban reconversion, and the networking of social actors constitute central topics that inform the spatial dimension of social innovation (Drewe, Klein, and Hulsbergen 2008; MacCallum et al. 2008; Moulaert and Nussbaumer 2008) as well as the social economy and socially oriented financial institutions.

This chapter begins with a brief overview of the city region profile and a review of recent policy documents and economic strategies that lay out the Montreal urban economy of the past and present. It then goes on to discuss innovation in the metropolitan economy and the role of talent attraction and retention, and finally, it highlights the impact of institutional density on the emergence of an inclusive mode of governance.

Recent Policies and Economic Strategies: Sources of the Cluster Strategy of the City of Montreal

The policies espoused by the City of Montreal since the 1980s support the idea of a network-based form of local economic development (Rifkin 2004) or cluster strategy (Porter 2000; Gertler and Wolfe 2005). Gerald Tremblay, former mayor of Montreal, introduced the concept of industrial clusters in 1991, when he was the Quebec minister of industry, commerce, science, and technology. He saw it as a model that, in his own words, is designed to stimulate the creation of conditions within which new ideas and processes can pass from embryonic to commercialized stages and provide returns for stakeholders. After twenty years and some experimenting with the concept at the provincial Industry Department, the City of Montreal has adopted the cluster strategy for innovation (Tremblay 2011).

A Short History

To trace the roots of the cluster strategy, one can go back some thirty years. In the Saucier Commission and Report, in 1985, the Quebec government first looked at proposals to improve the financing of firms, including small and medium-sized enterprises (SMEs), with good growth potential. For former mayor Tremblay, this is the first in a series of events that led to the "Greater Montreal Innovation system and the creation of the first four cluster secretariats" (Tremblay 2008, 24).

In 1986, as already noted, the Picard Report was a milestone. It recommended targeting seven competitive economic sectors: international activities; high technology; international trade and finance; design; cultural industries; tourism; and transportation. The report noted that revitalization would require joint action from the public and the private sectors. In 1991 Tremblay referred to the "urgency" of acting and developing a "value-added economy," and proposed the industrial cluster approach to restructure the Quebec economy. In that same year, Michael Porter wrote *Canada at the Crossroads*, suggesting a framework for focusing on the determining factors of Canadian competitiveness (Tremblay 2008, 24).

In 1993, a sectoral portrait of the economy of Quebec was published as *L'atlas industriel du Québec*. Prefaced by Michael Porter and supported by Gerald Tremblay, it advanced ideas that led to the adoption of the

Montreal Metropolitan Community's economic development plan in 2005 (Tremblay 2008, 25). The book examined competitive economies, synergy among the players in key sectors, and the issues and challenges facing Quebec. In 1996, a summit on the economy and employment was organized by the Quebec government, which then mandated a group of Montreal business people to determine the problems of the Montreal economy and present solutions to revitalize the city. In response, the task force presented some thirty initiatives, grouped into three large categories: "shifting to the new economy, modernizing established sectors, and improving overall development conditions" (25).

As a result of the Summit on the Economy and Employment, Montréal International (MI), a public-private organization, was created and assigned the mission of contributing to the economic development of metropolitan Montreal and increasing the region's international status. MI is funded by the Canadian and Quebec governments, the City of Montreal, the Montreal Metropolitan Community, and the private sector (Tremblay 2008, 25). In 2002, after being elected mayor of Montreal, Tremblay proposed to convene some 3,000 participants to a summit to draft a shared vision for the city's future. The new City of Montreal was created on 1 January 2002 following the merger of all municipalities of the island.[1] In the same year, MI worked with local industry to define an action plan to position the metropolitan region as one of the world leaders in the life sciences, and this cluster would adopt a brand strategy in 2005, renaming itself InVivo.

The Information and Communication Technologies cluster also developed an action plan in 2005 to support the economic development strategy (see City of Montreal n.d., 2005). In the same year, the MMC adopted its Economic Development Plan, which includes a metropolitan cluster-development strategy and a competitiveness fund to provide financial support to cluster development. This plan remains the dominant approach to economic development in the Montreal city-region. However, as we discuss below, it has not met the needs of all parts or sectors of the urban economy and has been complemented with alternative bottom-up strategies based on the social economy.

The Cluster Strategy and Sectoral Governance in Montreal

Montreal's cluster-development strategy is based upon identification of strategic sectors and mobilization of the principal stakeholders around a leader willing to rally the community around a common goal. The objective is to allow Montreal to project the international image of a city of knowledge that is also creative and prosperous.

In the MMC documents, the city initially identified four clusters: the aerospace cluster, created in 2006 after a concerted effort spread over two years; health sciences, which emerged in 2002; information and communications technology, launched in 2002; and the film and audiovisual production cluster, formally established when the Québec Film and Television Council became the secretariat for the film and television industry cluster in 2006. More recently, three clusters have been added to the MMC's strategy: Ecotech Québec, Finance Montreal, and the Montreal Fashion Bureau.[2] In 2005 the MMC Economic Development Plan identified four types of clusters: the *competitive* clusters, which bring together internationally competitive segments (aerospace, ICT; life sciences; textiles and clothing); the *emerging technology* clusters, which are cross-sectoral technologies with high, long-term growth potential (environmental technology; nanotechnology; and advanced materials); the *manufacturing* clusters, with growth potential based on natural resources (energy; paper and wood products; bio-food; petrochemicals, plastics and metallurgy); and finally *visibility* clusters, defined as strategic sectors for a city region's socio-economic development and branding, which include film, culture, tourism, and services (Tremblay 2008, 12).

While important administrative process leads to the creation of the cluster, which could be considered top-down, the overall approach to these clusters should be considered bottom-up, since initiatives are expected to come from firms, and the metropolitan-wide cluster was expected to demonstrate that it could organize itself. The MMC was responsible for the general planning and coordinating of activities but did not take the place of local actors and decision-makers. In order to qualify for financing, the firms that were part of a cluster had to develop a business plan with growth objectives, value-added projects, and performance indicators, and they were expected to operate by consensus. They had to develop a three-year action plan and a ten-year development strategy. Financing was normally provided by the three levels of government (municipal, provincial, federal) and the private sector at 25 per cent each.

Innovation

As noted above, we believe that innovation is not confined exclusively to high-tech sectors, as is often thought. An innovative society requires more than just technological change; it needs social and cultural innovation in the way wealth is generated and shared and in the governance methods that stakeholders propose (Klein and Harrisson 2007; Moulaert et al. 2013). Such change can occur when a neighbourhood or area interacts with the rest of the metropolis, becoming a node in a global network (Amin and Thrift 1992; Borja and Castells 1997; Hassen, Klein, and Tremblay 2011). The more these processes are inclusive and integrated – that is, the more all segments of society converge – the better the results in diversity and the more those results are appropriated by communities at large (Hillier, Moulaert, and Nussbaumer 2004). We regard this characteristic of inclusiveness and integration as the basis of a truly innovative society.

From that perspective, resources mobilized by social economy actors are crucial for integrating sectors into the innovation that would otherwise be excluded. These resources are the launching platform for socially and technologically innovative and entrepreneurial initiatives (Moulaert and Ailenei 2005) and foster links between economically depressed sectors and performing and dynamic milieus and networks (Amin, Cameron, and Hudson 2002). Many socially based productive experiments demonstrate the innovative potential of the actors and resources of the social economy (Klein, Tremblay, and Bussières 2010; Rantisi and Leslie 2010).

However, our research in a few of Montreal's main sectors or clusters (aeronautics, IT and multimedia, garment industry, and film) has shown that there is a diverse level and type of innovation in the urban economy. In general, it is difficult to identify specific sources of innovation in the region; rather, a complex series of factors, an elaborate web of interactions and knowledge exchanges contribute to innovation (social, product, process, or organizational).

From this perspective, our research has shown that intermediate organizations and business associations are important in the acceleration of knowledge flows, and in increasing the quality and the intensity of these flows (Hassen, Klein, and Tremblay 2011; Dossou-Yovo, Tremblay, and Klein 2008; Tremblay and Dossou-Yovo 2014). It appears that innovation is quite sectorally specific, and that intermediate organizations play a major coordinating role, especially in more concentrated sectors, such as aeronautics. On the other hand, in sectors like the garment industry or multimedia, where there are many small firms, not organized hierarchically as in the aeronautics sector, relations and knowledge flows between firms are less well developed, or at least they are less visible.

While it is apparent that, in creative sectors such as clothing design, innovative organizations have been developed, there are no major knowledge flows in this context. Rather, there is cooperation with the community economic development organization or other institutions and a sharing of resources. In the fur industry, whose innovative character is acknowledged by all apparel stakeholders, its success stems from the introduction of a flexible form of governance with sector-specific characteristics (Klein et al. 2007). Multimedia City offers examples of cooperation, but knowledge flows seem to be more important between individual workers than between firms. Some intermediate organizations were created to develop knowledge flows and information exchanges between firms in the city and in the cluster, but cooperation still appears limited (Tremblay and Rousseau 2006).

In product innovation, there are a few cross-sectoral knowledge flows, but they are difficult to identify and seem under-exploited. In the aeronautics industry, they appear to be rare. The same holds true in the garment industry, where designers tend to be individualistic and do not search for opportunities to collaborate. As well, in the film industry, it was pointed out that special effects in film animation and gaming should work together more closely, but since they are formally part of two different clusters, this has not happened to any great extent (Tremblay and Cecilli 2009; Cecilli and Tremblay 2009a, 2009b). So while cluster and district theory stresses the importance of knowledge flows within urban agglomerations, they seem to be concentrated mainly *within* sectors or clusters, and the Montreal cluster strategy tends to reinforce this perception, rather than create opportunities for crossovers (Tremblay and Yagoubi 2014; Tremblay and Klein 2014; Tremblay and Dossou-Yovo 2014).

When we tried to determine why cooperation was limited in the film and multimedia sectors, for example, we were told that Quebec represents a small market in which the players are very familiar with each other. And while this can be seen as a source of synergy and relational proximity, it does not prevent tensions and conflicts, and encourages fear of competition rather than a desire for cooperation. Similar difficulties can be observed in the fashion design sector (Tremblay 2012).

As we saw in the film, fashion design, and multimedia sectors, management of these conflicts is an important step to ensure that the performance of the sector feeds off the intensity of the local activity and the awareness of both local and non-local economic factors. The winning strategy for a cluster appears to be to assemble the greatest number of stakeholders within its structure, to have access to multifaceted points of view, and to develop relational proximity, possibly on the basis of physical proximity; the cluster must also attempt to resolve conflicts among participants and reach some form of consensus on its future and on the main actions to be taken. While this approach is difficult in sectors where there is a variety of small actors, such as multimedia, film, and most creative sectors – where there are also many self-employed – it appears to be easier to coordinate in the aeronautics cluster, where the large firms dominate the sector and, to a certain extent, can force or offer strong incentives for smaller firms to cooperate, since they are often subcontractors to the larger firms.

It appears that relational proximity is only beginning to appear in many clusters or that social capital – as defined in Bourdieu's (1972) work as the set of resources that are related to a durable network of relations, with "interconnections" and "interexchanges" – is only beginning to develop. While cooperation is presented to businesses as the competitive strategy of the future, they are not all convinced. However, many actors have seen enough areas of potential common interest to start moving in the direction of cooperation and exchange, many of them based on relational proximity. Also, in Montreal the inclusive form of governance may push towards stronger cooperation, as in the clothing sector, with the Lab Créatif bringing designers together.

The image of "glue" is often used to indicate how knowledge flows and "interconnections" can be useful, since they can reinforce the relationships among members of a group or a cluster; it is clear that even now the actors of the design, garment, IT, multimedia, film, and audiovisual cluster are not glued together, although some have started to develop connections and social relations. The aeronautics sector appears to be more closely connected, but this is largely due to the dominant role of the four major firms that can strongly reinforce cooperative relations through subcontracting and contractual relations.

We thus conclude that many of Montreal's clusters are at the start-up or development stage, while aeronautics is probably the only mature cluster. While we did observe some acceleration in the circulation of information among members of the clusters, and some development of professional exchanges and relational proximity, as well as learning and innovation (innovation usually coming later, when clusters are more established and connections between actors more developed), it would be difficult to conclude that innovation is strongly facilitated by local knowledge flows within and even more between clusters.

Talent Attraction and Retention

As mentioned above, innovative, participative institutional structures (including cluster strategies requiring firms to participate in order to get public support) have been a central focus of economic development strategies in Montreal as means for restructuring and revitalization. Another focus, which is linked with efforts to promote a cluster of economic activities, has been the promotion of a concentration of creative and knowledge workers (otherwise termed "talent"), which includes artists, scientists, and engineers. An aggregation of creative workers has been identified in recent works as an element fostering economic growth in metropolitan areas. In particular, the theory of the creative class put forward by Richard Florida has made cities and regions attentive to the ways to attract and retain these professional categories. The creative class thesis has emphasized the fact that the particular elements that shape the quality of place have a positive impact on the attraction of *talent* and on economic development (Darchen and Tremblay 2008).

From a general perspective, Montreal is often cited as an attractive city by creatives and the gay population because there are interesting amenities such as the Quartier des spectacles, the many festivals during the summer (Jazz, film, francofolies, Just for Laughs, etc.), and the gay district. Some CEDCs also stress quality of place when trying to attract business to their borough. While there has been little research on the issue, some scholars have recently started to look into factors that attract and retain talent in Montreal (Rantisi 2009b; Rantisi and Leslie 2009, 2010; Pilati and Tremblay 2007, 2008; Tremblay and Pilati 2008a, 2008b; Darchen and Tremblay 2009a, 2009b, 2010), and the next section presents key findings from research conducted in the current project (Rantisi 2009b).

With regards to the percentage of creative, artistic ("bohemian"), and technical workers, Rantisi (2009b) shows that Montreal ranks close to the other major cities and well above the Canadian average. However, limited consumer spending in Montreal and limited "markets" may represent a key constraint for independent creative workers and in many creative sectors, and possibly in other sectors (Craven 2009; Rantisi 2009a).

Why Creative Workers Come to Montreal

Rantisi (2009b) reports on a set of interviews with highly educated and creative workers living in Montreal. When the interviewees who relocated to Montreal were asked why they came, their answers were generally one of the following: work opportunities, school, or a partner (Rantisi 2009b). Of the twenty-eight people interviewed, only four said that they moved to Montreal because of Montreal's reputation for quality of life or its social/cultural offerings, and in all these cases, this factor was mentioned alongside work, school, or personal factors. Also, those who cited it were under thirty and single when they moved to the city.

Important distinctions can be made by sector. For example, for the videogame sector, the most common response was "work." That is not surprising, given Montreal's status as a centre for videogame development, particularly with the presence of Ubisoft's development studio and those of other major companies, such as Electronic Arts and Eidos (Nouri-Nekeoi 2007; Nouri-Nekeoi and Rantisi 2012). A concentration of such firms, as well as a of the key occupations (animation, music, computer programming) on which this sector draws, also contributes to Montreal's vibrancy as a videogame hub. When asked what initially attracted him to Montreal, one Ubisoft employee replied, "The simple truth is that Ubisoft is kind of a uniquely amazing place ... Montreal is cool, but I have a feeling that if they [Ubisoft] were in Reykjavik, people would still go to work for them in Iceland" (interview).

For the music and fashion sectors, by contrast, the most common responses were "school" and "partners," respectively (Rantisi 2009b). Montreal boasts a vibrant independent music and independent fashion design scene. However, barriers to entry for both sectors are low. Thus, fashion- and music-related jobs are available in most places (see, for example, Grant and Kronstal 2009 on Halifax; Lepawsky, Phan, and Greenwood 2010 on St John's; Leslie and Brail 2009 on Toronto). For this reason, it may be less likely that they would move to Montreal solely to take on such jobs.

While most people come to Montreal for work, school, or personal factors, the research findings indicate that quality of life can still play an important role in retaining artistic workers and facilitating social integration (Rantisi 2009b; see also Nouri-Nekeoi and Rantisi 2012). A similar sentiment was echoed by workers who migrated to Montreal, as well as by those who were from Montreal. One can group the positive amenities of a place under two broad headings: "social amenities" (most important being cultural diversity, small community, supportive work environment, friendly, welcoming, and the people) and "physical amenities" (primary being lifestyle, pace, cost of housing, art and culture, density / urban form, pool of creative workers, green spaces). More specifically, the key attribute cited under "social amenities" was cultural diversity. Interestingly, many respondents found Montreal to be more diverse than their own hometown, even among those migrating from cities with a relatively higher percentage of foreign-born residents (Rantisi 2009b). Some other interviewees suggested that because the city is bilingual, it may be more open to other languages and cultures. Other social attributes frequently cited were a supportive community and the friendliness of people. One fashion designer referred to the city as a "big village" when describing the presence of social networks and supports (see also Rantisi and Leslie 2009; Cummins-Russell and Rantisi 2012).

Under the "physical amenities" heading, apart from general references to Montreal as a "small, big city" and to the city's "quality of life," the most frequently cited attributes were the cost of living, the arts / cultural scene, a set of attributes relating to urban form, a pool of creative workers, and finally, the presence of green spaces (Rantisi 2009b).

Attraction of Science and Technology Creative Workers

The issue of talent attraction refers not only to artistic or creative professions, but also to science and technology workers in creative jobs or sectors (multimedia, for example). Our research on Montreal compares the relevance of criteria for quality of place with criteria for career opportunities (Darchen and Tremblay 2010a, 2010b). This study is based on interviews with students from the science and technology creative sectors and probes their interest in the amenities that could attract them and keep them in Montreal. The interviews confirm that students consider criteria for quality of place but these remain secondary in their decision and are always balanced with criteria for career opportunities (quality of work) or the social network. Although these are students and not active professionals, they appear to be a good approximation for scientific professionals, according to other research. While they cannot be considered totally representative of creative workers, their responses give an idea of the preferences of future creative workers.

Criteria on the quality of place do not appear to have a major impact on the retention of students. Moreover, a criterion like the presence of social networks has more impact on the retention of graduate students. Students in science and technology also prefer suburban living environments and the main reason mentioned is the availability of affordable space. It thus appears important to make a distinction between professional categories within the creative class, as not necessarily all of them strive for urban living environments (Darchen and Tremblay 2010a, 2010b).

Governance: The Role of the Third Sector and Social Economy in Montreal

We have concentrated to this point on the cluster and industrial strategy elements of Montreal's economic development and innovative performance, but it is important note a unique aspect of the broader Quebec situation, which is the importance of the institutional and social basis of economic development. While the City of Montreal has developed sectoral cluster strategies, the province has actively supported community participation. A strategy of local economic development has been developed over recent decades, with the first CEDCs appearing in the wake of the 1981–2 crisis in three deindustrialized zones of Montreal (Pointe-Saint-Charles, Centre-Sud, and Hochelaga-Maisonneuve).

The contribution of the social economy to innovation and socio-economic development in Montreal cannot be underestimated. In our view, under the imperatives of the new global economy, the restructuring of local spaces has relied on the innovating capacity of the productive sectors, of course, but also on the contribution of local social actors, including the associative sector and social economy, which are dynamic in Quebec and in Montreal (Klein et al. 2009; Klein, Tremblay, and Bussières 2010). From this perspective, innovation is not the exclusive domain of high-tech sectors, but all sectors contribute to the building an innovative society, which requires a social and cultural change in the way wealth is generated and in the governance approach adopted by stakeholders. Thus, it is important to emphasize that when we speak of economic policy development, social economy actors play a crucial role in this process in Quebec and Montreal. This is why we now turn to the issue of governance, in order to support the thesis of an *inclusive governance model* in Montreal.

In Montreal, a number of stakeholders are concerned with the problems facing the economy and have participated in governance mechanisms to plan for the future. These stakeholders include businesses and their representatives, of course, but also government agencies, the City of Montreal and its boroughs, unions, property owners, educational and research institutions, as well as third-sector or community organizations, the last constituting a distinctive characteristic of Montreal, in comparison with many other cities in Canada and abroad (Klein and Tremblay 2010; Klein, Tremblay, and Bussières 2010; Tremblay and Pilati 2013). The last group, chiefly the CEDCs established in the most affected neighbourhoods, are among the first to respond to the problems related to the economic crises. CEDCs operate at the level of city neighbourhoods and act as intermediary organizations, such as in support of entrepreneurship. In this respect, CEDCs have been frontline players, supporting entrepreneurs and fostering networks encompassing all actors and stakeholders involved. As such, they have played a very important role in the governance of the Montreal region, but also in developing innovation (social as well as product or process innovation), until the government of Quebec, as a measure involved within an austerity-based reform, changed their scale of action and their mission in 2015.

Other institutions play an important role in economic development governance in Montreal, including the local development centres (*centres locaux de développement*; hereafter CLD), and in Montreal both the CEDCs and CLDs were intimately related and both were reformed.

Origin and Mandate of CEDCs

CEDCs were locally based organizations created in the 1980s. In the wake of the crisis of the 1980s, community organizations in the most affected neighbourhoods devised locally based strategies for economic recovery. The community-based response first took shape in former industrial neighbourhoods and later across the city's less central districts. Headed by community leaders, these neighbourhoods mobilized to adapt development strategies to the needs and interests of their local populations (Hamel 1991). By the end of the 1980s, city hall had turned

CEDCs into local development bodies, and thereafter they had a recognized place in city boroughs. CEDCs were mandated to promote consensus among borough stakeholders. Their primary goal was to assist local stakeholders in identifying common objectives for partnership-based development projects. Their second goal was to support local entrepreneurship, thereby fostering local job creation. Their third goal was to improve the employability of the jobless in a changing economy. These objectives were shared by all Montreal CEDCs, which also created an action forum called "Inter-CEDC."

CEDCs also participated in other forums, such as the *Chantier de l'économie sociale* or forums that concern larger spheres of activity involving private enterprise and government agencies. CEDCs contributed to an important shift in community action, from pressuring political bodies to supporting economic development, as well as in the management of local economic development, from centralized state action to decentralized support. Such change did not occurred without debates in Montreal's social movements and in government circles.

The Quebec government had recognized CEDCs for their role as intermediaries in the wake of the 1998 reform aimed at modernizing local and regional development policies and programs. Inspired by the CEDC experience, the provincial government introduced the *centres locaux de développement* (CLD) (local centres for development) throughout the province. CLDs soon amalgamated different local development-cum-support agencies assigned to manage entrepreneurial support funds based on local development priorities and plans established within each locality. In Montreal, in the boroughs that were part of the former city, before the merger in 2002, as a result of negotiations with the provincial government, the management of CLD funds was assigned to CEDCs. In their role as supportive intermediaries of economic development, reinforced by their CLD status, Montreal CEDCs had access to organizational, human, and financial resources that were mobilized according to locally identified priorities. They could then assist private concerns or socio-economic projects. Their unique profile allowed CEDCs to aggregate diverse arrays of stakeholders and resources, whether local or external, private or public.

Access to these resources was, and already is, an important asset for innovative economic development projects and this highlights what appeared as an important characteristic of the Montreal socio-economic environment: namely, the strongly institutionalized character of an inclusive form of governance. The place obtained by CEDCs within the Montreal governance featured a specific coalition characterized by the participation of a plurality of actors and the hybridization of diverse forms of governance (Lévesque 2001; Fontan, Klein, and Tremblay 2005; Klein et al. 2009; Klein, Tremblay, and Fontan 2014). Driven at times by the government, by business organizations, and by social movements, this convergence contributed to the implementation of a hybrid form of governance. It was in fact Quebec's unique historical and cultural legacy that brought together public bodies, unions, community organizations, and employer representatives to collaborate in ensuring innovations that shaped the development of the Quebec model. The response to the crisis of the 1980s thus launched a cycle of mainly incremental social innovations that transformed the Quebec model. That cycle continued until the late 1990s, when the power of institutionalization limited the drive of experimentation.

In times of crisis or difficulty, this form of institutionalization of an inclusive form of governance makes it possible to tap into vital socio-territorial capital to launch innovative local initiatives and to support an inclusive model of innovation and socio-economic development. In order to succeed in deploying socially innovative collective actions, these local initiatives must also tap into more comprehensive, global dynamics. It is clear that these social economy or community economic development initiatives do not replace other actors, but they intervene actively with them, the city, government departments, the business community, and educational institutions. In this inclusive context, the CEDCs established ties between social, cultural, and economic actors, and thus assumed their responsibility as a community intermediary. Although they were not always welcome at the outset and often had views that conflicted with business or real estate promoters, they had become an unavoidable actor and their voices were respected, and this was a factor that allowed Montreal to implement an inclusive and distributed form of governance (Klein, Tremblay, Fontan 2014). In 2015, the government decided to focus public support on entrepreneurs and job creation rather than development-oriented organizations. This is an important loss for social cohesion and community development in the city, which can negatively affect the collective capability in local communities to launch creative and innovative urban development strategies. Nevertheless, the community spirit remains in boroughs and districts, as shown by thematic organizations in many domains, like creative and cultural activities, housing, local revitalization, etc.

Unions as Social Actors in the Regime of Governance

In the wake of the local community development initiatives and in the context of a difficult unemployment situation, unions have also taken up new roles in Quebec and have been at the forefront of social movements for employment and revitalization. From the crisis of 1981–2 onwards, unions have adopted a strategy that has reoriented their action and clearly given them new roles as important development actors. In reaction to de-industrialization and high unemployment, the unions have focused their action on the fight for jobs by creating investment funds and tools to prevent plant closures. With this view in mind, financial instruments were also created, especially two large funds established by Quebec's two largest unions to support employment in locally based firms in the various different regions of Quebec.

These funds are actually retirement funds, where individuals can place funds in registered retirement plans and thus benefit from tax deductions; the funds thus collected are used to avert business closures and invest in job creation. The first and largest fund of this type is the Fonds de solidarité (Solidarity Fund), created in 1983 by the Fédération des travailleurs et travailleuses du Québec (FTQ, Quebec Federation of Labour) with the explicit goal of creating jobs. In November 2012, the FTQ fund had 594,287 shareholders and assets of $8,763 million. The FTQ's experience inspired the second-largest labour confederation, the Confédération des syndicats nationaux (CSN, Confederation of National [Quebec] Trade Unions), to create a retirement fund in 1996, called Fondaction, with purposes similar to those of the FTQ fund, but focused more on venture capital investment in social economy and cooperative enterprises. In November 2012, Fondaction had assets of $991 million and counted 118,432 shareholders.

From the perspective of the fight to support job creation and reduce unemployment, the unions have collaborated with social-economy and community-based actors support collective initiatives. One interesting example of such a union implication in social and economic development is the creation in 2007 of the Fiducie du Chantier de l'économie sociale (Social Economy Trust), which offers patient capital to collective enterprises (Mendell and Nogales 2012). Many other funds (CLD funds, for example) are related to the social economy and CEDCs. They also constitute important financing bodies and institutions that support a more inclusive vision of economic development, actually a vision of integrated socio-economic development, and in some cases, these funds can support the same or similar projects in the Montreal region as elsewhere in Quebec.

It should be noted, however, that while unions have generally played a constructive role, some of their administrators have also sometimes played a heavy-handed corporatist role (opaque financing of political parties, links to the mafia, collusive practices in the construction trade). Increasing attention has been accorded such activity in the wake of what is now known as the Charbonneau Commission, which was authorized by the provincial government in 2011 to investigate corruption in the management of public contracts for the construction industry. Such practices have clearly presented a more negative vision of their action, and while one does not cancel the other, the vision of unions' role, in particular the FTQ and its Solidarity Fund, must be nuanced.

Culture Montréal also plays an important role in metropolitan governance, putting forward the crucial effect of the arts and cultural sectors in economic development. Culture Montréal is a lobby group for the cultural and artistic sectors. It has organized many activities and lobbies the government for the whole cultural sector and for continued support to the arts. For example, in 2007, they organized the "Rendez-vous 2007" with the Montreal Metropolitan Chamber of Commerce, to design activities and plan the cultural dimension of Montreal until 2017. The conference brought together many people from the business community and the arts and culture scene and served as a forum for discussion and exchanges between the two sectors (Cecilli and Tremblay 2008, 2009a, 2009b). With the CDEC's support, Culture Montreal is at the basis of the city's "Les quartiers culturels" strategy, which aims to decentralize public investments in the cultural sector and to support locally based cultural projects. To conclude, social and cultural (with Culture Montréal representing the cultural sector) agendas have been allowed some space in "strategic planning," and this appears to be an important characteristic to develop an inclusive society, not without conflict, of course, but it manages to go forward in many instances.

The perspective emerging from the above analysis views the social economy as intimately connected to innovation and the new economy, offering a more nuanced view compared to that of researchers such as Florida (see Stolarick and Florida 2006; Darchen and Tremblay 2008), who associate the new economy mainly with innovations by the most "talented," or with technologies and investments in leading-edge sectors. Instead, our approach focuses on combining strategies that concentrate on the local community (local development, community-based economy, solidarity-based economy, popular economy, community-based action, social creativity, and social innovation). Our research also identifies the reconnection of the local community to broader networks as a condition of their success. In this way, the social economy allows local initiatives to offer long-term solutions to local communities while contributing to building a more cohesive and pluralist city.

Conclusion

While Montreal presents a distinctive hybrid, inclusive, and distributed governance, and while actors from different social sectors are recognized as legitimate, thus facilitating collective learning and diverse kinds of partnerships, much remains to be done to ensure an easy transfer of knowledge between clusters or productive sectors, and to foster more innovative capacity within the city-region. Montreal definitely has many advantages and quality-of-life amenities, but they do not ensure smooth knowledge flows in all directions, or as much as might be warranted. However, the strong institutionalization of intermediate organizations and the inclusive character of governance do present a distinctive local asset for future development of all forms of innovation, and for socio-economic development. This strong institutionalization of the community and union sector can be viewed as an asset, but it can also sometimes slow changes down, especially when those changes threaten entrenched interest groups. However, except for the collusion and corporatist elements revealed by the Charbonneau Commission, the impact of consensus-building and concertation with social actors has generally been positive in terms of public policy. Nonetheless, the present situation indicates that the large array of social innovations carried out in Montreal (and in the province of Quebec) since the 1980s had not been sufficiently institutionalized, as is shown by the facility with which the Liberal Party governing the province since 2013 is attacking many of the previous gains (low-cost day care, local and economic development organizations, etc.), and it appears difficult for social groups to counter the austerity measures in all sectors.

A certain level of relational proximity and inclusiveness has been attained, but work still remains to ensure a continuous flow of knowledge between economic actors in the same and related sectors, the development of strong, mature clusters, and effective, socially motivated economic development. There needs to be more frequent interactions and collaboration between local actors in order to attain this objective. Time is needed to organize such a relational proximity and to foster social goals as part of economic development, with inclusiveness of all social actors, that appears to characterize the Montreal model.

We consider that the participation of social actors in the governance of economic change shapes the development of Montreal as a metropolitan region. According to this interpretation, Montreal is characterized by a generally inclusive governance model that sets it apart from many other North American metropolitan regions. Indeed, while a few other cities may include unions, community actors, and organizations in their debates and decision-making, this is far from frequent. Montreal illustrates a form of inclusive governance that contributes new dimensions to the theory on urban regimes, which is usually based on business coalitions. Our research shows that civil society organizations can play a significant part in metropolitan governance. In Montreal, organizations such as the chantier de l'économie sociale, Culture Montréal, and the CDECs act together to create a large, broadly based coalition; however, the Montreal coalition distinguishes itself by the inclusion and the influence of civil society organizations, related to the labour, social economy, and cultural communities.

It is also clear that consensus-building between the actors, who may have convergent as well as diverging views, does not exclude conflict. On the contrary, conflict is often a source of learning and compromise. Those compromises institute a mode of action, a "consensus-building culture," which characterizes Montreal's urban regime. The metropolitan region thus evolves with the rest of Quebec, inasmuch as many of the networks and resources mobilized by the Montreal coalition operate at the level of Quebec and within the Quebec model. However, given the specificities of Montreal, the civil society organizations at the centre of metropolitan governance are renewing the Quebec model, leading to a hybrid form of governance.

The Quebec model thus exhibits important specificities when applied to the metropolitan region – specificities that merit greater recognition and further analysis as they replace that model in the context of the "new economy" or "knowledge economy," where metropolitan regions have a determining role. Therefore, institutional leadership is needed, but it appears to be lacking, making the convergence of social and economic actors in Montreal somewhat precarious.

Big cities are part of a global network of metropolitan regions that compete with each other in order to attract investment and talent. What assets can be developed to increase the competitiveness of Montreal? From the point of view of the social actors, the city's main strength resides in the social cohesion that characterizes Montreal on the metropolitan level as well as, in terms of quality of life, at the neighbourhood level. While such factors – inclusive governance and quality-of-life attributes – are not conventionally viewed as determinants of economic growth, they provide a foundation upon which the networks that underpin creativity can develop and through which the gains from innovation can be shared. And, in the view of our interviewees in various projects over the course of the multi-year project, it is extremely important that this social cohesion be preserved and even, if possible, reinforced.

Notes

1 A few of them would later de-merge from the city, following a referendum.
2 *Clusters*: accelerating the development of industry clusters. See "Clusters" (n.d.). http://www.sdemontreal.com/en/collaborative-spaces/clusters.

References

Amin, A., and N. Thrift. 1992. "Neo-Marshallian nodes in global networks." *International Journal of Urban and Regional Research* 16 (4): 571–87. http://dx.doi.org/10.1111/j.1468-2427.1992.tb00197.x.

Amin, A., A. Cameron, and R. Hudson. 2002. *Placing the social economy*. London: Routledge.

Borja, J., and M. Castells. 1997. *Local & global: Management of cities in the information age*. London: Earthscan Publications.

Bourdieu, Pierre. 1972. *Outline of a theory of practice*. UK: Cambridge Studies in Social and Cultural Anthropology.

Cecilli, Elisa, and Diane-Gabrielle Tremblay. 2008. "La rencontre entre les entreprises et le monde des arts et de la culture à Montréal? Les résultats d'une recherche exploratoire." Paper presented at the INRS-Culture and Society conference, Quebec City, November 2008.

Cecilli, Elisa, and Diane-Gabrielle Tremblay. 2009a. "Art, culture et entreprises / À la recherche d'une direction pour surmonter obstacles et incompréhensions." Paper presented at the AIMAT International Arts Management Conference, New York, 23–5 June.

–. 2009b. "Il distretto del cinema e dell'audiovisivo di Montreal." *Tafter Journal* 16. http://www.tafterjournal.it/?s=Il+distretto+del+cinema+e+dell'audio visivo.

City of Montreal. n.d. "Le plan de développement." Montreal: City of Montreal. http://ville.montreal.qc.ca/portal/page?_pageid=7717,84077570&_dad=portal&_schema=PORTAL.

–. 2005. *Imaginer réaliser Montréal 2025*. Montreal: City of Montreal. http://ville.montreal.qc.ca/pls/portal/docs/PAGE/PES_PUBLICATIONS_FR/PUBLICATIONS/MTL2025-WEB.PDF.

"Clusters." n.d. Stratégie de développement économique. http://www.sdemontreal.com/en/collaborative-spaces/clusters.

Craven, R. 2009. "Mainstreaming the perception and practice of ethical fashion in Montreal." MSc thesis, Concordia University.

Cummins-Russell, T., and N.M. Rantisi. 2012. "Networks and 'place' in Montreal's independent music industry." *Canadian Geographer / Le Géographe canadien* 56 (1): 80–97. http://dx.doi.org/10.1111/j.1541-0064.2011.00399.x.

Darchen, Sébastien, and Diane-Gabrielle Tremblay. 2008. "La thèse de la 'classe créative': son incidence sur l'analyse des facteurs d'attraction et de la compétitivité urbaine." *Interventions économiques* 37: 1–20. http://www.teluq.uquebec.ca/pls/inteco/rie.entree?vno_revue=1.

–. 2009a. "La gouvernance locale des projets d'aménagement urbain: les cas de Griffintown et du projet du Casino-Cirque du soleil." Communication au colloque Acfas, Ottawa, 10–12 May.

–. 2009b. "La gouvernance de projets de reconversion et l'acceptabilité 'sociale': les exemples de Griffintown, du Casino-Loto Québec et du pôle St-Laurent." Communication au colloque étudiant du CRISES, Sherbrooke, 27 March.

–. 2010a. "The creative class thesis and the mobility patterns of knowledge workers considering the place of birth: The case of Montreal." *International Journal of Knowledge Based Development* 1 (3): 176–203.

–. 2010b. "What attracts and retains knowledge workers/students: The quality of place or career opportunities? The cases of Montreal and Ottawa." *Cities* 27 (4): 225–33.

Dossou-Yovo, Angélo, Diane-Gabrielle Tremblay, and Juan-Luis Klein. 2008. "Territoire, processus d'innovation dans les PMEs et acteurs intermédiaires: le cas du secteur des technologies de l'information dans la région métropolitaine de Montréal." Paper presented at the Association de science régionale de langue française, Rimouski, 25–8 August.

Drewe, P., J.-L. Klein, and E. Hulsbergen, eds. 2008. *The challenge of social innovation in urban revitalization*. Amsterdam: Techne.

Fontan, J.-M. 1991. "Les Corporations de développement économique communautaire montréalaises. Du développement économique communautaire au développement local de l'économie." PhD diss., Université de Montréal.

Fontan, J.-M., J.-L. Klein, and B. Lévesque, eds. 2003. *Reconversion économique et développement Territorial*. Quebec City: Presses de l'Université du Québec.

Fontan, J.-M., J.-L. Klein, and D.-G. Tremblay. 2005. *Innovation sociale et reconversion économique. Le cas de Montréal*. Paris: L'Harmattan.

Gertler, M.S., and D. Wolfe. 2005. "Spaces of knowledge flows: Clusters in a global context." Paper presented at DRUID Tenth Anniversary Summer Conference, Copenhagen, 27–9 June.

Grant, J., and K. Kronstal. 2009. "Smart city / cool city: Attracting and retaining talented and creative workers in Halifax." Paper presented at the Annual Meeting of the Innovation System Research Network, Halifax, 29 April–1 May.

Hamel, P. 1991. *Action collective et démocratie locale. Les mouvements urbains Montréalais*. Montreal: Presses de l'Université de Montréal.

Hassen, T.B., J.L. Klein, and D.G. Tremblay. 2011. "Building local nodes in a global sector: Clustering within the aeronautics industry in Montreal." *Canadian Geographer / Le Géographe canadien* 55 (4): 439–56. http://dx.doi.org/10.1111/j.1541-0064.2011.00384.x.

Hillier, J., F. Moulaert, and J. Nussbaumer. 2004. "Trois essais sur le rôle de l'innovation sociale dans le développement territorial." *Géographie, Économie Société* 6 (2): 129–52.

Klein, J.-L., J.-M. Fontan, D. Harrisson, and B. Lévesque. 2009. *L'innovation sociale au Québec: un système d'innovation fondé sur la concertation*. Collection Études théoriques. Montreal: CRISES. http://www.crises.uqam.ca/.

Klein, Juan-Luis, Jean-Marc Fontan, and Diane-Gabrielle Tremblay. 2009. "Social entrepreneurs, local initiatives and social economy. Foundations for an innovative strategy to fight against poverty and exclusion." *Canadian Journal of Regional Science* 32 (1): 23–42.

Klein, J.-L., and D. Harrisson, eds. 2007. *L'innovation sociale*. Quebec City: Presses de l'Université du Québec.

Klein, J.-L., J.L. Laville, and F. Moulaert, eds. 2014. *L'innovation sociale*. Toulouse: ÉRÈS.

Klein, J.-L., C. Manzagol, D.-G. Tremblay, and S. Rousseau. 2005. "Les interrelations université–industrie à Montréal dans la reconversion à l'économie du savoir." In *Les systèmes productifs au Québec et dans le Sud-Ouest français*, ed. Régis Guillaume, 31–54. Paris: L'Harmattan.

Klein, Juan-Luis, and Diane-Gabrielle Tremblay. 2010. "Social actors and their role in metropolitan governance in Montreal: Towards an inclusive coalition?" *GeoJournal* 75 (6): 567–79. http://dx.doi.org/10.1007/s10708-009-9270-0.

Klein, J.-L., D.-G. Tremblay, and D.-R. Bussières. 2010. "Social economy-based local initiatives and social innovation: A Montreal case study." *International Journal of Technology Management* 51 (1): 121–38. http://dx.doi.org/10.1504/IJTM.2010.033132.

Klein, J.-L., D.-G. Tremblay, and J.-M. Fontan. 2003. "Systèmes productifs locaux et réseaux productifs dans la reconversion économique: le cas de Montréal." *Géographie, Économie, Société* 5 (1): 59–75.

–. 2014. "Social actors and hybrid governance in community economic development in Montreal." In *Governing urban economies: Innovation and inclusion in Canadian city regions*, ed. Neil Bradford and Allison Bramwell, 37–57. Toronto: University of Toronto Press.

Klein, J.-L., D.-G. Tremblay, J.-M. Fontan, and N. Guay. 2007. "The uniqueness of the Montreal fur industry in an apparel sector adrift: The role of proximity." *International Journal of Entrepreneurship and Innovation Management* 7: 298–319.

Lepawsky, J., C. Phan, and R. Greenwood. 2010. "Metropolis on the margins: Talent attraction and retention to the St John's city-region." *Canadian Geographer* 54 (3): 324–46.

Leslie, D., and S. Brail. 2009. "The case of fashion talent in Toronto: A reevaluation of amenities based theories." Paper presented at the Annual Meeting of the Innovation System Research Network, Halifax, 29 April–1 May.

Leslie, D., and N.M. Rantisi. 2006. "Governing the design sector in Montreal." *Urban Affairs Review* 41:309–37.

Lévesque, B. 2001. *Le modèle québécois: un horizon théorique pour la recherche, une porte d'entrée pour un projet de société*. Montreal: Cahier du CRISES.

MacCallum, D., F. Moulaert, J. Hillier, and S. Vicari Haddock, eds. 2008. *Social innovation and territorial development*. Farnham: Ashgate.

Mendell, M., and R. Nogales. 2012. "Solidarity finance." *Universitas Forum* 3 (2). http://www.universitasforum.org/index.php/ojs/article/view/111.

Moulaert, F., and O. Ailenei. 2005. "Social economy, third sector and the solidarity relations: A conceptual synthesis from history to present." *Urban Studies* 42 (11): 2037–53. http://dx.doi.org/10.1080/00420980500279794.

Moulaert, F., D. MacCallum, A. Mehmood, and A. Hamdouch, eds. 2013. *The international handbook of social innovation: Collective action, social learning and transdisciplinary research,* Cheltenham, UK: Edward Elgar. http://dx.doi.org/10.4337/9781849809993.

Moulaert, F., and J. Nussbaumer. 2008. *La logique sociale du développement territorial.* Quebec City: Presses de l'Université du Québec.

Nouri-Nekeoi, M. 2007. "The social determinants of attraction and retention of creative workers: The case of Montreal's Ubisoft." BA thesis, Concordia University.

Nouri-Nekeoi, M., and N.M. Rantisi. 2012. "The enduring significance of economic factors for the attraction of creative workers: The case of Montreal's video game industry." *Northeastern Geographer* 4 (1): 1–16.

Pilati, Thomas, and Diane-Gabrielle Tremblay. 2007. "Cité créative et District culturel; une analyse des thèses en présence." *Géographie, économie et société* 9 (4): 381–401.

–. 2008. "Le développement socio-économique de Montréal: La cité créative et la carrière artistique comme facteurs d'attraction?" *Canadian Journal of Regional Science* 30 (3): 475–95.

Porter, M. 2000. "Location, competition, and economic development: Local clusters in a global economy." *Economic Development Quarterly* 14 (1): 15–34. http://dx.doi.org/10.1177/089124240001400105.

Rantisi, Norma M. 2009a. "Cultural intermediaries and the geography of designs in the Montreal fashion industry." In *Industrial design and competitiveness: Spatial and organization dimensions*, ed. Grete Rusten and John R. Bryson, 93–116. Hampshire, UK: Palgrave Macmillan.

–. 2009b. "'Montreal: The small, big city': Theme II report on the social foundations of talent attraction and retention." Research report for the ISRN project.

Rantisi, Norma M., and Deborah Leslie. 2009. "Creativity by design? The role of informal spaces in creative production." In *Spaces of vernacular creativity: Rethinking the cultural economy*, ed. Tim Edensor, Deborah Leslie, Steve Millington, and Norma M. Rantisi, 33–45. London: Routledge.

–. 2010. "Materiality and creative production: The case of the Mile End neighbourhood in Montréal." *Environment & Planning* 42 (12): 2824–41. http://dx.doi.org/10.1068/a4310.

Rifkin, Jeremy. 2004. "When markets give way to networks … everything is a service." In *Creatives industries*, ed. John Hartley, 361–74. London: Blackwell Publishing.

Shearmur, R., and N.M. Rantisi. 2011. "Montreal: Rising again from the same ashes, in Canadian urban regions." In *Trajectories of growth and change*, ed. Larry S. Bourne, Thomas Hutton, Richard Shearmur, and Jim Simmons, 173–201. Don Mills, ON: Oxford University Press.

Stolarick, K., and R. Florida. 2006. "Creativity, connections and innovation: A study of linkages in the Montréal region." *Environment & Planning A* 38 (10): 1799–817. http://dx.doi.org/10.1068/a3874.

Tremblay, Diane-Gabrielle. 2011. "Montreal's cluster strategy in culture and technology sectors." In *Economic strategies for mature industrial economies*, ed. Peter Karl Kresl. New York: Edward Elgar.

–. 2012. "Creative careers and territorial development: The role of networks and relational proximity in fashion design." *Urban Studies Research* 2012: 1–9. http://dx.doi.org/10.1155/2012/932571.

Tremblay, Diane-Gabrielle, and Elisa Cecilli. 2009. "The film and audiovisual production in Montreal: Challenges of relational proximity for the development of a creative cluster." *Law and Society* 39 (3): 157–87.

Tremblay, D.-G., and A. Dossou-Yovo. 2014. "Territory, innovation processes in SMEs, and intermediary actors: The case of the IT sector in the Greater Montreal Area." *International Journal of Technology Management* 69 (1): 1–19.

Tremblay, Diane-Gabrielle, and Juan-Luis Klein. 2014. "Innovation and social actors in Montreal: Intersectoral challenges of place-based dynamics." In *Innovating in urban economies: Economic transformation in Canadian city-regions*, ed. D. Wolfe, 123–50. Toronto: University of Toronto Press.

Tremblay, Diane-Gabrielle, Juan-Luis Klein, and Jean-Marc Fontan. 2009. *Initiatives locales et développement socioterritorial*. Quebec City: Presses de l'université du Québec.

Tremblay, D.-G., J.-M. Fontan, J.-L. Klein, and S. Rousseau. 2003. "Proximité territoriale et innovation: une enquête sur la région de Montréal." *Revue d'Économie Régionale et Urbaine* 5 (December): 835–52. http://dx.doi.org/10.3917/reru.035.0835.

Tremblay, Diane-Gabrielle, and Thomas Pilati. 2008a. "Les centres d'artistes autogérés et leur rôle dans l'attraction de la classe créative." *Géographie, économie et société* 10 (1): 427–47.

–. 2008b. "The Tohu and artist-run centers: Contributions to the creative city?" *Canadian Journal of Regional Science* 30 (2): 337–56.

–. 2013. "Social innovation through arts and creativity." In *International handbook on social innovation: Social innovation, collective action and transdisciplinary research*, ed. Frank Moulaert, Diana MacCallum, Abid Mehmood, and Abdel Hamdouch, 67–79. Elgaronline. http://dx.doi.org/10.4337/9781849809993.00015.

Tremblay, D.-G., and D. Rolland. 2003. *La nouvelle économie: où? quoi? Comment?* Quebec: Presses de l'université du Québec.

Tremblay, D.-G., and Serge Rousseau. 2006. "The Montreal multimedia sector: A cluster, an 'innovative milieu' or a simple colocation?" *Canadian Journal of Regional Science* 28 (2): 299–327.

Tremblay, D.-G., and V. Van Schendel. 2004. *Économie du Québec et de ses regions.* Quebec: Presses de l'université du Québec.

Tremblay, D.-G., and A. Yagoubi. 2014. "Knowledge sharing and development of creative fashion designers' careers: The role of intermediary organisations." *International Journal of Knowledge Based Development* 5 (2): 191–208.

Tremblay, G. 2008. "Clusters and innovation: Boosting creative capital." Paper presented at the 21st Annual Entretiens du Centre Jacques Cartier, October.

4 Vancouver and the Economy of Culture and Innovation

TOM HUTTON AND TREVOR BARNES

Introduction: Positioning Vancouver within the Urban Discourse

Vancouver's development as a city, as an experiment in urbanism, and as a site of innovation and restructuring has stimulated significant scholarly and policy interest, as reflected in a large and burgeoning research literature, perhaps unique in volume for a city of its size. This scholarly attention has included critical treatments of Vancouver's status as exemplar of post-industrialism, both as socio-economic process and as an expression of civic policy values and programs (Ley 1996), as well as the influence of global processes on the city's landscapes and its overall development trajectory (Olds 2001; Hutton 2004; Barnes and Hutton 2009; Barnes, Hutton, Ley, and Moos 2011). More particularly, the seductive imaginaries projected in the glittering landscapes of condominium point towers (slim, high-rise residential towers with a small floor plate) and urban amenity characteristic of the reconstructed central area have, since the 1990s, inserted "Vancouverism" as a privileged brand within the lexicon of contemporary city planning and development, although these are frequently juxtaposed against the deep deprivation of the proximate Downtown Eastside (DTES) in a somewhat crude binary construct that occludes much of the city's more complex development experience (Blomley 2004).

What makes the Vancouver case of larger interest within urban studies? First, the meshing of post-staples, post-corporate, and transnational development vectors shape a distinctive economy of small- to medium-size enterprises (SMEs) and social morphology, which, together with the built environment and amenity attributes and the city's ecological setting, comprise the essence of Vancouver's urban identity. Second, the emergence of a new cultural economy of production, consumption, and spectacle in Vancouver is not merely ancillary to an economy of propulsive industries and firms, as in many cities, but comprises, rather, in the aggregate a centrepiece element of a space economy configured by "diverse specializations" and framed by distinctive governance structures, innovation networks, and production systems. Third, Vancouver represents a particularly trenchant site for engaging some of the defining discourses of contemporary urban economic development. Here we can cite the cultural economy debate on the role of creativity in the contemporary urban economy and its socio-economic consequences; vigorous contestation over the centrality of production and consumption to the economy of the contemporary city; social class implications; and aspects of the industrial-residential interface and affiliated dislocations in the urban property market. In this chapter we propose to explicate both the localized and broader saliency of Vancouver in discourses of urban growth and change, informed primarily by a program of study and fieldwork conducted within the project framework of the Innovation Systems Research Network (ISRN) collaborative research on "innovation and creativity in Canadian city-regions."[1]

Following this introduction, first we present a concise review of Vancouver's development history, including the critical continuities and disjuncture associated with the city's staples economy vocation – essential to an appreciation of more recent aspects of innovation and transformation. Second, we examine defining features of Vancouver's emergence as an economy of culture and innovation, viewed through the lens of governance, labour, capital, production systems, and space. These factors produce a multiscalar relayering of capital and new divisions of labour in Vancouver, as well as multiple narratives of economic development, which project aspects of continuity as well as disjuncture, and complementarity as well as conflict. Our chapter concludes with summary observations on the specific trajectory of Vancouver's development as well as commentary on wider implications for urban studies and more particularly the contours of the economy of the contemporary city.

Prologue: Vancouver's Development in Local and Larger Contexts

The urban discourse tends to focus not unnaturally on the contemporary condition of cities in light of the forces of globalization and the sequence of innovations and restructuring episodes of the last decade or so, including recurrent downturns and crises. Of the latter, important events have been the technology crash of 2000 and afterwards, and the continuing fallout from the financial crash of 2008. But as Saskia Sassen (2006) argues, the "deep economic history" of cities has intrinsic study value as well as explanatory possibilities in the quest to understand the complex relayering of cities and their constitutive economies, societies, and landscapes. As is well known, Vancouver's provenance dates from its role in staples production, and more specifically as "milltown" in a forest-based economy from the 1870s (Morley 1969). The decisive event in this formative period of Vancouver's development was the decision to locate the western terminus of the Canadian Pacific Railway on Burrard Inlet. The ensuing strategic impacts included the connectivity between the nascent city on the inlet with resource regions, the agricultural economies of the prairies, and the industrial cities and consumer markets of central Canada. In addition, there was British Columbia's confederation with the Dominion of Canada in 1871, for which the completion of the Canadian Pacific Railway was sine qua non.

Within British Columbia the establishment of the CPR's western terminus at Vancouver also had the effect of truncating Victoria's development as (hitherto) primary city and underscoring its role as capital city rather than as a principal centre of commerce and industry. The marginalization of Victoria in this way, and the subsequent failure to develop the potential of a deep-water port at Prince Rupert, ensured Vancouver's primacy within the economy and urban system of British Columbia in the first half of the twentieth century. Manifestations of Vancouver's development pathway during this period included not only important resource-processing and transportation facilities, incorporating forest industry mills around False Creek and along the Fraser River, and a complex of salmon canneries in the settlements of the Fraser delta, but also a commercial and banking core centred on Victory Square, as well as a retail sector along Hastings and Granville Streets in the downtown.

While Vancouver was therefore by mid-twentieth century already a vibrant city, shaped by resource industries and transportation functions, the early post-war period saw an accelerated growth allied with the remarkable expansion of the provincial resource economy. Provincial government commitments to "opening up" British Columbia's interior resource bounty were realized though major public investments in railway and highway construction, as well as in infrastructure spending associated with the burgeoning resource communities and settlements of the coast and the interior. While much of this capital formation naturally occurred in situ, Vancouver was a principal beneficiary, reflected in the growth of head office and management operations, and banking and financial institutions, which stimulated the emergence of a corporate office complex centred on Georgia and Burrard Streets, as well as resource-processing and the expansion at the Port of Vancouver.[2]

The early 1980s, though, can be seen with the benefit of hindsight as the high-water mark of Vancouver's role within the BC resource economy. While important aspects of connectivity continued, notably the role of the Port of Vancouver as a site of bulk commodity exports, other staples economy functions declined, including resource-processing, and then also certain banking and business service industries. For example, Vancouver's speculative (and scandal-ridden) penny stock market on Howe Street closed in 1999, initially rolled into the CDNX exchange based in Calgary and later bought by the owners of the Toronto Stock Exchange who renamed it the TSX Venture Exchange. In the aftermath of the 1980s resource downturn that included both cyclical and structural effects, increasing core-periphery divergence took hold. Vancouver's service firms increasingly sought new markets abroad (Davis and Hutton 1991), creating a bipartite provincial, "two economies" model (Davis and Hutton 1989). Vancouver's economy became increasingly "decoupled" from the resource economy that dominated the rest of the province.

This new trajectory for Vancouver secured increased traction as the 1980s progressed, a decade that we can now acknowledge as the decisive period of comprehensive transformation for the city and region. The 1986 international exposition (Expo '86), with the theme of urban transportation innovation and marked in Vancouver by the construction of the initial "Expo Line" rapid-transit linking the city's downtown with the inner suburban centre of New Westminster, repositioned Vancouver from the metropolis of the "west beyond the west" in Jean Barman's evocative terminology (1991) to a node of the Asia Pacific (even then the leading global theatre of capital investment, economic growth, and urban development). This reorientation was, of course, dramatically accelerated by the new waves of immigration and investment from Asia, initially from Hong Kong, and then also from China and elsewhere in East, Southeast, and South Asia (Ley 2010).

Within the Canadian urban system, transnationalism plays a critical role in Vancouver's status as one of Canada's major metropolitan cities and urban growth centres, a roster that includes Toronto, Montreal, Ottawa, and Calgary. While growth in the last two city-regions is based largely on dominant specializations (government and public services, and more recently telecommunications and information technology, in the case of Ottawa, and the petrochemical sector for Calgary), Vancouver presents a more diverse industrial structure, including trade, transportation, cultural industries and labour, higher education, financial intermediaries, property, and construction. But Vancouver lacks the major manufacturing and banking/ financial sectors that characterize Toronto and Montreal at the peak of the Canadian urban hierarchy, and instead features an entrepreneurial economy of SMEs, shaped increasingly by the composition of international immigration, especially from Asian source societies (Bourne et al. 2011).

Creativity, Innovation, and Transition in Vancouver's Economy

Even in periods of large-scale innovation and change, the basic structures of urban economies are shaped by legacy effects as well as by the accretion of new industries and firms. In Vancouver, forestry is still important, and in the province as a whole it remains the largest manufacturing sector, generating significant provincial revenues. That said, its presence in the Vancouver region is much diminished. There are no sawmills left operating in Vancouver, the last one, the White Pines Mill, closing in 2001. The larger BC forestry sector has been increasingly squeezed both by low-cost jurisdictions with huge supply advantages (notably Russia) and by industries and companies in northern Europe who have committed to product innovation, advanced engineering, and design, all of which are clearly critical in the high-end market sector. To these troubles we can add the serious supply issues of resource depletion, especially in the coastal regions, and of course the devastating effects of the mountain pine beetle infestation in the interior regions. Vancouver's traditional management functions have also been eroded. McMillan Bloedel, formerly the largest BC-owned forest company in the province, was taken over by Seattle-based Weyerhaeuser, the Bank of BC was acquired by the Hong Kong and Shanghai Banking Corporation (now HSBC Bank), and as already mentioned, the Vancouver Stock Exchange (VSE) moved to

Calgary. Each of these events was imbued with deep symbolic portent and produced substantive effects.

These trends all affect the role of Vancouver's CBD, the largest agglomeration of firms and employment in the region. From its development in the 1970s and 1980s as "downtown BC," the attenuated linkages with the provincial resource economy and more particularly its steady loss of head office functions limit the CBD's control capacity and power projection relative to those of cities higher up the global urban hierarchy. Local policy has also shaped events in this realm, as the seminal Central Area Plan approved by Vancouver City Council in 1991 effectively halved the area zoned for commercial office development, privileging instead high-rise residential development, which has been exalted as the hallmark feature of Vancouver's experience of contemporary urbanism. As a result, the CBD has been recast as a domain of mostly smaller service intermediaries, with some large provincial utility companies and Crown corporations as important residuals of its former vocation as control centre within a core-periphery structure. In addition, a recent arrival is a cluster of new media firms forms part of the city's creative economy. In many ways the most interesting (and instructive) expressions of economic development in Vancouver are observed not in the CBD but rather in the inner city heritage areas and in the city's industrial districts, a theme we shall return to later.

Meta-narratives of Vancouver's Twenty-First-Century Economy

A quarter-century following the secular contraction of the tight interdependency between Vancouver and the provincial resource economy, scholars and urbanists have struggled to parse the meaning of successive periods of innovation and restructuring for the region's development trajectory. Frances Bula, a well-known journalist-commentator on the Vancouver scene, has suggested in conversation with scholars, business leaders, and policy specialists that there are three contending city visions: first, Vancouver as "gateway," notably linking Canada with the growth economies of Asia; second, a "residential-consumption" city, shaped by the rampant condominium development in the central area but also by high-rise housing in the suburbs, and by a burgeoning economy of urban amenity and consumption; and third, a more complex profile defined by an economy of diverse specializations, including film and video industries, other new media, and retooled design industries such as architecture, landscape architecture, and advertising/branding (Bula 2011), which in sum offer support for the continuing saliency of a productionist analytical viewpoint.

Each of these broad constructions of the Vancouver economy suggests different economic trajectories observed in multiscalar space, presenting marked contrasts as a result of the blend of capital, culture, technology, and attributes of place.

Vancouver as Asia-Pacific Gateway: Path Dependency and the Master Narrative

With respect first to the "Vancouver as gateway" model, the development program is dominated by massive infusions of capital in infrastructural works directed by senior levels of government, on the order of $3 billion in the aggregate, designed to realize the Vancouver–Lower Mainland region's destiny as linchpin between the limited Canadian economy and the notionally unlimited economies of the Asia Pacific region. The developmental scale is both regional and extra-regional. It is expressed in the construction of new highways to facilitate goods movement, notably in the north and south perimeter roads serving the Port of Vancouver and Roberts Bank Superport, and a new crossing of the Fraser. Culturally it is also represented by an unqualified enthusiasm for a modernist ideology, inflected with a belief in contemporary globalization. At the same time there are also investments in the software of international trade, including engineering, design, and marketing, each in turn requiring aspects of innovation and creativity.[3]

As senior government officials and business leaders have emphasized, the large quantum of capital allocated to the gateway project is justified by the relative importance of international trade to British Columbia and Canada as a whole. Measures of significance include throughput of seaborne trade facilitated by the Port of Vancouver, with massive tonnage of bulk cargoes destined for export, and mostly higher-value consumer products imported, as well as the impressive expansion of passenger traffic volumes utilizing Vancouver International Airport (Vancouver Airport Authority 2009). In employment terms, too, census data and other surveys point to the importance of gateway industries and installations, with employment in trade the largest single component of the labour force in Metro Vancouver (see table 4.1).

Table 4.1. Employment by industry for Greater Vancouver, 1996, 2001, 2006
Annual averages (thousands of employees)

	1996	2001	2006
Goods-producing sector	182.2	176.2	211.9
Agriculture	5.9	6.6	10.0
Forestry, fishing, mining, oil and gas	10.0	5.6	8.1
Utilities	5.3	5.5	3.7
Construction	59.4	53.5	85.3
Manufacturing	101.6	104.9	104.7
Services-producing sector	764.3	862.9	975.2
Trade	152.0	165.7	191.8
Transportation and warehousing	58.1	66.8	67.6
Finance, insurance, and real estate	78.2	77.8	88.0
Professional, scientific, and technical	74.1	95.8	112.0
Business, building, and support services	37.6	42.7	54.5
Educational services	55.8	72.5	92.4
Health care and social assistance	88.6	96.1	115.8
Information, culture, and recreation	50.4	66.3	70.3
Accommodation and food services	74.6	84.9	86.9
Other services	45.3	52.8	52.7
Public administration	49.5	41.4	43.3
Total employed, all industries	946.5	1,039.1	1,187.1

Source: Statistics Canada

That said, there are significant risks associated with Vancouver's twenty-first-century gateway vocation, and also no shortage of critics. Local advocacy groups have vociferously criticized the substantial environmental costs and future risks of the gateway projects, including the loss of agricultural land, while social activists have complained about the displacement effects of capital allocated to Gateway on spending ranging from social welfare to public transit.[4] Then there are the projected risks of facilitating the movement of oil tankers through the Georgia Strait. Anthony Perl and Richard Gilbert (2010) among others, have questioned assumptions about growth projections in trade in an era of peak oil. Finally, a looming strategic question concerns the long-term security of Vancouver's position within Asia-Pacific seaborne trade and travel rotation. The recent loss of a significant portion of the established cruise ship business to Seattle is particularly germane.

The gateway vision for Vancouver resonates with the globalization motif, and especially significant, given the shift both internationally from the Atlantic to the Pacific theatre, and nationally from central Canada to the West. But in important ways the trajectory represents continuity as much as it does a departure. Aside from Vancouver's positionality on the outer edge of the Innisian national core-periphery structure, the emphasis on Asia-Pacific trade and social networks and connectivity follows a pathway at least a century in the making: from the early immigration of Chinese and Japanese populations, and the trans-Pacific routes and itineraries of passenger and freight lines, including the Canadian Pacific steamships. The implication at some level is a form of path dependency rather than a radical deviation.

There is also a second layer of Vancouver's gateway vocation that parallels the senior government and corporate commitments to new capital formation: local business associations dedicated to fostering Asia-Pacific trade and investment. Illustrations of this important expression of urban transnationalism include the large Vancouver chapter of the Hong Kong–Canada Business Association (HKCBA). Established in 1984, it was at the front end of the inflow of Hong Kong immigrants and capital that transformed housing, labour, and property markets within Vancouver and other major receiving centres. HKCBA offers a range of services and networking opportunities, including trade missions and business seminars. The membership of HKCBA in Vancouver and other major Canadian cities includes a diverse sectoral representation of both Hong Kong and Canadian-born business people, as well as a sprinkling of public sector interests. But the principal concentrations are in the banking and finance, property, and trading sectors, with each contributing to Vancouver's SME entrepreneurial economy.

Another key agency is the Asia-Pacific Foundation of Canada, domiciled in downtown Vancouver. Its recent activities have included dialogues with specialized service firms having significant Asian practices, notably in legal and accountancy services, with a view to disseminating market knowledge within the Vancouver region. "Innovation" in this context can involve the shaping of hybrid practices that blend ideas about efficient business operations, collaborative co-production possibilities, and joint marketing, including the sharing of agents and sales offices. At the level of the firm, too, there are linkages between

Vancouver fashion designers and garment producers in China, demonstrating the possibilities of economies of scope, in which firms can transcend the limitations of the local market. In these examples we can acknowledge the (partial/selective) integration of Vancouver and its economy into the Asia-Pacific region, the leading theatre of growth in the global economy. Consequently, it enlarges the possibilities for stimulus to creativity, and to innovation in business practice.

While of course the City of Vancouver and Metro Vancouver each play significant roles in the evolution of the Asia-Pacific gateway program, such as in roadway construction, to a large extent the policy role of the local state has been essentially bypassed by other agencies. The strategic vision for the gateway and its propulsive impacts on the Vancouver economy have been authored and enunciated mainly by the federal and provincial governments, supported by the Vancouver Board of Trade, the Business Council of British Columbia, and other business interests. At the same time, the lack of an effective regional economic development strategy that might have explicated where the gateway fits (or conflicts) with the metropolitan planning program has constituted a recurrent problem in regional governance over the past forty years. Local (municipal) official community plans (OCPs), the principal vehicle for formal policy planning in British Columbia, each embody an implicit development strategy. But twenty-plus separate statements cannot in the aggregate offer an overall vision and program for the region as a whole. Given the absence of a master regional strategy and program, individual municipalities are left to promote innovation and creativity as instruments of economic development within their respective jurisdictions, as we shall now see.[5]

"LIVING FIRST": VANCOUVER AS HOUSING-LED URBAN DEVELOPMENT MODEL

Scholarship on the new economy of the city over the past two decades has included a revival of the debate concerning the relative weight of production and consumption in urban development. This discourse can be related in turn to the long-standing divide in urban studies generally between the social ecology (or Chicago) school, which emphasizes the saliency of social class, social morphology, and community structure as theory-building elements, in opposition to the genre of "industrial urbanism," which places greater weight on production systems, firms, and labour markets as motive forces in the city (Scott 1988).

This debate has naturally been influenced first by the decline (collapse in some cases) of traditional manufacturing and ancillary labour ("de-industrialization"), then more recently by the rise of a new cultural economy shaped ostensibly in large part by consumption amenities that appeal to a notionally footloose and self-regarding "creative class." Here we can trace a lineage of work that includes Terry Nichols Clark's exposition on the entertainment city (2004), Glaeser, Kolko, and Saiz's influential article (2001) on the rise of the "consumer city," and of course Florida's volume (2002) on the "creative class" and its ascendancy within the labour markets and social class configurations of the city.

While this body of work has attracted some vigorous criticisms, on empirical, theoretical, and ideological grounds, it does speak to some important aspects of urban development in the twenty-first century. To illustrate, first, the collapse of Fordist manufacturing has vitiated the production sector and seriously compromised the overall economy of important cities such as Manchester, Liverpool, Buffalo, and Detroit. While some older industrial cities have experienced significant regeneration, others are still struggling (Moulaert 2000). Second, the ascendancy of a new cultural economy, incorporating production, consumption, and spectacle, though sometimes exaggerated, now incontrovertibly represents a substantial element of the economy of an increasing number of cities including London, New York, Milan, Paris, and Toronto. Third, and as a corollary feature, cultural workers comprise a significant portion of the total urban labour force. There is general agreement, though, that Florida and his acolytes routinely inflate the numbers through a promiscuous taxonomical approach (Krätke 2011). Fourth, the growth of cultural workers clearly has social class implications for many cities, although whether they comprise a semi-autonomous cohort or more properly a subgroup within the larger "new middle class" is a subject of debate. Fifth, the emergence of a new cultural economy and its attendant economic and residential geographies and behavioural attributes has manifestly influenced the reconfiguration of the structure and morphology of the city.

VANCOUVER AS EXEMPLAR OF HOUSING-LED REDEVELOPMENT: ASPECTS OF INNOVATION

Vancouver constitutes a particularly fertile arena for testing or at least investigating these propositions. Although never an important centre of Fordist industrialism on the scale of other large Canadian cities, staples production was certainly a keystone feature of its economy through much of the last century (Barnes et al. 1992), and its obsolescence and associated negative externalities motivated a new urban policy discourse. The clear civic policy preference for housing was established in the municipal reformist era of the 1970s, a program that discounted the value of manufacturing and working-class labour and was most dramatically symbolized in the well-known False Creek South housing development (Ley 1980). This strategy was replicated on a much larger scale, and included a potent globalization inflection, in the sale of the former Expo '86 lands on the north shore of False Creek to Li Ka-Shing and Cheung Kong Holdings in 1988, with an intent to develop a new high-rise residential community (Olds 2001). This residential tendency was reaffirmed in city council's approval of the Central Area Plan in the fall of 1991, which in essence consolidated the commercial office complex within a much smaller CBD, privileging new housing in the downtown outside this zone.

While at one level this experience can be viewed as a normal (albeit strategic-scale) change in land use and zoning to respond to evolving social demand and market factors, there is a larger developmental motif that justifies its inclusion in this chapter. Important city actors and officials, including influential planners such as Larry Beasley as well as elected officials, proposed that the implications and attendant conditions of the land-use changes amounted to a new *development program,* rather than simply a straightforward rezoning. This new program, Living First, was mooted as an instrument of development for the twenty-first-century city, in accord with Vancouver's post-industrial trajectory. Essential features of the program were as follows. First, the combination of landownership, and the projected interest of buyers for the new residential units, which included a significant representation from Hong Kong and from elsewhere in Asia, were seen as accelerating Vancouver's inclusion within *Asia-Pacific circuits* of trade and capital. These inflows would be part of a new capital relayering in Vancouver, with Asian investors taking the place of domestic resource sectors' interests then experiencing a secular decline, and augmenting Vancouver's emergent "Asia-Pacific gateway" vocation described above.

Second, the new residential projects in Vancouver's central area would stimulate important innovation and creativity in the realm of *contemporary planning and urbanism.* Here we can cite the influence of "creative innovation" in governance and planning in the form of a complex system of discretionary planning as a departure from the usual practice of codified regulation and development control. Planning for the new developments included a heightened emphasis on innovation in urban design. This underscored the aesthetics of place-remaking in the city and collectively shaped by prominent local architects, design professionals, city staff and urban design review panels, and public consultation, with no fewer than 300 public meetings and consultations conducted during the planning for the Concord Pacific project on the former Expo '86 lands (Beazley 1993). The point tower with podium design model is widely acknowledged as an exemplary (and widely emulated) urban development feature for progressive cities. It is now actively marketed around the world, contributing to Vancouver's consistently enviable showing in annual rankings of liveable cities globally.

Third, the Living First program for Vancouver included not just innovative design features for the housing projects, but also a rich enhancement of the *public realm* in the central area. These included public space and pathways, environmental features, and community centres, together with an extravagant array of consumption amenities such as restaurants and cafés, coffee houses, fitness centres, and Internet and other social media outlets. These all combined with the new residential projects described above form what John Punter describes as the "Vancouver Achievement" (2004) in urban design, planning, and urbanism. Certainly these amenities are seen by some as inducements to the members of the "creative class," and there is evidence that these are valued by cultural economy workers in Vancouver's central area.

Fourth, the extraordinary new housing program realized in Vancouver's central area over the past twenty years prima facie provides both greater "*social density*" in the core as well as housing opportunities for skilled workers, including those in the cultural and innovation economy sectors. To the approximately 37,000 residents of the West End, developed in the 1970s primarily as an apartment rental community proximate to Stanley Park and English Bay, the Living First program has added capacity to bring the total to about 100,000 (distributed among the Concord Pacific mega-project, the Downtown South, Coal Harbour, and more recently Southeast False Creek and Victory Square, and the western margins of the Downtown Eastside), contributing notionally to the relational aspects (Yeung 2005) and social dynamics (Wolfe and Bramwell 2008) underpinning contact-intensive economic systems.

Finally, the processes of innovation and creativity associated with the city's Living First program include important initiatives in the sphere of *sustainable development*. The comprehensive development planning for Southeast False Creek, including the athletes' village for the 2010 Winter Olympic Games, was designed from the first to present an exemplar of a sustainable urban community. Here a critical process innovation took the form of leading roles for sustainability specialists at the front end of project planning over a decade ago. Consultation occurred with external experts such as William Rees, Mark Holland, and Mark Roseland; sustainability professionals, notably Sheltair; and local leaders drawn from the academy and public realm. Rather than offering a tokenistic gesture to selected elements of the sustainability agenda, the planning included local response to global climate change as a goal-setting marker. There was also a constructive policy dialectic with city staff in areas such as sustainable energy systems, green buildings technologies and systems, industrial ecology, transit and bicycle pathways, and around the principle of "compact and complete" community formation (Sussmann 2012).[6]

Living First as Urban Development Program: Toward an Assessment

While the developmental features of the city's Living First program have to be acknowledged, the overall balance of consequences suggest a mixed set of impacts for Vancouver's economy of culture and innovation. At one level the central area conforms in large measure to Florida's idealized vision of the creative city, replete with high-density housing, a rich amenity package, and high-integrity heritage landscapes on the CBD fringe and inner city. These have all added to what some observers maintain is a "sticky" labour market in the city and region, which sustains the presence of a skilled creative workforce in good times and bad (Murray and Hutton 2012). Vancouver certainly boasts a significant cultural economy ensconced in the heritage districts of Yaletown, Victory Square, and Gastown especially (Hutton 2008; Barnes and Hutton 2009). Some, like the film-production industry, have operated within the core (notably in Gastown) for several decades, suggesting a robustness of this sector "in place" (Coe 2001).

Set against this, though, we acknowledge that other outcomes of the Living First program may be prejudicial to the fortunes of Vancouver's

Table 4.2. Experienced labour force by occupations and gender: Vancouver CMA

Occupation (%)	Female	Male	All
Senior managers	0.7	2.2	1.5
Middle and other managers	8.0	12.7	10.4
Professionals	18.0	16.7	17.3
Semi-professionals and technicians	8.8	8.4	8.6
Supervisors	1.2	0.9	1.0
Supervisors: crafts and trades	0.5	2.1	1.3
Administrative and senior clerical personnel	10.1	2.1	6.0
Skilled sales and service personnel	3.8	5.2	4.5
Skilled crafts and trades workers	0.9	11.1	6.2
Clerical personnel	15.5	5.6	10.3
Intermediate sales and service personnel	17.3	8.8	12.9
Semi-skilled manual workers	3.3	12.0	7.8
Other sales and service personnel	10.4	8.2	9.2
Other manual workers	1.5	4.2	2.9
n cases	14,876	16,199	31,075

Notes: Includes employed labour force fifteen years of age and older. Differences statistically different from zero at $p < 0.001$.

Source: Authors' calculations using Statistics Canada, Census of Canada, 2001 (table by Markus Moos in Bourne et al. 2011)

economy of culture and innovation. While there is insufficient space here to provide a detailed accounting, several issues can be briefly mentioned. First, most of the new housing built in the core over the past twenty years is at price points unaffordable to many creative workers. Further, house-price inflation has spilled over from the new condo districts to the heritage districts of the CBD fringe and inner city, effectively dislocating creative workers from traditional communities of working life and residency. The price points characteristic of the new residential communities are geared to the social cohorts of the affluent "new middle class" of professionals and managers (see table 4.2) dominant in Vancouver and more specially a wealthy transnational élite. While this tendency is observed principally in global cities like London and New York, this is also an issue in Vancouver.

Second, Vancouver's central area residential market as a whole is essentially "internationalized." This mean it is marketed as a global commodity in Asia, Europe, the United States, and elsewhere, with property prices calibrated accordingly, rather than ensconced more firmly within the local housing market (and shaped by local demand and incomes).[7]

Third, a significant portion of the condominium capacity is always vacant, held as a speculative investment, thus taking away from the vibrancy that comes from fully inhabited urban neighbourhoods.[8]

Fourth, while there are vestiges of the neo-bohemian city popularized in the work of Richard Lloyd (2006) on the fringes of the central area, the general tendency is toward upscale consumption amenities (restaurants, bars, cafés), which cater mostly for the professional and managerial classes that dominate the new housing projects in the core.

Finally, all these factors combine to shape an increasingly residentialized vision for Vancouver's metropolitan core, placing increasing pressure both on creative industries and marginal communities, as exemplified by the continuing attrition of inexpensive practice and performance space for young creatives in the revalorized inner city.

VANCOUVER'S EMERGENT ECONOMY: INTERSECTIONS OF CREATIVITY, TECHNOLOGY, GOVERNANCE, AND PLACE

Innovation and creativity are critical determinants of urban and regional development among advanced societies, defining the trajectories of the "knowledge-based economy," the "learning region," or the "new cultural economy of the city." In particular, the metropolitan region has become the critical geospatial unit of the globalizing economy of the early twenty-first century, the centre of territorial innovation systems for national economies like Canada's.

The basic elements propelling creativity and innovation – production factors, critical independencies, processes, and practices – are found throughout the developed world, although they tend to be spatially "spiky," coalescing around particular places. Those elements include talent and human capital; propulsive industrial clusters and agglomerations of firms and labour; close-knit, embedded social networks; dynamic advanced production systems; and associative institutions of governance (Cooke and Morgan 1998). How such elements coalesce around a given site – indeed, whether they coalesce at all – as well as their precise combination and effects, depend often in large part on a set of historical and geographical local contingencies. The quality of creativity and innovation in metro Vancouver, whether viewed at the national urban system level, or within international/global settings, is powerfully bound up in a matrix of local-regional attributes, experiences, and interdependencies. This doesn't deny the force of larger, non-local, global factors. But the effects of such factors in shaping the particular systems and behaviours of innovation and creativity in Vancouver and region emerge only through their interaction with a set of contingent local circumstances.

Each of these conditions – marginality, eco-regional setting, and accelerated restructuring – is complicit in the particular forms of creativity and innovation the Vancouver ISRN team has studied over four years with respect to innovative firms, labour, and governance structure. The Vancouver region has engendered the development of an "alternative" innovation culture, comprising start-ups and SME firms, in contrast to the multinational corporations of Toronto, Montreal, or Ottawa (or, 200 km to the south on the I-5, Seattle). Moreover, the type of innovation sectors in which Vancouver has specialized were themselves initially marginal, like bio-pharmaceuticals, video games, the wi-fi sectors, and fuel cell research. But because there was no history of sustained manufacturing in Vancouver, they were able to fit quickly within the city culturally, institutionally, and physically. Especially, physically.

The new innovation-based economy of Vancouver expresses its "localism/regionalism" in the distinctive architectural idioms that now define "Vancouverism," and in the clothes of those who work in such spaces such as the eco-fashion of MEC and (at the higher end) Lululemon. Taken together, the region's ecological assets and recreational lifestyles, when combined with a metropolitan housing market that exhibits a long-run appreciation, tend to attract (and help retain) individuals, entrepreneurs, and creatives. Vancouver is a twenty-first-century manifestation of the "sticky place" enunciated by Ann Markusen (1996) that particularly fixes the city's labour market of talent.

Finally, there is Vancouver's distinctive governance structure, which, like its firms and labour, is diverse, creative, and experimental. It has not always been successful, with failures and sometimes rancorous discord among institutions, particularly around the city's endemic and growing homelessness. While in the city of Vancouver one can locate instances of clientelism in the politics of cultural administration, the city's Office of Cultural Affairs "controls a quantum of direct municipal funding for culture that is unparalleled in Canada on a per capita basis, been sustained over the years, and deploys a granting infrastructure with more staff than even the provincial bureaucracy" (Hutton and Murray 2013).

The ISRN research on the extent of collaborative governance institutions in providing innovative and essential services for the immigrant communities in Vancouver found scant evidence of strong, integrated networks among the range of organizations providing these services. Instead, there is a lack of formal linkages among the relevant organizations or institutionalized collaboration among various sectors. The collaborative governance structure in Vancouver thus remains nascent (Hutton 2012).

In many ways the critical activities that animate creativity and innovation in Metro Vancouver, and that supply vital rhythms of growth and change in the economy, society, and built environment, take the form of much smaller, almost micro-scale industries and boutique firms and enterprises and derive from the distinctive contingencies of development described above. As our field research and survey exercises have disclosed, these include a diverse array of industries shaped by synergies of technology and culture, mediated by place and by agency, and realized by talent and leadership. Further, in many cases they represent not stand-alone activities but highly interactive enterprises whose impacts are potentiated by both formal (traditional) and casual spillovers and crossovers of knowledge, conducted within the networked spaces of the metropolis. A representative sample of these key sectors comprises new media, applied design, and advanced-technology research, development, and production, intermediary finance and consultancies, and other specialized services. Within these sectors, specific industries studied in this project by members of the Vancouver team include film and video production and post-production, computer graphics and imaging, architecture, fuel-cell technologies, and bio-pharma industries. These sectors rely primarily on the generation of new ideas and the creation of intellectual property and are grounded in Vancouver by the presence of relatively dense concentrations of expertise in their respective labour markets (Wixted and Holbrook 2014).

To be sure, there are long-established firms and labour cohorts to be found within these emergent sectors and industries of the Vancouver economy especially in film production, within which we identified through interviews high levels of trust and collaboration among management, professionals, and unionized workers. But in many other cases we observed very high rates of turnover or "churn" at the level of the firm, and extraordinary fluidity of employment within specific industries. This is in contrast to the more durable ensembles of specialized production that characterized the classic industrial city (until the collapse of Fordism in the 1970s and 1980s), and that also defined the segmented labour of the office economy.

A second and related feature of the Vancouver economy lies in the *scalar characteristics* of key institutions and enterprises. The region generally lacks propulsive corporations, major private sector head offices, or "top thirty" global universities. Instead, it exhibits a dynamic profile of small business start-ups, entrepreneurship, and multiple agencies, which foster innovation and creativity. The limitations of the local market and lack of regional "champions" are no doubt problematic features, certainly in constraining the global power projection of the Vancouver economy, relative to Toronto (home to Canada's five largest banks, and many other industrial head offices), Calgary (Encana, Syncrude), and "nearest neighbour" Seattle (which boasts Amazon, Weyerhaeuser, Boeing, Microsoft, and Starbucks, among other multinationals). But in its stead we observe the formation of a distinctive SME economy, which has exhibited a high degree of dynamism and resiliency over the past quarter century. Many of the most innovative enterprises in Vancouver's economy have been typified by a "build to sell" business mentality (Richard Smith et al. 2009), for example in biotech, fuel cells, electronics, aerospace, and higher-value-added forest products), imparting a near-constant "churn" at the level of the firm. The innovation behaviours of these SMEs in Vancouver therefore assume the prospective sale of proprietary technology or designs to larger corporations. There is also a branch-plant syndrome characteristic of many Vancouver firms, notably in the production units of runaway film companies, a well-established strength of Vancouver's cultural economy. The dynamism of these small industries and firms in Vancouver tends to force a higher premium on experimentation, creativity, and innovation than for the rent-seeking resource industries of the city's staples developmental era.

Third, *intersections of process and place* have shaped local practices of creativity and innovation. More specifically, the transformations and restructuring of the Vancouver region have bestowed conditions (both directly and indirectly) that are propitious to the formation of a substantial "new cultural economy" within the city and in certain suburban districts. The precipitous contraction of the resource economy has created space conducive to the construction of a new economy of creativity and innovation, notably within the former wholesaling areas of the CBD fringe, within the resource-processing, warehouse, and distribution zones of the inner city, and within the obsolescent industrial zones of certain inner suburbs, observed notably in the major film-production facilities within Burnaby and North Vancouver. Indeed the erosion of head offices in the CBD proper has enabled the re-colonization of these office premises for creative industries such as computer graphics and imaging and video games. If there is a counterpart to Vancouver in Canada, we might acknowledge Montreal as sharing some of these features of transition and succession in a metropolitan core stripped of much of its former corporate power (Leslie and Rantisi 2006).

We can illustrate the saliency of space to creativity and innovation specialization of sites within Vancouver's emergent space-economy by reference to well-known examples in the urban core and certain inner suburban locations. Within the inner city, we can identify not so much a generic distribution of firms following a pure model of urban land economics and rents, or a stringently preference-based location model, but rather a diverse palette of specialized creative industries and firms filtered by choice, rents, building types, amenities, and policy factors. Thus, for many creative firms, Yaletown occupies the most prestigious of sites in the new cultural economy, with its stratospheric rents reflecting the intense competition for space among high-value creative industries as well as upscale housing and consumption; Victory Square and Gastown, with a mélange of film companies, media firms, and smaller creative start-ups; and False Creek Flats, a "failed" fin-de-siècle New Economy site in the wake of the collapse of the dot.coms, but now recast as a larger terrain of innovative firms in video games (Radical), and biotech (QLT).

Fourth, the education and training of talent is internal, organic, and cumulative. There is much learning on the job, and learning from others in the know. The fission that dominates new firm formation in creative industries contributes to transferring skills from one firm to another. Also contributing is the rapid inter-firm movement of labour, which is promoted in part by a project work system, but also by the larger cultural restlessness of the sector where the only constant is change. Consequently, while talent is brought into the city, sometimes from distant places in general, it is outside firms that move into Vancouver to tap into its established rich and deep talent pool.

Contributing to the growth of that talent pool have been educational institutions operating in the city, both public and private. The public side includes the two universities, UBC (the Film and Theatre

Department and Computer Science) and Simon Fraser University (the Centre for Contemporary Arts), as well as the community college, BC Institute of Technology, and Emily Carr University of Art and Design, as well as key federal government research laboratories, such as the National Research Council's Institute for Fuel Cell Innovation. The private side is represented by the Vancouver Film School. Opened in 1987, it now offers thirteen different programs, including acting, video-game design, animation, writing, and now spread over six buildings in downtown Vancouver. The latest addition to the educational pantheon is the Great Northern Way Campus, a unique collaboration among four quite different long-standing educational institutions in the city: UBC, Simon Fraser University, Emily Carr University of Art and Design, and BC Institute of Technology. The four have combined to create a "digital village" to change the way people think about art, science, learning, and commerce. It might not do quite that, but it does offer a curriculum where studies of the visual arts, industrial arts, writing and literature, technical expertise in computer hardware and software, and business studies are blended together, preparing the next generation of workers for Vancouver's Brave New World of creative industries. In addition, to the deep pool of talented labour that anchors many of these sectors in the Vancouver economy, these research and education institutions are also an important source of the intellectual property that is the key output of some of Vancouver's more innovative sectors (Wixted and Holbrook 2014).

Finally, there is distinctive *quality of life* associated with these systems of creativity and innovation in metropolitan Vancouver. While not accepting the more ebullient variant of the Floridian concept of "amenity as destiny," Vancouver's environmental package of ecological assets, amenities, and the built environment, along with an open and diverse culture and politics, consistently place Vancouver among global leaders in the urban liveability tables and are of value in the attraction and retention of creative talent. Those qualities are certainly advertised by firms in the creative industries to lure talent to Vancouver from elsewhere. Our panels of interviews across a spectrum of industries disclosed that for many in the creative industries, these (broadly defined) environmental assets can be drawn upon for stimulus to innovation in design, with notable examples in architecture, fashions and garment design, and graphic arts and design.

As a first principle, in Vancouver, as elsewhere, institutions play key roles in shaping innovation in the knowledge economy, including universities, colleges, and specialist agencies (such as film schools, digital training, and the like). This is consistent with Daniel Bell's (1973) forecast of a post-industrial society within which scientific knowledge is a marker of both economic transformation and the formation of a dominant social class. Second, innovation within advanced production systems is generated, transmitted, and absorbed within clusters, including, in the Vancouver case, biomedical, alternative energy, film, and new media, as well as more or less generic service industries such as intermediary finance and business services. In many instances, these clusters comprise highly localized sites or precincts of intense, proximate knowledge exchange, as well as taking the form of more extended production networks that range across regional space. Third, the waves of innovation and restructuring experienced since the 1990s have left their imprint on the patterns of innovation in the Vancouver region, including, notably, the digital revolution, which has created new industries (video games, software development) while retooling others (architecture, graphic design). And there is also the deep cultural inflection of production experienced across a range of sectors, including architecture, industrial design, and fashion design. Finally, the exigencies of globalization have shaped innovation in Vancouver as elsewhere, not least in exacerbating pressures of competition (and thus the search for competitive advantage through constant experimentation and innovation), and evidenced by the deployment of digital communications for the recruitment of talent, for sourcing inputs, and for marketing.

The broad contours of these innovation systems can be discerned in most city-regions, but our research conducted within the rubrics of the national ISRN project disclosed important signifiers of difference in Vancouver. These speak to the continuing saliency of contingency in advanced industrial development.

Conclusion: Reflections on Innovation and Creativity in Vancouver's Development

In this chapter we have attempted to explicate some key features associated with Vancouver's contemporary development, informed by our work on the Innovation Systems Research Network (ISRN) project, as well as ancillary research in the field. Rather than using a traditional sector- or industry-based model of analysis, we elected instead to deploy a framework we think works better for the Vancouver case study and accords with the region's overall trajectory and urban identity: first, the gateway vision – as some would see it, the "master narrative" of the metropolitan region; second, the Living First development program, which runs consistently through policy values and planning practices, and which many external observers see as the most innovative and influential feature of Vancouver's development experience; and, finally, a profile of the cultural economy, which constitutes a lead element of the urban and regional economy in Vancouver and other cities.

These visions of the Vancouver economy operate autonomously at some level, inasmuch as senior levels of government and Translink capitalize upon and manage the infrastructural elements of the Vancouver gateway, while, for the most part, the municipalities administer the regulatory and developmental aspects of the residential and culture-led development programs. Here the City of Vancouver is clearly the lead government in the region, endowed with a highly professional planning staff and enjoying the benefits of the "reputational capital" generated from four decades of generally successful redevelopment programming. But there are also serious conflicts and tensions among the three portfolios described above, seen most obviously perhaps in the displacement caused by the allocation of capital to gateway infrastructure. That allocation tends to reduce public resources available for other program areas, but increasingly it is also creating competition between housing and cultural economy enterprises for land resources in an increasingly revalorized inner city.

There is evidence of effective collaboration in multilevel governance in Vancouver, as in other major Canadian cities, in areas such as immigrant settlement, infrastructure, and image-building (see Horak and Young 2012). But within Metro Vancouver we noted a lack of regional awareness, despite the long-standing existence of a high-profile regional government (former GVRD, now known as Metro Vancouver). Effective strategic management of overarching views requires better coordination and/or alignment across the cities in the region. In particular, Vancouver and surrounding municipalities need to think of themselves as a metro region and share resources, initiatives, and amenities (Janssen-Jansen and Hutton 2011). A number of attempts to forge a regional economic strategy over the past two decades have each foundered on the shoals of parochialism and complacency. The power of Metro Vancouver to undertake strategic economic development in the region is severely constrained (or overridden) by sovereign provincial ministries, is marginalized by Translink's much larger capital budget capacity, and is further constrained and occasionally subverted by the stronger legal planning powers of the municipalities. That said, there is a rough congruence between the fragmented structure of governance in the Vancouver region and the metropolitan space-economy, managed principally at the municipal level by OCPs and land-use/zoning policies, but also involving special-purpose agencies, non-governmental organizations, and community-based organizations.

Despite this fragmentation in regional government and the longstanding lack of an economic policy vision for the region, there are aspects of governance that work well and support Vancouver's development as a site of cultural production and innovation. This is evidenced in the City of Vancouver's programming of a vernacular model of urban design and land use that is highly regarded and widely emulated, and in the cultural sector where informal alliances and collaborative networks underpin a vibrant economy of production and consumption.

Vancouver's lineage as a site of liveability has a provenance that goes back to the redevelopment and reimaging of False Creek South, explicated in David Ley's (1980) influential article in which consumption preferences are class markers and an expression of urbanism, and extending forward four decades to the redevelopment of the Olympic Village in Southeast False Creek. Throughout this extended narrative of planning in the service of innovative and progressive urbanism, a residential-consumption bias is evident in the construction of policy values and choices.

But we are resistant to the idea that consumption has supplanted production as a platform for Vancouver's development. After all, production is manifestly central to the contemporary economy of Vancouver, seen, for example, in the concentrations of *producer services* clustered in the CBD; in the importance of *cultural production* to the economy of innovation and creativity; in the *knowledge production* (fundamental and applied) associated with Vancouver's universities, colleges, and other institutions; and in the *(re)production* of landscapes and built form, which define in large part the city's planning values and policy successes, as recognized by scholars and other urbanists.

Further, Vancouver also continues to specialize in trade and exchange, which include not only the very large commodity export functions but also, increasingly, the ongoing exchange, diffusion (and fusion) of cultural values and practices, consistent with the city's transnational identity and particular form of multiculturalism. The "source materials" of creativity in Vancouver now include First Nations' traditions and symbols, elements of Vancouver's colonial and post-colonial past, and, increasingly, the cultural expressions of recent immigrant groups, notably but not exclusively from the Asia Pacific region. These hybridized cultural values and semiotic content feed into certain production processes, notably in garment and food products, architecture and the built environment, and new media industries, constituting another distinctive feature of creativity and innovation in Vancouver's economy. Thus production, trade, and exchange persist as central features of Vancouver's development, assuredly imbued with important aspects of innovation, and facilitated in some important respects by consumption and other amenity features, but constructed on a platform of capital, agglomeration, and labour markets – enduring features of both advanced and transitional economies across periods of insistent innovation and restructuring.

Notes

1 For a descriptions of the ISRN project and its approach to collaborative research on innovation and creativity, see Holbrook and Wolfe (2005).

2 The strength of the bond between Vancouver and the provincial resource economy presents an expression of the core-periphery structure of the Canadian staples economy explicated in the classic work of Harold Innis (Hutton 1997), which can be demonstrated empirically. To illustrate, until the early 1980s the City of Vancouver Planning Department employed a model that projected growth in housing demand as a lagged function of growth and change in the BC resource economy GDP. Similarly, empirical research demonstrated the interdependency between the expansion of the provincial resource sector and the growth of the city's central business district (Hutton and Ley 1987). As a trenchant demonstration of this interdependency, a severe global commodity price shock experienced in the early 1980s was transmitted from the resource-extraction regions in the provincial staples periphery to Vancouver, producing the deepest recession since the 1930s, with unemployment reaching 14 per cent in the 1982–4 period.

3 For an examination of advanced producer services (APS) in the development of Vancouver's gateway role, see Asia-Pacific Foundation of Canada (Vancouver) (2007).

4 Local organizations opposed to the Gateway Program include the Western Wilderness Committee, Against Port Expansion (http://againstportexpansion.org), and Gateway Sucks (http://gatewaysucks.org).

5 Karen Graham (2005) has documented four separate efforts to develop and implement a regional economic development strategy for Greater Vancouver over a ten-year period, none of which came to fruition, which she attributes in part to the lack of an effective policy network structure at the regional level. To this lacuna we might add a sense of complacency (or lack of urgency) associated with the region's record: while there are deep socio-economic problems experienced within the labour market in the Vancouver region, there hasn't been a major economic downturn since the deep recession of 1982–4.

6 In her doctoral thesis Cornelia Sussmann (2012) carefully documents the formation and operation of a "deep sustainability" advocacy and technical process associated with the city's plans for redeveloping South East False Creek. But she concludes that in the end only limited sustainability gains were achieved (relative to what the market would likely have achieved with the "standard" regulatory oversight of the City of Vancouver), as the result of institutional factors (notably in the form of resistance to deep subsidies by certain influential city actors and agencies, and also to an imperfect understanding of the imperatives of sustainability as reported by key informants), as well as the economic stress generated by the fallout of the 2008 financial crisis.

7 In support of this contention, Vancouver exhibits the highest housing prices among Canadian cities, while incomes are only a little higher than the national average (Bourne et al. 2011).

8 As Andy Yan observes, although the proportion of vacant condos is sometimes exaggerated, the 2006 census of Canada reported vacancy rates of about 14 per cent for Vancouver's downtown, to about 7 per cent for the city as a whole. See Yan (2009) for a more detailed elaboration of this phenomenon and its implications.

References

Asia-Pacific Foundation of Canada (Vancouver). 2007. "Building the Asia-Pacific gateway economy: The role of Vancouver-based professional services firms," 9 May. http://www.asiapacific.ca.

Barman, J. 1991. *The west beyond the west: A history of British Columbia*. Toronto: University of Toronto Press.

Barnes, T.J., D.W. Edgington, K. Denike, and T.G. McGee. 1992. "Vancouver, the province and the Pacific Rim." In *Vancouver and its region*, ed. G. Wynn and T. Oke, 181–200. Vancouver: UBC Press.

Barnes, T.J., and T.A. Hutton. 2009. "Situating the new economy: Contingencies of regeneration and dislocation in Vancouver's inner city." *Urban Studies* 46 (5–6): 1247–69. http://dx.doi.org/10.1177/0042098009103863.

Barnes, T.J., T.A. Hutton, D.F. Ley, and M. Moos. 2011. "Vancouver: Restructuring narratives in the transnational metropolis." In *Canadian urban regions: Trajectories of growth and change*, ed. L.S. Bourne, T.A. Hutton, R.G. Shearmur, and J. Simmons, 291–327. Toronto: Oxford University Press.

Beazley, M. 1993. "Public participation in urban mega-project planning: A case study of Pacific Place, Vancouver, BC." PhD diss., University of British Columbia.

Bell, D. 1973. *The coming of post-industrial society: A venture in social forecasting*. New York: Basic Books.

Blomley, N. 2004. *Unsettling the city: Urban land and the politics of property*. New York: Routledge.

Bourne, L.S., T.A. Hutton, R. Shearmur, and J. Simmons, eds. 2011. *Canadian urban regions: Trajectories of growth and change*. Toronto: Oxford University Press.

Bula, F. 2011. "The future of Vancouver's economy." *Vancouver Magazine*, 1 October

Clark, T.N. 2004. *The city as entertainment machine*. Amsterdam: JAI/Elsevier.

Coe, N. 2001. "A 'hybrid' agglomeration? The development of a satellite-Marshallian industrial district in Vancouver." *Urban Studies* 38 (10): 1753–75. http://dx.doi.org/10.1080/00420980120084840.

Cooke, P., and Morgan, K. 1998. *The associational economy: Firms, regions and innovation*. Oxford: Oxford University Press. http://dx.doi.org/10.1093/acprof:oso/9780198290186.001.0001.

Davis, H.C., and T.A. Hutton. 1989. "The two economies of British Columbia." *BC Studies* 82: 3–15.

–. 1991. "An empirical analysis of producer service exports from the Vancouver Metropolitan Region." *Canadian Journal of Regional Science* 14: 375–94.

Florida, R.L. 2002. *The rise of the creative class*. New York: Basic Books.

Glaeser, E., J. Kolko, and A. Saiz. 2001. "Consumer city." *Journal of Economic Geography* 1 (1): 27–50. http://dx.doi.org/10.1093/jeg/1.1.27.

Graham, K. 2005. "Establishing a regional economic development strategy in Greater Vancouver: The effective policy network." MA thesis, Simon Fraser University.

Holbrook, J.A.D., and D.A. Wolfe. 2005. "The innovation systems research network (ISRN): A Canadian experiment in knowledge management." *Science & Public Policy* 32 (2): 109–18. http://dx.doi.org/10.3152/147154305781779623.

Horak, M., and R. Young. 2012. *Sites of governance: Multilevel governance and policy making in Canada's big cities.* Montreal and Kingston: McGill-Queen's University Press.

Hutton, T.A. 1997. "The Innisian core-periphery revisited: Vancouver's changing relationships with British Columbia's staples economy." *BC Studies* 113: 69–100.

–. 2004. "Post-industrialism, post-modernism and the reproduction of Vancouver's central area: Retheorising the 21st-century city." *Urban Studies* 41 (10): 1953–82. http://dx.doi.org/10.1080/0042098042000256332.

–. 2008. *The new economy of the inner city: Restructuring, regeneration and dislocation in the twenty-first-century metropolis.* London: Routledge.

–. 2012. "Multilevel governance and urban development: A Vancouver case study." In *Sites of governance: Multilevel governance and policy-making in Canada's big cities,* ed. M. Horak and R. Young, 263–98. Montreal and Kingston: McGill-Queen's University Press.

Hutton, T.A., and D.F. Ley. 1987. "Location, linkages, and labour: The corporate office complex in a medium-size city, Vancouver." *Economic Geography* 63: 126–41.

Hutton, T.A., and C. Murray. 2013 . "The new cultural economy and its discontents: Innovation and policy disjuncture in Vancouver." In *The politics of urban cultural policy,* ed. C. Grodach and D. Silver, 141–53. New York: Routledge.

Janssen-Jansen, L.B., and T.A. Hutton. 2011. "Rethinking the metropolis: Reconfiguring the governance structures of the 21st century city-region." *International Planning Studies* 16 (3): 201–15. http://dx.doi.org/10.1080/13563475.2011.591140.

Krätke, S. 2011. *The creative capital of cities: Interactive knowledge creation and the urbanization economies of innovation.* Oxford: Blackwell-Wiley. http://dx.doi.org/10.1002/9781444342277.

Leslie, D., and N.M. Rantisi. 2006. "Governing the design sector in Montréal, Canada." *Urban Affairs Review* 41 (3): 309–37. http://dx.doi.org/10.1177/1078087405281107.

Ley, D.F. 1980. "Liberal ideology and the postindustrial city." *Annals of the Association of American Geographers* 70 (2): 238–58. http://dx.doi.org/10.1111/j.1467-8306.1980.tb01310.x.

–. 1996. *The new middle class and the remaking of the central city.* Oxford: Oxford University Press.

–. 2010. *Millionaire migrants: Trans-Pacific life lines.* Oxford: Blackwell-Wiley. http://dx.doi.org/10.1002/9781444319262.

Lloyd, R. 2006. *Neo-bohemia: Art and commerce in the post-industrial city*. New York: Routledge.

Markusen, A. 1996. "Sticky places in slippery space: A typology of industrial districts." *Economic Geography* 72 (3): 293–313. http://dx.doi.org/10.2307/144402.

Morley, A. 1969. *Vancouver: From milltown to metropolis*. Vancouver: Mitchell.

Moulaert, F. 2000. *Globalization and integrated area development in European cities*. Oxford: Oxford University Press.

Murray, C., and T.A. Hutton. 2012. "Vancouver: The enigmatic emerging cultural metropolis." In *Cities, cultural policy and governance*, ed. H. Anheier and Y.R. Isar, 310–21. London: Sage.

Olds, K. 2001. *Globalization and urban change: Capital, culture and Pacific Rim mega-projects*. Oxford: Oxford University Press.

Perl, A., and R. Gilbert. 2010. *Transport revolutions: Moving people and freight without oil*. Gabriola Island, BC: New Society Publishers.

Punter, J. 2004. *The Vancouver achievement: Urban planning and design*. Vancouver: UBC Press.

Sassen, S. 2006. "Chicago's deep economic history: Its specialized advantage in the global network." In *Chicago's geographies: Metropolis for the 21st Century*, ed. R.P. Greene, M.J. Bouman, and G. Grammenos, 75–86. Chicago: Association of American Geographers.

Scott, A.J. 1988. *Metropolis: From division of labor to urban form*. Berkeley: University of California Press.

Smith, R., A. Holbrook, T.J. Barnes, and T.A. Hutton. 2009. "Creativity and innovation in the Vancouver city-region." Paper prepared for a meeting of the ISRN, Toronto, ON, 5–6 November.

Sussmann, C. 2012. "Toward the sustainable city: Vancouver's southeast False Creek." PhD thesis, University of British Columbia.

Vancouver Airport Authority. 2009. "YVR passengers (enplaned + Ddeplaned) 1992–2009," accessed 12 August 2009, http://www.yvr.ca/authority/facts/index.asp

Wixted, B., and J.A.D. Holbrook. 2014. "Living on the edge: Knowledge interdependence of human capital intensive clusters in Vancouver." In *Innovation and knowledge flows in Canadian city-regions*, ed. D.A. Wolfe, 92–122. Toronto: University of Toronto Press.

Wolfe, D.A., and A. Bramwell. 2008. "Innovation, creativity and governance: Social dynamics of economic performance in city-regions." *Policy & Practice* 10 (2–3): 170–82. http://dx.doi.org/10.5172/impp.453.10.2-3.170.

Yan, A. 2009. "Downtown empty condos largely a myth." BTAworks Research Paper, May.

Yeung, H.W.-C. 2005. "Rethinking relational economic geography." *Transactions of the Institute of British Geographers* 30 (1): 37–51. http://dx.doi.org/10.1111/j.1475-5661.2005.00150.x.

5 Moving from Complaisance Revisited: Ottawa Trying Again to Define Its Regional Advantage

CAROLINE ANDREW AND DAVID DOLOREUX

Introduction

Ottawa began as a community dominated by the private sector: the forest industry and the "lumber baron" entrepreneurs. But after becoming the capital of the United Province of Canada in 1857 and, as a subsequent result, the capital of Canada, the city fell into a position of expecting that the federal public sector economy would guarantee the economic success of the community. The City of Ottawa complained about the federal government but accepted federal expenditure and expanding federal employment and adopted an essentially passive role in economic development.

This changed dramatically for a brief period, and our detailed examination of the social dynamics of the economic performance of Ottawa starts from the period of strong municipal support for the development of the high-tech sector in Ottawa with the vision of "Silicon Valley North." It was a period of strong municipal support but support in partnership with others, including the local post-secondary sector and of course the high-tech sector itself. However, this municipal activist period only lasted until 2001–2 with the collapse of the high-tech boom and the decline and disappearance of many of the giants, notably Nortel. The City of Ottawa then reverted to its more traditional dependence on the federal public sector economy and a seeming inability to set a municipal course, much less design a strategy of forward-looking development for Ottawa. However, there are recent signs, albeit tentative, of renewed interest and will on the part of the City of Ottawa to build a municipal strategy. It is a strategy of partnerships, both economic and social. The partnerships are largely between local government and civil society but they are also within the city, between economic and social sectors of the city administration. These partnerships, as all partnerships, involve both opportunities and challenges, and we will highlight both in our recounting of the recent signs of municipal Ottawa playing a more active role to counter the signs of economic stagnation in the capital.

This chapter is based on a multi-year research study that included approximately 100 interviews over the period of 2007 to 2012. The research focused on the social dynamics of economic performance, and subsequent research projects have added related interviews and participant observation, on municipal involvement in implementing the Equity and Inclusion Lens within the city administration, the municipal-community partnership in the Ottawa Local Immigration Partnership, and most recently in the municipal-community partnership in the Youth Futures program. The original research design included three related sets of interviews, with companies, engineers working in those companies, and civic leaders. The first set was carried out with 172 companies involved in the high-tech sector, focusing particularly on the knowledge-intensive business sector (KIBS), in order to better understand the links between economic performance and the local socio-political environment. This led, on the municipal side, to a focus on the important role played by OCRI (first called the Ottawa-Carleton Research Institute, then renamed the Ottawa Centre for Research and Innovation, and now recently reorganized as Invest Ottawa).

Our second set had as its objective to understand why the "talent" necessary to support the high-tech industry was attracted to Ottawa. Twenty-five interviews with engineers indicated that respondents were attracted by good jobs, a good place to raise a family and/or connect to family, and a safety cushion of federal employment if the high-tech private-sector job disappeared (Gulel 2009). These talented workers therefore exerted little or no pressure on the city to develop policies that would benefit them; Ottawa was a pleasant place to live, although "not exciting," and federal employment was an acceptable fallback position.

The third set of interviews explored the existence or absence of linkages between social and economic leaders in Ottawa. Thirty-three interviews (eight persons from the economic sector; fifteen persons from the social sector, including five immigrants; eight persons from the political/administrative sector, one provincial, two federal, five municipal;

and two persons from the education sector), conducted mostly in 2007, suggested there was an asymmetrical relationship: social leaders were aware of the economic leaders and generally suspicious of them, whereas the economic leaders were generally unaware of the social leaders. The social leaders were more aware of, and involved with, that part of the Ottawa population hidden by the overall statistics of a wealthy community and felt that the economic leaders were uninterested in those left out of Ottawa's prosperity. These three sets of interviews thus set the framework for understanding the social dynamics of the high-tech economic development. The support given by OCRI to the KIBS sector certainly contributed to a positive partnership, and the visible social dynamics of OCRI did much to link the post-secondary sector and locally focused high-tech activity. It harnessed strong support for activity from the city. This was much less true from the talented workers, who were, for the most part, content with their lives and careers in Ottawa and much less likely to exert pressure for municipal activity. And although economic and social actors appeared to be in separate silos with little partnering, both did feel that the City of Ottawa's overall leadership was disappointing. There was therefore pressure for a stronger municipal role coming from a relatively broad set of social and economic groups.

The Economic Profile of Ottawa

Ottawa is a relatively affluent community. According to family income data derived from 2009 personal income tax returns, Ottawa-Gatineau was the census metropolitan area (CMA) with the highest median total family income ($89,410), followed by Calgary ($88,410), Edmonton ($86,250) and Regina ($83,550) (Statistics Canada 2011). The 2011 population of the Ottawa-Gatineau city-region was 883,391, an increase of 8.8 per cent over the 2006 figure (Statistics Canada 2012).

Ottawa's industrial base is dominated by the services-producing sector: public administration, business services, and retail and wholesale trades.

> Employment in Ottawa-Gatineau has changed in recent decades, with a greater share of individuals finding employment in services-producing industries. In particular, employment in professional and specialist occupations has grown proportionally and numerically, particularly among women. The goods-producing sector, which has

> not constituted a large part of Ottawa-Gatineau's economy of most of the twentieth century, declined both in terms of the number of people directly producing goods or working as low-skill labourers and helpers in the trades, transportation, and equipment sector. To a considerable degree, Ottawa-Gatineau exemplifies an economy in which services (both high-and low-skill) play an extraordinarily important role, and in this sense the city exemplifies the qualities of a post-industrial economy. (Andrew, Ray, Chiasson 2011, 209)

There are interesting particularities in the industrial base of Ottawa that affect the localization of employment and on the gender and linguistic employment possibilities.

> We have portrayed Ottawa-Gatineau as a city that has been dominated by employment based on the production of services rather than goods for many decades. Yet as a post-industrial city, it is an unusual hybrid because investments by private corporations and the federal government have played an influential role in shaping the type of work performed and where people work in the region ... Because the federal government is a major employer, its gender equity and bilingualism policies have influenced both the number of women working in various employment nodes and the number of Francophones and Anglophones working on the opposite side of the Ottawa River from where they live ... [T]he federal government's planning initiatives have at times favoured the suburbanization of jobs, but for functional, symbolic and political reasons, the federal government has continued to invest in office space in the downtown core. (Andrew, Ray, Chiasson 2011, 232–3)

In 2013 Ottawa counted over 1,900 technology companies. The largest number is in the knowledge-based support-services sector, with 570 companies, followed by the software sector with 362 companies (Invest Ottawa 2013). Employment figures for the high-tech sector have varied greatly since the all-time peak in May 2000 with 72,700 employees, which dropped to 40,700 in December 2004, rose to 70,400 in October 2007, fell to 40,200 in December 2012, and climbed back to 50,400 in June 2013 (Bagnall 2013).

The early high-tech industry was situated in the western suburban edge of the metropolitan area, in Kanata. The employment profile was very different from that of federal employment, with men comprising the vast majority of employees and a far higher proportion of employees who were foreign born. As we will see later on, the more recent high-tech development is much more concentrated in the downtown area, and the federal government has been talking about moving some federal employment to Kanata.

The High-Tech Boom and Municipal Activism

When the high-tech boom began, it was very much as a result of federal decisions to carve off parts of the federal government technology sectors (Shavinina 2004). The rise of Ottawa's knowledge-intensive sector in the 1960s and 1970s is especially interesting, given that, prior to this time, the region did not have the reputation for being an established industrial centre (Steed and DeGenova 1983). In response to the federal demand for goods and services, the local economy developed a large employment base in business services. Moreover, the knowledge-intensive sector has grown significantly in recent years and has become an important player in the export industry. Since the 1990s, Ottawa has experienced a rapid and significant increase in industrial activity, and new islands of economic growth have developed, particularly in so-called knowledge-intensive and innovation-driven activities. Indeed, the principal sources of innovation in the high-tech sector came from the KIBS and from the high-tech manufacturing sector. The figures presented in table 5.1 are from the period of our first set of interviews, focusing on the KIBS sector.

As table 5.1 depicts, KIBS firms are strongly represented in Ottawa and accounted for 11.3 per cent of the regional workforce in 2006, whereas high-tech manufacturing accounted for 4.0 per cent. The share of KIBS employment in 2006 is three times the average of the high-tech manufacturing employment share. Ottawa is the only city in Canada where the share of workforce in services, and particularly in KIBS, is higher that the share of the manufacturing workforce. There is a high concentration of employment in computer systems design and related services, and in computer and electronics product manufacturing. Ottawa has a strong position in the information and communications technologies (ICT) industry, electronics, and semiconductors; additionally there has been a significant growth lately in opto-electronic

Table 5.1. High-tech and KIBS employment in Ottawa, 2006

Industry	Employment	% of total employment in Ottawa
High-tech manufacturing	22,255	4.0
Pharmaceutical and medicine manufacturing	280	–
Aerospace product and parts manufacturing	425	0.1
Computer and electronic product manufacturing	14,250	2.5
Electrical equipment, appliance, and component manufacturing	7,300	1.3
Knowledge-intensive business services	63,585	11.3
Software publishers	3,150	0.6
Telecommunications	8,365	1.5
Information services	2,975	0.5
Data processing services	525	0.1
Architectural engineering and related services	6,430	1.1
Specialized design services	1,795	0.3
Computer systems design and related services	20,335	3.6
Management scientific and technical consulting services	7,920	1.4
Scientific research and development services	8,870	1.6
Other professional scientific and technical services	3,220	0.6

Source: Employment data 2006, Statistics Canada

and life-science activities. These sectors have high growth rates and have developed in clusters of more than 1,000 employees. Figure 5.1 provides an overview of the growth in knowledge-intensive employment in Ottawa as compared to the growth for Montreal, Toronto and Canada overall, using comparable annual-employment data from 1971 to 2001. This period covers the peak of the late 1990s "dot.com" boom, the subsequent business recession, and the very slow recovery period. We can observe that KIBS employment in Ottawa has been the most dynamic component of regional employment growth. In Ottawa, the growth of KIBS firms since the 1980s has been driven by public-sector privatization and restructuring as well as regional-economy restructuring.

Interviews with representatives of these sectors showed clearly that the KIBS were much more local in their knowledge exchanges and partnerships. The high- and medium-tech manufacturing firms had

Figure 5.1. High-Tech and KIBS Employment Change in Ottawa, 1971–81, 1981–91, 1991–2001

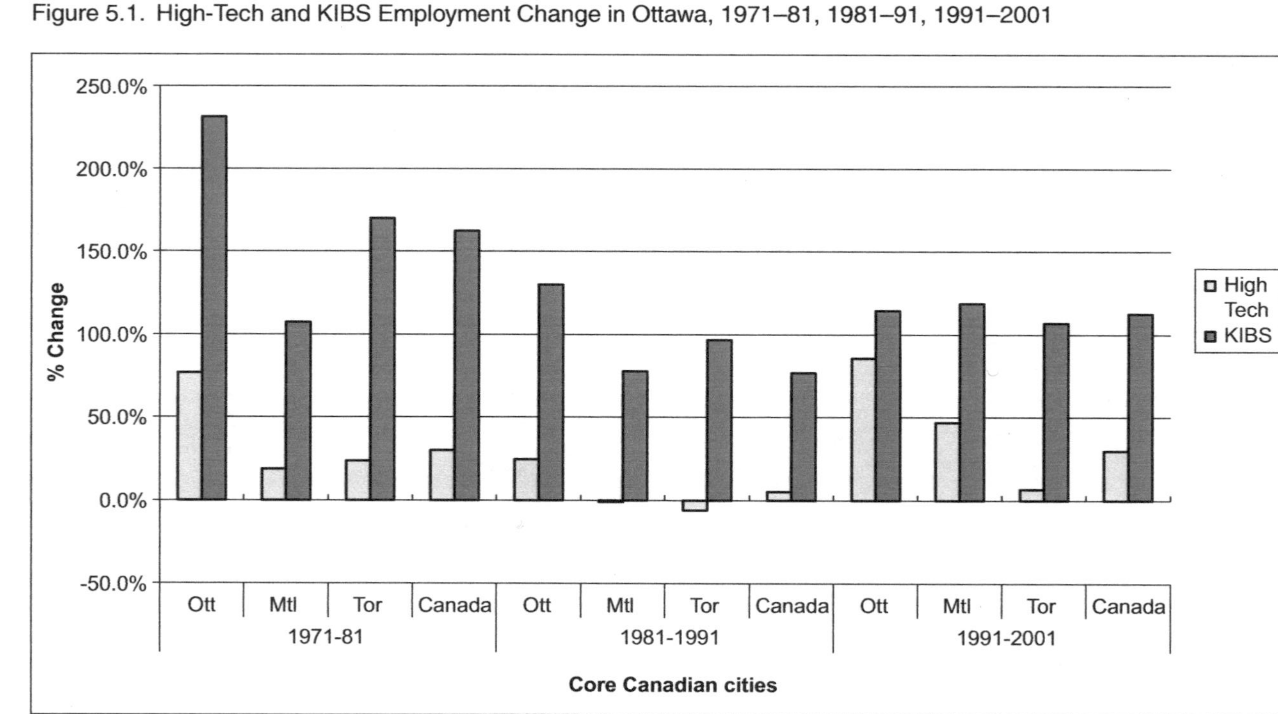

Source: Employment data from 1971, 1981, 1991, 2001, Statistics Canada

connections that were regional and global, whereas the KIBS firms were more resolutely local in their knowledge networks. These relationships emphasize the importance of the geographical proximity to the federal government and the interrelations between the different companies. The answers from the KIBS companies illustrated multiple collaborations, concentrated within the region. Of all KIBS respondents, 59 per cent collaborated with clients, 57 per cent with government agencies, 44 per cent with suppliers, 40 per cent with universities, 37 per cent with competitors and 32 per cent with research laboratories (Doloreux, Defazio, and Rangdrol 2010). And equally important, those firms that collaborated were more innovative (Doloreux and Mattson 2008); collaboration had an impact on the improvement of goods, services, and processes.

Turning to the municipal response, the early activities of OCRI were certainly congruent with the KIBS knowledge networks in that OCRI was preoccupied with creating and enhancing local connections and face-to-face interactions among all the regional high-tech players. This growth in the private sector stimulated the local government, and the chair of the Regional Municipality of Ottawa-Carleton (the precursor to the present City of Ottawa) was instrumental in the initial creation of OCRI in 1983. OCRI was a partnership between the local post-secondary institutions and the high-tech companies, and it established research chairs, organized conferences, set up networking opportunities, and organized trips to innovative centres. From relatively early on, under pressure from the large multinational corporations, OCRI developed activities to support the local education system, with awards for outstanding teachers, and programs to promote volunteers to read to children who needed extra help. OCRI was seen to be a great success and a model for economic governance (Wolfe 2009).

The city then created the Ottawa Partnership (TOP), co-chaired by a local high-tech leader and a president of a post-secondary institution, and, supported logistically by the city, TOP began a large-scale planning exercise based on cluster development and interested in the high-tech sector but also tourism and the life sciences (Andrew 2007). However, with the high-tech bust, the private sector members of TOP were too busy with their own problems to work on the partnership and, as a consequence, the city lost interest and TOP went into quiescence. However, as we discuss in a subsequent section of the chapter, there has been a recent regeneration of interest in strategic economic development with the folding of OCRI into Invest Ottawa, which was officially launched in 2012.

Despite the work of the economic development agencies, the city has not been able to increase the variety of the regional industry. "Overall, the Ottawa case provides a striking illustration of the difficulties encountered by a region in overcoming the legacy of an excessive reliance on a relatively small number of industrial sectors, despite the strong support of its governance institutions" (Wolfe 2009, 162). This municipal motivation was the result of development of diversified employment and of entrepreneurial success of local business leaders. It was also related to the long-standing negative relationship between the federal government and municipal Ottawa, whose origins go back to federal continuation of the British colonial view of Ottawa. This view was well illustrated by the advice to Queen Victoria to choose Ottawa as the capital for "its wild position, and relative inferiority to the other cities named" (Eggleston 1961, 103). That the federal government continued this view can be illustrated by its choice of a name for the first federal agency to plan the capital, as the Ottawa Improvement Commission. This view of municipal Ottawa as needing to be improved continued under the successors to the Ottawa Improvement Commission and underlay the National Capital Commission's (NCC) determination to play a strong role in planning the capital during the early post-war years, with no representation from municipal Ottawa on the NCC. Municipal enthusiasm and support for the high-tech development was therefore also support for the town against the Crown.

Municipal support for the high-tech expansion was strong and done primarily through supporting partnerships between the post-secondary institutions and the high-tech sector. At this early stage, the city preferred to have the partnership between the private sector and the post-secondary sector, with the latter as the visible part of the high-tech expansion, but its support was never in doubt.

The Talent Attractors

The second theme of the research focused on understanding why the workforce of high-tech development had been attracted to Ottawa and the answers were clear: pull of family and good employment. We interviewed engineers, as this group was the principal source of high-tech development in Ottawa. For many of them, family connections were a major attraction, either to settle near family or settling in Ottawa to raise a family. The overwhelming majority was very satisfied with life in Ottawa because it was a nice place to raise a family and a comfortable place to live. They acknowledged that Ottawa had neither vibrancy nor urban buzz, but only one person interviewed was simply waiting to find alternate employment before leaving Ottawa.

One result was that the talented workforce was not pushing the city into action. These were contented, talented workers: when there was an economic downturn in the high-tech sector, federal employment was always a viable option.

These talented workers also illustrate increasing diversity of Ottawa, as many had been born outside the country. But their general satisfaction with life in Ottawa indicated that they were not the ones to be pushing for new city policies and programs that might lead to a better integration of diversity. It also illustrates the vital importance of employment to the success of immigrant integration. The economic success of recent immigrants has been declining in Ottawa over recent years and has led to a broad-based community-municipal response, which we will describe later in this chapter.

Municipal Ottawa: Loss of Direction

As indicated in the introduction to this chapter, municipal Ottawa faded into indecision with the high-tech bust of 2001–2. The death of Nortel was a huge blow to the Ottawa economy and to the Ottawa high-tech identity. Not only was there loss of jobs but also loss of the "Silicon Valley North" image (Shavinina 2004). OCRI was increasingly criticized for having spread itself too thin and losing its focus on economic development. The endemic internal fragmentation of Ottawa, within and across sectors, was apparent (and also noted in the chapter on London in this volume). Our interviews with community leaders in 2007 indicated the lack of connections between economic leaders and social leaders, especially when compared with the situation in Calgary. The best-known and most appreciated person was a senior city manager, but although he was personally seen as efficient, the municipal government was criticized for its lack of leadership.

Lack of leadership from the municipal council only increased in 2007–10. The 2006 election saw the surprise election of Larry O'Brien, who entered the mayoralty race late, promising to "cut the fat" and to impose no tax increases in his term. The next four years saw an increasingly cantankerous council. In part, this was the legacy of the amalgamation of urban Ottawa, suburban Ottawa, and a large rural sector with little tradition of cooperation or shared goals, a weak mayor system of government, O'Brien's reluctance to spend time to create majorities for important votes, and an electorate increasingly divided between those wanting lower taxes and others worried about cuts in services necessary to if O'Brien was to keep his promise of no tax increases.

At the same time, economic development of Ottawa was facing challenges. The Ontario economy was heavily hit by the economic downturn, while the western cities, notably Calgary and Edmonton, were booming. The Conference Board of Canada's 2010 report, *City Magnets II*, called Calgary the most attractive of fifty Canadian cities. Calgary ranked first overall, based on its first place in the Economy and the Innovation categories and second in Housing (Lefebvre 2010, 48). Anecdotal evidence from Ottawa was that recent immigrants were leaving Ottawa to go west or to return to their countries of origin. Not only were the economies of the West booming, but the western cities had better and more pro-active municipal policies for integration of immigrants. Calgary was also very active on homelessness, both economic and social. Faced with these economic and social challenges, the City of Ottawa looked to its traditional pattern of action of partnering with the community.

The Ottawa Way: The City in Partnership with Community

In the chapters on London and Calgary, city government is described as the lead on many social innovations. But that has not been the pattern of the City of Ottawa, where partnering with the community has more often been the governance style. One classic and most successful example of this model was Operation 4000, when Mayor Marion Dewar invited the community to partner with the city in helping to settle and integrate Vietnamese refugees. Such an approach was seen by the Ottawa population as extremely successful, more so than the strictly government-assisted refugees, and this community-city partnership model continues to be seen as the desired model. OCRI can also be seen as the same kind of model; the region's role was deliberately less visible than that of the high-tech and the post-secondary sectors. In these two examples the municipal leadership played an initiating role with the community, but because municipal leadership was more risk-averse and divided, community participation became a prerequisite and not a consequence of municipal action.

As noted above, the city and local high-tech community attempted to reinvigorate Ottawa's local governance model by folding OCRI into Invest Ottawa, officially launched in February 2012. The *Ottawa Business Journal* (5 March, p.14) gave a positive evaluation to the launch, arguing that it seemed to have avoided some of OCRI's mistakes. Clearly, the focus was still on electronics but less specifically on the high-tech sector. The mayor was not only present at the launch but he also indicated in his presentation that the city was very engaged, politically and financially, in Invest Ottawa. The boy-wonder of economic Ottawa, the creator of Shopify (which is urban, young, and diverse), said at the launch, "Nice to see that not everyone here is old and white." It is too early to know what directions will be taken by Invest Ottawa, and overall comments in the *Ottawa Business Review* were mixed. However, this increased city involvement and some tie-in to immigrant integration (the articulation of immigrants as necessary risk-takers and therefore entrepreneurial) are positive signs of moving from complaisance once again.

The Ottawa governance model has both advantages and disadvantages. The combination of municipal and civic, or private-sector, participation can be a powerful lever for social change and effective action. Many of the examples described below illustrate the potential of partnerships that involve municipal and civic engagement. On the other hand, when the municipality is not fully engaged or gives only symbolic support to projects that must then depend solely on civic resources, those civic resources can be drained rather than empowered.

In one simple example of the Ottawa model, the chapter on London describes the city as getting the Age-Friendly certification from the World Health Organization, while in Ottawa it was given jointly to the city and to the Council on Aging for their collaboration to make Ottawa an age-friendly community.

The Council on Aging had been funded by Ontario's Trillium Foundation to create an age-friendly Ottawa. The council engaged with the city, which was developing a Senior Ottawa plan. City staff and representatives from the Seniors Advisory Committee were included on the Council on Aging Committee, and much effort was exerted on both sides to work harmoniously together, respecting the different timelines and reporting arrangements of city and community. In this case the innovative initiative emerged from both the community and the city.

Indeed, the Ottawa community has demonstrated considerable social innovation (Andrew and Doloreux 2014). Twenty years ago, the settlement sector in Ottawa was particularly creative with the establishment of Local Agencies Serving Immigrants (LASI), a coalition of the executive-directors of the major settlement agencies. LASI created LASI World Skills, an organization focused on immigrant employment, which spun off new organizations such as Immigrant Women's Services Organization (IWSO), and it has led to more specialization of member organizations and less competition. As an example, Ottawa Community Immigrant Services Organization (OCISO) does more work with the education sector, Catholic Centre for Immigrants does more work in housing and health, IWSO works specifically with women, LASI World Skills works on employment, and Conseil économique et social d'Ottawa-Carleton works primarily in French with the francophone immigrant population. Another local innovation was the Settlement Workers in Schools program, first created by OCISO in Ottawa and now funded nationally as part of the programming of Citizenship and Immigration Canada.

There are a whole new generation of social innovations in Ottawa: in information and data, economic innovation, and advocacy and civic engagement. Some have connections to the city and some have not. One such example is the creation in Ottawa of the Hub Ottawa, which opened in November 2012, both as a space that can be used for events and as an entrepreneurial incubator offering programs and activities to bring together young and socially minded entrepreneurs to "work, meet, and learn" and "to facilitate the creation of sustainable impact through collaboration."[1] Another example is Citizens Academy / Académie des citoyennes et citoyens, a community-based initiative that held pilot sessions of a democratic dialogue of citizens representing the full diversity of the city "to learn together what are the big challenges to our future, how the City works, how decisions are made, and how the community can be part of the solution."[2]

In this context, the city has recently undertaken partnership projects that may signal a renewed sense of direction by the city. One of the first projects related to municipal effectiveness, the Community Development Framework (CDF), an ambitious project to reorganize city development capacity in terms of need rather than political pressure, by designating priority areas according to indices developed by the Ottawa Neighbourhood Study and by horizontally coordinating city services in these priority areas. The Coalition of Community Health and Resource Centres of Ottawa[3] became the city's operating partner, with community developers in the designated priority areas playing a crucial role. In the next iteration of the CDF, the city supported the role of the CHRC and formalized the partnership relationship. This project has the potential for increased equity and efficiency in municipal services, through partnership with these uniquely Ottawa quangos (a quasi-autonomous non-governmental organization – essentially an arm's-length public sector agency). In an earlier period, the Community Resource Centres were fully part of the city administration but later the City of Ottawa "communitized" them by creating independent community-led boards while continuing to pay for part of the staff. The city is now trying to create closer links to the centres, and the partnership of the Community Development Framework can be seen as one illustration of the city's intentions.

Another partnership project that relates to city efficiency and to social inclusion has been between the City of Ottawa and the City for All Women Initiative (Initiative: une ville pour toutes les femmes).[4] CAWI is a community-based organization, with a steering committee composed of women from community-based women's organizations, city staff, and representatives from the Women's Studies programs at Carleton University and the University of Ottawa. CAWI advocates for more gender-friendly policies in the City of Ottawa, in partnership with the city. CAWI created the Gender Equity Lens, which the city partners liked, so when the city began to realize that a number of marginalized groups wanted to produce their own lens, the city engaged CAWI to develop a comprehensive lens. Following a very complex and interactive process, CAWI produced the Equity and Inclusion Lens, covering eleven marginalized communities; the five groups named in the city's diversity policy (Aboriginals, GLBTQ community, visible minorities, persons with disabilities, women), in addition to six other groups judged to be marginalized (youth, seniors, recent immigrants, people living in poverty, francophones, and rural residents).

The city is now implementing the Equity and Inclusion Lens, but given its financial constraints, the implementation moves slowly. The city very recently won a prize for being a good employer, and the Equity and Inclusion Lens was listed as the first reason for the prize. The city then awarded CAWI with a City Builder Award at a ceremony where the role of Status of Women Canada in funding CAWI was acknowledged. Implementation, particularly the evaluation of the implementation, is facilitated by a Partnership Development Grant by the Social Sciences and Humanities Research Council that began work in 2012 and is interviewing city decision-makers and participants in implementation of the Equity and Inclusion Lens.[5]

Another partnership between the city and the community is Youth Futures (Avenir Jeunesse), which engages disadvantaged youth from families with little or no experience in post-secondary education in a program that combines leadership training, paid summer employment through the city, and exposure to post-secondary education. The partners are the City of Ottawa, Ottawa Community Housing, the University of Ottawa, St Paul's University, Carleton University, La Cité collégiale, Algonquin College, and a host of community organizations that help to identify potential participants. The program participants come very largely from the recent immigrant population, so it is both an anti-poverty program and a program for the better integration of immigrants and refugees.

The partnership that most clearly covers both economic and social areas is the city's role in the Ottawa Local Immigration Partnership.[6] The host organization for OLIP is the CCI, and the City of Ottawa was an original partner. The city's social sector staff was the first to engage significantly in OLIP planning, but the city's economic development sector is now also deeply engaged in the OLIP implementation phase. An indication of its engagement was clear in 2011 when the city announced its policy priorities for the fall term of council (2011–14). On the social dimension, the first priority was better adaptation of city policies and programs to the demographic trends of aging and diversity, and on the economic side, the second priority was the better economic achievement of recent immigrants. The OLIP structure for the implementation phase is focused on sector tables: economic development, health, education, language policies, and integration, each of which includes city representatives and will implement the priorities from the planning phase. It will also take advantage of new opportunities to implement programs, projects, and policies that enhance the full integration of immigrants to the Ottawa community. Both the city's social sector staff and economic development sector staff seem fully engaged in the OLIP process, but for the moment it is clear that this engagement is much more on the staff side than on the political side of the council.

Conclusion

Two themes emerge from our description of the social dynamics of economic performance in Ottawa: the difficulty that the City of Ottawa has had in moving away from dependence on the federal government as the determining body in the economic development strategy for the city and the region; and the city's preference, even when most enthusiastic about supporting private-sector high-tech development, for partnering with other bodies, whether in the private sector or community-based.

We have described this as the Ottawa model of preferring partnerships over clear municipal initiative, and we have outlined the opportunities and challenges associated with this model. The opportunities can best be seen in the early period of OCRI's success. By playing a less visible role, the city was strategically prioritizing the development of links between the high-tech and post-secondary sectors, links that benefited both partners and therefore the city. A less successful partnership was that of the initial stages of the Community Development Framework. The city was "partnering" with Community Resource and Health Centres in priority neighbourhoods, without initially being clear about the precise nature of the partnership and without offering compensation for the time taken by the actual work that the partnership implied for specific Community Resource and Health Centres. The second stage of the partnership involved making the city's partner the Coalition of Community Resource and Health Centres, rather than individual centres, and the city agreeing to compensate the coalition for the work to be done.

More recently, some partnerships seem to be more like the early OCRI, with opportunities for bringing community pressure to bear on the city where there is an appetite for reacting positively to this pressure. This would certainly be true of the Ottawa Local Immigration Partnership and of the Equity and Inclusion Lens. The City of Ottawa's preference for partnering has worked well in a number of areas, but there are situations where a more direct initiative by the city would be called for in order to produce more systematic development.

There is no clear answer at the time of writing as to whether the City of Ottawa is convinced of the need for a much more coordinated and determined municipal development strategy. We have outlined positive signs, but history suggests how difficult it is for the city to abandon its reliance on the federal government to ensure economic prosperity of the region. It is too early to tell whether the city will follow a path-dependent approach or turn to new conditions that require innovative directions.

Notes

1 See http://ottawa.the-hub.net/.
2 See http://www.citizensacademy.ca.
3 See http://www.coalitionottawa.ca.
4 See http://www.cawi-ivtf.org.
5 This grant has been awarded to Fran Klodawsky as principal investigator, to Janet Siltanen, and to Caroline Andrew to develop our partnership with CAWI, the City of Ottawa, and the Federation of Canadian Municipalities. The grant is for a three-year partnership development.
6 See http://olip-plio.ca.

References

Andrew, C. 2007. "Trying to be world-class: Ottawa and the presentation of self." In *Urban communication: Production, text, context*, ed. T. Gibson and M. Lowes, 127–40. Lanham, MD: Rowman and Littlefield.

Andrew, C., and C. Doloreux. 2014. "Linking innovation and inclusion: The governance question in Ottawa." In *Governing urban economies: Innovation and inclusion in Canadian city regions*, ed. Neil Bradford and Alison Bramwell, 137–60. Toronto: University of Toronto Press.

Andrew, C., B. Ray, and G. Chiasson. 2011. "Ottawa-Gatineau: Capital formation." In *Canadian urban regions*, ed. L. Bourne, T. Hutton, R. Shearmur, and J. Simmons, 202–35. Oxford: Oxford University Press.

Bagnall, James. 2013. "Tech's time." *Ottawa Citizen*, 13 July.

Doloreux, D., D. Defazio, and D. Rangdrol. 2010. "The socio-economic landscape of knowledge intensive business services in the Ottawa region: A study using the regional innovation system approach." In *Knowledge intensive business services (KIBS): Geography and innovation*, ed. D. Doloreux, M. Freel, and R. Shearmur, 187–210. Aldershot, UK: Ashgate.

Doloreux, D., and H. Mattson. 2008. "To what extent do sectors 'socialize' innovation differently? Mapping cooperative linkages in knowledge-intensive industries in the Ottawa Region." *Industry and Innovation* 15 (4): 351–70. http://dx.doi.org/10.1080/13662710802239463.

Eggleston, Wilfrid. 1961. *The Queen's choice: A story of Canada's capital*. Ottawa: National Capital Commission.

Gulel, Cumhur. 2009. *Report on interviews of talented workers.* Ottawa.
Invest Ottawa. 2013. http://investottawa.ca.
Lefebvre, Mario. 2010. *City magnets II: Benchmarking the attractiveness of 50 Canadian cities.* Ottawa: Conference Board of Canada.
Shavinina, L., ed. 2004. *Silicon Valley North.* Amsterdam: Elsevier. http://dx.doi.org/10.1108/S1479-067X(2004)9.
Statistics Canada. 2011. *Daily*, 28 June.
–. 2012. *Focus on Geography Series, 2011 Census.* Ottawa: Statistics Canada.
Steed, G., and D. DeGenova. 1983. "Ottawa's technology-oriented complex." *Canadian Geographer* 27 (3): 263–78.
Wolfe, D.A. 2009. *21st century cities in Canada: The geography of innovation.* Ottawa: Conference Board of Canada.

6 Innovation from an Oil and Gas Platform: Calgary

COOPER H. LANGFORD, BEN LI, AND CAMILLE D. RYAN

Calgary has its own unique blend of site and circumstance, which has perpetuated a frontier image of individualism, freedom, and opportunity set in big sky country ... The history of Calgary has tended to mirror the ebullience and unpredictability of the frontier experience.

– Foran and MacEwan Foran (1982)

Never start into a business in [Calgary] that doesn't have direct implications and impact on the oil and gas business. This is an oil and gas town.

– Interview with a serial entrepreneur

Introduction

Discovery of oil and gas in the Turner Valley region south of Calgary early in the twentieth century, followed by construction of pipelines in the 1950s, re-invented Calgary's economic, political, and social structures. Alberta was transformed from one of the poorest provinces in Canada to one of the richest over several decades. Exploration and development in oil and gas have largely spurred the rapid growth of the Calgary census metropolitan area.[1] "Calgary's phenomenal growth after 1947 has been almost entirely due to its position at the forefront of Canada's burgeoning petroleum and natural gas industries ... Calgary found the prosperity that was denied by the cattle industry and railroad development ... [It] enabled Calgary to transcend the ... dependence on a limited agricultural ... hinterland" (Foran and MacEwan Foran 1982, 10).

Despite its broad characterization as an oil-and-gas-based economy, Calgary does not fit into a traditional mould that one would expect.

The activities in Calgary are those of a diverse knowledge economy. They combine technical knowledge, managerial knowledge, and financial knowledge facilitating petroleum resource extraction in the region, across Canada, and internationally. The knowledge base is characterized as diverse on the basis of industry codes (Conference Board of Canada 2009), but is that of a petroleum centre focused on an international commodity market.

Its early beginnings were as an oil-and-gas-producing centre, but relatively few well sites now remain near the Calgary city-region. The same is true for refining. Starting with the initiatives of Imperial Oil in the 1940s, Calgary temporarily enjoyed hosting oil refineries within its metropolitan boundaries, but this activity has subsequently migrated to Edmonton.

Through the 1970s, 1980s, and 1990s, Calgary's energy sector continued to grow, attaining critical mass by attracting the national head offices of many of the sector's leading firms to locate there. Now known as "Canada's global energy centre," Calgary is home to main offices of 87 per cent of the country's oil and natural gas producers (CED 2006). As a result, it represents the highest concentration of head offices per capita in Canada: 9.8 per 100,000 people, compared to 5.1 for Toronto and only 2.4 for Montreal (Miller and Smart 2011). What qualifies Calgary as the national energy centre is its tripartite expertise in management, finance, and technology that provides a *knowledge base* for oil and gas exploration and extraction in its hinterland, the Western Canadian region, and globally. Calgary's economy has thus become a knowledge economy in a knowledge-intensive industry.

This study of Calgary, which was undertaken as part of the Innovation Systems Research Network (ISRN) national project, focuses on three interrelated themes: the role of innovation and knowledge flows among firms in Calgary's leading economic sectors, the role of creative talent in driving the growth of the Calgary economy, and finally, the contribution of civic, cultural, and governmental organizations in fostering the economic development of the city-region.[2] The chapter analyses the primary characteristics of innovation and the character of requisite knowledge inputs in all three of the for-profit, not-for-profit, and government sectors. Similarly, the factors that influence the preferences of creative individuals for location in Calgary are reviewed. Finally, the chapter discusses the nature of civic governance in Calgary's regional economy and the role of key civic leaders in supporting the growth and development of the local economy.

Overview of the Calgary Economy

What was termed "phenomenal growth" in 1982 continued through the "oil boom" of 2006–7. The civic census of 1981 reported Calgary's population as 591,857. The 2011 census reports a population base of 1,214,839 for the Calgary CMA, more than double that of 1981 numbers. Between 2006 and 2011, Calgary's population increased by 12.6 per cent compared to the national average of 7.4 per cent for all Canadian CMAs. In contrast to some of the other major metropolitan areas in Canada, in-migration from the rest of the country has been an important factor in this growth, generally outweighing a healthy natural increase or international immigration. However, recent research suggests that Calgary is also a major beneficiary of secondary immigration, as international immigrants first move to one of Canada's major cities because of their higher international profile, but are subsequently drawn to settle in Calgary because of the high demand for workers in the local labour market driven by the continuing strength of the energy economy (Miller and Smart 2011, 272).

Within the overall net migration figures for 2001–6, Calgary led all CMAs in Canada in the rate of domestic in-migration of science and engineering professionals (just ahead of Ottawa-Gatineau), business and finance professionals (at almost twice the rate of Hamilton, which is the next leading CMA), chefs and cooks (just ahead of Windsor), and construction trades (just ahead of Edmonton). Calgary's in-migration rate for arts and culture professionals (third) is close to the numbers experienced by leaders (Moncton and Ottawa-Gatineau) (Spencer et al. 2010). The influx of chefs, cooks, and some construction workers may be seen as predominantly yielding basic employment serving internal needs of a rapidly growing CMA. The attraction of the other two groups and a significant part of construction contributes directly to that part of the "creative class" as defined by employment (Florida 2005) who are considered key players in the non-basic segment supporting the outward reach of the CMA. What will be seen as central, below, is that workers in these sectors are extensively engaged with oil and gas activity and offer a great deal of related variety[3] (Boschma 1999; Asheim, Cooke, and Martin 2008; Frenken, Van Oort, and Verburg 2007) through a mix of diverse professional knowledge that is finally focused on *one* overall outcome: extraction and marketing of oil and gas.

Despite the predominance of the oil and gas industry in Calgary's economy, the evidence from a Canadian statistical study of industry clusters indicates that a significant proportion of other sectors are clustered as well (Spencer et al. 2010). By this measure 42 per cent of Calgary employment is clustered, compared to a Canadian average of 22 per cent. The definition of Canadian clusters developed by Spencer et al. (2010) using location quotients[4] (LQs) as a key criterion identifies seven employment clusters defined by standard industry classifications (NAICS codes). The dominant cluster is the oil and gas cluster with an LQ of 5.02. The closely related mining industry is second with an employment LQ of 1.81, but the structure of employment is not broad enough to satisfy the overall cluster definition. Nonetheless, the sum of these two core industries accounts for only 6.5 per cent of the labour force. Clusters also exist in ICT manufacturing (1.06) and ICT services (1.15) as well as finance (1.00) and business services (1.44). The last three have close links to the oil and gas cluster and provide the high-end business services required to support the strong concentration of head offices located in Calgary. In fact, a conventional qualitative cluster study would include large parts of these clusters within oil and gas as "suppliers" or "infrastructure" (Wolfe 2003). This wide range of supporting clusters in the Calgary city-region provides a rich variety of related knowledge that can channel diverse knowledge inputs into innovation in the core cluster. Other clusters in the Calgary economy are found in construction (1.64), which is related to the rapid growth of the oil and gas industry, and in logistics (1.19).

The overall diversity of Calgary's economy stands in sharp contrast to the other major resource-based case studied, Saskatoon. In Saskatoon the economy responds to several resource bases and diverse markets in agriculture, potash, petroleum, and uranium. A key knowledge concentration is in agricultural biotechnology, and the local activity has an entrepôt character, where knowledge is imported and value is added and is passed on for exploitation elsewhere (Phillips and Webb, this volume). Where the major Saskatoon clusters can resemble knowledge islands, which might cross-fertilize by one occasionally passing genuine novelty to another (Jacobs 1961), the major Calgary "clusters" are deeply integrated into oil and gas activity, which requires diverse knowledge inputs with a common goal (and a common volatile market). This we identify as a "related knowledge diversity" (RKD) (Langford, Li, and Ryan 2014) unique in Canada.

Firm Innovation and the Paths of Knowledge Flow in Calgary Industry

Our understanding of firm-based innovation in Calgary is based on data from interviews identifying one to four innovation efforts from each (Langford, Li, and Ryan 2014). The interviews were chosen to represent the approximate distribution of firms among conventional sectors in Calgary's economy. Data were interpreted to connect innovations to their knowledge inputs. In contrast to the conventional OECD classification of innovations as new to the firm, new to Canada, or new to the world, it was deemed more useful to examine knowledge resources by the type of problem for the firm that the innovation ultimately addressed. The problem classes used were:

- satisfying a *client need*,
- firm *capacity building*,
- overcoming a *market barrier*, and
- creating a *new market*.

As well, types of innovation efforts were each categorized according to orientation to attaining individual *firm advantage* or yielding *collective advantage*.

Knowledge inputs were classified as:

- *internal* knowledge, which circulates within a particular firm or local innovative unit,
- *local* knowledge, which circulates primarily among innovative individuals and organization units within the CMA; or
- *non-local* knowledge, which arises from specific sources outside the CMA and is commonly transmitted to the CMA by "pipelines" for knowledge within the industry's field nationally and globally.

Our results reveal that problem-solving is a distributed cognitive process dependent upon knowledge sharing and acquisition. The results indicate that solving problems (by developing innovations) for *firm advantage*, rather than collaborative advantage, figured high across all knowledge types, yet local knowledge, which indicated a strong local system, ranked as the most common source, above internal or non-local sources. The knowledge inputs were also classified as primarily *codified* or primarily *tacit*. Tacit knowledge was not limited to the inherently non-codifiable, but also included elements of know-how where it may have proved uneconomic to codify. With this definition, tacit knowledge was found to be the most common type in local knowledge exchanges, suggesting the presence of intimate networking.

There is one central theme in the interviews that is not easily illustrated with one or two quotes or charts and tables. It is the pervasive description of innovations as complexes that might include products, but also entail customer consultation or knowledge-intensive services provided by the innovating firms (even for mass market items). Almost no innovations mentioned by interviewees were limited to individual products. This suggests a very close connection between knowledge flows and ongoing relationships among a network of firms, and emphasizes the importance of shared cognition in innovations that do not stop with product artefacts among the diverse professionals involved. Furthermore, much innovation was directed at assembling the competences required to provide a comprehensive suite of services.

A Platform of Related Knowledge Diversity

The most challenging issue that arose in examining knowledge flows was the question of inter-sector flows. The dominant oil and gas activity, which does not actually handle much oil or gas in Calgary, is not at all limited to activity within companies that are classified as oil and gas in the conventional NAICS codes. Strong linkages from the core sector to professional scientific and engineering services firms are obvious. ICT services play a key role in oil and gas. It is less widely appreciated that creative financial arrangements have been crucial to the growth of the oil and gas industry. Sophisticated business services are essential. Examination of the Canadian input-output tables (Statistics Canada 2008) shows that inputs to the oil and gas industry are concentrated in a very few sectors – mining and inorganic materials on the goods side. On the services side, business services (including professional and scientific services) and financial services are important components. The common view about the degree of integration of firms was captured in (perhaps) extreme language by a successful and widely influential Calgary serial entrepreneur: "I've learned over the years never start into a business in Alberta that doesn't have direct implications and impact on the oil and gas business. This is an oil and gas town … You can't do anything in Calgary if it's not connected to oil and gas" (confidential interview).

The reach of oil and gas activity in Calgary belies the apparent diversity of the regional economy. The non-basic activity in the city is concentrated in the assembly of the managerial, technical, and financial knowledge to manage resource extraction in its Alberta hinterland, regionally across Western Canada, and globally. The focus of this activity is *knowledge*. In contrast to common perceptions, oil and gas activity in Calgary is a knowledge-intensive multidisciplinary activity. It is best conceptualized as an integrated *platform* (Cooke 2007; Cooke et al. 2007). This is a *platform of diverse knowledge, related* by its focus on *outcomes for the oil and gas industry*, a platform of "related knowledge diversity" discussed in more detail in Langford, Li, and Ryan (2014). This insight will provide a guiding theme for understanding the governance coalition that frames the policy discussion for Calgary.

In consequence of the close integration of many firms into the oil and gas platform, the analysis of inter-sector knowledge flows represented in the interview data was based on four "sectors." The oil and gas platform is the most important. It is identified from the reported linkages and specializations of firms. A group of firms in environmental services that were not dominated by oil and gas was also identified in the data. Similarly, a group of firms in advertising and multimedia could be characterized. The remaining firms had to be simply lumped in a catch-all as "other." Table 6.1 displays the identified contributions of local knowledge supporting innovations in terms of the sector of origin to sector of use.

The dominance of the diagonal (highlighted) of this matrix confirms the partition that was adopted on independent grounds, as identifying knowledge communities.[5] The oil and gas platform is the largest supplier of innovation support knowledge to other sectors. This was even more evident in knowledge flows into the not-for-profit sectors. However, the low incidence of inter-sector exchanges does not imply a low value of "weak links" (Granovetter 1983). These links can in fact be the source of fresh insights not in circulation among those linked strongly (Jacobs 1961). An origin of inter-sector flows may emerge from features seen in the interviews with innovative individuals. Many of the attractions of Calgary for talented workers were activities and organizations from civic, cultural, or athletic vocations (from

Table 6.1. Intra- and inter-sectoral knowledge inputs (percentages of knowledge received from originating sectors)

	Originating Sector (%)				
Receptor sector	Oil and gas	Environment	Multimedia	Other	Not listed
Oil and gas	79	1	–	–	20
Environment	7	38	–	–	55
Multimedia	4	–	61	–	35
Other	1	–	–	53	46
Of all inputs identified	24	9	14	14	39

the opera, or the United Way to motorcycle clubs) that do not recruit members from any particular sector. These provide rich opportunity for development of strong personal links with accompanying weak professional ones.

A feature of the environmental services firms not integrated with the oil and gas platform is that they report a distinct advantage created by the expertise honed in their work with oil and gas problems. To some degree this sector is an oil and gas spin-off. Nevertheless, the pattern of local knowledge flow identifies the central role of a platform of related knowledge diversity (RKD). This is neither the type described by Frenken, Van Oort, and Verburg (2007) where related variety is found within a statistical sector, nor the type considered by Feldman and Audretsch (1999), where a common science base supports diverse activity. Nor does its special character promote resilience in the regional economy, because the activity is all directed to serving a common global commodity market.

Innovation in the Not-for-Profit (Mainly Services) Sector

Innovations in the not-for-profit (cultural, civic, charitable, and government organizations) sector were classified by problem type in a manner parallel to those for firms. The problem classes used are:

- providing a client service,
- organization capacity building,
- overcoming a social barrier, or
- introducing new models or exemplars.

The first two are very close to those for firms. Barriers were not to access to markets but more appropriately social barriers to delivery of some service that needed to be overcome, and *exemplars* (models) was the term chosen to categorize introduction of entirely fresh types of services. We chose the term *exemplars* (Kuhn 1977) because the new services were often found to introduce approaches that were readily used as models by other organizations in a way that might evolve into a new service paradigm across providers.

The analysis of the not-for-profit sector, using a framework parallel to that for analysis of firms described above, suggests several contrasts between innovations in the two categories of organizations. Of the four varieties of innovation in not-for-profit organizations, the highest numbers of innovations were in capacity building, and in implementing new models or exemplars. Local (and tacit) knowledge led sharing, but non-local knowledge was a major source. Capacity-building contrasts, as expected, with firms' primary inspiration from customer need. Altogether, this suggests that not-for-profit innovators have been bringing new capabilities into Calgary from elsewhere (especially national networks of parallel organizations – "knowledge pipelines"), while innovators in firms deliver capabilities to end users. Consistent with the differences just cited, we find 71 per cent and 78 per cent of knowledge input to client need and capacity-building innovations (top two kinds) for firm advantage are local, while for not-for-profit organizations, local knowledge is responsible for 48 per cent and 57 per cent of new models and capacity-building (top two kinds) for collective advantage. A similar (perhaps stronger) pattern holds for internal sources of knowledge, which, in not-for-profits, includes private-sector board members and volunteers, indicating the importance of the internalization of knowledge in the Calgary innovation system via knowledgeable individuals.

In the scope of innovations conducted by not-for-profits and firms, we find a significant contrast, insofar as it is possible to classify. There appear to be firms innovating for a global market, whereas not-for-profits tend to bring new ideas from the outside, especially elsewhere in Canada.

A number of innovations generated by firms and identified as new to the world were inventions eligible for patents, or innovations gained from basic science research. In contrast, half of the not-for-profit sector's identified innovations were new to the city, but not new to the world. This finding is consistent with the varieties of innovation brought to Calgary by firms and not-for-profit organizations in their roles: internally focused firms innovate for competitive advantage, while not-for-profit organizations in Calgary are not inventing new things as much as bringing such new things to the city to be shared. Important linkages are with national and international associations concerned with the problem area. Such pipelines to outside specialized knowledge seem to be even more important than they are in the private sector, perhaps because the private sector obtains much specialized knowledge by recruiting talent and later describes this as "internal" knowledge.

Linkages of the Private Sector to Innovation in Culture, Charitable, and Civic Organizations

Both the role of board members as internal knowledge sources and the differences in focus and scope of the "innovation problem" indicate the relationship between innovation in the two domains. Representatives of not-for-profit organizations regularly referred to the contributions from private-sector figures as board members and volunteers. A number of the innovations by those organizations were identified as dependent on the contributions of private-sector board members. This was especially true for innovations in business models where private-sector practices served as analogues. However, the contributions were not limited to business models. In fact one interviewee who had become an officer of a charitable organization had started as a volunteer employed in the oil and gas industry. The commitment of private-sector volunteers is highly regarded. However, there are some areas of tension. Private-sector leaders have initiated importation of novel approaches that have offended some established social agencies. This intimate engagement of the private sector contrasts with the other city of similar size in the ISRN study, Ottawa (see Andrew and Doloreux, this volume). Apparently, government is seen as the responsible sector in a government centre, whereas the private sector accepts a broader community role in Calgary.

The attitude and motives within the private sector for linkage to the not-for-profits were clearly expressed as a desire to "give back." This applied to both firms and individuals. However, there was a second commonly expressed motive. Executives of firms recognized support for not-for-profit as important to retention of talent. Policy governing firm financial contributions commonly followed special interests of employees. "Beyond that we have community investment policy ... we match dollar for dollar everything that the employees donate" (confidential interview).

Firms recognize that their employees' interests extend over a wide range beyond the job, as seen in the variety of attractions of the Calgary location identified among creative individuals. The employers' donation policies are well adapted to recognizing diverse motivations of employees. Convergence between sectors around the idea that quality of life and satisfaction of a diverse spectrum of interests is important to the attraction and retention of the talent that supports economic growth has been articulated by city government spokespersons (Ryan, Li, and Langford 2014)

A "Creative Class" in Calgary

A key theme that arose throughout the interviews with senior officers of firms, organizations, and institutions was the role played by creative individuals in their innovative activities.[6] There was no doubt that a concern for the "creative class," according to Richard Florida's precise definition, was pervasive.[7] In interviews with individual creative workers, responses concerning satisfaction (or lack thereof) with Calgary as a site for their profession versus other cities were grouped around major hypotheses about the attractors. Among these were references to the positive business climate of a young city ("entrepreneurial spirit" was mentioned especially often): "There's an entrepreneurial spirit in the city ... an open-for-business attitude ... you can't duplicate that anywhere in the world" (confidential interview). Alternatively, that the physical environment supports an outdoor lifestyle. "I moved here to be near the mountains, to ski, and to mountain bike, and to do all those kinds of things" (confidential interview).

Professional and personal (e.g., family) networks also figured often, as did, of course, the availability of job opportunity. There was little explicit mention of social factors such as inclusiveness (where it was cited, some of the comment was a bit negative).

The single most striking feature was that almost all interviewees gave prominence to *a number of different factors* that make Calgary personally attractive (or not). Examination of the *perceptions* from semi-structured interviews emphasizes the *complex character* of attitude formation among creative workers. Nevertheless, questions about possible alternative locations support interpretation of this complex "expressed factor" matrix as characterizing preferences of considerable significance to attraction and retention.

Essentially, reports in all segments of the community recognize the importance of creativity in all areas of work and the presence of a thick labour market in Calgary (except in health services). The richness and diversity of this labour market depends in significant measure on the wide range of professional and technical competences required to supply knowledge needs of oil and gas activity. Recognition of knowledge diversity and the importance of its maintenance are incorporated in policies of the City of Calgary.

On the whole our respondents paint a picture of Calgary as a suitable site to pursue creative careers, but it is essential to appreciate that any individual's reasons are typically diverse. Important interests range from the opera to a motorcycle club. No "magic attractor" characterizing Calgary emerges. Many of the attractions of Calgary for talented workers were activities and organizations from civic, cultural, or athletic vocations (from the opera, or the United Way to special interest clubs) that do not recruit members from any particular sector. These provide rich opportunity for development of strong personal links with accompanying weak professional ones. A positive deviation from the Canadian trend of CMA size to in-migration attraction (Bettencourt et al. 2007) is found for Calgary. It may be attributable to a concentration around oil and gas of the greater "density" of the RKD, enhancing the "gravitational" attraction of the city (Bettencourt et al. 2007). Yet no single dimension or character of attraction controls the value of that attractive "mass."

Governance in the Context of an Oil and Gas Platform

"Policy outcomes ... [are] the product of a complex pattern of interaction between several levels of government and an array of social and economic actors in the community where the policy is implemented" (Wolfe 2009, 110).

Discussion above reasonably reflects the array of social and economic actors in the community. To understand their roles in the "complex pattern of interaction," we borrow a concept from actor-network theory (Latour 1987). A functional network may stabilize around congruent goals. In some cases, civic networks form as a consequence of the entrepreneurial skill and persuasive force of a champion group, and often championing is accomplished through, or in the name of, a specific spokesperson (Latour 1988, 14). It is this that leads to effective "grand" regional plans. No evidence of such an effective entrepreneur has emerged[8] in the Calgary study. However, stabilization can also be achieved by bringing actors together through a number of means (Callon

1986). One is through proposing that the route to another's specific goal is best approached through the goal articulated by the actor seeking to enrol those others (Latour 1987, 112). Certain common themes around which divergent groups of actors could converge did emerge. These have significant consequences for policy.

The common themes emerged most directly from reports of spokespersons for organizations around which segments of the community converge. One set of key organizations included the Calgary Chamber of Commerce, Calgary Economic Development, and Calgary Technologies, Inc. (now Innovate Calgary), who are related by their common goal to advance the cause of *economic development and growth*. An excerpt capturing the goal from Calgary Economic Development (CED) is "Working with stakeholders from business, the community, and government, CED capitalizes on Calgary's abundant energy and entrepreneurial spirit to facilitate sustainable economic growth. The organization's mission and mandate are to foster business growth for community prosperity and to lead, facilitate and advance Calgary's economic development efforts. *Vision*: Calgary is the location of choice for people and business. *Mission*: To foster business growth for community prosperity within the Calgary Region" (CED 2009). The role of the city in this organization indicates significant city government endorsement of the goals.

The Calgary Foundation, imagineCalgary, and Plan It – the city's long-range plan – the Epcor Centre, and the United Way are representatives of another category, related by their common goals to advance the cause of a *healthy and sustainable community*. As major coordinator of philanthropy (affiliated with Community Foundations of Canada), the Calgary Foundation has as its vision "A giving and caring community that values sharing, collaborating and learning; A community with citizens engaged in community building at all levels; A healthy, vibrant community that embraces diversity and supports all of its people; A strong and sustainable charitable sector serving the existing and emerging needs of the community" (Calgary Municipal Government 2009).

The clearest expression of a sustainability goal comes from the imagineCalgary Plan. ImagineCalgary, an ongoing project, was launched as an eighteen-month public engagement project in 2005 to achieve a 100-year vision, to which 18,000 citizens contributed. Over fifty organizations, mainly in the public not-for-profit sector, are formally affiliated. A few of the "100 year goals" are: "*Energy*: The energy used by Calgarians comes from a diverse portfolio ... [having] a low impact on the environment and contribute to the positive development of our society. *Transportation*: Calgary is built at a human scale with a transportation system that serves the access and mobility needs of all … *Economic well-being*: Calgary is a city with a vibrant, resilient, environmentally sound and sustainable economy that fosters opportunity for individual economic well-being" (imagineCalgary 2006). Several organizations firmly associated with economic development participate in the quality of life / sustainability organizations. A major example is the homeless initiative. The Calgary Chamber of Commerce, whose individual public positions always include core business issues such as low taxes and limiting government involvement in business, is quite active.

The two streams of goal formation are not independent of each other. Positions of the City of Calgary commonly reflect a synthesis (see City of Calgary 2007). The linkage of goals arises from private, growth-oriented sector recognition of the importance of talent and the attraction offered by a healthy, sustainable community to talented individuals and their families. At the same time, the sustainability goal is seen to require a healthy economy, as articulated by imagineCalgary.

The 300 "Who Make a Difference"

There are also important organizations based on informal contacts that bring together like-minded individuals who share, especially, the economic goals – such as the Petroleum Club. As one interviewee noted, there is an influential informal group coming mainly from industry of "300 Calgarians who make things happen." Interviews with civic and cultural agencies emphasized how informal networking among influential Calgarians plays a central role in initiatives. A key example has been the effort to deal with homelessness. Here accounts agree that a single individual became convinced of the seriousness of the problem and was able to recruit from his network an active alliance that obtained government funding, fostered a new agency, and influenced the importation of the "housing first" model on the basis that it has been successful in other cities. It was clear that setting a policy direction came from an informal group whose influence derives from positions in the private sector. Social agency executives were by no means all convinced that the new initiative was correct (and it is too soon to evaluate the outcome). The role of influential individuals with strong informal networks of private-sector peers in energizing initiatives of charitable, social, and cultural agencies is clear. These informal networks cannot be said to be inclusive.

In this context, do the two goal streams become reconciled to produce policy outcomes? *First,* it is clear that the streams converge not only on the need to attract and retain creative talent, but also on the requirement for a good quality of life covering many dimensions in order to achieve this goal. Policy initiatives in this direction are emerging in the City's long-range plan (Calgary Municipal Government 2009). The plan deals explicitly with the two major areas of city jurisdiction: land use regulation and transport. Policy for both is oriented to making the city more compact, with infrastructure favourable to alternatives to the automobile. Neighbourhoods ("pods") combining residence and work that support the development of an atmosphere of social connection, basically in the tradition of Jane Jacobs (1961), are recommended. Transport should effectively link these pods. The formulation of this policy has been much more inclusive with extensive consultation behind imagineCalgary and Plan It Calgary. Since 1998, principles of sustainability have been built into city policies. Members of the major growth-oriented informal networks of influential private-sector individuals have played a part in the consultations. Perhaps at this stage only some real estate developers, important actors in city politics, remain opposed.

However, it is clear that the ambitions behind the sustainability and growth plans extend beyond the areas of direct city jurisdiction. The success of the overall direction for the growth of the city will not be realized without the continued creativity and innovation by the charitable, civic, and cultural sectors illustrated by the work of the Calgary Foundation, the United Way, and the Epcor Centre for Performing Arts. Moreover, these sectors will depend on the continued support of both money and talent they receive from private-sector actors, as illustrated by the work of the Chamber of Commerce on homelessness. This support clearly reflects the convergence with the private-sector interest in talent retention. It is interesting to compare the Calgary experience with that of the other Canadian city of similar size in, Ottawa. Andrew and Doloreux (this volume) report that the private and social/charitable sectors do not enjoy the same level of engagement from the private sector, despite the fact that more formal organizations exist to bring private groups together. An interesting possibility is that

Calgary's strong informal network is a by-product of the dominance of the RKD platform.

Second there is a goal that has a long history in Alberta that implicitly recognizes the dominance of the oil and gas platform and the still-limited role in the Calgary community played by industries independent of that platform. This is the goal of diversification of the economy. It has federal support in the activities of Western Economic Diversification and has been a part of Alberta policy since the era of the government led by Premier Peter Lougheed (Marsh 2005). The 2008 provincial government strategy prioritized established industries in energy, agriculture, and forestry, but does focus on enhancing value-added opportunities and on commercialization of the products of Alberta research institutions. Leading the government's statement of five priorities for Albertans is "creating opportunity": "Enhance value-added activity, increase innovation, and build a skilled workforce to improve the long-run sustainability of Alberta's economy" (Alberta Ministry for Advanced Education and Technology 2009).

The context provided by the development of a knowledge platform focused on oil and gas with development, over time, of a rich fund of related knowledge in engineering technology, IT, capital management, structuring strategic alliances, and risk management strongly indicates a regional policy based on exploitation of the oil-and-gas-related knowledge platform as a basis for diversification. Closest to the oil and gas industry, Calgary firms now export geophysical knowledge for application globally. Other important examples include a wireless telecommunications industry forming the core of IT manufacturing (Langford, Wood, and Ross 2003), Nova Chemicals Corporation in polymers (Nova Chemicals 2015), and a global positioning systems industry (Langford, Wood, and Ross 2003). A specialized example is ATCO (2015), which operates frontier-worker housing and facilities and now has a global military service business. A recent example illustrating the reach of the knowledge base from the oil and gas platform is a digital X-ray company, IDC, that has been listed among Canada's fastest growing companies. Its core technology is in image-processing, which is important in the geophysics of reservoirs.

In support of a platform policy (Asheim, Cooke, and Martin 2008), the provincial government focus on added value is a useful component. The provincial focus on commercialization of products of research institutions may give too much emphasis to the input of analytic (science-based) knowledge (Asheim and Gertler 2005). It suggests insufficient attention to the synthetic (engineering-based) knowledge, which is richly represented in the technology and finance elements of the oil and gas knowledge platform and is the strong suit of a resource-based knowledge economy.

Concluding Remarks

Innovation in Calgary depends critically on two dimensions of human performance: creativity (talent) and entrepreneurship (including "intrapreneurship"). Nurturing the former is achieved through a coalition of agencies in the not-for-profit sector with the support of the for-profit sector. Coalition members share the interest in a multidimensional quality of life (from the opera to the motorcycle club) satisfying a wide variety of citizen interests. It is recognized by all that maintaining the economic health to attract and retain talent and protect against boom-bust cycles is essential. A central agency of coordination is the city government. However, the success or failure of entrepreneurship is largely a matter of attitudes in the private sector. Will this entrepreneurship favour rent-seeking innovation that simply redistributes wealth, or can it favour productive innovation (Baumol 1990) of the type seen in the spin-off industries?

As of the publication date of this analysis, Calgary is now experiencing the strains of an oil price collapse and displaying the lack of resilience inherent in diversity of talents that converge in support of a single global market. The opportunities created by the industries serving distinct markets that spin off the diverse knowledge accumulated in the oil and gas platform are long-term opportunities. They probably require more careful and active incubation than the present configurations of government and industry are providing. It is interesting to ask if there is an opportunity for a major initiative materially engaging all sectors, similar to initiatives leading to innovations in oil sands technology that created that industry.

Appendix: The Interviews: Some Methodological Notes

This examination of Calgary was undertaken based on questionnaire guidelines developed by the Innovation Systems Research Network (ISRN) national project for interviews with: firms (theme 1), creative talent (theme 2), and civic, cultural, and governmental organizations (theme 3). The instruments were edited to support semi-structured interviews of approximately one hour in length that could begin with open-ended questions. All interviews were conducted in Calgary between 2007 and 2009. Interviewers did probe to ensure coverage of the guidelines. The interviews (123) were transcribed and coded, tagging full phrases referring to particular issues. At the first level, this coding involved identifying statements responding to questions raised in the guidelines. Beyond this, the process involved tagging across the "questions," such as correlation of innovations and their associated knowledge factors, or the positive and negative concerns expressed by representatives of creative talent on Calgary as a place to pursue their careers in relation to alternative locations. The primary characteristics of innovation and the character of requisite knowledge inputs in all three for-profit, not-for-profit, and government sectors are summarized above. Similarly, the factors in expressed preferences of creative individuals for location in Calgary are reviewed.

Firms for interview were selected to achieve a distribution roughly matching the distribution of firms in major statistical categories. Once a potential emerging cluster was discovered, added emphasis was given to the advertising, multimedia group.

Theme 3 organizations were identified by initial interviews with leaders of the obvious major organizations, followed by some "snowballing."

In order to select interviewees representative of the "creative class," the qualitative method enabled identification going beyond usual statistical indicators such as employment category, educational credential, or earning level. Interviewees were selected by asking firm and organization senior officers to identify individuals, in or associated with the organization, whose contribution would be "difficult to replace." The term *creative* was avoided, since it tends to elicit responses limited to the subcategory of arts, graphic design, and writing. The suggested candidates' profiles were probed to eliminate those who were not easily substitutable only because they occupy organizational nodes.

Interviews with those identified (Langford et al. 2014) were examined, and twenty-eight categories of expressions characterizing the features of Calgary they described as attractors or negative features were isolated in the transcripts.

More methodological detail can be found in individual chapters of the three earlier volumes in this series devoted to each of the three interview themes.

Notes

1 The boundaries of the city-region correspond closely to the Statistics Canada definition of the Calgary census metropolitan area (CMA). A census metropolitan area is defined by Statistics Canada as a core city of over 100,000 and the surrounding communities, with a large fraction of the work force employed in the central city. The Calgary CMA includes Airdrie, Beiseker, Cochrane, and other areas of the Rocky View municipal district.
2 The research methodology used for the case study is described in more detail in the Appendix to this chapter.
3 A community may have industrial diversity where there is a low level of exploitation of overlapping knowledge, or it may have diversity (measured by conventional industrial categories) that involves industries sharing the utility of many types of knowledge in common. The latter is captured by the concept of related "variety."
4 LQ is defined as the ratio of a sector parameter to the value of that parameter for the CMA divided by the ratio of sector parameter to overall parameter in national statistics. It measures the intensity of localization of the parameter normalized to the national averaged ratio. The most commonly used parameter is employment.
5 The magnitude of the diagonal element in a knowledge-flow matrix may offer an interesting approach to mapping a cluster.
6 In order to select interviewees representative of that "class," recommendations from senor organization officers were combed for interviewees having substantial control over the direction, management, and quality of work, and who commonly employed abstract concepts as a primary vocational tool.
7 "Creative class is the shorthand I use to describe the roughly one-third of … workers who have the good fortune to be compensated monetarily for their creative output" (Florida 2005, 4).
8 Former Alberta premier Peter Lougheed may have been such an entrepreneur. The network he built may persist in the convergence described below.

References

Alberta Ministry for Advanced Education and Technology. 2009. *Advanced education and technology business plan, 2009–2012*. www.finance.alberta.ca/publications/Budget/budget2009/adved.pdf. Accessed 1 February 2016.

Asheim, B., P. Cooke, and R. Martin. 2008. "Clusters and regional development: Critical reflections and explorations." *Economic Geography* 84 (1): 109–12. http://dx.doi.org/10.1111/j.1944-8287.2008.tb00394.x.

Asheim, B., and M. Gertler. 2005. "The geography of innovation: Regional innovation systems." In *The Oxford handbook of innovation*, ed. Jan Fagerberg, David C. Mowery, and Richard R. Nelson, 291–317. Oxford : Oxford University Press.

ATCO. 2015. http://www.atco.com. Accessed 21 December 2015.

Baumol, W.J. 1990. "Entrepreneurship: Productive, unproductive, and destructive." *Journal of Political Economy* 98 (5): 893–921. http://dx.doi.org/10.1086/261712.

Bettencourt, L.M., J. Lobo, D. Helbing, C. Kuhnert, and G.B. West. 2007. "Growth, innovation, scaling, and the pace of life in cities." *Proceedings of the National Academy of Sciences* 104 (17): 7301–6. http://dx.doi.org/10.1073/pnas.0610172104.

Boschma, R.A. 1999. "The rise of clusters of innovative industries in Belgium during the industrial epoch." *Research Policy* 28 (8): 853–71. http://dx.doi.org/10.1016/S0048-7333(99)00026-8.

Calgary Economic Development. 2006. "A global energy leader energy: Sector profile." Calgary: Calgary Economic Development.

–. 2009. Calgary Economic Development, Calgary. http://calgaryeconomicdevelopment.com/.

Calgary Municipal Government. 2009. "Municipal development plan" and "Calgary transportation plan." http://www.calgary.ca/PDA/pd/Pages/Municipal-Development-Plan/Municipal-Development-Plan-MDP.aspx. Accessed 1 February 2016.

Callon, M. 1986. "Some elements of a sociology of translation: Domestication of the scallops and the fishermen of St Brieuc Bay." In *Power, action, and belief: A new sociology of knowledge*, ed. J. Law, 196–233. London: Routledge.

City of Calgary. 2007. "The Calgary plan: Municipal development plan."

Conference Board of Canada. 2009. "Metropolitan outlook spring 2009."

Cooke, P. 2007. "Regional innovation, entrepreneurship and talent systems." *International Journal of Entrepreneurship and Innovation Management* 7 (2–5): 117–29. http://dx.doi.org/10.1504/IJEIM.2007.012878.

Cooke, P., C. De Laurentis, F. Tödtling, and M. Trippl. 2007. *Regional knowledge economies: Markets, clusters and innovation – New horizons in regional science*. Cheltenham, UK: Edward Elgar Publishing. http://dx.doi.org/10.4337/9781847206930.

Feldman, M., and D. Audretsch. 1999. "Innovation in cities: Science-based diversity, specialization and localized competition." *European Economic Review* 43 (2): 409–29. http://dx.doi.org/10.1016/S0014-2921(98)00047-6.

Florida, R. 2005. *Cities and the creative class*. New York: Routledge.

Foran, M., and H. MacEwan Foran. 1982. "Calgary: Canada's frontier metropolis." Windsor, ON: Windsor Publications (Canada).

Frenken, K., F. Van Oort, and T. Verburg. 2007. "Related variety, unrelated variety and regional economic growth." *Regional Studies* 41 (5): 685–97. http://dx.doi.org/10.1080/00343400601120296.

Granovetter, M. 1983. "The strength of weak ties: A network theory revisited." *Sociological Theory* 1: 201–33. http://dx.doi.org/10.2307/202051.

imagineCalgary. 2006. "imagineCALGARY Plan for Long Range Urban Sustainability." City of Calgary.

Jacobs, J. 1961. *The death and life of great American Cities*. New York: Vintage Books.

Langford, C.H., B. Li, and C. Ryan. 2014. "Firms and their problems: Systemic innovation and related diversity in Calgary." In *Innovating in urban economies: Economic transformation in Canadian city-regions*, ed. David A. Wolfe, 151–72. Toronto: University of Toronto Press.

Langford, C.H., J.R. Wood, and T. Ross. 2003. "Origins and structure of the Calgary wireless cluster." In *Clusters old and new: The transition to a knowledge economy in Canada's regions*, ed. David. A. Wolfe, 161–86. Montreal and Kingston: McGill-Queen's University Press.

Latour, B. 1987. *Science in action: How to follow scientists and engineers through society*. Cambridge, MA: Harvard University Press.

–. 1988. *The Pasteurization of France*. Cambridge, MA: Harvard University Press.

Marsh, J. 2005. "Alberta's quiet revolution." In *Alberta formed: Alberta transformed*, ed. M. Payne, D. Weatherell, and C. Cavanaugh, 650–76. Edmonton and Calgary: University of Alberta Press and University of Calgary Press.

Miller, B., and A. Smart. 2011. "'Heart of the New West'? Oil and gas, rapid growth, and consequences for Calgary." In *Canadian urban regions*, ed. L. Bourne, T. Hutton, R. Scharmur, and J. Simmons, 269–90. Don Mills, ON: Oxford University Press.

Nova Chemicals. 2015. http://www.nova.com. Accessed 21 December 2015.

Ryan, C., B. Li, and C.H. Langford. 2014. "Exploring 'creative' talent in a natural resource–based centre: The case of Calgary." In *Seeking talent for creative cities*, ed. J.L. Grant, 178–98. Toronto: University of Toronto Press.

Spencer, G.M., T. Vinodrai, M.S. Gertler, and D.A. Wolfe. 2010. "Do clusters make a difference? Defining and assessing their economic performance." *Regional Studies* 44 (6): 697–715. http://dx.doi.org/10.1080/00343400903107736.

Statistics Canada. 2008. "National Symmetric Input-Output Tables: Aggregation Level L." 15-208-XCB. Ottawa: Statistics Canada. Accessed 21 December 2015.

Wolfe, D.A., ed. 2003. *Cluster old and new*. Montreal and Kingston: McGill-Queen's University Press.

–. 2009. *The geography of innovation: 21st century cities in Canada*. Ottawa: Conference Board of Canada.

PART III

Innovation and Growth in Medium-Sized Cities

7 Innovation in an Industrial City: Economic Transformation in Hamilton

PETER WARRIAN AND ALLISON BRAMWELL

Dramatic changes driven by globalization pose particular challenges for mid-sized industrial cities. The innovation required to drive economic competitiveness privileges large, dynamic, "global" city-regions with flows of "people, capital, and ideas" to support diverse and knowledge-intensive economic activities. Manufacturing cities are often dismissed as having experienced their "best before" dates and written off as sorry relics of a bygone industrial age (Gertler 2001; Bluestone and Harrison 1982). Although some deeply distressed cities may have passed the point of no return, others appear to be holding their own, stimulating important questions about why some industrial cities are more resilient than others to the shocks of economic change (McGahey and Vey 2008; Kodrzycki and Munoz 2009). A literature linking economic resilience and regional innovation identifies three core factors: knowledge-intensive specializations that build on the foundation of earlier industrial activities; evolving labour markets that drive innovation in these new activities; and institutional structures to facilitate knowledge transfer and strategic management of local assets (Storper 2010, 2013; Rodríguez-Pose 2013; Gertler 2001).

Research on the impact of economic change on industrial cities in the United States and Europe has not been matched in Canada. Numerous plant closures and the loss of over 300,000 manufacturing jobs in Ontario since 2004 have had a devastating effect on many workers and their families, yet we know little about how mid-sized Ontario cities with historic specializations in manufacturing such as Oshawa, Windsor, Sarnia, Kitchener, Cambridge, St Catharine's, London, and Hamilton have responded to the challenges of de-industrialization (Anastakis 2010). This chapter engages with the question of resilience in industrial cities through a detailed case study of Hamilton, Ontario, a city that has experienced its fair share of plant closures and job loss but that also demonstrates remarkable resilience and the ability to innovate. Drawing on Storper's (2010) framework that captures the interplay of industrial specialization, human capital, and institutions to explain different urban economic development trajectories, we find that specialization and human capital dimensions in Hamilton are evolving in important ways to support resilience and adaptation to economic change, but that the institutional dynamics considered critical to economic performance are not similarly keeping pace. Hamilton has a relatively diverse, knowledge-intensive economy and labour market based on steel manufacturing and health sciences, yet the disjuncture among its development-oriented networks has thus far precluded community-wide civic governance to facilitate local strategic planning.

This chapter traces three dimensions of Hamilton's transformation in detail.[1] First, we present an account of Hamilton's shift from domestic hub to global node in knowledge-intensive steel production, and how innovations in health sciences education have driven the development of diagnostic and other health services specializations. Second, we chart how the transfer of engineering knowledge and skills from the steel industry has applications to knowledge-intensive activities in health services and digital fabrication. Finally, we discuss civic governance dynamics that have failed to align local agendas, interests, and resources for strategic planning. This finding underscores the need for further refinement to theoretical assumptions about the role of these dynamics in local economic development.

Industrial Restructuring and Urban Resilience

Attention to the local dynamics shaping economic competitiveness and regional innovation is reflected in the preoccupation of economic geography and urban planning research with the interaction effects of economic specialization and human capital at the firm level, an empirical focus that captures economic growth in places well poised to benefit from the knowledge economy. Large, dynamic, and growing city-regions with diverse regional economies, concentrations of highly educated human capital, large stocks of investment capital, strong research institutions, and robust knowledge networks have the innovation infrastructure that allows them to weather economic shocks and benefit from shifts to knowledge-intensive economic activities.

In contrast, industrial cities and peripheral regions lacking the factor endowments required for new economy activities find themselves handicapped by specializations in mature manufacturing industries. These de-industrializing "Silicon Valleys of the second industrial revolution" like Detroit, Akron, Youngstown, and Buffalo are often lumped together and dismissed as having enjoyed their heydays as hotbeds of post-war economic growth but are now seen to be collapsing under the weight of current misfortunes and written off as "shrinking" Rust Belt cities (Bluestone and Harrison 1982).

As Storper and Manville (2006) observe, however, not all "old, cold, dense city-regions" in the industrial North have suffered the same fate; recent population and employment growth in some of these places is directly linked to shifts in regional economic geography and industrial activity. Mounting evidence that some cities that have managed comebacks from economic adversity has drawn attention to the economic *transformation* in "resilient" or "resurgent" cities (Christopherson, Michie, and Tyler 2010; McGahey and Vey 2008). For example, dividing restructuring Rust Belt cities that have manufacturing histories based on metals-based production into "stable," "struggling," and "devastated" categories, Hobor (2013) finds that while all have lost many of their manufacturing activities, "stable" cities have been able to shift specializations to new manufacturing industries by building on capacity in old ones. While still not "high-tech post-industrial production sites," these cities have numerous small, high-skilled manufacturers engaged in production for new high-tech markets, albeit lower on the value chain. Struggling and devastated cities remain locked into globally vulnerable auto and metals–based production. In all three categories of cities, hospitals and other health-care providers are dominant employers, calling into question the wisdom of economic transformation strategies based solely on "eds & meds" industries.

In this context, accounting for why some urban economies perform better than others has opened up rich opportunities for theory-building and comparative research, stimulating the development of analytical frameworks to capture variation in urban responses to economic change. While questions about the factors affecting the performance of city-regions have been framed largely in terms of the relative degree of specialization or diversity that characterizes their economic structure, other underlying factors exert a determining influence, and current research locates much of the explanation on how local institutions shape the *adaptive capacity* of regional economies. However, Storper observes that "the area of institutions is perhaps the most complex and least well-explored space" in the regional economic development puzzle (2010, 2036). Finding clues in the actor networks that "constitute the basic tissue of political life in a city-region" (2045), Storper echoes other current research focusing on the role of social networks and civic leadership. Growing theoretical interest in local agency focuses on how collaboration among civic leaders and social networks shapes the ability of cities to strategically mobilize regional assets and alter their economic growth trajectories (Safford 2009; Simmie and Wood 2002; Wolfe 2010).

In this analytical context, we examine how the dynamics of industrial transformation are unfolding in Hamilton, Ontario, Canada's leading industrial city and the ninth-largest city in the country, which is located in the geographic centre of a densely populated industrial region known as the Golden Horseshoe.[2] To situate the subsequent analysis, the following section provides a snapshot of the city, including recent evolutions in primary economic activities, human capital, and spatial dimensions.

"Hamilton's Dead. Or Is it?" Tracking Economic Transformation in an Industrial City[3]

Like many mid-sized industrial cities in the U.S. "Rust Belt" directly south of the border, steel and its related industries, from railways in the nineteenth century to auto parts in the twentieth and twenty-first centuries, have formed the backbone of Hamilton's economy. Although Hamilton's steel industry has demonstrated remarkable resilience, other manufacturing industries including textiles, agricultural equipment, tires, and major appliances have fared less well in the face of global competition. The sting of de-industrialization has accelerated since the early 1980s with the closure or relocation of numerous large firms, some of which were indigenous and dated back to the turn of the previous century, such as Firestone, International Harvester, Westinghouse, Proctor & Gamble, Life Savers, and Levi Strauss.[4] Hamilton lost 35,000 manufacturing jobs from 2003 to 2013, with over 11,000 in 2006 alone (Cole 2009).

A caricature of a de-industrializing city, Hamilton was described in 2009 as a "dazed and bloodied" fighter and a "city that fortune betrayed" (Cole 2009). However, like a proverbial underdog, recent developments suggest that predictions about the city's precipitous decline are premature. Hamilton is "taking stock of itself, its assets and its flaws," and "pushing itself to its feet and daring to think that some good might yet come of it all" (Cole 2009). Recently buoyed by its ranking as one of the top ten "business-friendly" mid-sized cities in North America by fDI Intelligence (Walls 2013), its transformation from "beleaguered to bountiful" is reflected in a low unemployment rate of 5.9 per cent, low commercial vacancy rates, and high numbers of construction permits (Ministry of Research and Innovation 2012). Hamilton appears to be charting stronger post-recession growth than many of its industrial counterparts in Southwestern Ontario, making its good-news story worthy of closer attention.

A quintessential "steel town," specialized in steel production and related heavy manufacturing in automotive and related industries, Hamilton also has a relatively diverse knowledge-intensive economy for a city of its size, suggesting that it is evolving into a post-industrial economy, building on its traditional configuration of industrial and human resources in the steel industry to develop new specializations in knowledge-intensive economic activities. Standard metrics indicate that between 2001 and 2006 Hamilton had seven industry clusters, of which three (food, steel, and automotive) are primary manufacturing industries and, if grouped together with logistics, accounted for more than twelve times as many jobs as the biomedical sector, indicating that it continues to have an unusually high proportion of its employment based in primary manufacturing (table 7.1). While Hamilton's industrial identity will continue to be associated with steel for the foreseeable future, it will be less for domestic steel production and more for its expanding capacity in knowledge-intensive steel manufacturing and its growing reputation as a knowledge hub in the global steel industry.

At the same time, Hamilton is well known for the strength of its regional health care sector; Hamilton Health Sciences has emerged as the largest single employer in the community, and a related medical diagnostics sector has developed as a result of research linkages with local research and teaching hospitals. Although this dual specialization suggests a somewhat bipolar economic geography of innovation with steel, industrial suppliers, and manufacturers spatially concentrated in Hamilton East, and Hamilton Health Sciences, McMaster University, and government laboratories in Hamilton West, as will be discussed later, there is in fact substantial synthetic cross-sector activity between the two.

With a labour market reflecting a more diverse and nuanced picture of its economy and population than its traditional steel town label would suggest, human capital in Hamilton has similarly evolved. With

Table 7.1. Clusters and employment, Hamilton 2001–6

Cluster	No. labour force	Labour force LQ* (%)	Industry LQs* > 1 (%)	Growth 2001–6 (%)
Food	11,760	1.16	66.7	1.4
Steel	18,880	2.67	83.3	−16.3
Automotive	14,860	1.54	76.9	−8.6
Biomedical	3,490	1.06	50.0	14.1
Finance	24,180	1.07	56.3	5.4
Logistics	21,365	1.20	65.4	10.2

* Location Quotient

Source: Spencer and Vinodrai (2009)

higher-than-average levels of income existing alongside lower-than-average levels, the distribution of educational attainment is highly correlated with the industrial structure of the local economy.

Because historically Hamilton has been seen as a blue-collar, lunch-bucket town reliant on unionized, skilled, and low-skilled manufacturing jobs, major losses of these types of jobs has been correlated with high levels of poverty and increasing numbers of the working poor reliant on precarious employment in the city. This reflects the impact of downsizing of traditional manufacturing in the past decade. Hamilton's population change from 2001 to 2006 lagged behind the national average (Spencer and Vinodrai 2009). However, currently at 5.7 per cent, unemployment in Hamilton is low in comparison to that of other restructuring cities like Windsor, which hovered between 9 and 10 per cent in the first quarter of 2013, and St Catharines at 7.3 per cent.[5] A large proportion of the local labour market is still employed in the manufacturing and transportation and logistics sectors, and Hamilton's list of top ten employers includes four large manufacturing companies centred on steel and related industries.[6]

At the same time, Hamilton exceeds the national average in percentage of PhDs in the population, and the number of people in "creative" occupations is slightly higher than average for other Canadian cities of its size.[7] An economy whose economic pillars are largely in steel and health sciences will inevitably have a more polarized distribution of educational achievements. However, the city has a lower level of science and technology occupations and slightly fewer "bohemians" than other Canadian cities of its size, at least currently resident in the city, but a significantly larger proportion of foreign-born residents, 24.4 per cent versus 19.8 per cent (Spencer and Vinodrai 2009).

Among the important spatial changes evident in Hamilton has been its gradual merger with the economy of Metropolitan Toronto. The most obvious expression is the amendment of political and policy language from that of the Greater Toronto Area (GTA) to the Greater Toronto and Hamilton Area. The new regional transportation plan now incorporates this in both policy and physical infrastructure planning, with boundaries extending as far as Waterloo. Transportation improvements are intended to facilitate movement of talent and skills throughout the broader regional economy to which Hamilton belongs. Many young professionals working in the city of Toronto now look to Burlington and Hamilton to find affordable housing. In return, faculty, students, and researchers regularly commute the other way, with direct Metrolinx connections between downtown Toronto and McMaster University.

In summary, as a city in the midst of fundamental industrial transformation Hamilton has a complex political economy with contradictory and complementary dynamics simultaneously at play. It appears to have the economic diversity and human capital to support the innovation required for transformation to high-value and knowledge-intensive activities. However, it may lack the institutional infrastructures to shape strategic planning for the region. Drawing on Storper's (2010) framework, the remainder of this chapter examines Hamilton's economic transformation, focusing on a detailed discussion of the interplay of specialization, human capital, and institutions in this industrial city.

Dual Specialization in Hamilton: Steel and "Meds"

Urban economies evolve over long periods of time in a path-dependent manner, with multiple dynamics intersecting to shape the scope and trajectory of future development. A key function of local innovation systems is to provide windows on relevant knowledge frontiers, supported by local organizations and institutions to develop the capacity to absorb and combine both internal and external knowledge into new practical and commercial forms (Martin and Simmie 2008; Wolfe 2009). As is evident in the Hamilton case, new pathways do not emerge in a vacuum, but rather in the context of existing technological and industrial structures and institutional arrangements.

Although not on the playlist of most economic innovation researchers, the city of Hamilton and its economy are undergoing a fundamental transformation to a post-industrial economy. This traditional "steel town" previously dominated by the Steel Company of Canada (Stelco) has become an important hub of the global steel industry, merging with broader manufacturing processes and integrating digital technologies. Not by accident, however, recent industrial evolutions have been built on two primary innovations generated over the past thirty years, each which has had global impacts. Invented in the 1980s, the Stelco Coil Box solved a fundamental quality and energy-consumption problem for the Japanese-led revolution in automotive steel manufacturing, and is now used as the global industry standard. Evidence-based medicine emerged out of the McMaster medical school in the 1970s, which departed from the conventional approach in other medical schools to build its research and educational models around clinical practice rather than conventional bioscience. Evidence-based medicine has since become the global standard for health policy and management of health systems. Both originating in Hamilton, these innovations were based on the scale and configuration of local resources.

Of particular relevance, however, is the emerging synthesis between the two. Although the Hamilton economy appears to be spatially polarized between steel, industrial suppliers, and manufacturers in Hamilton East, and McMaster University, Hamilton Health Sciences, and government laboratories in Hamilton West, there is more cross-sector and synthesis than the caricature would suggest, and there are multiple – if somewhat unconventional – interactions between these two pillars of the "new" Hamilton economy. For example, the creation of the new Hamilton Health Sciences complex drew heavily on the expertise and resources in the East End; steel executives with critical expertise in managing large capital intense, multi-locational, highly unionized enterprises, continue to be key leaders on the Board of Directors of Hamilton Health Sciences. The generous benefit plans of the United Steelworkers and other labour contracts have provided funding streams to finance new health innovation firms in the biomedical cluster emerging around Hamilton Health Sciences. Ironically, it is these often-criticized high-cost union benefit plans that have made up for the shortcomings of the venture capital market in Hamilton.

On another dimension, Hamilton's engineers and physicians share epistemology – their fundamental orientation is to tacit knowledge and communities of practice, the drivers of innovation for Hamilton's two dominant economic sectors. In a classic case of synthetic knowledge transfer, these industries "learn by doing" and are based on the application of pre-existing primary knowledge or the development of technology derived from international networks or "global pipelines." While there have been occasional breakthroughs like the Stelco Coil Box and evidence-based medicine, the ongoing story is incremental progress through process improvement and clinical practice. However, while emerging strengths in health-care and health sciences are a critical part of the economic story in Hamilton, here we focus on a more detailed discussion of recent developments in the steel industry.

The New Global Steel Industry

Known as Canada's industrial city for over a century, the dominant narrative in Hamilton remains that of steel. Within the time frame of this study, the Canadian steel industry has been fundamentally changed from independent, Canadian-owned firms into local facilities of the new global steel companies; Stelco was sold to US Steel, Dofasco was sold to Arcelor Mittal, and Algoma Steel was sold to Essar, all in the mid-2000s.

Three phenomena are at the heart of the current phase of globalization in the steel industry. First, the internationalization of ownership structures is most evident in primary steel production, where there has been a change of ownership from domestic control to international control in every steel-producing company (with one minor exception). A direct consequence of the transformation of ownership structures is significantly increased international flows of capital, technology, managerial norms, and talent. While attention most often focuses on capital and technology, the adoption of international managerial norms and the international flows of talent may have the most far-reaching impact. These international managerial norms include productivity benchmarking, new approaches to work organization, and distinct strategies in training and human resources development (O'Grady and Warrian 2011). Shifts in management systems and benchmarking have become critical elements in the local/non-local interaction of senior management of Hamilton's leading economic sector. They also mark a decisive shift away from the traditional indigenous model of innovation that characterized the Stelco era.

The second phenomenon that defines globalization is the accelerated integration of international markets. The signature development that marks this integration is a sharp increase in both exports and imports of steel products. Hamilton steel now overwhelmingly produces for the integrated NAFTA steel market (Warrian 2010). Third, the technology intensiveness of production and design equipment – especially the application of information technologies to product and design processes – has increased both the number of technicians and technologists employed in the steel sector and their share in the sector's workforce. A further consequence of the increased application of information technologies to production processes has been an increased need for skilled tradespersons with technology skills.

At the same time, the location of these facilities in global steel networks is critical for Hamilton's economic future. The evolution of the steel industry in Hamilton can be traced through the fate of Stelco and Dofasco, since the late nineteenth century, Hamilton's two dominant steel firms. Taken over by US Steel, production rose at Stelco (Hilton Works) in 2007 and 2008, but the number of product lines was significantly reduced, and by the downturn of 2008–9 it became clear that the former Stelco facilities had become second-tier, standby facilities as US Steel concentrated its production and resources at its primary facilities in Fairfield, Alabama, Mon Valley, Pennsylvania, and Gary, Indiana. Research and development was eliminated in Hamilton and concentrated at US Steel's Research and Technology Center in Munhall, Pennsylvania, leaving the former Stelco Hilton steel facilities to more resemble the classic U.S. branch plant operation than the former leader of the Canadian steel industry. In its final days, it was relegated to drawing slabs from the Lake Erie Works, before its closure was announced in 2014, marking the end of primary steelmaking at the Hamilton Works (Warrian 2010).

Dofasco displaced Stelco as the Canadian industry leader in the 1990s with a major marketing and rebranding campaign under the banner of Solutions in Steel. Their intellectual property strategy was traded knowledge in the form of the licensing of new metallurgical technologies from Japan and Europe, with a commercial focus on local application development in the Southern Ontario automotive industry. Dofasco successfully pursued this strategy for a decade and became the most profitably integrated steel company in North America, and its CEO John Mayberry, the first Canadian chair of the American Iron and Steel Institute. Unlike the US Steel takeover of Stelco, since its acquisition by Arcelor Mittal, Dofasco has been used as a strategic asset; key local engineering talent has been circulated around the world to other

Arcelor centres, and international talent has been recruited to Hamilton (Warrian 2010; Warrian and Mulhern 2003, 2005).

As can be seen in the differing trajectories of Dofasco and Stelco, not only were they subject to different corporate strategies, they also learned differently. Absorptive capacity, or the ability to utilize externally held knowledge, is path dependent. Building on prior investments and developing cumulatively, it depends on the organization's ability to share knowledge and communicate internally. In the halcyon days of the steel industry, university research centres were marginal players in steel research and technology development. However, the university research infrastructure may be getting a second chance. The movement of the Canadian government's Metal Technology Laboratory (CANMET) to Hamilton is a critically important shift in the intellectual landscape of Hamilton.

Manufacturing, Global Supply Chains, and the De-localization of Industry

Closely related to the globalization of the steel industry is the increasing integration of steel and manufacturing in the modern economy, making the links between the steel industry and other local manufacturing in Hamilton another important locational theme. Prime movers in shifting the boundaries of the local industrial economy and a major source of interaction between local and non-local actors, global supply chains have transformed Ontario's manufacturing economy. These changing manufacturing dynamics are critical to understanding how knowledge networks operate in Hamilton (Birnbaum et al. 2010). As Hamilton-based industries have become integrated with these supply chains, a process has emerged that can best be described as "de-localization."

Herrigel (2010) suggests that, a firm's position and functioning within global supply chains turn on its learning capabilities, indicating that knowledge networks are vital to the future of manufacturing. Manufacturing supply chains and specifically the relationships between original equipment manufacturers (OEMs) and their suppliers have undergone substantial evolution. The classic industrial supply chain was marked by arm's-length market relationships, which characterized most Hamilton manufacturing companies at the height of the post-war steel industry and their association with General Motors in its heyday. The job of the supplier firm was simply to meet contract requirements for specified parts and components. This was the dominant form of local and regional manufacturing for most of the post-war period.

The Japanese auto manufacturing revolution brought Toyotaism – an integrated though captive supplier relationship involving joint development of design, manufacturing, and quality functions shared between OEM and supplier. This model now dominates the auto industry and is copied by other major manufacturing OEMs and defines the environment in which Hamilton's remaining auto parts manufacturers now function. Contract manufacturing takes place at the other end of the spectrum, where design and manufacturing are completely separate, and in which the supplier takes on the manufacturing and assembly functions as agreed with the OEM. Relational contracting is a more integrated form of production relationship in which the OEM and supplier form long-term relationships and plan future developments. This strategic model of modularization is pursued by Magna, an indigenous Canadian auto parts firm and global purchaser of over 3 million tons of steel.

Recent research in industrial studies identifies sustained contingent collaborative relations as the norm for manufacturing supply chains in which OEMs and suppliers have close and mutually dependent relations around design, quality, and manufacturing. Both labour under the unrelenting pressure of continuous cost-reduction pressures and the need to constantly innovate. It is towards this norm that Hamilton companies and its educational institutions, like Mohawk College, are adapting.

In summary, Cooke (2005, 2007) has argued that for biotech and optics, disaggregation of manufacturing means that asymmetric knowledge networks will become normative, and innovation will be driven from multiple local sources. The global R&D centre may be fading from the corporate architecture of twenty-first-century manufacturing, and the steel fabrication-architecture case described here is a clear example.

Three large inter-sectoral knowledge transfer themes emerge in the Hamilton economy, all of which continue to evolve. First, the steel mills are importing Japanese (kaizen) techniques and processes from the auto industry to rebalance their production flows and scheduling from batch to continuous flow, in order to better align with their leading-edge customers in steel-consuming industries. This is a fundamental challenge to traditional steel industry managerial norms in production processes, managerial control, job structures, and the established hierarchy of skills. Second, there is an important shift underway in the skills profile of the steel mills which are following other manufacturing industries in pursuing a thickening of the engineering labour market. The rising trend is to merge the boundaries between traditional skilled trades and engineering technologists. At the same time, the impact of ICT on steel manufacturing and logistics is pushing traditional steel engineering further out onto the information technology learning curve. Third, the health sciences and health services sectors are learning from steel. Managerial skills from steel management have directly affected health-system management in Hamilton in governance, operations, and human resources. In a related observation, innovation in health-service firms is being enabled by the financial flows from industrial unionized benefit plans as well of the availability of workers' bodies and those of their families to health practitioners and researchers. This is a phenomenon unique to Hamilton where, beyond the well-identified transfer of skills and talent from old economy to new economy enterprises, old economy labour market institutions have a major impact on the demand side for innovative new economy firms.

Adaptable Human Capital in Hamilton: Skills Transfer from Steel to Digital Fabrication

Clearly, highly skilled and educated talent looms large in the recent industrial evolution of Hamilton's economy where local talent pools – and the attraction and retention strategies to maintain them – are characterized by diversity and depth, a pattern that has recently been supplemented by Hamilton's integration into the larger labour market of the GTA. Managers and entrepreneurs interviewed consistently remarked that the Hamilton labour market is characterized by significant breadth and depth; whatever level of skill and capacity is needed, it can be met in the local labour market. This holds equally true for industrial labour and trades skills, and for technicians, technologists, and engineers. It also applies to nurses, health sciences technicians, physicians, and other health-care professionals. Whatever may be required to fuel growth in innovative ventures and firms, Hamilton is seen as having all the labour inputs required.

Respondents overwhelmingly identified the attraction and retention of talent in Hamilton in terms of quality of place – low-cost, good-quality housing stock and the city being a good place to raise a family. Secondary reasons were sometimes identified, such as the presence of industrial and research organizations for engineers and health scientists. Ethnicity and immigration are also important in attracting and retaining engineering and scientific talent through family or friendship networks. Hamilton is ranked third after Toronto and Vancouver in immigration and the ethnic diversity of the population. This is a critical factor in the ongoing attraction and replenishment of the Hamilton economy in industrial trades, engineering, health, and scientific talent. However, this orientation is much less imbedded in educational, business, and civic leaders' minds than the housing and family narrative.

The traditional sources of talent attraction and retention in Hamilton were the industrial companies and their surrounding working-class communities. The local industrial base of Hamilton generated one of the largest engineering labour markets in the country. Ironically, to this day, Hamilton has more engineers than Waterloo, the technology capital of the country. The engineering aspect of the immigration story is particularly important in such an industrial city. The thickening of labour markets for engineers, technicians, and technologists, and the need for post-secondary institutions to train more engineering and science talent is well established. However, surveys of industrial establishments and employers present a more nuanced view of the engineering labour market.

Talent Attraction and Retention in Steel

Workers who are over fifty – especially workers in the skilled trades – have acquired knowledge about production and the maintenance of machinery and equipment that is typically undocumented. Transferring this tacit knowledge smoothly and efficiently to new hires is important for maintaining high levels of effective utilization of machinery and equipment. Indeed, failure to transfer tacit skills and knowledge efficiently could jeopardize the high steel productivity levels that were achieved in this decade.

Given that access to capital and to new technology depends on meeting international benchmarking standards, it is strategically important that managers of Canadian steel facilities meet the knowledge transfer challenge. It is noteworthy that one senior executive in the industry reported that 10 per cent of the company's workforce was now engaged in documenting work processes for knowledge transfer.

There are two distinct mismatches between the demand for persons with technology skills and the supply for steel and manufacturing in locations like the Hamilton regional economy. The first pertains to recent graduates from college technology programs. Efficient integration of recent graduates into jobs for which they have been trained requires bridging programs. Three types of programs are relevant: co-op placements, which are concurrent with college training; internships, which follow college training; and specialized programs, which blend industry-specific training with paid or unpaid placements. The Canadian Steel Trade and Employment Congress, a joint labour-management training organization, has started an innovative apprenticeship consortium in Hamilton to bridge the gap between company needs and students' desire to gain experience while in the classroom component of their apprenticeship training, as well as ameliorating employer costs and risks. The program has 150 apprentices in training and placement (O'Grady and Warrian 2011).

Employers who participate in such programs almost invariably report that they provide a valuable screening opportunity and also increase the value-added contribution of these individuals when they are subsequently hired. Students who participate in these programs express greater satisfaction with their training and report greater ability to obtain work in the technical field for which they were trained. As a consequence, the most motivated technology students gravitate to programs that offer experience-based components.

The second aspect of the mismatch between the supply and demand for persons with technology skills pertains to internationally trained professionals. This is particularly important in a city like Hamilton, which is third in the country in scale of immigration. In the main, these individuals have university-level training in engineering. In recent years, approximately 4,000 persons have immigrated to Canada with university-level qualifications in engineering and an intention to work in a technical field. Data from engineering regulators indicate that only a minority will pursue professional licensure and find employment as engineers. By far the majority will seek jobs as technologists. The Canadian labour market has been notably inefficient in integrating these internationally trained professionals.

As information technologies are linked directly to every aspect of production, the line between the technology skills of technicians and technologists and the trade skills of a skilled tradespersons are becoming blurred. Some steel companies are addressing this evolution of skill requirements by raising the training requirements for apprentices. Consequently, in some companies, apprentices are required to have at least some college training in technology in addition to their regular trades training. Indeed, one company requires successful completion of two years of training in a community college as a technician before a worker is hired into an apprenticeship.

Mobility and Creativity: The Rise of Digital Manufacturing

Hamilton draws upon the broader talent base in the GTA to boost its transition to the new economy. Two cases of the emergence of digital manufacturing arose during the interviews, one artisanal, the other scientific. For example, with declines in Ontario automotive and general manufacturing, higher-value-added products have been identified as a survival strategy for the steel industry (Warrian 2010). Critical shifts are underway in the skills composition of the fabricating companies, and the traditional knowledge base of craftsman welders and fitters are being displaced by CAD/CAM and BIM software systems. However, at the design-fabrication interface, the critical visualization skills of the traditional craftspeople is still required in order to formulate how a structure goes together. Steel manufacturers have increasingly teamed with graphics design studios in Toronto to help produce the next generation of digital fabrication. By combining traditional craft skills with graphic design skills, steel fabricators are seeking to position themselves as owning and controlling the DNA of building structures for the future.

An illustrative case is the conjoining of a traditional steel fabricator's competencies with new media and design talent in the Toronto economy. Both were skills-based, involving the attraction and retention of talent. The steel fabricator faced a skills crisis: with a rapidly aging traditional base of welder-fitters, it was a special challenge to replace the key tradespeople who had the capacity to visualize the assembly of steel structures. Because few replacements were available in the local economy, firms recruited designers from Toronto. The key recruit was a Hamilton-born steel sculptor with a background in design, new media, and welding who ran his own graphics design company. In itself, this was an interesting transfer of knowledge and skill from the Hamilton arts sector to manufacturing. To this were added new media grads from the Ontario College of Art and Design and Sheridan College. Interestingly, they did not seek architectural students. The fabricator bought the design house, a trend followed by several of their competitors. This unusual combination of talents has become the technical anchor for an emerging $500 million digital manufacturing and fabrication company in Hamilton, reflecting an increasing convergence between Hamilton steel manufacturing and the Toronto-based new media and design industries. It is also a story of the merger of the Hamilton economy into the larger city-region of the GTA. However, it also signifies a merger of two types of workers, traditional industrial skilled trades with a new media design talent and its synthesis into a new form of digital manufacturing.

A second example is based more on scientific occupations. The federal CANMET Materials Technology Laboratory's state-of-the-art research facility moved from Ottawa to Hamilton and opened in 2011. The CANMET facility is a major enhancement for steel manufacturing capacities in the Hamilton and regional economies. The arrival and commissioning of world-class equipment allows researchers and technical staff to develop and test high-performance metals and materials for use in the automotive, pipelines, and energy-production industries (CANMET 2011). For instance, it is being used by the Innovative Casting and Advanced Materials Processing research team to perform the first magnesium melts in Hamilton. Its advanced sheet-metal-forming press can simulate real-world manufacturing situations, for study of how different materials and alloys behave under a variety of metal-forming conditions. Researchers can now carry out computer simulations based on their theoretical models and record the actual motions and forces at work during metal-forming. The simulation laboratory is able to process test samples taken from ingots, melts, and cast components and perform metallurgical simulations, including melting, melt treatment, solidification, and heat treatment for specialized alloys (CANMET 2011). These represent a major importation of technical talent and applied research capabilities that did not previously exist in Hamilton and are a major contributor to the rebirth of advanced manufacturing in the city and region. Taken as a whole, the CANMET facility is a platform for steel manufacturing to migrate towards the digital, post-industrial economy.

In summary, there is dynamic interplay between industrial specializations and human capital dimensions in Hamilton that continues to enable and facilitate economic transformation. Cross-sector and synthetic knowledge transfer across and between mature steel manufacturing and knowledge-intensive health sciences and digital fabrication sectors is facilitated largely by human capital and the large numbers of highly trained and educated engineers, technicians, and skilled trades people with transferable skills applicable to a wide range of industrial activities. In this context, publicly funded educational institutions have become critical nodes providing knowledge infrastructure and human capital, as traditional sources of talent in skilled trades have declined. The definition of infrastructure clearly includes public laboratories and educational institutions, but it should also include programs and institutions facilitating immigration. Immigration has developed as an important pipeline for technical talent at the trades, engineering and scientific levels. McMaster University and the CANMET labs are additional attractors. At the industrial end of the spectrum, the community colleges have taken over virtually all of the responsibility for training apprentices. Most firms interviewed suggest that the regional talent pool is excellent and that this is due to the presence of good universities and colleges. The most important contribution of universities to industry is producing a highly talented workforce, and they are especially supportive of co-op programs.

Fragile Institutions in Hamilton: Misaligned Networks and the Politics of Coalition-Building

A third pillar that interacts with industrial specialization and human capital to facilitate industrial adaptation consists of local formal and informal institutions (Storper 2010, 2013; Rodríguez-Pose 2013; Wolfe 2010). Recent theories of urban politics and governance focus on how interactions between state and societal actors shape governance outcomes at the city-region level, arguing that some cities are more successful than others because they are able to collectively make choices about how social and economic processes should unfold (Clarke and Gaile 1998; DiGaetano and Strom 2003; Savitch and Kantor 2002; Bradford and Bramwell 2014). Formal and informal institutional arrangements support stable governing coalitions that "bridge state and market, city hall and civic leaders, and take on various forms under different economic and policy conditions" (Giloth 2004, 16). A feasible common agenda, boundary-spanning civic leadership, and linkages among political leaders and senior municipal officials are seen to be essential ingredients that underpin the formation and durability of stable urban development coalitions.

However, while cross-boundary collaboration is positively correlated with economic transformation, it is by no means assured. Conflict over the strategic direction of urban growth is as likely – if not more so – than cooperation, and the diffuse linkages and relational nature of power among public, private, and community actors in urban regions makes stable governing coalitions challenging to build and sustain (Clarke and Gaile 1998; Clarke 2004; Stone 1989, 2005). Much of the literature on urban governance emphasizes the role of social networks in coalition-building and how societal interests interact within communities to shape and influence local political agendas (Pierre 2011; Safford 2009). Different interests organize around different developmental agendas, and, given "contending views within cities about the purpose and goals of the city's policies," conflict over local development discourses will be more likely than consensus, resulting in "governance gaps" that inhibit effective strategic problem-solving in the face of complex economic and social change (Pierre 2011).

On this institutional dimension, it is less clear that Hamilton has the civic infrastructure to take it where it needs to go. Numerous networks representing multiple social, cultural, economic, and environmental interests are active in the community. Research reveals at least seven different identifiable constituent networks in the community, operating at varying degrees of formality, but each aligned around distinctive objectives and discourses.[8] However, there appear to be few sustained linkages among them, a disjuncture that appears to have precluded community-wide strategic planning. As theories of urban governance would predict, the lack of overlap between social and economic networks in Hamilton is not particularly surprising (Pierre 2011). What is somewhat unusual, however, is the apparent disconnect *within* the business community over the future economic growth trajectory of the city.

Often wistfully compared to Waterloo with its robust civic associations supporting regional strategic planning (see Vinodrai, this volume), Hamilton has specialization and human capital in knowledge-intensive industries, but lacks supportive civic governance institutions. Respondents emphasized the fragmented nature of the community and the fact that local actors tend to operate in isolation rather than engaging with community development: "In Hamilton it has been very fragmented. The university has functioned on its own. Mohawk has functioned on its own. Industries have suffered on their own. The education system operates on its own. The city ... typically operated on its own ... In three or four different pieces where you have powerful committees and powerful groups which have responsibility for certain parts of the city or certain aspects of the city. They don't interfere with each other and they don't align with each other about anything, either ... So it's been, in my opinion, a very fragmented city" (confidential interview).

Fragmentation and misalignment among the numerous networks operating in Hamilton is evident in interactions between and within social and economic development networks. Interviews suggest that "Hamilton is quite well organized in terms of community development" but lacks a similar voice for strategic economic development (confidential interview). Rather than between social and economic development agendas, conflict over the future of economic development in the city plays out in competing agendas – or "two camps" – between those who emphasize Hamilton's traditional industrial manufacturing economy and those who seek to encourage innovation and the transition to knowledge-intensive forms of economic activity (confidential interview).

What follows is a brief description of the three most influential and visible networks in Hamilton, one focused on social service delivery, and the other two on economic development, followed by a more detailed examination of the successful formation but subsequent failure to sustain a broad, community-wide coalition for inclusive local strategic planning, the Jobs Prosperity Collaborative (JPC). These findings suggest that networks in Hamilton may not be as politically fragmented as some might think, but are also not sufficiently robust to sustain a cross-boundary network that spans social equity and economic growth objectives for inclusive strategic planning.

The Hamilton Roundtable for Poverty Reduction (HRPR) is a particularly successful example of a multi-stakeholder equity-focused development network that provides a regular forum for social welfare organizations to share information, discuss ideas, coordinate services, and engage in policy advocacy. Including large not-for-profit charitable organizations and service providers such as the United Way and the YMCA, as well as local representatives of all three levels of government and most other local service providers, the HRPR provides a strategic focus for coordinating poverty reduction across the city.

Driven by senior municipal staff, with political commitment from two successive mayors, and core funding for the executive director's salary from the municipal government, the City of Hamilton plays a critically important role as a "convener and partner" in the HRPR, demonstrating strong evidence of policy activism in areas typically outside municipal jurisdiction. The HRPR has also benefited from sustained influential civic leadership and high levels of trust and social capital.[9] Not only has the HRPR model been replicated in several other communities, it also acts a policy forum to advocate for a province-wide anti-poverty strategy (Weaver and Makhoul 2009). However, despite heavy initial involvement in the JPC, there appear to be few other linkages between social and economic development discourses in Hamilton.

Like chambers of commerce everywhere, the Hamilton Chamber of Commerce is a membership-based organization whose basic mandate is to represent the interests of local businesses, regardless of size or economic sector. The dominant economic development narrative advanced by the chamber tends to promote the interests of firms in manufacturing, transportation, and logistics sectors, rather than of firms in technology-based sectors, and to support greenfield and brownfield development in order to increase the amount of warehousing and serviced employment lands within the City of Hamilton, much of which is spatially concentrated around the Hamilton airport.

In recent years the chamber has spearheaded and hosted three Hamilton economic summits, one-day meetings to bring sector leaders together to discuss the future trajectory of economic growth in Hamilton. These meetings were initially broadly inclusive of the local community and were well attended by civic leaders from all sectors of the economy as well as local educational institutions, social service agencies, arts and culture organizations, and perhaps most importantly, local politicians and senior municipal staff. Despite an initially broad agenda, however, subsequent meetings have tended to emphasize traditional urban economic development issues such as firm attraction, stadium-building, and business opportunities arising from the 2015 Pan Am games, rather than facilitating the transition to knowledge-intensive economic activities and sustainable economic development.

Although social and economic development networks like the HRPR and the chamber of commerce are active in Hamilton, it is not clear who represents the innovation agenda in the city. There is a robust public research and educational infrastructure, much of which is attributable to the increasing activism and engagement of McMaster University with the local economic community over the past ten years. For example, located on the site of a former appliance manufacturing plant, the university, with the support of all three levels of government, has renovated this former industrial space to develop the McMaster Innovation Park (MIP) which houses research labs and spin-off incubators in materials manufacturing and biosciences. In addition, the provincial government, through the Ministry of Research and Innovation pledged $10 million and the City of Hamilton $5 million to help relocate the federal CANMET Material Technology Laboratory, Canada's principal national lab for metals research to the MIP.[10]

However, there is no formal civic association to integrate and advocate for the "innovation agenda" in Hamilton, and at the time of this research, public discussion of innovation-led economic growth was conspicuous by its absence in the city. When asked about the main actors and activities driving technology-based economic development, few respondents identified relevant actors and institutions such as McMaster University, Hamilton Health Sciences, or the Golden Horseshoe Biosciences Network.[11] One respondent observed, "There's a huge defensiveness in Hamilton in certain quarters. If you don't phrase it right you're walking on eggshells. If there's any tone in your voice about lost manufacturing, old economy, defunct day-is-done, it's over ... the gloves come off ... So framing a conversation within the creative age, within innovation, new products, streamline, globalism, that conversation is taking some time to get there" (confidential interview).

Because of these tensions, many business people were reported as choosing not to participate in local economic development activities and instead to prefer closed, informal networks that operate "under the radar" because "they don't feel understood or respected" (confidential interview). One respondent referred to an emerging informal network of entrepreneurs who have "as big or bigger impact on investments and job growth here as formal networks" and that "a lot of the stuff that happens is quietly done by fifty or sixty people, and it isn't the usual old guard industrialist third-generation money, it is a new breed of both social entrepreneurs and private sectors entrepreneurs" (confidential interview).

Crossing Boundaries? The Short Life of the Jobs Prosperity Collaborative

Against this backdrop, the formation of Jobs Prosperity stands out as an important, if failed, exercise in community-building. Despite perceptions of Hamilton as a socially and politically divided city that has difficulty establishing consensus on city-wide priorities, there is an emerging sense that civic engagement in the city has improved and that collaboration is starting to take shape after a long period of conflict and fragmentation.[12] When asked about key actors and institutions supporting local collaboration, every interview respondent mentioned the Jobs Prosperity Collaborative and emphasized its potential to bring "a real breath of hope" to a "very fragmented city" by facilitating alignment of different community agendas and discourses (confidential interview). As one respondent put it, "People in successful communities ... get aligned about what they are doing and what they are aiming to do ... Alignment is really about having a big enough purpose that the whole community can embrace, and leadership that keeps that purpose in the front of everybody ... it's about tearing down the silos, getting a common direction that we can all be supportive of. So if you get the community all heading down that same road it's much easier to get things done" (confidential interview).

Evolving out of the Hamilton Civic Coalition, an earlier attempt to establish a forum for community-wide collaboration, the JPC was launched in 2008 with funding from the Ontario Ministry of Training, Colleges, and Universities and the City of Hamilton as a broad multi-stakeholder network aligned with the common goal of job creation in Hamilton.[13] Bringing together civic leaders representing a wide range of community interests to discuss issues such as economic development, community revitalization, quality of life, environmental and cultural issues, and support for job creation, the JPC enjoyed strong civic and political leadership, as well as direct and formal linkages with the City of Hamilton.

Architects of the JPC learned valuable lessons about attracting and sustaining community engagement from its precursor, the Hamilton Civic Coalition, one of which was the importance of building a feasible agenda on which all participants could agree (Mossberger and Stoker 2001). To avoid disabling political conflict, the focus of the JPC was structured around the discourse of job creation, which was seen as a "strategic focus that everyone could understand and buy in to" (confidential interview). The JPC also featured an organizational structure to facilitate inclusive participation and minimize conflict by providing the hub through which different social, economic, and political interests could interact and intersect without having to directly confront one another. Supplying the institutional space to facilitate ongoing dialogue, the JPC consisted of seven working groups, each focusing on a different priority area.

In this way, the JPC was seen by many respondents to fill the economic development governance gap in Hamilton, underscoring the close relationships between city politicians, senior staff, and civic leaders to improve the connection between the community and the city's economic development efforts. The well-known local anti-poverty activist and entrepreneur Mark Chamberlain worked closely with Mayor Fred Eisenberger to get the JPC off the ground, and the current iteration of the city's economic development strategy was developed in conjunction with the economic development working group of the JPC.[14]

However, it is one thing for a development coalition to form and quite another for it to actually make and implement policy. Not only does a "guiding vision that expresses the collective aspirations of a community" need to be developed, it needs to be durable over time and linked to specific projects and outcomes to have discernible impacts on the communities they seek to serve (Bradford 2005, 11). Despite the inclusive institutional space created by the JPC, cracks began to appear not long after the initial flurry of activity that accompanied its launch. Unable to live up to high expectations, it languished shortly after funding ran out.

Although its demise occurred after the formal research was completed, several observations offer some insight. The JPC attracted a lot of initial attention because it was "the new kid on the block," but many expressed doubts that it would "exist in three years" (confidential interview). Some working groups accomplished their original objectives, but others reported difficulty sustaining momentum as a result of complex and cross-cutting mandates in the absence of a funded secretariat to sustain momentum. Even though relations between the JPC and the chamber of commerce improved over time, sustaining the initial participation of the business community became a challenge. Finally, a new mayor was elected and it was unclear if the leadership of the JPC and the new mayor were closely aligned.

Conclusions: The Interplay of Specialization, Human Capital, and Institutions in Hamilton

We have found that Hamilton has the economic diversity and human capital to effect the successful transition to knowledge-intensive economic activities, but lacks the civic institutions to support innovation, management of local assets, and strategic planning for future economic development. Contrary to common perception, the steel industry in Hamilton has not gone away, and the medical and health-services sector continues to gather momentum; tacit knowledge and communities of practice will remain the dominant mode of learning and innovation in Hamilton's post-industrial economy. In fact the challenge is not that there will be no jobs but that there will not be enough people with the right skills to do the thousands of jobs that will be available. There will also be a shift in the skills profile, particularly in production jobs and skilled trades that will be not easily met within the existing training system.

Hamilton's greatest challenge appears to be governance. Networks representing social and economic interests lack sustained linkages between them, presenting a disjuncture that appears to have precluded durable community-wide strategic planning. These findings underscore the challenges of coalition-building for social and economic development in Canadian cities; while economic restructuring calls for strategies that balance innovation and inclusion, mobilizing diverse interests behind a shared agenda and institutionalizing the civic capacity for change is a daunting task. In Hamilton, the community was unable to sustain the Jobs Prosperity Collaborative, a comparatively ambitious effort to establish the civic infrastructure deemed critical to economic transformation (Wolfe 2010).

Economic transformation in Hamilton continues to unfold through the interplay of economic specialization, human capital, and civic institutions. While the outcome remains uncertain, two variables are in play and the third continues to evolve, suggesting that Hamilton is on the right track. In the wake of the failure of the JPC, however, it remains to be seen if Hamilton has the strategic leadership and broad-based commitment to balance Hamilton's future social development with its emerging economic fortunes.

Notes

1 This chapter summarizes the key insights derived from the extensive interviewing for the three different themes under the ISRN project. The number of interviews for all themes combined is in excess of 200. This includes additional interviews done on theme 1 studying knowledge networks in the steel, automotive, and advanced manufacturing industries through funding provided by the Toronto Regional Research Alliance.

2 Hamilton is a single-tier municipality that, like many other Ontario city-regions, underwent amalgamation in 2001, during which the new City of Hamilton was formed out of the Regional Municipality of Hamilton-Wentworth and its six municipalities. As a result of the amalgamation, and according to the 2006 census, Hamilton has a population of 504,559.

3 This title is borrowed from a newspaper article of the same name in the *Globe and Mail, Report on Business*, 29 August 2009.

4 Of particular note were the departures of Dominion Glass (established 1864, departed 1997), Otis Elevator (established 1902, departed 1987), International Harvester (established 1902, departed 1992), Canadian Westinghouse (established 1903, departed 1997), Proctor & Gamble (established 1913, departed 1998), and Firestone Tire (established 1919, departed 1988).

5 Human Resources and Skills Development Canada (2013). Figures are for March/April 2013.

6 These include: ArcelorMittal Dofasco, U.S. Steel Canada, National Steel Car, and Orlick Industries. Both Dofasco and Stelco were acquired by large multinational steel companies over the course of this research and are now known as ArcelorMittal Dofasco and U.S. Steel Canada.

7 The city also has a lower level of science and technology occupations and slightly fewer "bohemians" than other Canadian cities of a similar size, but a significantly larger proportion of foreign-born residents, 24.4 per cent versus 19.8 per cent. The percentage of the population with college or above is higher than average: 41.3 per cent versus 39.8 per cent, but those with BAs or MAs is slightly below the average. At the PhD level, 7.2 per cent versus 6.9 per cent reflects the presence of McMaster University and Hamilton Health Sciences (Spencer & Vinodrai 2009).

8 A detailed discussion of other networks is beyond the scope of this chapter, but include the Hamilton Roundtable for Poverty Reduction, a network of social service providers; environmental protection and sustainable economic development advocates; civic groups focused on increasing civic participation and democratic accountability; arts and culture network; and an innovation-led economic growth network that will be alluded to below.

9 Co-established by Joanne Priel, manager of Social Services for the City of Hamilton; Caroline Milne, executive director of the Hamilton Community Foundation; and Mark Chamberlain, the well-known business leader and civic entrepreneur, who is also chair of the JPC; other community leaders such as the presidents of McMaster University and Mohawk College, City Councillor Brain McHattie, and the mayor were or continue to be involved regularly.

10 Among other innovations supported by or housed in McMaster are the Golden Horseshoe Manufacturing Network and the McMaster Institute for Transportation and Logistics.

11 The Golden Horseshoe Biosciences Network was the local Regional Innovation Network (RIN) funded by the Ontario Ministry of Research and Innovation. Since the time of the research, the RIN program has been

changed to the Regional Innovation Centres delivered by the Ministry of Economic Development and Innovation's Ontario Network of Excellence. The RIC centres are tasked with supporting entrepreneurialism in knowledge-intensive economic activities. The Hamilton RIC was renamed the Innovation Factory.

12 For example, in addition to longstanding perceptions of fractious local politics divided along "left" and "right" lines, one of the most divisive issues in Hamilton has historically been virulent debates between advocates of greenfield expansion of employment lands and the development of a transportation and logistics hub, and advocates of environmental protection and sustainable economic development. This conflict played out most publicly and divisively in the long fight over the building of the Red Hill Expressway.

13 The HCC, first established in the early 2000s, and inspired by the Toronto City Summit Alliance, was an effort to establish a regular forum where community leaders could meet regularly to discuss issues of importance to the Hamilton community, but strong initial participation in the HCC began to attenuate when political conflicts emerged over whether the coalition should focus on social welfare or economic development, and the work of the coalition languished until 2007.

14 Mark Chamberlain is also the chair of the Hamilton Roundtable for Poverty Reduction. He is a well-known anti-poverty activist, and a very active and influential member of the local business community with a track record as a highly successful high-technology entrepreneur.

References

Anastakis, D. 2010. "An exaggerated demise." *Literary Review of Canada*, 8 October. http://reviewcanada.ca/magazine/2010/10/an-exaggerated-demise/

Birnbaum, E., D. Cohen, M. Harris, and P. Warrian. 2010. *Ontario manufacturing, supply chains, and knowledge networks.* Report for the Toronto Region Research Alliance, TRRA Toronto.

Bluestone, B., and B. Harrison. 1982. *The deindustrialization of America.* New York: Basic Books.

Bradford, N. 2005. *Place-based public policy: Towards a new urban and community agenda for Canada; Research report.* Ottawa: Canadian Policy Research Networks.

Bradford, Neil, and Allison Bramwell, eds. 2014. *Governing urban economies: Innovation and inclusion in Canadian cities.* Toronto: University of Toronto Press.

CANMET. 2011. "CANMET Materials Technology Laboratory." CANMET news release, 25 July.

Christopherson, S., J. Michie, and P. Tyler. 2010. "Regional resilience: Theoretical and empirical perspectives." *Cambridge Journal of Regions, Economy and Society* 3 (1): 3–10. http://dx.doi.org/10.1093/cjres/rsq004.

Clarke, S. 2004. "The politics of workforce development: Constructing a performance regime in Denver." In *Workforce development politics: Civic capacity and performance*, ed. R.P. Giloth, 30–74. Philadelphia: Temple University Press.

Clarke, S., and G. Gaile. 1998. *The work of cities*. Minneapolis: University of Minnesota Press.

Cole, T. 2009. "Hamilton's dead. Or is it?" *Globe and Mail*, 29 August, Report on Business.

Cooke, P. 2005. "Regionally asymmetric knowledge capabilities and open innovation." *Research Policy* 34 (8): 1128–49. http://dx.doi.org/10.1016/j.respol.2004.12.005.

–. 2007. "Regional innovation, entrepreneurship and talent systems." *International Journal of Entrepreneurship and Innovation Management* 7 (2–5): 117–39. http://dx.doi.org/10.1504/IJEIM.2007.012878.

DiGaetano, A., and E. Strom. 2003. "Comparative urban governance: An integrated approach." *Urban Affairs Review* 38 (3): 356–95. http://dx.doi.org/10.1177/1078087402238806.

Gertler, M.S. 2001. "Urban economy and society in Canada: Flows of people, capital and ideas." *Isuma* 2 (3): 119–30.

Giloth, R.P. 2004. "The 'local' in workforce development politics: An introduction." In *Workforce development politics: Civic capacity and performance*, ed. R.P. Giloth, 1–29. Philadelphia: Temple University Press.

Herrigel, G. 2010. *Manufacturing possibilities*. Oxford Scholarship Online. http://dx.doi.org/10.1093/acprof:oso/9780199557738.001.0001.

Hobor, G. 2013. "Surviving the era of deindustrialization: New economic geography of the urban rust belt." *Journal of Urban Affairs* 35 (4): 417–34. http://dx.doi.org/10.1111/j.1467-9906.2012.00625.x.

Human Resources and Skills Development Canada. 2013. "EI employment figures by Ontario region – Hamilton." http://srv129.services.gc.ca/ei_regions/eng/rates.aspx?id=2013#data.

Kodrzycki, Y., and A.P. Munoz. 2009. *Lessons from resurgent cities*. Boston: Federal Reserve Bank of Boston.

Martin, R., and J. Simmie. 2008. "Path dependence and local innovation systems in city-regions." *Innovation: Management, Policy & Practice* 10 (2–3): 183–96. http://dx.doi.org/10.5172/impp.453.10.2-3.183.

Ministry of Research and Innovation. 2012. *The comeback kid*. Hamilton, ON: Ministry of Research and Innovation.

McGahey, R.M., and J.S. Vey, eds. 2008. *Retooling for growth: Building a 21st century economy in America's older industrial areas*. Washington, DC: Brookings Institution.

Mossberger, K., and G. Stoker. 2001. "The evolution of urban regime theory: The challenge of conceptualization." *Urban Affairs Review* 36 (6): 810–35. http://dx.doi.org/10.1177/10780870122185109.

O'Grady, J., and P. Warrian. 2011. *Human resources in the Canadian steel sector: Final report*. Toronto: Canadian Steel Trade and Employment Congress.

Pierre, J. 2011. *The politics of urban governance*. Basingstoke, UK: Palgrave Macmillan.

Rodríguez-Pose, A. 2013. "Do institutions matter for regional development?" *Regional Studies* 47 (7): 1034–47. http://dx.doi.org/10.1080/00343404.2012.748978.

Safford, S. 2009. *Why the garden club couldn't save Youngstown: The transformation of the rust belt*. Cambridge, MA: Harvard University Press.

Savitch, H.V., and P. Kantor. 2002. *Cities in the international marketplace: The political economy of urban development in North America and Western Europe*. Princeton: Princeton University Press.

Simmie, J., and P. Wood. 2002. "Innovation and competitive cities in the global economy: Introduction to the special issue." *European Planning Studies* 10 (2): 149–51. http://dx.doi.org/10.1080/09654310120114454.

Spencer, G., and T. Vinodrai. 2009. *ISRN City-Region Profile, 1006: Hamilton*. Toronto: Munk School of Global Affairs, University of Toronto.

Stone, C. 1989. *Regime politics: Governing Atlanta 1946–1988*. Lawrence: University Press of Kansas.

–. 2005. "Looking back to look forward: Reflections on urban regime analysis." *Urban Affairs Review* 40 (3): 309–41. http://dx.doi.org/10.1177/1078087404270646.

Storper, M. 2010. "Why does a city grow? Specialisation, human capital or institutions?" *Urban Studies* 47 (10): 2027–50. http://dx.doi.org/10.1177/0042098009359957.

–. 2013. *Keys to the city: How economics, social interaction, and politics shape development*. Princeton: Princeton University Press.

Storper, M., and M. Manville. 2006. "Behaviour, preferences, and cities: Urban theory and urban resurgence." *Urban Studies* 43 (8): 1247–74.

Walls, J. 2013. "American cities of the future 2013/14." *fDI Intelligence*, April/May.

Warrian, P. 2010. *The importance of steel manufacturing in Canada*. Toronto: Munk School of Global Affairs.

Warrian, P., and C. Mulhern. 2003. "Learning in steel: Agents and deficits." In *Clusters old and new: The transition to a knowledge economy in Canada's regions,* ed. D.A. Wolfe, 37–62. Montreal and Kingston: McGill-Queen's University Press for Queen's School of Policy Studies.

–. 2005. "Knowledge and innovation in the interface between the steel and auto industries: The case of Dofasco." *Regional Studies* 39 (2): 161–70. http://dx.doi.org/10.1080/0034340052000599934.

Weaver, L., and A. Makhoul. 2009. *Hamilton roundtable for poverty reduction: Setting the table for change.* Community Stories. Ottawa: Caledon Institute for Social Policy, March.

Wolfe, D. 2009. *21st Century cities in Canada: The geography of innovation.* Ottawa: Conference Board of Canada.

–. 2010. "The strategic management of core cities: Path dependency and economic adjustment in resilient regions." Special issue, *Cambridge Journal of Regions, Economy and Society* 3 (1): 139–52.

8 A City of Two Tales: Innovation, Talent Attraction, and Governance in Canada's Technology Triangle

TARA VINODRAI

Introduction

Technology-based regions have long been held up as examples of successful local and regional economic development. While places like Silicon Valley, Boston's Route 128, and North Carolina's Research Triangle are routinely identified as iconic in this regard and attempts are regularly made to imitate their success, the received wisdom suggests that such regions develop over time and are the product of regionally specific cultures and institutions, regional political, business, and civic leadership, historical events, and specific investments and decisions made by various levels of government (Saxenian 1994, 2006; Best 2001; Malecki 2011). In the Canadian case, the Waterloo region is often compared to these U.S. examples, especially given its regional economic strengths in information and communication technologies (ICTs).[1] However, Waterloo's regional economy is more diverse than this narrative suggests; the region has a long industrial past and has been a key centre for Canadian manufacturing over the past century (Wolfe 2009, 2012; Rutherford and Holmes 2008). Waterloo has also been the location of a thriving insurance industry and a range of other business activity. Thus, the region is at once the poster child of Canada's technology success and well recognized as a leading-edge hub of technology-based economic growth; yet as a major manufacturing centre it has also been exposed to significant industrial restructuring and plant closures. Most accounts of the region highlight the key role of the University of Waterloo and a few critical private sector firms (e.g., Christie Digital, OpenText, Desire2Learn, and Blackberry – formerly Research in Motion or RIM) as driving technology-led growth, yet there are other dimensions to this story that remain underexplored.

Drawing upon research on the social dynamics of innovation, talent attraction and retention, and civic governance, this chapter explores the tension between the dominant narrative of a successful technology-based region and some of the potential dark sides, contradictions, and conflicts this development approach introduces. This chapter is greatly aided by the wealth of studies of innovation, economic development, firm formation, and cluster dynamics in the Waterloo region conducted by research team members (Bathelt and Hecht 1990; Bramwell and Wolfe 2008; Nelles, Bramwell, and Wolfe 2005; Bramwell, Nelles, and Wolfe 2008; Wolfe 2010, 2012; Bathelt, Munro, and Spigel 2011; Bathelt, Kogler, and Munro 2011; Vinodrai et al. 2012; Nelles 2014), as well as the extensive network of established contacts produced by these efforts that allowed access to local actors. The findings reported in this chapter draw upon over 150 interviews conducted between 2007 and 2012 with a diverse range of local actors including firms, workers, government officials, and representatives from universities, colleges, industry, and professional associations and other organizations. The chapter begins by providing an overview of the Waterloo region and then explores the dynamics of business innovation focusing on ICT and manufacturing firms, talent attraction and retention, and the evolving forms of regional governance arrangements that shape innovation and economic development. On balance, the chapter confirms many aspects of the dominant explanation of the region's success, while emphasizing the cracks and potential contradictions revealed through the research.

The Waterloo Region: Diverse, Mid-Sized City or Technology Hub?

The Waterloo region, located about 100 km west of Toronto, has received a great deal of attention from policymakers because of its success in maintaining high regional growth rates and the ability to upgrade its economic basis. The region comprises three mid-size cities (Kitchener, Waterloo, and Cambridge) and four rural townships (Woolwich, North Dumfries, Wilmot, and Wellesley); the seven municipalities are part of a regional municipality – resulting in a two-tiered local government structure. By most accounts, the region has benefited from its long-standing role as a traditional manufacturing centre, as well as its cluster of dynamic and globally oriented ICT firms established over the past several decades. Over the past century, the region has housed major national and international corporations, from Dominion Electrohome Ltd (now Christie Digital) to Blackberry and OpenText. Waterloo's diversified industrial base, and the success of leading local industrial firms, such as Christie Digital, in making the transition from older industrial technologies to newer digital technologies, have been identified by some observers as sources of Waterloo's continuing economic resilience (Wolfe 2010, 2012).

The regional economy has been characterized as having immense industrial diversity. Beckstead and Brown's (2003) analysis of Canadian cities revealed that Waterloo had much higher levels of industrial diversity than other mid-sized cities; its level of economic diversity was on par with that found in large Canadian cities. The region's above-average level of economic performance according to indicators such as job growth, the unemployment rate, or average household income (see table 8.1) is often attributed to this industrial diversity. In economic performance, between 2001 and 2006, the Kitchener CMA experienced an increase in population and jobs that was higher than the national growth rates, and similar to the Toronto CMA (Spencer and Vinodrai 2006, 2009). The Kitchener CMA ranks above the national average in the percentage of population born outside the country, and research suggests that the region acts as a secondary gateway for new immigrants (Walton Roberts 2008). Despite the presence of several higher-education institutions and its technological prowess, the proportion of the population with a bachelor's degree or higher is close to the national average, although the region scores above the national average in the number of PhDs per 1,000. The rate of employment growth has been well above the national average, and conversely, unemployment rates are among the lowest in Canadian metropolitan areas. The region ranks about average in the percentage of creative occupations in the regional economy, slightly above average in scientific occupations, and below average in number of individuals in artistic occupations per 1,000 population, confirming its image as more of a high-tech centre than a "cool" place. Overall, average employment income was slightly higher than the national level.

Figure 8.1 compares the performance of seventeen industrial groups (or clusters) in the Kitchener CMA. The horizontal axis shows the employment growth rate between 2001 and 2006, while the vertical

Table 8.1. Key socio-economic and demographic characteristics of the Kitchener CMA, 2006

Characteristic	Kitchener CMA	Canada
Population	451,240	31,612,890
% population change, 2001–6	8.9	5.4
% foreign born	23.1	19.8
% BA or higher	18.4	18.1
PhDs per 1000	9.5	6.9
% employment growth	26.4	19.8
% unemployment rate	5.6	6.6
% in creative occupations	32.1	33.2
% science tech occupations	7.5	6.6
Bohemians per 1000	12.2	14.2
Number of clusters	7	255
% employment in clusters	20.3	22.1
Average full-time employment income	$53,510	$51,221
% change in income, 2000–5	6.1	5.5

Source: Spencer and Vinodrai (2009)

axis shows the employment location quotient comparing the proportion of the Kitchener CMA's employment in an industrial sector to the Canadian average. The diameter of each "bubble" is proportional to employment in the specified industrial group in 2006. Industrial groups that appear in the upper-right quadrant have positive growth rates and have a higher-than-expected proportion of employment (specialization) in this group of industries. As shown in figure 8.1, the largest industrial groups in the Kitchener CMA are automotive manufacturing, business services, ICT services, finance, and higher education. A more sophisticated analysis of industrial structure involves cluster analysis. Clusters represent groups of interrelated firms and industries that gain competitive advantage by concentrating geographically in certain locations. Using a methodology developed by Spencer et al. (2010), industrial groups that meet a set of quantitative criteria can be identified as clusters. Clusters are identified on the basis of their relative size (employment), their relative specialization (location quotient), as well as the breadth or scope of activities undertaken in the region. According to these criteria, in 2006, seven of these industrial groups were clusters: textiles and apparel, steel, automotive, plastics and rubber, biomedical, ICT manufacturing,

Figure 8.1. Growth, Size, and Industry Specialization in the Kitchener CMA, 2001–6

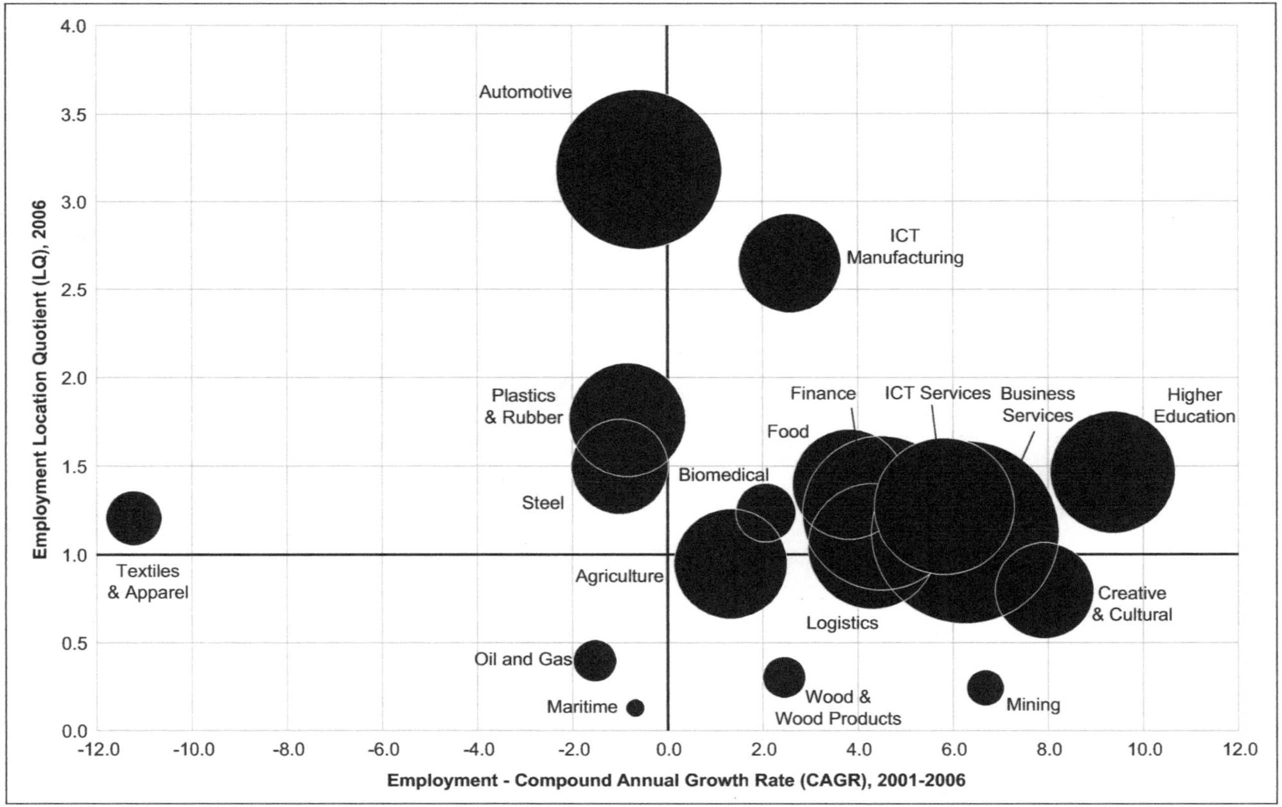

Source: Statistics Canada, 2001–6 (author's calculations)

Table 8.2. Industrial clusters in the Kitchener CMA, 2001 and 2006

	Location quotient 2006	% growth 2001–6
Textiles and apparel	1.21	–44.6
Steel	1.50	–4.9
Automotive	3.18	–2.9
Plastics and rubber	1.76	–4.1
Biomedical	1.24	10.5
ICT manufacturing	2.65	13.7
Logistics	1.05	23.7

Source: Spencer and Vinodrai (2006, 2009)

and logistics. Job growth was substantial in the ICT manufacturing, biomedical, and logistics clusters (see also table 8.2). However, other industrial groups (food, ICT services, finance, business services, and higher education) also demonstrated high levels of growth between 2001 and 2006, highlighting the growth, dynamism, and industrial diversity of the region as a whole.

As the above discussion highlights, ICT manufacturing and services have been a key source of growth for the region. Certainly, Waterloo's tech sector is viewed as one of the most dynamic sources of high-tech activity in Canada. No single company has symbolized this success in recent years more than the iconic Blackberry. However, the company, viewed as a key anchor firm, a Canadian technology success story, and a major source of regional employment, has experienced changes in senior management to leaders who are not embedded in the local economy, poor business and market performance, and several rounds of layoffs. The future of Blackberry – a company once viewed as a critical regional anchor tenant – remains uncertain. Despite the challenges faced by this global tech company, there are over 1,000 other companies involved in the high-technology sector, and the region has developed a reputation for fostering tech-based start-ups. As Wolfe (2012) notes, the emergence and dynamism of Waterloo's high-tech sector owes its success, in part, to decisions made by local industrial leaders in the 1950s, leading to the creation of the University of Waterloo (UW). Waterloo's high-technology cluster grew out of its strong industrial base in advanced manufacturing, combined with the early focus of the new university in engineering, math, and computer science. Two of the cluster's earliest established firms, WATCOM and Dantec Electronic, were spun off from the university in 1974. A subsequent generation of firms followed in the 1980s, including Dalsa (1980), Virtek Vision (1986), and Open Text (1989). Blackberry, although not technically a university spin-off, was also founded in the early 1980s. The university remains central to the continuing development of the regional economy, although its primary contribution is no longer through new firm formation, as relatively fewer firms have spun off directly since the late 1980s, and other mechanisms for knowledge transfer have played a more significant role (Nelles, Bramwell, and Wolfe 2005; Bathelt, Kogler, and Munro 2011; Wolfe 2012).

Unlike other concentrations of high-tech activity in Canada or elsewhere, Waterloo's economy is not dominated by one technological specialization, such as telecommunications or Internet-based forms, nor is the regional economy dominated by any sector. This diversity of economic activity has enabled the regional economy to weather economic shocks – such as the post-2000 dot.com meltdown – that devastated employment in other leading ICT regions across North America. However, the region is at once both a high-tech region and a diverse mid-size city, which combine to allow the region continued economic success and may help it to weather the difficulties of its flagship company. The next sections of this chapter turn to exploring how this context shapes innovation and knowledge flows, talent attraction and retention, and governance.

Innovation and Knowledge Flows in a Tech Region

The literature on firm learning and innovation emphasizes critical conduits that facilitate knowledge circulation and information-sharing within the regional economy. Prime among these processes are university-industry technology transfer mechanisms, particularly related to spinoffs; job-hopping (or labour market mobility) by local talent; and the development of local industry or inter-sectoral networks that facilitate firm learning (Cooke 2001; Fagerberg et al. 2006; Cooke et al. 2011). These are particularly important activities that promote innovation within regional clusters, as well as spillovers to other regional industries. Although Waterloo is usually portrayed as a dynamic technology region that draws from university-related start-up/spinoff processes, knowledge transfers, and corresponding regional networks, research conducted for this project portrays a mixed picture of innovation and knowledge flows in the region. In other words, the dominant narrative of Waterloo as a dynamic and innovative technology region is somewhat misleading.

Universities and Spinoffs

Although there is substantial hype regarding the University of Waterloo's role in promoting the growth of the regional economy through university commercialization, technology-transfer, and spinoffs, recent evidence suggests that this narrative may be based more on historic performance rather than its current performance. While key regional firms such as OpenText are spinoffs, it is important to recall that, controversially, the most famous spinoff firm in the region, Blackberry, is in fact not technically a university spinoff. While the firm was started by University of Waterloo students, the company's initial product line was unrelated to the BlackBerry, and the original intellectual property (IP) behind the BlackBerry did not originate from within the university. Bathelt, Kogler, and Munro's 2011 study of university spin-offs and start-ups indicated that even the absolute number of spinoffs appears grossly overstated and showed that most university spinoff/start-up firms operated in very specific cross-regional networks along market and technology linkages that adhere to their particular technological expertise. Local linkages with customers and suppliers, and the existence of regional industry networks, such as those described in conventional cluster approaches, were quite limited in their extent, or absent altogether. Regional industry organizations also played a limited role in stimulating innovations, playing a minor role in deepening social and industry networks and generic skill sets. Firms frequently turned to specialized Internet-based user groups as their initial problem-solving tool and rarely found opportunities to collaborate with other firms in the region, typically citing that nobody else in the region was working on the same type of products and problems that they were encountering. In other words, although many spinoff firms had clear links to the community (e.g., being founded by local students, hiring UW students out of school or in co-op), there were limited linkages to regional actors or institutions with respect to innovation. The results suggest that the role of local universities in spurring start-ups/spinoffs is most likely overstated (Bathelt, Kogler, and Munro 2011).

While the university may have a more limited direct role in new venture creation within the region, our research did reveal the critical role of other regional actors in supporting entrepreneurship and fostering a regional start-up culture. Student entrepreneurs and other local entrepreneurs are well supported by key regional organizations and facilities. In particular, the Accelerator Centre (located in the University of Waterloo's research park) and the Communitech Hub (established in 2010) offer a suite of services to start-up companies, as well as programming intended to support entrepreneurs and firms in the region. Programs include an executive-in-residence program, hosting start-up firms, mentoring, assistance in access to financing and venture capital, and on-site access to the necessary legal, accounting, and other business services, in addition to a variety of networking events. The Hub's 30,000 square foot state-of-the-art facility in a redeveloped tannery in downtown Kitchener offers a highly attractive location for entrepreneurs, established and new firms, and academic institutions to interact regularly, with the prime goal of fostering regional expertise in digital media and mobile technologies. Indeed, the universities have both established student-oriented start-up programs within the facility, and larger technology firms in the region also have space, including Desire2Learn and Google. The Hub has several noteworthy features, including the 3D Hub Interactive Virtual Reality Environment (HIVE) showcasing the technology of the local Christie Digital, a 3D-capable event space, and virtual conferencing facilities. Between the Accelerator Centre and the Hub, the latest data from Communitech indicate that it has provided support for more than 1,500 start-up firms in the region (see also Wolfe 2012); Communitech's role is discussed in greater detail in subsequent sections.

Innovation, Local Industry, and Inter-sectoral Networks

The innovation literature also emphasizes how local networks are a critical ingredient for the transfer of knowledge and ideas between firms, particularly for high-tech regions (Saxenian 1994; Lawton Smith 2008; Malecki 2011). Again, the Waterloo story is mixed. There is evidence of both *formal* and *informal* inter-firm networking; however, it was unclear whether this contributed to cross-industry learning and knowledge-sharing in all cases. As noted above, as a result of the disparate needs of local firms, firms often sought out solutions to problems from extra-regional sources (Bathelt, Munro, and Spigel 2011). Nonetheless, networking is greatly facilitated by the relatively small size of the region. As one respondent noted, "I am likely to see [a colleague working for another firm] at my children's swimming lessons or at an event at the Perimeter Institute." In addition to these informal social interactions, the local technology industry association (Communitech) has been a leader in facilitating conversations across firm boundaries through their activities, which include hosting weekly breakfast events on a variety of topics of interest to local firms, organizing peer-to-peer networks that involve groups of managers or specialists discussing common problems, and other similar events. Communitech and several other actors are seen as critical in local governance of innovation and knowledge circulation, as well as being participants in and catalysts or brokers for several economic development initiatives (see below).

However, Bathelt, Munro, and Spigel (2011) note that there are few relationships between traditional manufacturing firms and the high-tech firms in Waterloo. Moreover, relationships that do exist are reported by firms to not be relevant to innovation processes. Indeed, linkages across industry value chains are so rare as to have little influence on regional innovation. So while traditional manufacturers in the region have been more innovative than might be expected of the sector, this has not been the result of collective innovation; instead, regional successes can be more attributed to the individual efforts of firms and their specific competencies (ibid.). As such, this raises questions about dominant narratives of the region that suggest there are high levels of inter-firm knowledge flows or evidence of knowledge flows across diverse industrial sectors. To the extent there is knowledge-sharing in Waterloo region, it tends to be on the how-to of starting and growing firms and the sharing of managerial experience.

Labour Market Mobility

Finally, most accounts of regional innovation – particularly in high-tech regions – emphasize the importance of labour market mobility (Angel 1991; Almeida and Kogut 1999; Malecki 2011). However, research on the Waterloo region indicated that firms did not identify inter-firm labour-market mobility as an important contributor to innovation, firm-learning, or circulation of knowledge (Bathelt, Munro, and Spigel 2011). Moreover, interviews with major regional employers, as well as with employees, did not reveal unusually high levels of local inter-firm labour mobility. Despite portraying the technology community as being tightly knit and highly interconnected, there is little evidence that the local talent base moves between local firms, thereby contributing to cross-sectoral ties and local knowledge flows. Limited mobility between firms may reflect the nature of the local high-technology sector itself. While there is a perception that the high-technology sector is homogeneous, the companies themselves view the firm population as being particularly heterogeneous, working in very different technology areas that require very different specialized skills. For that reason, there was a view that the companies did not necessarily always compete with one another for talent.[2] As noted by a human resources manager for a large technology company, "If we compare ourselves to other tech centres, Toronto, Chicago, the Silicon Valley, our turnover is almost half of what the turnover is in those other areas. We have a lot more stability and resources … [T]here aren't fifty companies like ours sitting within a couple of miles of each other for people to move in and about and between. So we tend to have people stay a little bit longer, and if people raise their families here, they tend to want to stay a little longer as well" (confidential interview, 2009).

Lower levels of employee turnover suggest that workers are more dedicated to working for specific local firms than might be expected. Furthermore, as the quote above indicates, family life plays a key role in retaining talent in the region (see below).

The interviews indicate that while the university may not play as large a role in direct technology transfer (above), it does facilitate knowledge transfer, even if not directly. UW's computer science, math, and engineering programs are cooperative education programs that require students to participate in several four- to eight-month work terms with different employers; often undergraduate students will therefore work for several local firms before receiving their degree. Some interviews with entrepreneurs and other high-tech workers suggested that the ideas for their firm start-ups or for solving problems came from their cooperative experiences. Interviews indicate that, through their co-op rotations, undergraduate students act as a key conduit for knowledge circulation in the local economy. The close relationship established through co-op rotations also allows the curriculum to keep pace with the ever-changing technological frontiers of industry, as students bring the experience and questions acquired through their work experience back with them to the classroom. Co-op student placements also provide an effective means of knowledge circulation among local firms, as they take the knowledge acquired in one work placement to their next employer. Finally, co-op students also provide a mechanism for linking local firms in need of technical assistance with the academic expertise found within the university, thus acting as almost a tech transfer office in reverse (Bramwell and Wolfe 2008).

"Waterloo, couldn't escape if I wanted to"

These words, sung by the Swedish pop band ABBA in their 1974 hit single *Waterloo*, aptly describe the dynamics of talent attraction and retention in the region. Despite the downsides of the region, talented workers move to the Waterloo region to access leading-edge work in their fields. The area is held in high regard as a hotbed of software, engineering, computer science, and mathematical talent. Once in the region, these same individuals often became embedded in the community; as noted by one expert in the tech community, "Waterloo is a sticky place, not an attractive place." Interviewees emphasized the relative affordability, the "family-friendly" environment, or an attachment to place developed through growing up or attending school in the community. Other amenities related to outdoor recreation, green space, easy access to the countryside, a strong K–12 school system, and the presence of several local universities and colleges were also highlighted. Yet there was also recognition that the lack of urban amenities posed a challenge. These dynamics of quality of place, the relative size of the region, and its proximity to a larger urban centre (Toronto) provided significant advantages and drawbacks. Moreover, the spatial structure of the region has had a strong influence over the quality of the built environment. This has led local institutional actors to engage in place-making. One the one hand, it is intended to develop new industries and sectors to further enable the region's transition to a knowledge-based, digital economy. On the other hand, it is intended to redefine the character of the urban environment, thereby addressing perceived shortcomings of the region.

Finally, local universities play a key role in attracting, retaining, and producing local talent. More recently, the universities have been more involved in shaping the conditions that underscore these processes. Each of these key themes is elaborated upon below.

Cool Jobs, Boring Place?

Interviews with technology-based and other highly skilled workers revealed that the primary draw of the Waterloo region was access to cool jobs and exciting and meaningful work; amenities and quality of place were mostly secondary considerations. The presence of the high-technology sector, the finance and insurance industries, the universities, as well as newer institutions that are loosely affiliated with the local universities and established through the philanthropy of Blackberry's co-founders, such as the Perimeter Institute and the Centre for International Governance Innovation, means that there are plenty of job opportunities that require highly educated workers. Often these types of jobs are on the leading edge of workers' respective fields; a critical mass of individuals doing work in similar and related fields acted as key draw to the region for many of the interviewees. Several noted that they did not really know much about the region but had taken a job with an institution or firm because of its reputation for doing cutting-edge and interesting work in their field. For example, several recent hires in UW's Faculties of Math and Engineering had been recruited from leading U.S. schools such as MIT, Stanford, and U.C. Berkeley. However, upon arrival, these same individuals, while expressing satisfaction with *working* in the region, expressed some disappointment about *living* in the region.

Employers, city officials, and representatives from local agencies and organizations alike noted that a primary challenge to the region is in the quality of the built environment, including a lack of vibrant downtown, nightlife, restaurants, and other urban amenities – issues that officials were actively seeking to address (Kulha 2013). However, most interviewees quickly noted that some key benefits of living and working in the region compared to Toronto or other larger metropolitan centres were in levels of traffic congestion and housing prices, which are perceived to be significantly lower. However, anecdotal evidence provided by a number of interviewees suggested that while this might be true in some parts of the region, the presence of the high-tech community placed upward pressure on housing prices, particularly in the City of

Waterloo. In addition to these considerations, interviewees also pointed to the proximity to the countryside, outdoor recreational opportunities, abundant green space, easy access to the countryside, a strong K–12 school system, and the presence of several local universities and colleges. Mentions were also made of easy access to local food, particularly given the presence of both the Kitchener Downtown Farmers Market and the St Jacob's Farmers Market.

Strong primary and secondary school systems were consistently identified as an important feature of the region, pointing to one of the most consistent findings regarding quality of place. There was a common perception among employers, university officials, and local government policymakers that the region was well suited for raising families, a point that was often raised when discussing recruitment. As one key informant noted, "If we marry them to a job first, they will then marry a local girl and have kids, then they will end up being married to the region" (confidential interview 2009). Such comments were common and reflect a narrow perception of the gender (male) and sexual (heterosexual) identities of workers who are considered the target of talent attraction and retention efforts. However, it does begin to address an early criticism of the work of Florida (2002) and others. Critics have suggested that Florida's 3Ts hypothesis overlooks several important issues (Peck 2005; Scott 2006), including gender and social reproduction, such as raising a family (Donald and Morrow 2003). Moreover, this emphasizes the diversity of quality of place that can be important to attracting and retaining talent and highlights the importance of taking into consideration life cycle and career stage.

Geography Matters: Relative Size, Proximity, and Spatial Structure

When asked to consider the relative strengths and weakness of working, living and locating in the region, interviewees often discussed Waterloo in comparison to Toronto and its surrounding suburban communities. On the one hand, the proximity of such a large metropolitan region meant that some of the urban amenities that were not readily available in the region could be accessed quite easily. On the other hand, some viewed this as a "crutch" or an "excuse" to not invest in the soft infrastructure that employers and employees alike have identified as a weak spot for the region in talent attraction and retention. It should be noted that the two largest technology companies in the Waterloo region, Blackberry and OpenText, despite having their origins in the region, opened offices in the Greater Toronto Area. This has raised some concerns about the ability of the region to maintain and expand its talent base without investment in upgrading the built environment.

As noted earlier, the Waterloo region comprises three distinctive cities (each with a population between 100,000 and 225,000), as well as several surrounding rural townships. In fact, Cambridge itself is the product of a municipal amalgamation dictated by the provincial government in the mid-1990s to reduce the number of municipalities in Ontario. Cambridge comprises the former towns of Galt, Hespeler, and Preston, as well as the settlement of Blair. This underlying spatial structure has been critical to shaping the specific quality of place that defines the region and influences the conditions that govern it. In other words, rather than the region having one single, distinctive downtown, as well as related patterns of land use, there are at least three separate downtowns, which means that none of the downtowns has achieved a critical mass of employment, amenity-oriented businesses (e.g., retail, entertainment, and restaurants), or residential housing stock. However, each of these downtowns is undergoing revitalization and industrial upgrading that are driven by creativity-oriented economic development agendas to improve the quality of the built environment to attract and retain a new generation of highly skilled workers.

Moreover, there are differences in the approaches taken by the three main municipal governments to attracting and retaining talent. The City of Kitchener has perhaps been the most active in reformulating and reorienting its economic development policies towards a creative economy (Vinodrai et al. 2012). This can perhaps be attributed to an added sense of urgency in seeking out new engines of local economic growth, given the erosion of its traditional employment base. Once the Town of Berlin, dubbed "busy Berlin," the City of Kitchener was a thriving manufacturing centre. Yet as Vinodrai (2010) has shown, between 1971 and 2006, the proportion of employment accounted for by the manufacturing sector decreased from 41.5 to 23.1 per cent. While manufacturing still accounts for a high proportion of employment relative to the national and provincial averages and some of this manufacturing is design-intensive (e.g., Krug Inc., a furniture manufacturer) and uses advanced technologies (e.g., Christie Digital), there have been a number of substantial employment losses and plant closures. In response, the City of Kitchener has invested in several initiatives that recognize this erosion of the traditional manufacturing employment base in the city.

In the wake of the restructuring of the manufacturing sector, large tracts of downtown urban lands have been left vacant as factories have closed. Like in many cities in more developed industrial societies, these buildings have come to be viewed as territorial assets ripe for adaptive reuse – for employment and residential applications. It comes as no surprise then that several of the abandoned factories in Kitchener's downtown have been converted into loft-style condominiums, as well as open-concept offices, including those for a small outpost of Electronic Arts (EA), the well-known video game producer, and the Hub, a digital media convergence centre. This latter project fits with a broader economic development strategy to diversify the region's economy and facilitate the transition to more knowledge-based activities. However, it is also focused explicitly on developing new local talent, recognizing that the region is most successful at producing local talent rather than attracting it from elsewhere (confidential interview, 2009). In addition, the City of Kitchener – in articulating a desire to revitalize the downtown by bringing new employers to the downtown core – has brokered land development deals with several key actors, including the University of Waterloo and other universities in southern Ontario. Of particular note, the City of Kitchener provided UW with $30 million to build its School of Pharmacy in its downtown to anchor a new health sciences campus and broader life sciences cluster. Similarly, the City of Cambridge brokered a deal with UW to relocate UW's School of Architecture; each of these initiatives is part of each city's economic development plan to diversify the economy and revitalize their respective downtowns (Wolfe 2012).

The Role of Universities in Attracting and Retaining Talent

The initiatives led by the City of Kitchener and other municipal governments described above underscore the important role that universities can play and are playing in economic development. It is shifting away from one focused more strictly on technology transfer and commercialization to a much wider set of roles that make it an anchor in the creative economy (Gertler and Vinodrai 2005; Bramwell and Wolfe 2008; Vinodrai 2009). For example, in speaking with several of the parties involved, there was an underlying assumption that UW's Stratford Institute would be critical in producing a steady stream of new talent with skills that would match local companies' needs, as well as matching those in emerging initiatives centred on digital media technologies, linking the university to initiatives such as the envisioned digital media corridor between Toronto and Stratford and the City of Kitchener's support for digital media, centred on the Hub. Thus, there seems to be a concerted effort by local universities, firms, and government actors to create conditions that will attract and retain highly skilled workers with skills sets that are targeted to producing talent that will also align with the perceived emerging needs of the local economy.

In addition to these land-development-related initiatives that further the educational aspirations of the university, as well as the economic development goals of local governments, the university has also played two other key roles in talent attraction and retention. First, interviews with major regional employers suggested that their main connections to the local universities and colleges were through hiring graduates (see also Bramwell and Wolfe 2008). Both UW and Wilfrid Laurier University have been key suppliers of talent to local firms and – although there are few available statistics – there is an understanding that many UW students find jobs with local firms. Indeed, Mike Lazaridis, co-founder of Research in Motion (RIM), has emphasized the critical role of students to local technology commercialization; as Bramwell and Wolfe (2008, 1180) note, "The best tech transfer is a pair of shoes." This connection is reinforced through the cooperative education programs that have been viewed as pillars of the University of Waterloo's success story. Second, the universities have also played an important role in creating a more open and tolerant community. This point is critical, given one of the more troubling findings revealed in the interviews, which suggested that the local community was often perceived as unwelcoming to newcomers, particularly those with non-European backgrounds. Data from the University of Waterloo indicate that foreign student enrolment in graduate programs has grown rapidly in the past decade and draws heavily from Middle Eastern and Asian countries (Vinodrai 2009; see also Walton Roberts 2008). These data suggest that there is an increasing flow of highly educated immigrants into the region. Walton Roberts (2008) has shown that the region's local universities attract highly skilled immigrants. This role in improving the level of social cohesion within the community and creating a safe and welcoming space should not be underestimated. Her interviews and focus groups with recent immigrants in the Waterloo region found that the local universities attracted immigrants and were critical in assisting in their subsequent integration into the community by creating spaces that were perceived as safe and free from discrimination. This suggests that universities – particularly in smaller and mid-sized cities – may become increasingly important institutions in talent attraction and retention, given the increasing internationalization of higher education, the global nature of labour markets for highly educated workers, and the growing importance of immigration as a source of new talent in Canada.

The Waterloo Way: Inclusive or Divisive Governance?

More than the specifics of attracting talent or firm level innovation, one of the most interesting features of the Waterloo region is its system of governance that is celebrated by academics and policymakers. Waterloo is one of the most prosperous and internationally recognized regions of its size in Canada. In a relatively short time it has carved out a niche in high technology, advanced manufacturing, and higher education and has become a much-touted model for city-regions seeking to replicate its success in regional economic governance. Much of the success of the Waterloo region can be attributed to its unusually active civil society and the proliferation of mechanisms of regional strategic coordination and collaborative governance (Wolfe 2010, 2012; Nelles 2014). In local circles, there is an almost uncritical explanation for Waterloo's success, and references are consistently made to "barn building," the Mennonite traditions of the community and the Waterloo Way. The "Waterloo Way" is a powerful trope that provides a shorthand explanation for the region's culture and governance approach. As noted in one of Canada's national newspapers, the *Globe and Mail*, "Call it the Waterloo Way. It's a cultural and economic model that provides a beacon as Canada enters a new age of embattled manufacturing accompanied by massive investments in energy. It's the blueprint for how other communities can become economic warriors in the global battle for jobs and growth. It holds the key for Canada's economic survival and perhaps dominance" (Keenan, Pitts, and Scoffield 2006).

Indeed, the region is well known for its ability to build coalitions across industrial sectors through decentralized, civic-led governance, and the region has a rich history of collaboration to develop regional institutions (Nelles, Bramwell, and Wolfe, 2005). And, as the region has evolved, governance initiatives at the regional scale have proliferated and expanded in scope. There is (relatively) broad-based participation in regional strategic management. This section traces this evolution and suggests that the dominant narrative of a region where everyone works together obscures biases towards specific economic development goals, in part due to the dominance of economic actors (see also Vinodrai et al. 2012; Nelles 2014).

The Foundations of Strategic Governance

As Nelles (2014) discusses, the dawn of regional strategic governance can be traced to the foundation of two associations in the mid-1980s: Canada's Technology Triangle Inc. (CTT Inc.) and Communitech. Each was established independently by different communities of actors interested in developing the regional high-tech economy. As the two associations evolved, they have developed stronger ties and coordinate more closely, and each has expanded its mandates significantly. CTT Inc. is a regional marketing and economic development association, founded in 1987 by economic development officials in Kitchener, Waterloo, Cambridge coordinate regional marketing and business attraction. CTT Inc. was originally constructed as a political partnership of the three local governments but evolved into a public-private partnership in 1999 (Parker 2001; Leibovitz 2003). In adopting the public-private form, control over the direction and strategy of the association passed from public to largely private hands. This transition marked an expansion in the vision and mandate of the association from marketing to include other areas of regional economic development. Representation on the board of directors and corporate partners reflects the economic development mission of the association. In recent years, the composition of community partners has expanded to include new associations involved in regional economic governance, such as the municipal chambers of commerce, the regional manufacturing association (the Manufacturing Innovation Network), and the regional tourism marketing association (the Waterloo Region Tourism Marketing Corporation). While neither the membership nor the leadership of CTT Inc. is broadly inclusive of social or cultural actors, as part of its expanding mandate it has participated in regional initiatives supporting these goals.

Communitech began in 1997 as a member-based organization supporting the high-tech industry in the Waterloo region. Its original mandate was to facilitate the exchange of ideas, improve networking relations between high technology firms, and intervene with governments on behalf of the industry. Although these functions remain central to its mission, Communitech has embraced a broader role in regional governance. Like CTT Inc., its leadership and board of advisors represents private sector and economic development interests. However, it has also led and supported a wide variety of initiatives in social and cultural areas, including the local symphony and Oktoberfest. In addition, the organization has been involved in the Intelligent Community Task Force, the Physician Recruitment Task Force, the Waterloo Region Immigration Employment Network, and the Prosperity Council. Members include officials from all levels of government, the local chambers of commerce, the universities, and other community groups.

These two organizations (CTT, Communitech) have transcended their narrowly economic initial mandates to become leaders in regional governance (Wolfe 2012; Nelles 2014). Both associations have been described as catalysts of regional initiatives with the critical mass and political weight to bring people to the table in a wide variety of areas beyond economic development. While the associations themselves cannot be described as widely inclusive – despite the relative increase in the diversity of their membership and partners – the scope of their activities shows a growing commitment to diversity, cultural vibrancy, and regional health. However, at their cores CTT Inc. and Communitech remain economic development associations, and their involvement in cultural and social spheres is consistently in the name of regional prosperity. In addition, the support of both organizations is viewed as critical for any new, large-scale regional initiative. As a result, these organizations act as de facto gatekeepers to the evolution of strategic management and governance in the Waterloo region (Nelles 2014).

In 2003, the Prosperity Council was created by the Kitchener-Waterloo Chamber of Commerce and includes the Cambridge Chamber of Commerce, CTT Inc., and Communitech among its founding members. The council was established as a federation to "collectively create an environment that supports opportunities for prosperity in Waterloo region" (Prosperity Council of Waterloo Region 2009) following a visioning exercise that united local business, government, and community interests to discuss regional development. It has a broader mandate and membership compared to CTT Inc. and Communitech, which have an economic development focus.

The Prosperity Council acts as a locus of regional debate and discussion and has been a launch pad for several regional initiatives (but not a leading organization). Nevertheless, the council has played a significant role in opening up discussions on broader issues underpinning regional prosperity, such as physician attraction and retention, post-secondary education, and the role of arts and culture, which ultimately led to the creation of the Creative Enterprise Initiative. While the Prosperity Council has the most broadly inclusive regional initiative, interviews conducted for this study indicated that it may yet remain too economic in focus, even as it tackles issues of broader social and cultural importance to the region. This economic bias is hardly surprising, given the involvement of core economic actors.

The Deepening Pool: Recent Governance Initiatives

With these foundations in place, several regional governance associations and forums dealing with narrower mandates emerged, including the Waterloo Region Immigration Employment Network (2006), Manufacturing Innovation Network (2007), and the Waterloo Region Tourism Marketing Corporation (2008). Each initiative emerged relatively recently to address specific regional challenges or capitalize on opportunities for development, and each plays a role in strategies to support the future prosperity of the region. Moreover, each has involved a diverse range of regional actors in its work. These emerging governance initiatives cover a wider range of issues and include a wider diversity of interests than ever before. They demonstrate an increasing commitment to regional coordination. However, despite accelerating regional governance, the degree to which these initiatives can be considered inclusive – as genuine bridges that link economic, social, and cultural actors and interests – is in question (Nelles 2014).

As noted, two organizations – CTT Inc. and Communitech – are ubiquitous actors in almost every regional forum imaginable. In interviews conducted for this project, subjects were asked to name key individuals and associations active at the regional level in the three sectors of interest: economic, social, and cultural/arts. No matter the sector of the interview subject, without exception each interviewee named the same core associations and leaders in the economic sphere. CTT Inc., Communitech, and the Prosperity Council were all cited repeatedly as the key associations concerned with economic governance in the region (Nelles 2014). The support of these organizations lends legitimacy and resources to emerging partnerships. This raises some interesting questions about the consequences of this participation in shaping regional agendas, or which initiatives succeed or fail. Thus, despite inclusivity in some initiatives, the degree to which non-economic and/or non-central participants are able to steer agendas remains unclear. These organizations seem to lead, or at least play an important catalytic role, in every major regional initiative that has emerged since the early 1990s. So deep is their involvement that one might ask whether a regional program can be successfully launched without their (at least tacit) support. As Nelles (2014) notes, merely considering this possibility raises important questions about the implications of having such a consistently strong group at the centre of regional governance. On one hand, these organizations have been catalysts in cooperation, bringing diverse groups together, achieving critical mass to move forward, and bringing legitimacy to the projects that they support. On the other hand, to what extent are these organizations becoming gatekeepers of the regional governance agenda in Waterloo? What of the projects that fail to gain their support? And to what degree are problems that don't serve the interests of these associations being seriously addressed regionally as a result? (Nelles 2014). What is clear, however, is that, regardless of potential bias, these organizations have been invaluable in promoting a regional agenda and successful in expanding the scope of discussion to ever-wider issues related to the region's future. In this respect, they are anchor institutions that have produced increasing collaboration and awareness of regional issues.

Has Waterloo Met its Waterloo?

The discussion above reveals cracks in the dominant and accepted narrative of the Waterloo region. On the one hand, Waterloo is a dynamic and innovative technology-based region and a hotbed of talent, with the institutional and civic leadership capacity to allow the region to evolve and adapt over time (see Wolfe 2010, 2012). On the other hand, the research conducted for this project suggests that Waterloo has pockets of innovation and some ability to attract talent, with institutions and civic-leadership capacity that are focused primarily on economic development and led by two powerful regional development actors with the ability to shape the region's trajectory in specific ways. Thus, the story of Waterloo needs to be retold or interpreted carefully.

With regards to innovation in the region, there is a mixed story. A robust and evolving institutional architecture supports entrepreneurship and start-ups, including in the emerging digital media industries. However, findings indicate that the university plays a far lesser role than expected in traditional technology transfer; the university does, however, play several important regional roles in attracting, producing, and retaining talent and land development, thereby contributing to innovation and quality of place. With respect to talent, the region depends more on its reputation as a destination for cool jobs and meaningful, cutting-edge work than recent theories emphasizing amenities and quality of place would suggest. Our research contributes to the debate about how well the creative-class thesis stands up under empirical scrutiny. Recent evidence suggests that the dynamics of talent attraction and retention in smaller and mid-sized cities are different, particularly in tolerance and diversity (Sands and Reese 2008; Lewis and Donald 2010; Vinodrai 2014). The Waterloo case adds additional empirical weight to such claims. However, there is a view that Waterloo's cool jobs will not be enough in an age of global talent wars; as this chapter has outlined, there are efforts to alter this dynamic, although it is too soon to evaluate the efficacy of such initiatives.

Finally, in terms of governance, the region has an unusually well-developed set of organizations that act as regional stewards (Nelles 2014). However, these organizations are focused primarily on economic development and wield significant power in which projects gain legitimacy and – ultimately – funding. Membership and involvement in these organizations reflects an entrenched business elite, rather than a truly inclusive group of local actors. In other words, one interpretation of Waterloo's economic resilience might be that regional economic resilience has much to do with the nature of the elite business networks, which – while increasingly open and inclusive – are quite closed in some ways and represent specific economic interests.

In summary, this chapter suggests both a narrative and counter-narrative of Waterloo's success. The region's success encompasses contradictory stories that are not easily reconciled. These contradictions are part of the region's story and deserve recognition through a more nuanced analysis of the regional economy that recognizes the often contradictory and power-laden processes at play. In a post-mortem note, this chapter would be remiss in not taking account of the ongoing saga of Blackberry. While it is too early to know whether the company will be sold, be taken private, or continue in a different form, the implications of its fate for the future of the regional economy remains an open question. Nonetheless, the local institution building and investments made by Blackberry's founders may create part of the foundation for future regional prosperity. Thus, Waterloo remains a living regional laboratory for understanding long-term regional resiliency and economic dynamism and one well worth studying.

Acknowledgments

This research was funded by the Social Sciences and Humanities Research Council of Canada (SSHRC) grant no. 412-05-1001. The author acknowledges the editorial assistance, patience, and valuable comments provided by David Wolfe and Meric Gertler. The author is especially grateful for the insights provided through the research conducted by Harald Bathelt, Allison Bramwell, Dieter Kogler, Andrew Munro, Jen Nelles, Ben Spigel, and David Wolfe. The author would also like to thank Jordan Katz, Nirvana Micoo, Lynn Despatie, Jordan Hypes, and Michael Seasons for research assistance in this project.

Notes

1 While the region can be referred to as Canada's technology triangle, Kitchener census metropolitan area (CMA), Waterloo region, and the Kitchener-Waterloo region, throughout this chapter, the city-region will be referred to as "Waterloo," except when presenting statistical data, when the term *Kitchener CMA* is used.

2 Managerial, communications, marketing, and human resource talent were viewed as more mobile within the region, whereas technical talent was viewed as having more specialized skills that were not always transferable to other local firms.

References

Almeida, Paul, and Bruce Kogut. 1999. "Localization of knowledge and the mobility of engineers in regional networks." *Management Science* 45 (7): 905–17. http://dx.doi.org/10.1287/mnsc.45.7.905.

Angel, David. 1991. "High-technology agglomeration and the labor market: The case of Silicon Valley." *Environment & Planning A* 23 (10): 1501–16. http://dx.doi.org/10.1068/a231501.

Bathelt, Harald, and Alfred Hecht. 1990. "Key technology industries in the Waterloo Region: Canada's Technology Triangle." *Canadian Geographer / Le Géographe canadien* 34 (3): 225–34. http://dx.doi.org/10.1111/j.1541-0064.1990.tb01081.x.

Bathelt, Harald, Dieter F. Kogler, and Andrew K. Munro. 2011. "Social foundations of regional innovation and the role of university spin-offs: The case of Canada's technology triangle." *Industry and Innovation* 18 (5): 461–86. http://dx.doi.org/10.1080/13662716.2011.583462.

Bathelt, Harald, Andrew K. Munro, and Ben Spigel. 2011. "Challenges of transformation, innovation, re-bundling and traditional manufacturing in Canada's Technology Triangle." *Regional Studies* 47 (7): 1111–30. http://dx.doi.org/10.1080/00343404.2011.602058.

Beckstead, Desmond, and Mark Brown. 2003. *From Labrador City to Toronto: The industrial diversity of Canadian cities, 1992–2002.* Ottawa: Analytical Studies Branch, Statistics Canada.

Best, Michael. 2001. *The new competitive advantage: The renewal of American industry.* London: Oxford University Press. http://dx.doi.org/10.1093/0198297459.001.0001.

Bramwell, Allison, Jen Nelles, and David A. Wolfe. 2008. "Knowledge, innovation and institutions: Global and local dimensions of the ICT cluster in Waterloo, Canada." *Regional Studies* 42 (1): 101–16. http://dx.doi.org/10.1080/00343400701543231.

Bramwell, Allison, and David A. Wolfe. 2008. "Universities and regional economic development: The entrepreneurial University of Waterloo." *Research Policy* 37 (8): 1175–87. http://dx.doi.org/10.1016/j.respol.2008.04.016.

Cooke, Phil. 2001. "Regional innovation systems, clusters, and the knowledge economy." *Industrial and Corporate Change* 10 (4): 945–74. http://dx.doi.org/10.1093/icc/10.4.945.

Cooke, Philip, Bjørn Asheim, Ron Boschma, Ron Martin, Dafna Schwartz, and Franz Tödtling, eds. 2011. *Handbook of regional innovation and growth.* London: Edward Elgar. http://dx.doi.org/10.4337/9780857931504.

Donald, Betsy, and Doug Morrow. 2003. *Competing for talent: Implications for social and cultural policy in Canadian city-regions.* Ottawa: Strategic Research and Analysis, Canadian Heritage.

Fagerberg, Jan, David C. Mowery, and Richard R. Nelson, eds. 2006. *The Oxford handbook of innovation.* Oxford: Oxford University Press. http://dx.doi.org/10.1093/oxfordhb/9780199286805.001.0001.

Florida, Richard. 2002. *The rise of the creative class.* New York: Basic Books.

Gertler, Meric S., and Tara Vinodrai. 2005. "Anchors of creativity: How public universities create competitive and cohesive communities." In *Taking public universities seriously*, ed. F. Iacobucci and C. Tuohy, 293–314. Toronto: University of Toronto Press.

Keenan, Greg, Gordon Pitts, and Heather Scoffield. 2006. "Waterloo a place that doesn't hold back its best." *Globe and Mail*, 25 April 2006. http://www.theglobeandmail.com/technology/waterloo-a-place-that-doesnt-hold-back-its-best/article22504053/

Kulha, Shari. 2013. "With a tech-sector-aided boom, Kitchener is rethinking everything from its housing to its nightlife." *National Post*, 16 January 2013. http://news.nationalpost.com/homes/with-a-tech-sector-aided-boom-kitchener-is-rethinking-everything-from-its-housing-to-its-nightlife.

Lawton Smith, Helen. 2008. "Inter-firm networks in high-tech clusters." In *Handbook of research on innovation and clusters*, ed. C. Karlsson, 107–23. Cheltenham, UK: Edward Elgar. http://dx.doi.org/10.4337/9781848445079.00013.

Leibovitz, Joseph. 2003. "Institutional barriers to associative city-region governance: The politics of institution-building and economic governance in 'Canada's technology triangle.'" *Urban Studies* 40 (13): 2613–42. http://dx.doi.org/10.1080/0042098032000146812.

Lewis, Nathaniel M., and Betsy Donald. 2010. "A new rubric for creative city potential in Canada's smaller cities." *Urban Studies* 47 (1): 29–54. http://dx.doi.org/10.1177/0042098009346867.

Malecki, Edward J. 2011. "Technology clusters." In *Handbook of regional innovation and growth*, ed. Philip Cooke, Bjørn Asheim, Ron Boschma, Ron Martin, Dafna Schwartz, and Franz Tödtling, 315–32. London: Edward Elgar. http://dx.doi.org/10.4337/9780857931504.00040.

Nelles, Jen. 2014. "Myth making and the 'Waterloo way': Exploring associative governance in Kitchener-Waterloo." In *Governing urban economies: Innovation and inclusion in Canadian city-regions*, ed. Neil Bradford and Allison Bramwell, 88–109. Toronto: University of Toronto Press.

Nelles, Jen, Allison Bramwell, and David A. Wolfe. 2005. "History, culture and path dependency: The origins of the Waterloo ICT cluster." In *Global networks and local linkages: The paradox of cluster development in an open economy*, ed. David A. Wolfe and Matthew Lucas, 227–53. Montreal and Kingston: McGill-Queen's University Press.

Parker, Paul. 2001. "Local-global partnerships for high-tech development: Integrating top-down and bottom-up models." *Economic Development Quarterly* 15 (2): 149–67. http://dx.doi.org/10.1177/089124240101500204.

Peck, Jamie. 2005. "Struggling with the creative class." *International Journal of Urban and Regional Research* 29 (4): 740–70. http://dx.doi.org/10.1111/j.1468-2427.2005.00620.x.

Prosperity Council of Waterloo Region. 2009. "Our mission." Accessed 9 September 2009. http://www.prosperitywaterloo.ca

Rutherford, Tod, and John Holmes. 2008. "Engineering networks: University-industry networks in Southern Ontario automotive industry clusters." *Cambridge Journal of Regions, Economy and Society* 1 (2): 247–64. http://dx.doi.org/10.1093/cjres/rsn001.

Sands, Gary, and Laura A. Reese. 2008. "Cultivating the creative class: And what about Nanaimo?" *Economic Development Quarterly* 22 (1): 8–23. http://dx.doi.org/10.1177/0891242407309822.

Saxenian, AnnaLee. 1994. *Regional advantage: Culture and competition in Silicon Valley and Route 128*. Cambridge, MA: Harvard University Press.

–. 2006. *The new argonauts: Regional advantage in a global economy*. Cambridge, MA: Harvard University Press.

Scott, Allen J. 2006. "Creative cities: Conceptual issues and policy problems." *Journal of Urban Affairs* 28 (1): 1–17. http://dx.doi.org/10.1111/j.0735-2166.2006.00256.x.

Spencer, Greg, and Tara Vinodrai. 2006. *Waterloo city-region profile, 2001*. Toronto: Innovation Systems Research Network.

–. 2009. *Waterloo city-region profile, 2006*. Toronto: Innovation Systems Research Network.

Spencer, Gregory M., Tara Vinodrai, Meric S. Gertler, and David A. Wolfe. 2010. "Do clusters make a difference? Defining and assessing their economic performance." *Regional Studies* 44 (6): 697–715. http://dx.doi.org/10.1080/00343400903107736.

Vinodrai, Tara. 2009. "The university as an anchor in the regional economy: Evidence from Kitchener-Waterloo, Canada." Paper presented at "The Larger Role of the University in Economic Development" conference, University of North Carolina at Chapel Hill, Chapel Hill, NC, 22–4 April.

–. 2010. "The dynamics of economic change in Canadian cities: Innovation, culture and the emergence of a knowledge based economy." In *Canadian cities in transition*, 4th ed., ed. Trudi Bunting, Pierre Filion, and Ryan Walker, 87–109. London: Oxford.

–. 2014. "Attracting and retaining talent in Canadian cities: Towards a holistic view?" In *Seeking talent for creative cities: The social dynamics of economic innovation*, ed. Jill L. Grant, 31–56. Toronto: University of Toronto Press.

Vinodrai, Tara, Riaz Nathu, Emily Robson, Scott Ross, Paul Parker, and Steffanie Scott. 2012. *Taking regional action? Understanding networks in the local food, green energy and creative sectors in Waterloo region*. Report prepared for the Economic Developers Council of Ontario.

Walton Roberts, Margaret. 2008. "Immigration, the university and the tolerant second-tier city." CERIS working paper 69. Toronto: Centre of Excellence for Research on Immigration and Settlement.

Wolfe, David A. 2009. *21st century cities in Canada: The geography of innovation*. Ottawa: Conference Board of Canada.

–. 2010. "The strategic management of core cities: Path dependence and economic adjustment in resilient regions." *Cambridge Journal of Regions, Economy and Society* 3 (1): 139–52. http://dx.doi.org/10.1093/cjres/rsp032.

–. 2012. "Civic governance, social learning and the strategic management of city-regions." In *Creating competitiveness: Entrepreneurship and innovation policies for growth*, ed. David B. Audretsch and Mary L. Walshok, 6–25. Cheltenham, UK: Edward Elgar. http://dx.doi.org/10.4337/9781781954058.00006.

9 Ordinary City at the Crossroads: London, Ontario

NEIL BRADFORD

Introduction[1]

In recent years, studies of economic development in OECD countries have stressed the importance of innovation – the generation of new ideas and institutions that enable firms and communities to thrive in the knowledge-based competition that drives the global economy. Importantly, this research also reveals innovation to be iterative and interactive, engaging a host of economic actors in relationships that circulate different forms of specialized knowledge. It follows that some of the most dynamic "innovation systems" have emerged in geographically localized places that supply a creative milieu for learning and collaboration. Those places containing a supple infrastructure of knowledge supports and networks, as well as an attractive mix of urban amenities and cultural openness, can expect ample flows of investment and talent (Wolfe 2009; Florida 2002).

Not surprisingly, innovation studies have concentrated on large cosmopolitan city-regions that are the knowledge economy's "creativity hotbeds" (OECD 2006; Sands and Reese 2008). However, in many countries, Canada included, there are only a handful of such urban powerhouses. A clear majority of citizens still reside in smaller places, typically mid-sized cities with knowledge infrastructures, amenity mixes, and demographic profiles quite different from the aspiring global cities of Toronto, Vancouver, and Montreal. Yet these places must find their way in the new global economic competition. How can they build their niche by leveraging a quite different, arguably more mundane set of local assets? What innovation strategies are available to cities without an identifiable economic brand or convincing creativity narrative? (Lewis and Donald 2010).

This chapter takes up these questions through case study analysis of one such city with its share of innovation gaps and creativity deficits in today's knowledge-based economic competition: London, Ontario. For context, we draw on recent literature analysing "ordinary" cities (Benneworth 2007; Todtling and Trippl 2005). This literature convincingly argues that ordinary cities are distinguished by certain innovation system failures and further, that these can be tackled through concerted mobilizations that strategically couple local planning with extra-local resources. In these terms, we report on both London's limitations and on recent civic collaborations to make change.

The chapter is organized in three parts. We begin by first locating London as an ordinary city, highlighting its fit within the conceptual frame. Second, we report on aspects of London's innovation and creativity profile, moving from business clusters to labour markets and governance arrangements. Finally, we track the emergence of an interesting set of collaborations and networks designed to reposition the city, a civic effort with considerable urgency in the wake of the recent global financial crisis that devastated London's traditional economic pillars.

Innovation and Creativity in the Ordinary City: Locating London

The much-discussed "place turn" in economic development research has spawned two robust bodies of urban and regional literature. On the one hand, there has been much analysis of the high-performing city-regions with well-developed clusters of leading-edge firms embedded in learning communities that capture knowledge spillovers and exchange ideas. These success stories have their own tensions, but their robust innovation systems enable research breakthroughs and product innovations (Scott 2006). On the other hand, there are many case studies of places at the other end of the continuum, the "less-favoured" cities and regions that economic modernization has bypassed. With an over-specialization in older industries relying on outdated technologies or raw materials, these places confront massive restructuring challenges and do so without the knowledge networks or compelling amenities that facilitate change in the dynamic urban centres. Over the past three decades a number of such marginalized places have managed quite remarkable comebacks, and scholars have been almost as keen to tell their stories as those of the "new economy hotbeds" in Silicon Valley or the Third Italy (Cooke and Morgan 1998).

While the scholarly preoccupation with the drama of the hotbeds and hinterlands is understandable, it leaves another category of cities largely on the analytical sidelines. These are the in-between places, neither the cosmopolitan hubs nor the crisis-ridden outposts. On several grounds these cites are unexceptional. Mid-sized in population, lacking flagship firms or cluster profiles to distinguish the local economy, these places also are without cultural claim to either the hip buzz of the big cities or the quaint identity of many smaller cities (Chatterton 2000).

Yet there is little evidence to suggest that such cities are not performing well enough to maintain a reasonable place quality and living standard (Statistics Canada 2008). In their ordinariness, they contain elements of a local innovation system but lack the full complement of networked assets that distinguish the high performers. They are not the "places to be" – innovative milieux where talented professionals and leading-edge firms congregate to access the latest know-how or know-who. Ordinary cities are pressured to adapt their economies, not only to hold their middle ground but to advance rather than fall back as competitive conditions change. As such, their developmental agenda exhibits a particular logic – adjustments less encompassing than the wholesale reinventions called for in the less-favoured cities, yet involving something more than the ongoing fine-tuning sufficient at the leading edge (Bradford 2003).

For all these reasons, the ordinary city and its development trajectory are an important research subject. A good starting point comes from Todtling and Trippl, who offer a useful conceptualization of the challenges, identifying three broad categories: lock-in, organizational thinness, and internal fragmentation (Todtling and Trippl 2005). *Lock-in* refers not just to an economic specialization in mature industries, but to wider cognitive blockages that reinforce traditional mindsets, thereby limiting renewal possibilities through different ideas and people. *Organizational thinness* reflects the relative absence of knowledge generation and transfer networks that compromises the local economy's cluster growth. *Internal fragmentation* arises when cities house the assets of innovation, including research and educational institutions and entrepreneurial talent, but lack the social relations and governance networks to leverage or assemble the parts.

The identification of these cognitive, organizational, and institutional gaps provides a template for interpreting the challenges in cities without robust innovation systems. For their part, Todtling and Trippl return the focus to the less-favoured regions, classifying places on the basis of which of the three "system failures" precipitates economic collapse. However, we propose that the specificity of the ordinary city innovation challenge lies precisely in the *presenting mix of elements of all three system gaps*. Where a less-favoured region or city may fail in one dimension on an order of magnitude producing structural economic crisis, in the ordinary city, conditions and signals are more ambiguous.

It follows that the ordinary city's economy requires a more balanced set of interventions and middle-range adjustments. Civic leaders in the ordinary city are likely to find themselves addressing all three gaps identified by Todtling and Trippl, at the same time but in forms less intense than that expressed in the less-favoured region. For the ordinary city, the default position of allowing embedded development trajectories to continue to deliver less than optimal performance is always at hand. Such passive resistance to change, however, may consign local leaders to managing long-term decline. For ordinary cities, the question of how to initiate change and sustain momentum is complex. Issues of "local agency" become more salient than in either the less-favoured regions or the leading-edge centres (Benneworth 2007).

These descriptions of the ordinary city speak directly to the case of London, Ontario. Long known as the "typically Canadian city," London has been relied upon by corporations for test marketing new consumer products from drugs to doughnuts. In a series exploring the city's elusive identity, the *London Free Press* summarized, "Life in London may be as ordinary, statistically speaking, as it can get" (Richmond 2011a). Across a number of economic and demographic indicators, London's post-war performance gravitated close to provincial and Canadian averages. A mid-sized Canadian city, with a population of about 350,000 and the urban centre of a census metropolitan area of some 460,000 people, London is the country's tenth-largest market area, a regional hub for Southwestern Ontario, for both its agricultural producers and smaller cities and towns. Located at the junction of three important 400 series highways and the Ontario city closest to all three major U.S. border crossing (Detroit, Buffalo, and Port Huron), London prospered in the second half of the twentieth century as a site of choice for many subsidiaries of American manufacturers, notably in food and beverage, automotive parts, aircraft and locomotive assembly.

The foundations of this unremarkable yet stable trajectory began to come apart in the 1990s (London Economic Development Corporation 1998). As continental and global restructuring took its toll on Ontario's economy, London lost several of its corporate head offices, and many branch-plant manufacturers closed. London's economic performance, population growth, and median family income fell behind those of its key mid-sized municipal competitors. Moreover, the head-office flight drained away business leaders and philanthropic families heavily invested in the community, and signalled that, in the new knowledge economy, London's labour market would not offer the same opportunities for either senior advancement or professional mobility. London consistently places in the lower half of the field of Canadian mid-sized census metropolitan areas on measures of innovation such as cluster employment, educational attainment, employment, and employment in creative industries (Spencer and Vinodrai 2009). As the Martin Prosperity Institute stated in their mid-sized city technology, talent, and tolerance rankings, "London has some advantages but would benefit from improved performance on the 3Ts as it positions itself to compete in a creative economy" (Martin Prosperity Institute 2009, 7). While civic leaders were miffed when a national coalition of Canadian Technology Cities – the so-called C-11 – declined to include London, one observer noted, "London's steady-she-slows economy has put it far down on a new ranking of Canadian cities" (Richmond 2011b).

In fact, London's capacity for change and renewal has been constrained by the three barriers associated with the ordinary city. The city's business culture, forged by an impressive post-war generation of corporate elites in insurance and banking, was conservative and risk-averse – an "old boys club" with high barriers to entry, resistant to new ideas, and embodying "London's traditional bland modesty" (Pedro 2011). Experiencing such cultural lock-in first-hand, one young technology entrepreneur was dismayed at the "destructive and self-propagated" image of closed-minded conservatism (MacLean 2005). When the municipal government established an economic development agency to lead renewal, its initial priorities were "old economy thinking": attracting branch plants by making available serviced industrial land at the city's edges and waiving development charges for incoming investors (Pedro 2011). Concerns surfaced about the business sector's organizational thinness as knowledge assets in the city's two post-secondary institutions and several health research centres remained disconnected from the local economy. Internal fragmentation was another challenge. London evolved few leadership networks that connected the economy and the community, and there were no institutional structures that in many other cities engage civic dialogue around longer-term challenges. A major public engagement exercise in the mid-1990s produced little substantive policy change as the municipal administration became embroiled in a series of internal disputes and scandals (Cornies 2002). A detailed study of London's downtown revitalization efforts in the 1990s found "no evidence that a stable, informal, and cross-sectoral governing coalition guided development policy-making in London" (Cobban 2003, 352). Young people, it was reported, found the city "hard to penetrate if you don't know how to get in to know people, to get into the different organizations" (Richmond 2011a, 2011b, 2012).

Simply put, key aspects of London's urban development resonate with the ordinary city experience. However, this is not the whole story. Over the last decade, civic leaders in London have exercised *local agency*, mobilizing on several innovation and creativity fronts to enhance the city's economic prospects in a far more demanding continental and global context. The rest of this chapter examines in more detail London's evolving "innovation journey" (Benneworth 2007). The analysis focuses on three central dynamics: business innovation, creative talent, and governance capacity.

Innovation in London: Firms and Knowledge Flows

Scholarly study of innovation processes makes three key points about local economic development (Gertler 2001). First, the innovative capacity of a city or region has less to do with its size or even location; rather, "place matters": the social and institutional milieu enables firms in related industries to forge trust relations and learning networks. Second, in a knowledge-driven economy, innovation depends on the breadth and quality of knowledge that is locally available, the degree to which it circulates widely and rapidly, and the extent to which actors can put it to productive use (Malmberg and Maskell 2002). Third, global-local knowledge interactions are crucial everywhere, but their form and content can vary across cities. While spatial proximity is important, research also shows that innovation does not spring from local sources of knowledge alone (Wolfe and Gertler 2006). A consensus has emerged among innovation scholars on the importance of firms accessing both global and local knowledge pools, with the optimal mix determined by particular city-region economic profiles and specializations.

In these terms, London presents an interesting innovation case, confirming the variable mix of knowledge sources and flows. To capture London's dynamics, our analysis focused on a selection of 25 firms classified as "innovators" by the chamber of commerce. The most significant finding is that interactions and connections among firms in the local economy are quite infrequent. For most firms, networks of knowledge exchange tend to be global with firms and researchers in related sectors. In terms of local attachments, firms lack opportunities or are unwilling to collaborate with other firms in the London region. Similarly, ties to local research capacity have also been weak. These findings echo the message of a London technology audit that reported that the city's 250 or so high-technology firms exhibited few cluster synergies. They operated without the "glue" of anchor companies that branded the sector and seeded start-ups or spinoffs, and lacked the "local buzz" flowing through collaborative networks in research, finance, and entrepreneurship (London Economic Development Corporation 2006). In fact, our research reveals that many leading firms in London are innovative while not embedded in any identifiable or thick local "regional network-based industrial system" (Saxenian 1996, 2). Instead, these firms are globally networked through strategic interfaces with, and position in, global value chains to access the ideas and information that drive innovation. Such firms seldom engage in local technology consortiums or learning communities, reflecting the marginal value they place on local knowledge flows. Indeed, our research found that global orientations and connections were often the reason why interaction with other co-located firms and the universities, community colleges, and laboratories remained a low priority.

Among the firms in our sample, most base their competitive advantage in the market on factors such as product quality and design, responsiveness to customer needs, and efficiency of production and/or service delivery. Customers are often cited as important sources of product ideas and market feedback but are rarely considered as partners in innovation. They are more providers of feedback to which firms can be more or less responsive. Similarly, suppliers were also cited as sources of innovation, generally to the extent that their own product innovations open up new possibilities. In general, it falls to in-house development departments to adapt to these market inputs and drive innovation. Foreign-owned firms also cite parent companies and affiliates as important sources of innovation. As with suppliers, foreign parents or affiliates were most instrumental in developing products or processes that the London firm then incorporated into its development cycle. Therefore, the transmission of knowledge and innovation through globally linked firm networks can be characterized in most cases as passive – a simple transfer – rather than a collaboration.

These observations reveal that *internal* sources of innovation – through in-house R&D divisions – have typically been the most important for firms in the London region. Where customers, suppliers, and foreign parents and affiliates were cited as factors, these were overwhelmingly non-local. As a result, knowledge flows most frequently between the London firm and its individually developed, industrially specific, and primarily non-local customer/supplier network, and does not typically extend to firms in the region or outside the sector. The attitude prevails that the benefits of engaging local firms in knowledge exchange are imperceptible or not worth the effort, with some firms arguing that such sharing with other firms would be too risky to justify collaboration. A small number of firms mentioned that informal collaboration with co-located firms occurred, but stressed that this was only on general areas of the business and not on proprietary issues. Interviews revealed that instances of informal cooperation on broad matters such as "best practices" rarely extended to "technology development" involving exchange or sharing of intellectual property.

One of London's latent strengths is the quality of its higher education institutions (such as Western University [WU] and Fanshawe College) and research organizations in areas like health sciences and advanced manufacturing. The richness of these local knowledge assets is widely recognized, yet few firms in our study have formalized local research linkages. Many firms feel that academia and public research organizations have little to offer their businesses and, further, that public research entities and universities are too slow, are too difficult to deal with, and ask too much in return for formal partnerships to justify the effort. As one CEO summarized, "They [external R&D labs/universities] move at the speed of institutions and we have to move at the speed of industry" (confidential interview, 2008). While many firms announced a general interest in engaging university researchers, most had no concrete plans to do so and were wary of dealing with technology-transfer officials.

In addition, few firms in our sample found the resources or influence of London's economic development organizations to be significant to their growth and business planning. With the municipally supported London Economic Development Corporation (LEDC), strong support in principle was tempered by limited practical engagement. Responses varied from very positive support for the organization to frustration with the narrow focus of its strategies. Very few interviewees referred to the LEDC as a significant actor in the region, and for most firms in the sample, the organization's impact was viewed as limited. Responses for the high-technology network TechAlliance were similar. Most firms in the region are aware of its existence and support its mission. But engagement, for the most part, was either passive – dues-paying members and event participants when invited – or more expressions of community service quite unrelated to core business needs.

Finally, local flows of labour as a potential source of knowledge exchange between firms tended to be relatively rare. Neither the knowledge workers involved in the innovation nor senior management had typically worked in other firms in the region. Hiring in these areas was also described as a global process, and these firms rarely advertised positions in general job forums. Reputational factors were cited as an important magnet for talent. People on the research or technical side, interested in working in a given field, knew the most innovative firms and contacted them for employment, even when positions were not advertised. Senior management frequently commented that they needed professionals who understood the intricacies of their unique type of business – knowledge that is much harder to find locally – and therefore emphasized more global talent pools. This external orientation to talent also limited the degree to which knowledge flows between firms in London. People who chose to leave these firms usually also left the region.

In sum, London's innovation profile features limited local knowledge flows, thin inter-organizational networks, and few institutional focal points of interaction. The dynamic arises from a combination of firm reliance on global customers, suppliers, and talent, and a guarded or "closed" innovation process that places a high premium on in-house knowledge as a form of protected intellectual property on the local scene. Several broader implications arise from this innovation pattern. Here, AnnaLee Saxenian's classic account of industrial and institutional change in different regional settings offers useful perspective (Saxenian 1996). She highlights the particular adjustment challenges facing firms in regions lacking sophisticated local knowledge infrastructures when markets, technologies, and tastes all suddenly change. While some leading-edge firms managed the transition, many more in traditional sectors or start-ups foundered. While it is difficult to predict the potential foregone when city-region economies evolve with weak local knowledge flows, an important message is that there will be less resilience in periods of significant restructuring.

Since the 2008 Great Recession, London has faced precisely the kind of challenges described in Saxenian's account. Southwestern Ontario's key secondary manufacturing sectors, notably automotive assembly and parts sector have been hollowed out. London's economy was plunged into its worst recession since the Great Depression. Within a year, the city-region's unemployment rate skyrocketed to over 11 per cent, the second-highest in the country, social assistance claims increased 20 per cent, and only part-time work showed any resilience (Hunter 2009). Two years later, things had yet to improve – in July 2011, London had the highest unemployment rate of any urban centre in Canada, with major plant closures in both manufacturing and service sectors. Complicating London's challenges were economic studies (Martin Prosperity Institute 2009; Conference Board of Canada 2010) from national think tanks that took a dim view of the city's economic prospects, especially in comparison with key mid-sized competitors such as Waterloo and Ottawa. As a beleaguered mayor put it, "Every time we see a report like this, it means we have to work just that much harder" (Richmond 2011b).

In Saxenian's terms, London has confronted the major economic challenges of the early twentieth century with an industrial culture and innovation pattern that makes broad-based economic transformation – as distinct from "ordinary growth" – difficult.

Are there signs that London's economic infrastructure may evolve to support such transformation through a better balance of global and local knowledge flows? Saxenian emphasizes that major economic shocks can be the catalyst for economic and institutional change. She specifies two steps to success. First, city-region economic leaders must recognize the need to act differently and embrace new mindsets. Second, they need to deliver on the "shared understandings," creating opportunities for a range of economic knowledge-holders to join together for collaborative problem-solving (Saxenian 1996, 167).

In these terms, London's recent history is noteworthy. Partnerships and networks are emerging to embed firms locally, engage talent, and bridge the economy and community. The next two sections of this chapter track a series of civic initiatives to leverage London economy's global connectedness *and* local embeddedness.

Creativity in London: Growing Talent, Seeking Diversity

Scholarship on urban creativity concentrates on the large cosmopolitan city-regions with their thick knowledge infrastructures, interesting amenity mixes, and culturally diverse populations (Lewis and Donald 2010). London stands for the many ordinary cities without credible claim to either "hip buzz" or "quaint character." London is regularly overlooked in Canadian urban creativity tables, and it trails several competitor cities in its attraction of immigrants and retention of its own university graduates. A former WU president described the university – and the city – as a "pass through," with 85 per cent of students not from London leaving upon graduation (Graham 2008). More generally, London is perceived as a conservative, insular community and boring city – "all elements of an ordinary city [but] not the foundations upon which to build a distinct identity" (Richmond 2011a). While these images are partial, various factors contribute to their perpetuation: local institutions and clubs that long excluded women and ethno-racial minorities, the refusal of a 1990s mayor to proclaim Gay Pride Week, thereby breaching Ontario human rights legislation and resulting in a fine for the municipality, and an uninspired city-region form with a deteriorating downtown core and sprawling suburbs (Currie 2006).

By the early 2000s, such attitudes and practices came under fire. Important here was the recruitment of a new chief administrative officer, Jeff Fielding, from Kitchener in 2004, who delivered "a wake-up call" to the city council (Miller 2004). Pulling together trend line data, Fielding documented London's declining population growth rate in comparison to competitor cities and drew attention to looming labour shortages rooted in a failure to either retain young professionals or attract skilled immigrants. Challenged by Fielding as to whether London sought to play in the municipal "big leagues," the deputy mayor conceded that the city had been sliding over the past decade, that it lacked a focused development strategy, and that it had no clear economic profile or political influence on provincial and national stages.

Fielding's wake-up call set in motion two novel policy and planning processes, each facilitated by the city, representing a form of what Gertler and Wolfe term "organized social learning" (Gertler and Wolfe 2004). Such exercises are initiated in periods of uncertainty and aim to alter both the community mindset and its development priorities. Particularly important, Gertler and Wolfe note, is the intelligence-gathering and vision-building: they need to include diverse interests, question established ways, and engage local leaders beyond the "usual suspects." London's two learning exercises aligned with these criteria, notably the absence of outside consultants and the commitment to diverse representation. Further, the particular mandates of the two exercises complemented one another in seeking fresh perspectives on the city and its challenges and opportunities. The first was the Creative

City Task Force (CCTF), a sixteen-member inquiry with extraordinary cross-sectoral membership from the arts, technology, business, immigrant settlement, municipal, architecture, and tourism sectors (Creative City Task Force 2005). With a mandate to change "the way London thinks" and determine a "strategy to help London become a leader in mid-sized cities in North America," the CCTF tackled cultural diversity, workforce development, and urban design. The second report, *London's Next Economy* (*LNE*) was written by a local technology entrepreneur who was mandated by the four key economic development organizations in London to recommend a framework for ensuring that London leveraged its business-development and research assets to become a "new economy hotbed" (City of London et al. 2005).

Significantly, both reports converged on London's creativity and talent deficit. The *LNE* noted that London's growth gap with its key mid-sized municipal competitors was "particularly concerning in the high value 25–54 year old age group" and that, absent new strategies "to keep its best and brightest at home," the community's long-term prosperity and quality of life would be compromised. "Providing this new economic base," the CCTF declared, "must become a top priority of the City, and its business and labour communities" (2005, 25). From this common perspective, each report addressed key aspects of the three systemic gaps in the innovation systems of ordinary cities. First, with respect to problems of cognitive lock-in, the CCTF was especially blunt, describing a city that was isolated, complacent, and smug, and "perceived as not having an exemplary reputation for welcoming newcomers." It declared that London was "at a crucial stage in strategizing for its future economic development." The *LNE* spoke about the city's inaction in the face of a "stealth-like erosion" of high-end jobs and talent, and perceptions of London "as a comparatively lethargic business community" known for its "modesty and conservative style." London, it declared, was "at an economic crossroads" (6).

Breaking through these cognitive barriers, both reports argued, required tackling the other two systemic problems – organizational thinness and internal fragmentation. The CCTF proposed "partnerships, collaborations, and other joint initiatives" to institutionalize a new development strategy. These included a cultural division in city government to catalyse sectors, a public-private city-wide prosperity congress, an immigrant entrepreneurship council, and networks bridging historical divides between the post-secondary institutions and the local economy. Under the heading "Consolidate, Coordinate and Regionalize," the *LNE* called for a rationalization of the city's economic development services that would unite three existing agencies with intersecting mandates under a single board for "organic growth" and "business attraction." Referencing biomedical and information technology sectors, it questioned why "London has never deliberately leveraged these knowledge assets" (City of London et al. 2005, 8). An innovation infrastructure was proposed, including a local venture-capital fund for start-ups, a research commercialization organization to connect laboratories and markets, and an advanced manufacturing technology park or "downtown tech alley" to enable clustering of knowledge-based enterprises.

These two highly visible social-learning exercises provided a rationale and a roadmap for London to alter its course, while also mobilizing new civic leadership. In their wake, analysts began to refer to London's "brain drain" and "demographic time bomb" (London Economic Development Corporation 2007). They also framed a novel research and policy question: what talent strategies apply in cities missing much of the urban creativity literature's favourite attractors – vibrant downtown cores, compelling urban design, ethno-racial and lifestyle diversity, and a distinctive city "place" brand?

Our interviews with creative workers, their employers, and intermediary organizations offer some answers. London's primary foundations for attracting and retaining talent were identified as economic conditions, with certain characteristics related to "family life" – most notably housing affordability and commuting times – playing a secondary role. Attractors such as a lively downtown, an edgy urban cultural scene, or openness to diverse lifestyles were not locational drivers in London. As one member of the CCTF summarized London's talent challenge, "If you asked any student on the UWO campus if they would consider staying in London, they would answer 'if I can find a job'" (Anderson 2005).

In employment, London's appeal is mixed. On the one hand, high-technology workers appreciated developmental opportunities that were not necessarily available in larger centres such as Toronto, with its deeper talent pools. In London, knowledge workers more rapidly can obtain a breadth of professional experiences and enjoy a more rounded form of creativity autonomy. On the other hand, this advantage, particularly valued by junior professionals, was tempered by general recognition that London's lack of head offices limited upward mobility and senior management progression. In the health and medical science sector, the depth of research opportunities through WU were identified as providing a stimulating and supportive environment for leading-edge work, and increasingly, spin-off enterprises. However, leaders in the smaller information-technology sector pointed to the need for stronger networks, such as between the sector's emerging digital gaming firms and WU's Engineering Department and Fanshawe College's creative media programs.

The other important talent attractor for London is best termed the "pull of family." Several interviewees mentioned a desire to relocate or remain in close proximity to parents or relatives. A complicating factor for professional couples, reported by several intermediary organizations and employers, was the difficulty of finding suitable spousal employment in the London labour market. Overall, there was strong endorsement of London as a good place to raise a family. This theme was elaborated in a variety of ways – affordable housing and overall cost of living, community safety, commuting time, recreational services, and good schools.

London's "physical place quality" either in its built environment or natural assets was not celebrated by our interviewees. They referred to the mundane physical features of the city – its downtown was at best a "work in progress" – and that the city lacked inspired urban design, with an underutilized river front that offered no memorable physical identity or sense of place. The notion that London was a cultural city valuing experimentation or a distinctive built environment conducive to creative industries did not resonate. Here our interviews reinforce the findings from a 2007 LEDC workforce survey that found that persuading candidates to work in London was a greater challenge for London firms than persuading them to work for their company. A final significant issue facing London's talent recruiters was immigrant settlement. When interviewees were asked about barriers, they mentioned difficulties with labour market access and credentials recognition. But these problems were understood as endemic to the federal immigration and provincial regulatory systems rather than arising from local obstacles. At the same time, they expressed the view that London needed to work harder to recognize its own multicultural character and welcome newcomers.

Thus, our data suggest that the creative city variables highlighted by Richard Florida and other cosmopolitan analysts are not leading indicators for London. More prosaic elements come to the fore, specifically jobs and families. When it comes to place quality, continued investments in London's long-standing areas of strength – the social infrastructure of community including housing, transit, schools, and safety – appear most salient. In several of these measures, such as the quality and affordability of the housing stock and commuting distances, London performs above provincial and Canadian averages. In an interesting twist on the usual age-cohort focus of urban creativity, London, in 2010, became the first Canadian municipality to earn the Age-Friendly City designation from the World Health Organization. The mayor noted that retirement homes represent an economic opportunity (Turner 2010). As well, its public school board has been recognized as a provincial leader in creating a tolerant learning environment for children and youth, with notable initiatives in violence prevention and proactively addressing the needs of gay and lesbian students (Rayside 2008). For London, such investments in the fundamentals of urban and *suburban* living are likely to deliver greater community benefit and economic return than "creativity makeovers" that often ignore local context and undervalue enduring strengths. City planners launched a strong neighbourhoods project that included new urban design and sustainability goals for the growing suburbs. In the ordinary city, indicators of urban creativity resonating in large cosmopolitan centres need to give considerable ground to more familiar quality-of-life measures.

In their respective creativity and innovation stock-takings, both London social learning exercises triggered a wide civic discussion about change, underscoring the long-term journey ahead. As the CCTF wrote, "It took the City a number of years to get in this position, and it will take the City a number of years to reverse these trends." The *LNE* projected a "15 year end state" describing London's change process as an "economic evolution" requiring risk and patience (Creative City Task Force 2005, 21).

Of course, the influence of such organized learning exercises should not be overstated. Certainly, both reports were greeted with considerable enthusiasm: about the *LNE*, the mayor stated, "The timing of this bold and insightful report could not be better," and the dean of business at Western University's prestigious business school lauded both reports as groundbreaking, signalling that London was "embarking on an all-important, community-wide partnership" (Stephenson 2005). From the outside, former Winnipeg mayor Glen Murray deemed the London effort "the best creative cities plan in Canada" (Coulson 2005). London CAO Jeff Fielding joined the parade but with an important qualifier. Describing the CCTF as "an outstanding attempt to get something started," he also noted that "London doesn't execute very well" ("The idea of London" 2005).

The next section takes up this issue of translating new ideas into action in London. We report on several novel governance processes playing out across the economic, cultural, and social dimensions of the ordinary city.

Governance in London: Towards an Economic Community

Research on innovative and creative cities highlights the strategic importance of collaborative governance. Beyond the "silos and stovepipes," cities can "improve their prospects for economic development [through] the presence of strong, responsive relationships between the economy and the community that give both firms and the community a sustained advantage (Wolfe 2009, 126). American researchers studying local and regional resilience confirm that the most successful places are "economic communities" that "have learned how to connect their clusters of economic specialization with responsive community competencies such as education, infrastructure, and quality of life" (Henton, Melville, and Walesh 1997, 2).

In these governance matters, London has not been a high performer. Key informants frequently mentioned London's silo mentality, the lack of collaboration, and the absence of an institutional space – a "council of councils" – where the city's economic, social, and cultural interests could meet regularly to consider cross-cutting issues and overall direction (confidential interview 2008). Far from functioning as an "economic community," London, for most of the first decade of the twenty-first century, featured heated conflict between supporters of a development strategy based on industrial recruitment to serviced greenfield sites, and advocates for an organic growth alternative based on local knowledge assets and urban growth boundaries. Close observers of council debates worried about a stalemated political system with "camps that are so divided there is no bringing them together" (Belanger 2010). In 2007, when the Council Planning Committee refused to expand the city's urban growth boundary to accommodate a developer's request for an $80 million industrial park without a prior assessment of the financial implications for the city, the Board of Control's deputy mayor complained that a "whining socialist cabal" was stopping progress (Belanger 2007). The chamber of commerce CEO went so far as to call for a "ceasefire" and urged appointment of an outside facilitator to help councillors find common ground (London Chamber of Commerce 2008).

As noted above, the onset of the 2008 Great Recession altered both the material context and discursive terms of London's economic development strategy. The years since have witnessed several collaborations in economic, social, and cultural development, suggesting a growing governance capacity.

Economic Development: From Growth Machine to Ideas Laboratory?

In 1998, the city established the LEDC after forty business leaders, led by the chamber of commerce, mobilized a campaign for stronger economic leadership in London, with a particular concern to expedite municipal approvals for industrial and commercial development. It is accurate to describe the relationship between the city and the LEDC as a clear example of an *urban growth machine* (Molotch 1976). Growth machines feature the kind of development policy division of labour evident in London: the city supplies plentiful, cheap serviced land while the development agency pursues external investors through ambitious place marketing. In London, the city delivered a twenty-year $65 million Industrial Lands Strategy that the LEDC helped package into seven industrial parks across the city's outer edges with development charges waived for prospective tenants (Perspective London 2007). London's growth machine made rapid progress, and the LEDC soon was "considered by many economic development professionals to be the 'Gold Standard' in Canada as a business attraction initiative in the manufacturing sector" (City of London et al. 2005, 14).

However, concerns surfaced about London's development strategy. The *LNE* drew attention to dependence on "old economy" branch plants, an absence of venture-capital networks, and fragmented leadership that privileged external manufacturing attraction over local technology development. In 2006, the LEDC was reorganized and refocused. CEO John Kime, the architect of the manufacturing attraction approach, was replaced by a younger leader with much deeper roots in the high-technology sector. In partnership with London's key technology organizations, the LEDC made the *LNE*'s "organic growth strategy" a new priority. The WU Research Park was repositioned to bridge local research and business worlds, with the author of the *LNE* recruited to lead WORLDiscoveries, a technology and knowledge-transfer consortium. A technology alliance – TechAlliance – brought together a group of local investors and WU's Ivey Business School to launch London's first angel investor network, the Southwestern Ontario Angel Group.

In 2010, London's old and new development thrusts began to merge (London Economic Development Corporation 2009). Following the city's first-ever "economic summit," the municipal government established a nearly $70-million Economic Development Fund with six priorities balancing traditional industrial development with knowledge economy supports. While the fund's single major investment of $25 million was in 400 series highway interchanges to facilitate industrial expansion, it also included partnership investments in five pillars of London's "new economy": an international composite materials centre, a wastewater research facility, a digital media centre of excellence, a downtown Fanshawe College campus for digital and theatre arts, and a medical devices initiative for start-ups. While some observers saw in the priorities the perpetuation of "two very different visions of the city and its economy," the director of the UWO Research Park offered a different view, calling such debates a "false dichotomy." He elaborated: "There is a third way London is uniquely positioned to take advantage of. We can make video games and then manufacture the chip boards they run on, and we will need Hwy 401 manufacturing space for that. You cannot do that at a research park" (De Bono 2011).

In 2011, the Mayor's Economic Prosperity Council was established, co-chaired by the dean of the Ivey Business School and a former bank executive, to forge such a third way (City of London 2011). Calling on London "to be bold," the council declared that the city's sector leaders "must not be afraid of striking up new partnerships beyond the confines of our region or our traditional partners." To follow up, the city announced two organizational innovations to strengthen economic linkages and focus. A chief investment officer was proposed for strategic management of municipal economic assets and partnership development, as well as a standing council committee on investment and economic prosperity for coordinating economic development. As London's city manager remarked, "It can't be business as usual" (Maloney and De Bono 2011). A common platform was envisioned to align resources and target supports.

Cultural Development: Forging a Diversity Coalition

Efforts to make London a more diverse city built on the CCTF's call for a community-based network of immigrant service providers, municipal departments and agencies, businesses and trade unions, and university researchers (City of London 2006b, 2008). Co-sponsored by the City of London and the United Way of London and Middlesex, this network aims to welcome and retain newcomers to London by upgrading immigrant employment and enhancing cultural diversity. Leadership has come from enhancing different local sources, with the municipal government establishing a Culture Office to coordinate a stream of initiatives, including an immigrant settlement portal and a business-led immigrant employment council to tackle economic marginalization of newcomers.

Co-chaired by two executives from RBC and 3M, the council coordinated forty business and training organizations to recruit and retain immigrant workers. Settlement agencies similarly realigned their efforts to link immigrant social, cultural, and economic opportunities through regional and national partnerships for newcomer attraction and labour market integration. Proposals emerged for a Multicultural Economic Council, led by London's prominent immigrant entrepreneurs.

The value of these local collaborations has been confirmed in two forms of external recognition (Bradford and Esses 2012). First, London won a national multiculturalism award for its partnerships in "fighting racism, creating inclusive work places and stimulating dialogue and action on making Canada a nation open to the diversity of the human condition" (City of London 2008). Second, upper-level governments have made substantial investments in support of the coalition and its inclusion work. The provincial government established in London its first credential-recognition centre outside Toronto. The federal government funded a Local Immigration Partnership Council as a focal point for the local settlement efforts. Consistent with a new emphasis on university-city linkages, WU's Centre on Migrant and Ethnic Relations was awarded a five-year federal community-driven research grant to study immigrant experiences in mid-sized cities, including London.

The second key diversity gap in London's labour market – professional talent – has also been tackled through network development. Research has shown that the most creative workers in the new economy pursue careers that span multiple firms and work experiences and that they value professional organizations and other work-related associations that circulate knowledge both about fluctuating job opportunities and new developments in their field (Scott 2006). Such networks have taken two forms in London. First, several recent "town and gown" initiatives focus on embedding the city's post-secondary education institutions in the local economy. WU's strategic plan strengthens its presence in the local economy with strong endorsement for such community collaboration from the President (Chakma 2009). Second, associations for the city's young professionals have formed. Emerging Leaders and InterNetwork expand participation in political and economic decision making, helping to open London's traditionally closed governance networks. One young professional leader identified a "real tipping point" in London's business culture: "In terms of the grassroots community initiatives out there ... it's a great matrix of opportunities depending where your passion is" (Richmond 2011b).

Social Development: Bridging the Governance Gap

Urban social analysts have long observed that many of the most innovative and creative cities are also the most polarized and segregated (Hulchanski 2010). Critical in turning the tide is a vibrant local civil society populated by efficacious popular movements and professional organizations able to participate in civic governance. By this standard, London's social development forces have never exhibited much collective capacity. Missing in London were peak association networks or inter-sectoral councils that can tackle a city- or community-wide agenda. London has no social planning council, and agencies such as the United Way and Community Foundation that pursue broad community-building mandates in other Canadian municipalities have until very recently confined their work to conventional fundraising. London's business leaders have not sought partnerships with social groups on economic development. The LEDC ignored overtures from autoworker representatives to contribute to business recruitment, and calls for wider community representation on the LEDC Board were never acted upon.

The consequences for London's social development agenda have been twofold. First, social groups function more as external critics than partners in development. The Urban League of London has been a vocal opponent of the traditional business attraction and industrial lands strategy. Second, social development has remained largely within the purview of the municipal government, distinct from any governance partnerships. Indeed, the Department of Community Services produced an impressive Social Policy Framework that included a broader reflection on London's social development: "While each of the 'three pillars' – public, private, and voluntary sectors – has clear roles in the success of local efforts to identify and respond to social issues, one of the notable gaps in our community is the absence of a coordinated community body that guides this work. While other communities across the country may have social planning councils or similar mechanisms that work to address broader social issues (such as poverty or quality of life) in a more coordinated way, this does not exist in London" (City of London, 2006a, 26).

However, as in the economic and cultural domains, over the past several years there have been notable developments in London's social governance that address the fragmentation. In 2008, a Child and Youth Network, comprising more than 140 agencies and individuals from the education, health, recreation, and social service sectors, was formed (Child and Youth Network 2008). Acting as a catalyst for partnership with governments and the private sector, the network developed an agenda for a "family-centred service system" on poverty, literacy, and health. The municipal government led in chairing the network and linking it to neighbourhood-based community hubs. The network has received provincial recognition for its innovations in community development and neighbourhood-based planning.

At the same time, London's leading charitable organizations transformed themselves into purposeful community change agents. The United Way of London and Middlesex County launched its "community impact agenda" with extensive public engagement that identified key priorities and cross-sectoral leadership for new "impact councils." The London Community Foundation began to issue annual *Vital Signs* reports providing benchmarks for "networking and collaboration among organizations" on evidence-based priorities. On the release of its 2010 report, it was observed that the issues provided "fertile ground for partnerships because they're similarly intertwined: immigration and language, poverty and employment, leadership and youth-mentoring programs" (Van Brenk 2010).

Conclusion: The Next London?

This analysis of London's development trajectory suggests a city in transition. Images of a conservative, self-satisfied insurance and finance town are clearly outdated – overtaken by events and rejected by civic and economic leaders. Several social learning exercises have generated new development agendas built around knowledge assets, talent attraction, and collaborative governance. These learning processes also revealed the depth and breadth of changes required to overcome the attitudinal, organizational, and institutional challenges of this ordinary city. As such, we have situated London at a crossroads. Consensus about an unsustainable past and present is matched by an uncertain future. No longer conducting business as usual in the ordinary city, London's economic, social, and cultural sectors are all experimenting with novel forms of collective action.

It is precisely this theme of "transition and crossroads" that makes London an intriguing case study in innovation, creativity, and governance research. It engages major scholarly and policy debates in challenging ways. In matters of economic innovation, London's trajectory aligns with AnnaLee Saxenian's depiction of an independent firm-based industrial culture with limited local knowledge flows. Yet London's civic leaders have recognized the gaps and are forging multiple business-research networks. With talent retention and attraction, London's experience reminds that creativity strategies must be multifaceted and locally contextualized, addressing the fundamentals of urban quality of life as well as the cultural amenities of place. Imported creativity makeovers make little sense in the ordinary city.

Finally, London's emerging governance relations offer insights into the dynamics of collaboration. Actors from different sectors have recently come together for joint work, but rather than the formalized and durable governance institutions depicted in much urban and regional development literature, the focus has been project-based and time-limited (Pierre 2011). London's "pragmatic join-ups" can't draw on stocks of social or civic capital that elsewhere sustain development coalitions and institutionalize multi-sectoral collaboration (Wolfe 2009). London's story reminds us that cities evolve their own adjustment pathways. Local histories and institutional settings – network relations, leadership styles, and policy cultures – all combine to shape unique development trajectories and innovation possibilities. While ordinary cities cannot escape today's extraordinary challenges, their response remains an open question demanding context-sensitive study.

Note

1 I would like to acknowledge the excellent research assistance of Kadie Ward, Paris Meilleur, Kate Graham, Matthew Patterson, and Jen Nelles in preparing this chapter. The analysis is based on seventy-five key informant interviews conducted between 2007 and 2009 with London civic and business leaders, and knowledge workers.

References

Anderson, J. 2005. "How do you create a creative city?" *Western News*, 3 March.

Belanger, J. 2007. "'Socialists' handcuff city, Gosnell fumes." *London Free Press*, 1 August.

–. 2010. "Councillor bickering a natural part of politics." *London Free Press*, 2 January.

Benneworth, J. 2007. "The role of leadership in promoting regional innovation polices in 'ordinary regions': A review of the literature." NESTA working paper, Newcastle University, U.K.

Bradford, N. 2003. *Cities and communities that work: Innovative practices, enabling policies*. Ottawa: Canadian Policy Research Networks.

Bradford, N., and V. Esses. 2012. "A city in transition: Immigration, integration and diversity in London." In *Immigration integration and inclusion in Ontario cities*, ed. C. Andrew, J. Biles, M. Burstein, V. Esses, and E. Tolley, 103–21. Montreal and Kingston: McGill-Queen's University Press.

Chakma, A. 2009. "Western active partner in London economy." President's News Archive, University of Western Ontario.

Chatterton, P. 2000. "Will the real creative city please stand up?" *City* 4 (3): 390–7. http://dx.doi.org/10.1080/713657028.

Child and Youth Network. 2008. *The best for our children, youth and families: The first three years of London's child and youth agenda to 2015*. London: Child and Youth Network.

City of London. 2006a. "Social policy framework." Department of Community Services, Social Research and Planning.

–. 2006b. "Welcoming cultural diversity in London: A community action plan."

–. 2008. "EMCY award winner." News release.

–. 2011. *Mayor's Economic and Prosperity Council report and summary*. London: City of London.

City of London, LEDC, TechAlliances, and Stiller Centre. 2005. "London's Next Economy: A game plan for accelerating new business development in the London region."

Cobban, T. 2003. "Timothy Cobban's reply to Christopher Leo's comment 'Are there urban regimes in Canada?'" *Canadian Journal of Urban Research* 12 (2): 349–52.

Conference Board of Canada. 2010. *City magnets II: Benchmarking the attractiveness of 50 Canadian cities*. Toronto: Conference Board of Canada.

Cooke, P., and K. Morgan. 1998. *The associational economy: Firms, regions, and innovation*. Oxford: Oxford University Press. http://dx.doi.org/10.1093/acprof:oso/9780198290186.001.0001.

Cornies, L. 2002. "City's empty leadership cuts through entire organization." *London Free Press*, 6 April.

Coulson, S. 2005. "Focus on a strong local identity, not a generic style, Glen Murray says." *London Free Press*, 10 June.

Creative City Task Force. 2005. *Creative City Task Force report*. London: City of London.

Currie, P. 2006. "Welcome to the club." *London Free Press*, 18 September.

De Bono, N. 2011. "City's $67.8 million in question." *London Free Press*, 7 February.

Florida, R. 2002. *The rise of the creative class*. New York: Basic Books.

Gertler, M.S. 2001. "Urban economy and society in Canada: Flows of people, capital and ideas." *Isuma* 2 (3): 119–30.

Gertler, M.S., and D.A. Wolfe. 2004. "Local social knowledge management: Community actors, institutions and multilevel governance in regional foresight exercises." *Futures* 36 (1): 45–65. http://dx.doi.org/10.1016/S0016-3287(03)00139-3.

Graham, K. 2008. *The role of the university in the local economy: A case study analysis of the City of London and the University of Western Ontario*. MPA Major Research Report. London: Department of Political Science, UWO.

Henton, D., J. Melville, and K. Walesh. 1997. *Grassroots leaders for a new economy*. San Francisco: Jossey-Bass.

Hulchanski, D. 2010. *The three cities within Toronto*. Toronto: Cities Centre, University of Toronto.

Hunter, T. 2009. "Enhance London: A strategy for economic and societal prosperity." Prepared for London Economic Development Corporation.

"The idea of London, creative city gains critics and energy." 2005. *The Londoner*, 10 August.

Lewis, N., and B. Donald. 2010. "A new rubric for 'creative city' potential in Canada's smaller cities." *Urban Studies* 47 (1): 29–54. http://dx.doi.org/10.1177/0042098009346867.

London Chamber of Commerce. 2008. "Chamber presents effective governance." News release, 14 May.

London Economic Development Corporation. 1998. *Investing in prosperity: A commitment to innovation, initiative and competitiveness*. London: London Economic Development Corporation.

–. 2006. *London technology audit*. London: London Economic Development Corporation.

–. 2007. *A workforce development strategy for London*. London: London Economic Development Corporation.

–. 2009. *Advantage London: London economic summit; Creating the action plan for the next economy*. London: London Economic Development Corporation.

MacLean, J. 2005. "Competitive future depends on people." Next London series. London: London Free Press.

Malmberg, A., and P. Maskell. 2002. "The elusive concept of localization economies: Towards a knowledge-based theory of spatial clustering." *Environment & Planning A* 34 (3): 429–49. http://dx.doi.org/10.1068/a3457.

Maloney, P., and N. De Bono. 2011. "Fontana wants to create investment post." *London Free Press*, 29 June.

Martin Prosperity Institute. 2009. *London 3Ts reference report*. Toronto: Martin Property Institute.

Miller, D. 2004. "London losing economic clout." *London This Week*, 15 September.

Molotch, H. 1976. "The city as growth machine: Toward a political economy of place." *American Journal of Sociology* 82 (2): 309–30. http://dx.doi.org/10.1086/226311.

OECD. 2006. *Territorial reviews: Competitive cities in the global economy*. Paris: Organization for Economic Co-operation and Development.

Pedro, K. 2011. "Vitality in a word: Neighbourhoods." *London Free Press*, 7 May.

Perspective London. 2007. "City's Innovation Park providing room to grow." Oakville: Perspective Media.

Pierre, J. 2011. *The politics of urban governance*. London: Palgrave Macmillan.

Rayside, D. 2008. *Queer inclusions, continental divisions*. Toronto: University of Toronto Press.

Richmond, R. 2011a. "Are we so average we'll never stand out?" *London Free Press*, 14 May.

–. 2011b. "London short on sizzle in survey." *London Free Press*, 19 July.

–. 2012. "They're young and bright and want to stay. Really?" *London Free Press*, 28 May.

Sands, G., and L. Reese. 2008. "Cultivating the creative class: And what about Nanaimo?" *Economic Development Quarterly* 22 (1): 8–23. http://dx.doi.org/10.1177/0891242407309822.

Saxenian, A. 1996. *Regional advantage: Culture and competition in Silicon Valley and Route 128*. Cambridge, MA: Harvard University Press.

Scott, A. 2006. "Creative cities: Conceptual issues and policy questions." *Journal of Urban Affairs* 28 (1): 1–17. http://dx.doi.org/10.1111/j.0735-2166.2006.00256.x.

Spencer, G.M., and T. Vinodrai. 2009. *Innovation systems research network city-region profile, 2006: London*. Toronto: Munk School of Global Affairs, University of Toronto.

Statistics Canada. 2008. *Tracking trends in London: 2006 Census*. Ottawa: Statistics Canada.

Stephenson, 2005. "The urban economy." Speech to the Next London Community Forum, Huron University College, 24 September.

Todtling, F., and M. Trippl. 2005. "One size fits all? Towards a differentiated regional innovation policy approach." *Research Policy* 34: 1203–19.

Turner, G. 2010. "Senior-friendly London lands WHO title." *London Free Press*, 7 July.

Van Brenk, D. 2010. "Failure to reach out hurts all: Report." *London Free Press*, 5 October.

Wolfe, D.A. 2009. *21st century cities in Canada: The geography of innovation*. Toronto: Conference Board of Canada.

Wolfe, D.A., and M. Gertler. 2006. "Spaces of knowledge flows: Clusters in a global context." In *Clusters and regional development: Critical reflections and explorations*, ed. B. Asheim, P. Cooke, and R. Martin, 218–35. London: Routledge.

10 The Social Dynamics of Economic Performance in Halifax

JILL L. GRANT[1]

In many ways the Halifax city-region represents an interesting test of theories about the social dynamics of economic innovation. Despite its modest size (with a population under 400,000) and vast area (almost 5,500 square kilometres), Halifax has scored surprisingly well on several indices of creative cities (Florida 2002a, 2002c). Gertler and Vinodrai (2004) reported that the city-region ranked fourth among Canadian cities on the Talent index (proportion of the population with bachelor's degree or higher), seventh on the Bohemian index (proportion of the workforce in creative industries), and tenth on the Techpole index (the share of high-tech employment to overall employment). Halifax's weak points have been its relatively slow rate of growth and its limited ability to attract and retain international migrants (Grant and Kronstal 2013). With respect to the proportion of foreign-born residents in relation to the total population (the Mosaic index) the city-region was nineteenth in Canada (Gertler and Vinodrai 2004), but as Lewis and Donald (2010) noted, most small cities score weakly on this measure. The key question posed then is what factors explain the relative success Halifax has enjoyed in "punching above its weight" in attracting talented and creative workers from within Canada, while it struggles to draw international migrants. To what extent does Halifax fit the creative-class model of a tolerant and inclusive social context? Our investigation of Halifax suggests that in several ways the city-region defies the expectations of current theories that attempt to link the social characteristics of city-regions with innovative characteristics and economic performance.

We conducted the research for our case study between 2006 and 2009, as part of the comparative study of the social dynamics of economic performance in Canadian city-regions.[2] We found that while the quality and social dynamics of place contribute to economic performance, theoretical premises about the role of social and cultural diversity in stimulating innovation may not explain the Halifax context (Grant and Kronstal 2009). For instance, in some industries in Halifax, overlapping social and professional networks facilitate the development of trust within communities that prove relatively socially homogeneous, yet innovative (Grant, Holme, and Pettman 2008). Although Halifax is a popular destination for young Canadians – with a vital music and arts scene, a beautiful natural environment, and well-respected post-secondary institutions – job growth has failed to keep pace with the labour supply in some sectors, and the city-region has a reputation for political and social conservatism. Our research suggests that talented and creative young people come to Halifax to take advantage of its dynamic incipient cognitive-cultural economy, despite perceiving that the city-region's governing elites may be intolerant. Their decisions about whether to stay in Halifax depend primarily on job availability rather than on social diversity or tolerance.

Overview of the Halifax Economy

Halifax is a mid-sized Canadian city that serves as the economic hub of Atlantic Canada. Between 2001 and 2006 its population grew 3.8 per cent while the country as a whole expanded by 5.4 per cent (Spencer and Vinodrai 2009). As table 10.1 shows, Halifax has a well-educated population more likely than the Canadian average to be engaged in a creative occupation. While almost one in five Canadians immigrated to the country, over 90 per cent of Haligonians were born in Canada; thus Halifax lacks the ethnic diversity of larger centres. Incomes are lower than the Canadian average, but residents of Halifax are slightly more likely to be employed than other Canadians.

Originally settled in 1749, Halifax owes its history and character to its excellent port, which provides multi-modal service for sixteen container lines (Port of Halifax 2013). While shipping volumes decreased in the last decade, Maritime services remain a cornerstone of the local economy. The harbour plays a major role in the tourism sector in the city as well: the port receives about 250,000 cruise ship visitors a year. Since its early days Halifax has served as a centre of government and military activities. Governments are major employers in the city-region. The provincial capital also hosts several federal government departments for the Atlantic region. Canadian Forces Base Halifax employs

Table 10.1. Halifax population characteristics

Characteristic	Halifax 2001	Canada 2001	Halifax 2006	Canada 2006
Population	359,185	30,007,085	372,855	31,612,890
% foreign born	6.8%	18.2%	7.4%	19.8%
% BA or higher	21.1%	15.4%	24.0%	18.1%
Employment rate	63.0%	61.5%	64.5%	62.4%
% in creative occupations	37.4%	29.2%	38.0%	33.2%
% science tech occupations	7.1%	6.4%	7.0%	6.6%
% employment in clusters	21.7%	22.1%	19.0%	22.1%
Average employment income	$30,614	$31,757	$48,092	$51,221

Note: 2001 data cite average employment income; 2006 data provide average full-time employment income.

Sources: Spencer and Vinodrai 2006, 2009

about 14,000 personnel. In this respect, the city-region bears a strong affinity to other city-regions – such as Kingston and St John's – that are highly dependent on public-sector employment as a foundation of the urban economy.

As table 10.2 indicates, over 24,000 people work in health-care services. With six universities and several colleges, the city-region has a large workforce in educational services. It hosts the largest shopping centres in Atlantic Canada as well as tourism and hospitality activities. The city-region also benefits from its acknowledged status as the hub of the regional economy (Lefebvre and Brender 2006).

Analysis of data from the 2001 census revealed that Halifax had five industrial clusters: maritime, ICT services, business services, higher education, and logistics. By 2006, Halifax had added a cluster, while some Canadian cities and the nation as a whole lost industrial clusters over the five-year period. Logistics had declined in size (shedding 675 jobs to total 10,890) and no longer qualified as a cluster. Two new clusters had appeared: biomedical and creative/cultural. The maritime and biomedical clusters grew more than 25 per cent in the five-year period between censuses, while creative/cultural and higher education grew about 15 per cent (see table 10.3). Employment in the biomedical industry increased by 445 to 2165, while the creative/cultural sector added 3615 jobs to reach 9140 people (Spencer and Vinodrai 2006, 2009).

Table 10.2. Industry characteristics in Halifax, 2006

	# labour force	Labour force (%)	Average FT income ($)
Construction	11,590	5.5	43,687
Manufacturing	11,015	5.2	52,069
Retail trade	25,045	11.9	34,778
Educational services	16,355	7.8	51,708
Health care and social assistance	24,485	11.7	46,462
Accommodation and food service	14,750	7.0	25,189
Public administration	23,375	11.1	59,645
All industries in Halifax	210,135	100	48,092

Source: Spencer and Vinodrai 2009, 8

Table 10.3. Industrial clusters in Halifax, 2001 and 2006

	Location quotient 2001	Location quotient 2006	Growth from 2001–2006
Maritime	1.59	2.02	26.6%
Biomedical	[1.06]*	1.14	25.9%
ICT services	1.46	1.47	6.2%
Business services	1.49	1.36	8.2%
Creative and cultural	[1.00]*	1.14	15.3%
Higher education	1.75	1.57	14.8%
Logistics	1.20	[1.06]*	–5.7%

* Not identified as a cluster in the year indicated

Sources: Spencer and Vinodrai 2006, 2009

Halifax: The Social Dynamics of Economic Performance

The case study of Halifax focused on three key sets of questions on innovation, social dynamics, and economic performance in city-regions. First we explored knowledge flows within and among sectors to assess potential for mutual learning, innovation, and growth. Then we sought to understand factors affecting the city-region's ability to attract and retain talent. Finally, we examined the extent to which civic governance in the city-region was inclusive and associational.

Knowledge Flows and Innovation

Innovation depends not only on individual inspiration and perspiration but also on the effective flow of knowledge among workers, businesses, and sectors (Wolfe 2009). Jacobs (1969) argued that cities are the engines of economic growth in part because they provide good conditions for knowledge to flow across sectors and industries: diversity and proximity create optimal contexts for innovation and growth. In our analysis of this theme of the study, we tried to identify the sources of innovation in particular sectors or clusters. The research focused on how knowledge flows within and among sectors and considered local versus global dimensions of knowledge flows. We conducted interviews with employers in three sectors spanning creative/cultural industries and business services: music, built environment consulting, and advertising.

The primary source of innovation in the music industry was individual musicians working within a social context that encouraged and rewarded creative performance in somewhat unpredictable patterns. Changing technologies of distribution – with the rise of music downloading and file sharing – have altered the dynamics of the music industry in ways that favoured smaller cities like Halifax, where the costs of living were relatively low but the density of opportunities and connections in the music community was relatively high (Grant, Haggett, and Morton 2009b; Hracs et al. 2011). Halifax musicians relied on touring to earn income; they saw Halifax as a great place to be creative. A music intermediary explained,

> All you have to do is take twelve CDs and read the credits and you won't believe you are looking at the same thirty names over and over and over again. But they are playing different instruments, they are singing different things. It is different kinds of music. It's bizarre, but it's wonderful. It's what makes this industry unique and saleable from my perspective ... It becomes fascinating as a sales feature – part of our brand. We work it from all angles, that this is a community. We're selling a community. It didn't use to be like this. It's very nice. It was really dog-eat-dog when I worked in the music business. But the Internet changed the world. Information is so easy to get to. All of that stuff you used to guard, your business before ... it is all here. Why not just tell people?

In the built-environment consulting sector, firms often competed with each other for projects. When they believed it improved their odds of winning contracts, they worked with other firms and shared information. Employers in the built-environment consulting industry indicated that they followed what their competitors did within the Atlantic region and sometimes collaborated on projects or hired new staff from other firms to gain knowledge. They watched developments in the field to identify new ideas or strategies to bring to their clients. In general, the companies reported few independent innovations in products or processes. Some design firms indicated that the city-region provided few opportunities for innovation or creativity and reported that they looked for projects outside Atlantic Canada to find the creative challenges employees craved. More complex projects generated partnerships with well-known firms in larger cities: such collaborations thereby contributed global knowledge to the local scene. Larger firms in Halifax proved more likely to describe themselves as innovators than did smaller firms.

Advertising firms varied markedly in their approaches to innovation and knowledge exchange. Some firms highlighted their particular creativity and saw the quality of their employees as key to innovation and to market success. Such firms were competing internationally for contracts, and winning international awards for their work: their innovation and creativity drew new clients. Other firms worked primarily with others in their firm or with a limited number of partners, and depended on long-term relationships with clients for projects. Some firms had developed patented processes for addressing client needs.

Knowledge flows differed among the industries studied (Grant, Haggett, and Morton 2009a). Knowledge sharing and mutual learning proved especially important in the Halifax music scene, where musicians worked together to "jam" and challenge each other (Morton 2008). Similarly, in the health-research sector, researchers contrasted the collaborative learning environment in Halifax with competitive work environments they experienced in other cities. By contrast, respondents in the advertising industry indicated little interest in sharing knowledge: they criticized other local firms' approaches and work. They looked to firms in other cities or countries for collaboration. While knowledge-sharing within the local context was vital to innovation in the music scene, it seemed to play a lesser role in the advertising business. In the health-research sector, knowledge-sharing occurred both locally and globally.

As noted, two new industrial clusters emerged in Halifax between 2001 and 2006. The biomedical cluster clearly involved talented workers with significant cognitive skills and educational achievements. The creative and cultural cluster reflected the growth in cultural industries in the city-region. Does such growth indicate the emergence of a cognitive-cultural economy linking creative/cultural industries, design industries, and higher-order knowledge-intensive business services? Scott (2000, 2009) described cognitive-cultural capitalism as involving an economy with clusters of high technology, service, and cultural production activities encouraging exchange of knowledge in innovative ways, but revealing a polarized structure of high-wage and low-wage segments. Is an increase in employment in relevant sectors sufficient to denote the emergence of a cognitive-cultural economy? Would change require a new governance approach or development philosophy? While employment in these sectors has grown, and local and provincial policy encouraged a focus on knowledge and cultural industries in the mid- to late 2000s (Nova Scotia Arts and Culture Partnership Council 2006), we found limited evidence that the overall structure of the local economy or the emphasis of economic development strategies changed in ways that facilitated innovative knowledge exchanges among sectors. Certainly the sectors we profiled were doing well nationally and internationally. Yet many respondents suggested that traditional economic concerns and approaches remained significant in limiting growth and innovation in Halifax.

For instance, the ability of some Halifax-based advertising companies to win international commissions and awards garnered recognition for the city-region and helped the firms attract talented workers. Rapid growth in some of these firms brought talented and creative workers from larger centres (like Toronto) that traditionally were seen as the hub of the industry and characterized by thick labour markets for workers in the field. Technological innovations via the Internet make design and creative work possible anywhere. Some companies that began in Halifax have stuck with their roots and have not relocated, despite international success. However, respondents suggested that the shortage of educational programs in advertising, copy writing, and art direction limited the local talent pool and prevented growth of the industry. They discussed the need for local training. Although the provincial government has been quick to address labour requirements for traditional manufacturing industries, such as shipbuilding (Government of Nova Scotia 2013), it has evinced less commitment to enhancing educational opportunities to ensure that cognitive-cultural industries grow.

Attracting and Retaining Talent

Richard Florida's (2002c) argument that cities grow primarily by attracting talented and creative workers had a major influence on development policy in many Canadian cities during the 2000s. Florida (2002b, 2005) suggested that talented people are attracted to places that are tolerant, diverse, and dynamic, and urged cities to recognize they had to compete for talent. Like many other Canadian cities (Kipfer and Keil 2002; Wolfe 2009), Halifax developed strategies to attract and retain young workers who they hoped would stimulate growth and innovation (Grant and Kronstal 2009).

Early in our research we discovered that development intermediaries often pointed to key sectors such as health research, music, and business services as examples of successful innovation in Halifax. Our research on the foundations for attracting and retaining talent focused on three sectors – built environment consulting (business services), music (creative / cultural), and health research (biomedical / higher education) – with highly specialized requirements. The interviews with employers, workers, and representatives of organizations in these sectors probed for the factors affecting the decisions of talented and creative workers to come to and stay in Halifax (Kronstal et al. 2009).

Although almost everyone interviewed pointed to the natural beauty of the region and the easy pace of life, those factors did not account for the ability to keep people in Halifax. Respondents in the health and built-environment consulting sectors indicated that the availability of jobs in the city-region was a key factor in their decisions to come to or stay in Halifax. Many respondents talked about friends, family members, or colleagues who would like to live in Halifax if jobs were available, but noted that work is often hard to obtain. Employers found it relatively easy to recruit talented workers to the city-region because of the quality of place (both natural and built environment), quality of life (pace, lack of traffic, affordability), and the amenities in the region (Grant and Kronstal 2009, 2010).

Within the music sector and the health-research sector, respondents suggested that strongly supportive social environments gave Halifax special appeal for talented workers (Grant and Kronstal 2009; Hracs et al. 2011). The work environment within these sectors proved highly collaborative; workers described themselves as creative with limited resources. A health research employer explained, "We're underresourced in this region ... but we're able to do a lot with very little. And we're able to pool our skills and pool our ideas and resources, and there is that willingness to work together and to collaborate. And that's maybe just the Nova Scotia way. I mean, you may not see that in other big cities, but we're small and we can do it, and there's a willingness to do it."

Several respondents indicated that the city-region could be more welcoming and inclusive of immigrants. A manager in provincial economic development explained, "If you are a newcomer from the Maritimes, I think the answer is yes [it is easy to integrate]. If you are a newcomer from somewhere outside the Maritimes, I think it is somewhat more difficult. If you are an immigrant in the true sense of the word, it's not easy at all." Issues such as recognizing foreign credentials and finding employment for spouses were seen as hindering talent attraction and retention (Grant and Buckwold 2012).

Sectors examined differed in the degree of labour mobility and knowledge flows within and across sectors. The size of the sector and employment incomes may affect mobility. Those in the music sector indicated that creative workers typically have to find multiple employment opportunities to make ends meet (Grant, Haggett, and Morton 2009b). Few music-sector workers earn a living wage from music. Many take multiple roles in the industry or find employment in other sectors. Where alternative employment may occur in related sectors, then knowledge flows do occur. For instance, some musicians also taught music; others worked for venues that employ or promote musicians.

Mobility seemed limited among health-sector workers not because opportunities do not arise but because workers seemed highly committed to their research agenda and content to remain with their colleagues and facilities. While some workers may relocate to gain access to better funding in larger centres, those interviewed generally appreciated the lifestyle possible in Halifax. Respondents suggested that the small scale of the city-region and the collaborative culture facilitated knowledge exchange within the sector.

Labour mobility was relatively high in some occupations in the built-environment consulting sector. Some skills were sought after, so that workers demand a salary premium and can work where they want. Such employees played important roles in transferring knowledge between firms. Talented workers in occupations that were over-supplied (like junior architects) may have lower incomes and less job mobility. Some respondents worried about the lack of innovation in building in Halifax. An employer in a consulting firm said, "One of the issues we're having now is that ... not much is happening ... You lose some of those people to international jobs and bigger cities to do the exciting work."

We found few specific examples of cross-sector knowledge flows in the sectors profiled. It seems reasonable to conclude, however, that knowledge flows occur between higher education and other clusters, as they are often linked by research projects, by students making the transition to workers, and by high-profile workers joining the higher education workforce. The small size of Halifax provides many opportunities for people to meet those working in other sectors.

Civic Governance

In recent years a growing number of scholars and community practitioners concluded, "The need to forge better linkages among relevant institutions and associated actors is a critical factor in urban economic development policy" (Wolfe 2009, 19). While innovation is a necessary condition for growth, it may not be sufficient. Bradford (2004) suggested that only inclusive places will rise to the top. To what extent does the Halifax experience indicate that inclusive mechanisms of civic governance contribute to innovation and economic performance?

DEVELOPMENT POLICIES

A key aspect of the governance question concerns the manner in which the local government and the private sector collaborate in forging local economic development strategies. In 1996 the Province of Nova Scotia amalgamated the City of Halifax, City of Dartmouth, Town of Bedford, and Halifax County into Halifax Regional Municipality (known as HRM or Halifax). Creating a regional municipality was designed to reduce administrative costs but also to improve the national and international competitiveness of the city-region. The Greater Halifax Partnership (GHP) formed the same year as a public-private partnership to promote economic development in the region. It initiated several campaigns, including an advertising initiative branding Halifax as a "Smart City." Gertler and Vinodrai's (2004) study for the GHP revealed that Richard Florida's (2002c) ideas about the role of creativity in economic development had begun to influence policy in the city-region. Local authorities invited Florida to address business leaders in 2004 (HRM 2004).

At the behest of the municipality, the Halifax Chamber of Commerce (2004) organized an economic summit to offer recommendations about development directions. The chamber's report discussed themes such as attracting and retaining talented people and the role and impact of post-secondary institutions. It advocated interventions, such as enhancing the qualities of place, to improve the city-region's performance on Richard Florida's indicators. It suggested that the GHP may need to broaden its traditional approach to economic development.

Halifax adopted important development policies in the period from 2005 to 2009. With the GHP support, a blue-ribbon panel of business leaders, university presidents, and government staff advised the municipality on policy for a new strategy to promote greater economic growth (MacDonald 2005). The resulting economic strategy (HRM 2005b) pursued creative cities and smart growth agendas, urging investments in social and cultural infrastructure and other changes to encourage talented and creative workers to come and stay in Halifax. Under the direction of a steering committee of government representatives, and following focus groups and interviews with individuals, management consultants prepared an immigration strategy for the region (HRM 2005a).

Council adopted two other plans in 2006. After several years of public consultations led by a community-based planning advisory committee, the regional plan was approved (HRM 2006b). It advocated smart growth planning principles and set in motion implementation strategies to promote interventions to enhance the attractiveness and potential for growth in the urban core. Staff produced the first cultural plan for the region the same year. The plan "challenges the notion that Culture drains public resources; new public agendas are highlighting Culture as a pillar of economic and community growth. The Cultural Plan delivers this new message and marks the beginning of a long-term policy shift" (HRM 2006a, 4).

In 2007 consultants hired by the GHP offered advice on strategies that the region could use to attract and retain creative young people (Next Generation Consulting 2007). Consequently, the GHP helped to found (and fund) an organization called Fusion Halifax to help young professionals meet and network.[3] Fusion Halifax organized action teams around themes such as sustainability, health and wellness, diversity, and urban development. The urban development group became a vociferous force promoting the region's new urban design plan for downtown in early 2009 (Fusion Halifax 2009; Leung 2013).

HRM's urban design plan (HRM 2009a) was approved in June 2009 following three years of consultations. Toronto-based consultants worked with staff and a task force comprising residents, business community representatives, municipal councillors, design community representatives, and representatives from heritage and cultural advisory committees (HRM 2009b).

In sum, by 2009 various plans showed the influence of creative cities and smart-growth thinking. Consultation processes used for the regional plan and for the urban design plan were most broadly based and participatory; others tended to involve constituencies particularly focused on thematic issues. By 2011 Halifax should have begun revising many of its plans. The regional plan review got off to a slow start while staff focused on a city centre plan but gathered steam by 2013. The cultural plan languished: the department managing it disappeared during a municipal reorganization in 2012, with the cultural planners leaving the municipality's employ. Staff began reviewing the immigration plan in 2013, after facing several challenges with implementation (Kronstal 2009); the process was abandoned shortly thereafter. Only the economic development plan was completed on schedule. While weak economic performance reinforced the perception that government needed to act to promote growth, a close reading of various plans in Halifax suggests that the fundamentals of economic development policy changed remarkably little over time, despite the temporary overlay of new theories and discourses. For instance, while the 2006 economic development strategy referred to being a talent magnet, ensuring a vibrant community, and employing smart growth ideas, it also highlighted the importance of a good business climate to encourage growth (HRM 2005a). The revised 2011 economic strategy essentially reverted to a traditional development approach of focusing on growth and improving conditions for business, although it acknowledged the importance of smart people and a vital regional centre (HRM 2011).

ECONOMIC STRATEGY AND CIVIC GOVERNANCE

To gain greater insight into the governance mechanisms that may have emerged to undertake "strategic planning" or related exercises in Halifax, we conducted interviews with development intermediaries, including representatives of associations and government agencies or departments involved in economic, social, or cultural development. Respondents suggested that Halifax remained relatively conservative and traditional in its approach to governance (Kronstal and Grant

2009). A manager for a cultural development association told us, "I often find that it is a very small-*c* conservative government where some forms of innovation are concerned," and a federal economic development worker said new ideas were rarely welcomed. Although the city-region established new organizations (such as the Greater Halifax Partnership) and community-based committees (such as the Urban Design Task Force), those responsible for the direction of economic development in the region remained essentially attuned to business interests. While the varying plans discussed social, economic, and cultural matters, respondents expressed concerns that the immigration strategy and the cultural strategy lacked sufficient means for implementation. While the city-region committed financial resources to bringing the economic development strategy to fruition, social and cultural agendas failed to receive the investment necessary to advance them.

How socially inclusive are Halifax's governance mechanisms, and to what extent do they link economic, cultural, and social development agendas? The merger of the Greater Halifax Partnership and the Halifax Regional Development Agency in 2007 improved Halifax's ability to engage in strategic management. The GHP has proven effective in linking local government with business interests in a way that effectively promotes economic development and investment in the region. By creating organizations like Fusion Halifax, the GHP moved towards engaging young professionals and linking economic, social, and cultural development agendas. Several initiatives at GHP seek to engage immigrants and help them integrate into local social and economic networks (Greater Halifax Partnership 2009).

At the same time, however, many social and cultural associations and interests felt excluded from the development agenda and from civic governance mechanisms. "If you're not politically acceptable in terms of politics, irrespective of the fact that you may have a great cultural contribution to make, you're not included. So the best thing to do is to be totally neutral politically. But if you have the unfortunate position of being politically active and at the same time being able to contribute, they won't even talk to you, won't even talk to you in this province. It's unique here: it's probably the only place in the country where it's like that" (manager of a cultural development association).

Economic development intermediaries considered social and cultural agendas in a utilitarian way: they advanced them where they saw them as contributing to economic growth, while limiting attention to inclusion or social justice. Social development and cultural development were treated not as ends in themselves but as means to growth. The advocates of social and cultural development felt marginalized and excluded from discussions of economic development policy and priorities. The civic governance mechanisms set up to advise council on economic development policies disenfranchised some social and cultural sector interests while privileging business interests.

We noted perceived differences between urban and rural interests, and occasional animosities between municipal and provincial authorities. While Halifax's population is concentrated in the urban centre, a vast rural hinterland expects services and amenities from local government. A staff person working for federal economic development authorities explained, "Our [city] council is set up to be concerned about the outer, outer parts of the city ... Most of the time they're going to be more concerned about putting money in their own communities: that's where their constituents are, so you won't get a consensus to develop the peninsula."

Some respondents pointed to innovation resulting from successful alliances, such as the Seaport Redevelopment (Grant, Holme, and Pettman 2008). Many of those interviewed described Halifax as a friendly and small community where it is easy to get to know people and develop collaborative networks. Although creative-class discourse suggests that diversity might create bridges to innovation, in the Halifax context respondents more often pointed to opportunities initiated through the bonds of common activities and interactions in venues such as grocery stores or recreational events.

Knowledge Flows, Talent, and Governance of the Cognitive-Cultural Economy in Halifax

Our research tested three key sets of ideas that have figured prominently in recent literature on innovation and creativity in city-regions. The case study of the Halifax city-region supports some hypotheses in the literature, but finds little evidence to substantiate others.

With respect to knowledge flows, our interviews revealed dense and overlapping social and professional networks that contributed to building trust, collaboration, and knowledge-sharing in many sectors. They confirmed a mix of local and non-local ties and a range of economic actors participating in social and professional networks. However, they offered little evidence that economic performance depends on local knowledge circulation between industries or clusters that we investigated.

On questions concerning the attraction and retention of highly educated and creative workers, our findings supported the hypothesis that quality of place and cultural dynamism facilitated the economic performance of the city-region, at least inasmuch as people want a beautiful city and a dynamic arts and culture environment. In contrast with some common hypotheses in the literature about the importance of diversity, however, respondents indicated that social homogeneity contributed to the region's appeal and effectiveness in socially integrating newcomers, at least those from within Canada (Grant and Kronstal 2013).

Although respondents described Halifax as not always inclusive, tolerant, diverse, or open, they nonetheless found it a welcoming environment for them personally. They valued diversity in theory but felt comfortable in a relatively homogeneous city (Grant and Kronstal 2013). Such views suggested that the appealing lifestyle and affordability of the city-region may compensate for other missing social dynamics valued by contemporary urban and creative class theorists (Florida 2002c; Putnam 2000; Sandercock 2003).

As for the questions about civic governance, our core hypothesis holds that economic performance depends on the ability of city-regions to generate new forms of associative governance and collaborative leadership. Halifax has remained conservative and traditional in its governance mechanisms. Although council created advisory committees to assist in planning and policy exercises, those engaged in economic development were almost entirely from business and government. Social development and cultural development interests have been marginalized in decision-making. Policy- and decision-makers have yet to appreciate fully the potential of the cognitive-cultural economy and to adopt more inclusive governance structures that reflect its growing importance, despite some statements in recent policy documents. The trajectory of agencies like the Greater Halifax Partnership reflects continuing growth-machine dynamics rather than new forms of associative governance.

In many ways the economic success of Halifax challenges some hypotheses central to the larger research project documented in this volume. The city-region benefits from its coastal setting, relatively affordable housing costs, laid-back lifestyle, friendly people, and rich arts and culture environment. Talented and creative workers looking to avoid the hectic pace and competitive life of larger urban centres like Toronto and Vancouver see Halifax as an attractive option. They recognize its shortcomings but appreciate the comfortable scale and socially supportive workplaces they find in the city-region. Its vibrant creative sectors make it attractive to an educated population. Strong universities and colleges contribute to innovation in the region, and to the social ambience. Students flock to Halifax despite high tuition rates relative to the rest of Canada, at least in part because it is a "party town" replete with live music and vibrant bars: their presence in the city creates a pool of potential talent that employers can recruit to enhance the economic performance of their organizations. Halifax does not enjoy the ethnic diversity or wealth of larger cities, but residents are generally comfortable nonetheless.

While the research revealed signs of an emerging cognitive-cultural economy in Halifax, local authorities have done relatively little to acknowledge its potential role or to invest in its growth. Current government policy focuses on issues such as infrastructure investment, construction, and improving the business climate. While these contribute to long-term growth, local authorities cannot continue to sideline other important issues of social and cultural development if they hope to provide a stronger foundation for Halifax's long-term economic performance and competitiveness.

Notes

For information on the Halifax case study findings visit http://theoryandpractice.planning.dal.ca/creative-cities/index.html.

For more on the overall project, visit Innovations Systems Research Network, sites.utoronto.ca/isrn.

1 I am grateful to the research assistants who made this work possible: Robyn Holme, Aaron Pettman, Jeff Haggett, Jesse Morton, Rebecca Butler, and Karin Kronstal. Funding for this research was provided by the Social Sciences and Humanities Research Council of Canada under MCRI grant 412-2005-1001 led by Dr David Wolfe of the University of Toronto. Thanks to Meric Gertler and David Wolfe for insightful comments on the work.
2 As part of the research we conducted ninety interviews and reviewed myriad reports, statistics, and other materials related to social and economic development in Halifax.
3 Fusion Halifax employs staff members, hosts regular events for its members, and produces buttons and other materials to distribute in its lobbying. However, membership is free to those who wish to join. Its funding sources are not public knowledge.

References

Bradford, Neil. 2004. "Place matters and multi-level governance: Perspectives on a new urban policy paradigm." Canadian Policy Research Networks. http://www.cprn.org/documents/26856_en.pdf.

Florida, Richard. 2002a. "Bohemia and economic geography." *Journal of Economic Geography* 2 (1): 55–71. http://dx.doi.org/10.1093/jeg/2.1.55.

–. 2002b. "The economic geography of talent." *Annals of the Association of American Geographers* 92 (4): 743–55. http://dx.doi.org/10.1111/1467-8306.00314.

–. 2002c. *The rise of the creative class, and how it's transforming work, leisure, community, and everyday life*. New York: Basic Books.

–. 2005. *The flight of the creative class: The new global competition for talent*. New York: Harper Business, Harper Collins.

Fusion Halifax. 2009. "Action teams." Accessed 2009. http://www.fusionhalifax.ca/en/home/FUSIONactionteams/default.aspx.

Gertler, Meric S., and Tara Vinodrai. 2004. *Competing on creativity: Focus on Halifax*. Report prepared for the Greater Halifax Partnership.

Government of Nova Scotia. 2013. "Nova Scotia welcomes jobs, next step in shipbuilding preparations." News release, 7 March. http://novascotia.ca/news/release/?id=20130307002.

Grant, Jill L., and Benjamin Buckwold. 2012. "Precarious creativity: Immigrant cultural workers." *Cambridge Journal of Regions, Economy and Society* 6 (1): 113–26.

Grant, Jill L., Jeff Haggett, and Jesse Morton. 2009a. "Halifax City Region Study, report on theme 1: Knowledge flows." http://theoryandpractice.planning.dal.ca/_pdf/creative_halifax/isrn/summary_theme1.pdf.

Grant, Jill L., Jeff Haggett, and Jesse Morton. 2009b. "The Halifax Sound: Live music and the economic development of Halifax." http://theoryandpractice.planning.dal.ca/_pdf/creative_halifax/isrn/halifax_sound.pdf.

Grant, Jill L., Robyn Holme, and Aaron Pettman. 2008. "Global theory and local practice in planning in Halifax: the Seaport redevelopment." *Planning Practice and Research* 23 (4): 517–32. http://dx.doi.org/10.1080/02697450802522848.

Grant, Jill L., and Karin Kronstal. 2009. "Smart city / cool city: Attracting and retaining talented and creative workers in Halifax." Draft. http://theoryandpractice.planning.dal.ca/_pdf/creative_halifax/isrn/smartcity_coolcity.pdf.

–. 2010. "The social dynamics of attracting talent in Halifax." *Canadian Geographer* 54 (3): 347–65. http://dx.doi.org/10.1111/j.1541-0064.2010.00310.x.

–. 2013. "Old boys down home: Immigration and social integration in Halifax." *International Planning Studies* 18 (2): 204–20. http://dx.doi.org/10.1080/13563475.2013.774148.

Greater Halifax Partnership. 2009. Connector program. http://www.halifaxpartnership.com/en/home/get-connected/connector-program/default.aspx.

Halifax Chamber of Commerce. 2004. *Halifax Economic Summit, final report.* http://www.halifaxchamber.com/content/Economic_Summit.

Hracs, Brian, Jill L. Grant, Jeffrey Haggett, and Jesse Morton. 2011. "A tale of two scenes: Civic capital and retaining musical talent in Toronto and Halifax." *Canadian Geographer / Le Géographe canadien* 55 (3): 365–82. http://dx.doi.org/10.1111/j.1541-0064.2011.00364.x.

HRM (Halifax Regional Municipality). 2004. "Richard Florida's world tour arrives in Halifax." http://www.halifax.ca/regionalplanning/Florida.pdf.

–. 2005a. "Halifax region immigration strategy." Business case and strategic action plan. Prepared by Christa Hornberger, Halifax Global Management Consultants. http://www.halifax.ca/Council/agendasc/documents/ActionPlanSept05_WebRes.pdf.

–. 2005b. "Strategies for success: Halifax Regional Municipality's economic development strategy 2005–2010." http://www.halifax.ca/EconomicStrategy/EconomicStrategy.html.

–. 2006a. "HRM cultural plan." http://www.halifax.ca/culturalplan/documents/CulturalPlan112007.pdf.

–. 2006b. "Regional plan." http://www.halifax.ca/regionalplanning/Final-RegPlan.html.

–. 2009a. "HRMbyDesign: Urban design plan." http://www.halifax.ca/CapitalDistrict/RegionalCentreUrbanDesignStudy.html.

–. 2009b. "Project team." http://www.halifax.ca/CapitalDistrict/UrbanDesignTaskForce.html.

–. 2011. "A GREATER Halifax: Economic Strategy 2011–2016." http://www.halifaxpartnership.com/en/home/economic-data-reports/economic-strategy/2011-2016-economic-strategy.aspx.

Jacobs, Jane. 1969. *The economy of cities.* New York: Random House.

Kipfer, Stefan, and Roger Keil. 2002. "Toronto Inc? Planning the competitive city in the new Toronto." *Antipode* 34 (2): 227–64. http://dx.doi.org/10.1111/1467-8330.00237.

Kronstal, Karin. 2009. "A place for everyone: A formative evaluation of the Halifax Regional Municipality Immigration Action Plan." Master's research project, School of Planning, Dalhousie University. http://theoryandpractice.planning.dal.ca/_pdf/creative_halifax/metropolis/kkronstal_10.pdf.

Kronstal, Karin, and Jill L. Grant. 2009. "Halifax city region study, theme 3: Inclusive communities and civic engagement." http://theoryandpractice.planning.dal.ca/_pdf/creative_halifax/isrn/summary_theme3pdf.pdf.

Kronstal, Karin, Jill L. Grant, Rebecca Butler, and Jeff Haggett. 2009. "Halifax city region study, theme 2: Social foundations of talent attraction and retention." http://theoryandpractice.planning.dal.ca/_pdf/creative_halifax/isrn/summary_theme2_revised.pdf.

Lefebvre, Mario, and Natalie Brender. 2006. "Canada's hub cities: A driving force of the national economy." Ottawa: Conference Board of Canada. http://www.conferenceboard.ca/e-library/abstract.aspx?did=1730.

Leung, Gladys. 2013. "The role of Fusion Halifax in the Halifax urban development dialogue." Undergraduate thesis, School of Planning, Dalhousie University. http://theoryandpractice.planning.dal.ca/_pdf/creative_halifax/leung_thesis_2013.pdf.

Lewis, Nathaniel, and Betsy Donald. 2010. "A new rubric for 'creative city' potential in Canada's smaller cities." *Urban Studies* 47 (1): 29–54. http://dx.doi.org/10.1177/0042098009346867.

MacDonald, Betty. 2005. "Economic development strategy update." Report to HRM council, 8 September. http://www.halifax.ca/Council/agendasc/documents/EconomicStategy.pdf.

Morton, Jesse. 2008. "'There's a reason why I love this town': Exploring the Halifax music scene." Master's research project, Dalhousie University. http://theoryandpractice.planning.dal.ca/_pdf/creative_halifax/jmorton_thesis.pdf.

Next Generation Consulting. 2007. "Attracting and retaining talent to Greater Halifax: Executive summary." Report for the Greater Halifax Partnership.

Nova Scotia Arts and Culture Partnership Council. 2006. "Creative Nova Scotia: How arts and culture can help build a better Nova Scotia." http://0-nsleg-edeposit.gov.ns.ca.legcat.gov.ns.ca/deposit/b10643734.pdf.

Port of Halifax. 2013. "Cargo." http://www.portofhalifax.ca/english/cargo/index.html.

Putnam, Robert D. 2000. *Bowling alone: The collapse and revival of American community*. New York: Simon and Schuster. http://dx.doi.org/10.1145/358916.361990.

Sandercock, Leonie. 2003. *Cosmopolis II: Mongrel cities of the 21st century*. London: Continuum.

Scott, Allen J. 2000. *The cultural economy of cities*. Thousand Oaks, CA: Sage.

–. 2009. "Human capital resources and requirements across the metropolitan hierarchy of the USA." *Journal of Economic Geography* 9 (2): 207–26. http://dx.doi.org/10.1093/jeg/lbn051.

–. 2006. Halifax: Innovation Systems Research Network City-Region Profile 2001. University of Toronto. http://www.sites.utoronto.ca/isrn/city%20profiles/index.html.

–. 2009. Halifax: Innovation Systems Research Network City-Region Profile 2006. University of Toronto. http://www.sites.utoronto.ca/isrn/city%20profiles/index.html.

Wolfe, David A. 2009. *21st century cities in Canada: The geography of innovation*. Ottawa: Conference Board of Canada.

PART IV

Innovation for Survival or Growth in Canada's Small Cities

11 Saskatoon: From Small Town to Global Hub

PETER W.B. PHILLIPS AND GRAEME WEBB[1]

Context

Saskatoon is often overlooked in the context of Canadian development. As the most northerly metropolitan city in Canada that is not also a provincial or territorial capital, it has spent more than a century attempting to craft an identity that reflects the reality of local strengths and resonates beyond the city limits. In the context of Garreau's typology of regionalization of North America, Saskatoon is situated on the border between the "empty quarter" and the breadbasket (Garreau 1981). In many ways it qualifies for the empty quarter, in that it is land-locked and dependent on exploiting the natural resources of the region. But its recent history suggests that typology may not be the most appropriate for this or other centres in the interior regions of Canada and the United States. In spite of all the constraints imposed by location, this smallish city has created what appears to be a new development trajectory, unambiguously anchored to resource development but firmly attached to global innovation networks.

Along the way, the city has been buffeted by booms and busts. Global economic cycles in the twentieth century delivered price surges for core commodities produced near and served by Saskatoon, which boosted employment, incomes, and wealth; all too often those booms were quickly followed by commodity price collapses, which undercut incomes, wiped out wealth, and forced released workers to migrate (mostly to Calgary and beyond). In contrast, Regina, until recently the largest and most vibrant city in the province, is the capital and the host for the head offices for the key cooperatives and Crown corporations, which until the 1980s secured its economic base and ensured modest if unspectacular growth.

Since the Second World War, Saskatoon, partly by plan and partly by chance, has laid the foundation for what appears to be a vibrant present and prosperous future. Resource development in Saskatchewan accelerated after the war, differentially helping Saskatoon, as potash was centred on the city, and most of the minerals and forestry in the North are served by Saskatoon. Similarly, fundamental economic restructuring in the agri-food sector helped Saskatoon, as new crops and livestock opportunities emerged in the dark brown soil zone across the northern half of the farm belt, which sustained on-farm activity and generated new opportunities for processing or serving the sector.

For much of this period no one would have said Saskatoon was an innovation hub. Rather, it was a resource town, with all of the attendant challenges. The Saskatoon economy and population began to accelerate and lock onto a new development trajectory beginning in the 1980s, in the first instance because of rural exodus and later due to consolidations and expansion in the resource and research areas. Both interprovincial and international migration accelerated in response. The single most important shift was the decision to focus agri-food and biotechnology research at the University of Saskatchewan. This ultimately put Saskatoon on the map as one of the earliest and most successful agricultural biotechnology innovation clusters in the world. The lessons learned in biotechnology – that community leadership, strategic investment in university-based and public research infrastructure, and selected industrial support could build a world-class sector – have now been translated into efforts to expand research and development in other resources.

This chapter examines the social foundations of both innovation and talent attraction and examines the efforts to use more inclusive governance processes to broaden and deepen this transformation.

The Scope of Saskatoon's Transformation

As recently as 2000, per capita incomes in Saskatoon lagged, relatively slow employment and demographic growth were more related to intra-provincial restructuring than net provincial economic growth, and the asset value of homes, businesses, and property was significantly lower than in comparably sized communities elsewhere in Canada. However, with the relatively strong global commodity markets in 2000–10, the situation changed. New and potentially more profitable resource deposits have been delineated and prepared for development, including oil, heavy oil, potash, uranium, gold, and diamonds. An array of technologies has also made some of the province's products more profitable. Meanwhile, over the decade, more than $1 billion in investment was directed to facilities on the University of Saskatchewan campus.

Saskatoon after 2005 led the province and nation in many economic indicators; perhaps most impressively the city economy remained vibrant throughout the 2008–11 global economic downturn, which shocked other "empty quarter" centres. Saskatchewan's provincial GDP per capita rose from 93 per cent of the national average in 2001 to 105 per cent in 2006 and, with a surge in commodity prices in 2008, Saskatchewan's per capita GDP jumped to more than 30 per cent higher than the national average. Given that much of the new activity is centred in Saskatoon, this suggests the local economy is delivering strong local returns. Moreover, Saskatoon has one of the highest labour force participation rates, with 71.7 per cent of the potential labour force working, 4.7 percentage points higher than the 2010 national average, and an employment growth rate of more than twice the national average since 2007.

While Saskatoon's economic prosperity has caught the attention of the national media and economic forecasters and pundits, a more fundamental and important transition has been largely overlooked. Saskatoon has converted from a town that overwhelmingly relied on brawn to a town that now increasingly defines itself as a city of "brains." As the home for the largest provincial university and a major polytechnic, Saskatoon has historically produced a relatively large number of trained and skilled workers, but until recently the majority of the graduates migrated to areas with more or better jobs (Calgary is jokingly referred to as Saskatchewan's third-largest city, on the basis of migration of more than 120,000 skilled workers since 1945). Now, with better local economic prospects and stronger job growth, more graduates stay in Saskatoon and a few are returning. In 2006 Saskatoon had a higher stock of talent than the national average, with a larger proportion of workers with higher degrees (BA or higher) and PhDs (10.9/1000 in Saskatoon versus 5.4/1000 for Canada). Similarly, Saskatoon has a higher percentage of the population engaged in creative occupations (33 per cent versus 29 per cent for Canada). Somewhat counter-intuitively, Saskatoon has a smaller share of its population in the science and technology (S&T)

occupations and a smaller share of its activity in clustered sectors.[2] This new reality is slowly translating into a new image for the city. In the 1960s the city described itself as the POW (potash, oil, wheat) city; in recent years Saskatoon has both self-labelled and been singled out by others as "Canada's science city," "Paris on the Prairies," and one of Canada's "cultural capitals."

The Social Nature of Innovation

Sustained economic vitality in Saskatoon is due only partly to commodity prices. An important aspect of this transformation is the focus on science, technology, and innovation. To understand the roots and impact of this effort, one can address two interrelated questions. First, what are the primary sources of innovation in key sectors or clusters of the city region? How do knowledge flows occur? What evidence is there of knowledge flows across sectors or clusters? How important are the local versus the global dimensions of knowledge flows? Second, is there any evidence of a new cognitive-cultural economy emerging in the city that links the creative or cultural industries, design industries, and higher-order business services?

The short answer for Saskatoon is that codified knowledge (often in the forms of published academic research and patented technologies) flows through global pipelines while contextual, intangible knowledge is embedded in relatively self-contained, sector-specific local labour and knowledge markets. There is limited evidence that there are significant links across the creative platforms; the domains tend to remain relatively distinct.

Strength of Local Knowledge Flows within Individual Clusters or Industries

The local innovation system has been characterized as an entrepôt, drawing on global pipelines and exploiting local buzz (Phillips 2002; Bathelt, Malmberg, and Maskell 2002). In this context, none of the clusters are self-contained or self-sustaining. Each cluster accesses critical inputs from other markets (especially knowledge and money) and uses those to craft a differentiated product or service that is then marketed to the world, often in a primary or semi-finished form. Recent research on aspects of the community and its clusters offer evidence in support of this interpretation.

For example, a survey undertaken in the Saskatoon agricultural biotechnology community in 1998 illustrated the critical role of the local education system (Phillips and Khachatourians 2001). Virtually all technicians were trained in Canada, and more than 80 per cent came from the city-based polytechnic. Looking up the knowledge and training ladder, local influence declined – about two-thirds of those working in the sector with undergraduate degrees graduated from the University of Saskatchewan, but at the graduate level more than half the workers came from other parts of Canada, with only about one-quarter of the employees with doctorates having training in Saskatchewan. Thus the local labour market depends critically both on local educational systems and on attracting key personnel from away.

Meanwhile, about one-third of companies report that they get new employees from non-local markets, with firms relying relatively heavily on other markets for marketing, management, science, technology, and engineering research staff. Local markets were more important for production and design workers. Nevertheless, the local labour market exhibits some thickness, as 82 per cent of those surveyed in 1998 indicated that they had previous employment experience in the local labour market, with the university and the commercial sector providing most of the early career opportunities (ibid.).

Equally important is the flow of intellectual property within the clusters. An analysis by Niosi and Bas (2001) showed that in 1989–99 Saskatoon ranked fourth in Canada for patents issued (behind Montreal, Toronto, and Edmonton, or Vancouver, depending on the measure). The biotechnology-related patent activity was proportionately much higher in Saskatoon (67 per cent of all university patents) relative to other universities in Canada (average 16 per cent for all universities).

Beyond the education and research areas, there is some evidence that the Saskatoon biotechnology cluster offers unique opportunities for competitive intelligence and foresight. A survey in 2004 concluded that once the companies were operating, they used a range of methods to keep track of opportunities and threats, most of which depended on face-to-face relationships, many with some local component (Phillips et al. 2004). Firms in the biotechnology cluster, in particular, report tangible and intangible benefits of co-locating with competitors and collaborators (Phillips et al. 2004; Phillips and Khachatourians 2001). Surveys reveal that few companies think that it is important to be located near their key customers, and few would consider relocating simply to be near customers. There is more diversity of opinion about the importance of locating near suppliers. While most firms report they rely on a mix of local and non-local suppliers, few would consider relocating simply to establish closer ties with a supplier. In contrast to ambivalence about co-location with customers or suppliers, more than three-quarters of firms interviewed reported strong value from locating near their competitors. These actors – many at the R&D and early commercialization stage – reported that co-location improved their odds of competing.

More recently, this issue was tested with a broader group of firms from a range of clusters in Saskatoon. Many of the firms interviewed were early-stage start-ups, and they generally asserted that they were innovative – most noted that their firm has offered a new or significantly improved good or service or introduced a new or significantly improved production or manufacturing processes in recent years (many "new to the world"). When they were probed about how the local milieu affects their innovative activities, most reported accessing only informal feedback systems, either from customers or through collaboration with large-scale research projects executed with other firms and organizations. Firms tend to look first to the university, then clients, consultants or contract workers, other firms, research or product-testing firms, research organizations outside Saskatoon, and with Saskatoon-based research institutions (i.e., Saskatchewan Research Council, NRC/Plant Biotechnology Institute, POS Pilot Plant, Agriculture Canada, NRC/IRAP, the Innovation Place Bioresource Centre, and the Vaccine and Infectious Diseases Organization). While all firms acknowledged collaboration takes place, they often described relationships directly related to a specific step in the innovation process, such as funding or product testing. Few firms could describe any project in which the firm had worked closely with a partner throughout development. When asked to describe the motivation underlying collaboration, the most common answer was the need to cut costs. Others reported they seek to gain access to knowledge and expertise in order to stay at the cutting edge of advancements in science and technology. Smaller firms, such as start-ups in biotechnology and junior mining companies, often asserted that their limited capacity forced them to collaborate to access specific services, equipment, and infrastructure.

A deeper probe into the nature of firm collaborations in research and development and commercialization revealed that while life-science firms generally look for help from academics, many of these connections were informal – they often described this as simply picking up a phone and calling an acquaintance at the university or elsewhere to seek assistance. Only a few firms reported that they have dedicated science boards (see Zucker, Darby, and Brewer 1998). In contrast, mining and engineering firms tended to turn to consultants for advice or to seek help from parent or sister companies or competitors in their field (often based elsewhere).

Many policymakers assert that innovation can be nurtured through direct government services or through government-supported trade or industry associations. But it was rare for any firm respondent to indicate that trade associations or any level of government had significant impact on the firm's commercial success. Even if a firm indicated it was involved with a trade association, it was seldom able to identify what benefit, if any, it received from its engagement. Even when an organization was mentioned, that does not automatically imply it generated any benefit; many firms actually derided associations for not doing enough. Those mentioning benefits cited information, networking, client identification, lobbying, financing, market analysis, and training and recruitment. Only one firm (a very large employer) mentioned ever interacting directly with the municipal government.

In Saskatoon, it appears that a large proportion of collaboration and cooperation between firms and other organizations in the local economy occurs informally through personal contacts and loosely structured network (Phillips and Webb 2014b). While formal connections can still be important, especially connections with public research organizations and universities, the perception from the interviews is that informal connections between individuals is a more important conduit of information in the average firm's day-to-day operations. Firms seldom refer to collaboration and cooperation with other firms as a major part of their business strategy. Those firms that see interfirm collaboration as a strategic advantage usually reported working with a parent or sister firm. While many firms report they collaborate for components of their innovation process, such as product testing, in many cases this is indistinguishable from merely purchasing services from the market.

In general, Saskatoon entrepreneurs and business leaders appear open to exchanging information whenever this is not a direct threat to their company. That the default would be to share knowledge was seen as the natural order of things. Key individuals appear to have a number of knowledgeable acquaintances outside their company whom they can phone in order to seek help on specific issues. Furthermore, there is every indication that they would likely assist if the roles were reversed – interview respondents report a high degree of reciprocity in the Saskatoon system. Compensation is rarely received for brief consultations; interactions that run over an extended period may be crystallized into a contract. Generally, consultations are based on pre-existing contacts and, while these interactions may occur with individuals located anywhere, most of the examples referred to connections with individuals in Saskatoon.

One could conclude that most knowledge sharing is done within a framework of social norms instead of market norms. The concepts of social and market norms come from behavioural economics. While they seem simple – the difference is that interactions regulated by the market require compensation while those regulated by social norms do not – these concepts represent two fundamentally different ways in which individuals think about commercial interactions. Whether an interaction is regulated by social norms or market norms radically changes the nature and outcomes of that interaction. Other research has, somewhat counter-intuitively, shown that the expectation of payment can radically decrease an individual's willingness to render a service to another individual in certain situations (Benkler 2006). As a result, Saskatoon's environment of informal connections based on social norms may facilitate a greater level of knowledge transfer and willingness to assist other firms and individuals than if paid consultations were the norm. In environments where social norms predominate, reputation is critical – Saskatoon's small size likely contributes to social norms–dominated exchanges by allowing for easier tracking of reputational factors.

Strength of Local Knowledge Flows between Industries or Clusters

Theory suggests that communities that host more than one cluster may generate spillovers between and beyond innovative agglomerations that contribute to local economic prosperity. One test is simply to ask whether the local economy supports mobility of knowledge between jobs and sectors. A 2008 survey of 115 creative individuals in Saskatoon investigated whether there is mobility between sectors (Phillips and Webb 2008). Respondents on average pegged mobility at 6.5 out of 10

(10 = high; standard deviation was 1.6) and the ability to use knowledge gained in other sectors in their current work at 6.6 out of 10 (2.2 standard deviation). Interestingly, a correlation analysis between the personal creativity of respondents (dubbed the talent index, discussed in Phillips and Webb 2014c) and the responses to these questions revealed no significant relationship. In short, labour and skills may be mobile, but it is not clear that mobility differentially assists creative people to contribute in their own unique way.

Interviews conducted with firms in Saskatoon suggested similar findings to those revealed in the 2008 creative individuals survey. While some firms reported benefits from co-location with other sectors in Saskatoon – e.g., mining firms are well-served by Saskatoon's metal-working and manufacturing infrastructure – the overwhelming response to these questions was bafflement at the idea of learning from other sectors. While some suggested they could learn from other sectors in such activities as human resource management and importing/exporting, most firms reported only minimal opportunities to do so. Larger firms, presumably because of their greater range of activities, were more likely to report cross-sectoral learning – but in those cases it was usually from a closely related industry, such as a gold miner learning from a uranium firm.

Similarly, most workers were strictly confined to their particular industry and sector and did not work across fields in any significant way. In fact, the majority of firms in Saskatoon deny recruiting workers from other sectors. However, because of the city's thin workforce, there are many instances of firms being forced to hire from outside of their sector. Interestingly, a number of firms in the local industrial clusters have some sort of special relationship with a local post-secondary educational institution – the relationships seemingly vary from participation in job fairs to providing internships and to guiding curricula.

One test of how community features might influence creativity within and between clusters is to examine whether firms believed Saskatoon is a multicultural city and whether that positively affects their firm. The challenge is that only 7.5 per cent of the Saskatoon population is foreign born, compared with more than 18 per cent for Canada (note, the aboriginal population makes up an estimated 15 per cent of Saskatoon's total population, providing diversity of another kind). Moreover, Saskatoon has only 11.6 bohemians (defined as artists and artisans) per 1,000 labour force, compared with 13.1/1000 for Canada. Firms reporting that diversity offers benefits usually point to the value of a variety of perspectives and the enhanced ability to integrate new members of the workforce in a multicultural community. To test whether this mattered practically, firms were asked how many of their employees were born outside of Canada. While many had difficulty in answering, they hazarded best estimates: about a third of the firms reported all their employees were Canadian-born; the rest reported foreign-born employees, in most cases much higher than the migrant share of the local population.

Symptomatic of these findings, firms acknowledged limited local buzz. Only firms located in Innovation Place reported their location facilitated creativity and innovation. Located on the grounds of the University of Saskatchewan, Innovation Place has been one of the most successful university-related research parks in North America since 1980. Praised for its attractive buildings and grounds, its range of amenities and a vibrant research culture, Innovation Place is home to over 130 firms or organizations employing about 3,300 people. It was the only location in Saskatoon that was said to have "buzz" (primarily for biotechnology firms). One explanation is that Saskatoon might simply be too small to have districts with buzz distinguishable from that for the city as a whole.

Strength of Knowledge-Based Linkages between Local and Non-Local Actors

A third issue is how localized communities of actors interact with the world. As noted earlier, both clusters and the community recruit labour, technical services, and codified knowledge from away. One study (Phillips 2002) investigated these linkages specifically in the context of knowledge flows in the canola industry, the core of the local biotechnology cluster. The resulting global pipelines and local buzz suggested the canola research system in Saskatoon exhibited entrepôt features, having variable local capacity to create knowledge, use knowledge, and commercialize new products. While one might *a priori* conclude that Canada was the main canola innovator (on the basis of its record as the developer and first adopter of all the new-to-the-world traits over the past fifty years), analysis showed that a significant share of the research to develop the techniques needed to create those varieties was done in other countries; similarly, much of the research into downstream uses for the oil happened elsewhere. This suggests that Saskatoon is a niche operator in this global knowledge-based industry – an entrepôt undertaking and assembling the know-why, know-how, and know-who of varietal breeding and primary production – but that the bulk of the activities upstream and downstream were done elsewhere.

A related survey in 2004 further examined local–global relationships. More than three-quarters of the firms and organizations surveyed reported that they had formal intellectual property (IP) strategies. More than a third relied exclusively on non-local management of their strategies, and most firms accessed key skills related to valuation of IP both locally and non-locally. An analysis of the most innovative firms (i.e., those firms defined as innovative as calculated by Procyshyn 2004) showed that they had a number of common approaches: they had formalized IP strategies and a team approach to decision-making; their IP strategies were managed locally; but the critical IP valuation was generally handled non-locally by a multidisciplinary team (Ryan and Phillips 2004).

Conclusions

Saskatoon offers mixed evidence that the theory on the social nature of innovation is sustained, at least for mid-sized centres, in the empty quarter. First, the data offer some (but not universal) support for the importance of knowledge flows within sectors and clusters. Both employees and firms indicated that thick labour markets and fluid systems for accessing advanced knowledge are important in highly innovative sectors, but it is less clear that these matter for less knowledge-intensive industries. Second, the data do offer little support for the hypothesis of positive externalities between innovative clusters and the rest of the economy – if anything, they are solitudes. Third, there is some support for the need for global pipelines. Firms (and highly skilled individuals) acknowledge the need to be globally aware and connected, but there is limited evidence that this interconnectivity generates greater innovation – it seems that the creative spark that drives innovation, at least in the Saskatoon context, is locally centred.

Social Foundations of Talent Attraction and Retention

Florida (2002) asserts that people are more important than systems. The foregoing analysis of the social nature of innovation highlighted the critical role of highly trained and motivated individuals in innovation. We investigated this hypothesis further by addressing two core questions. First, what are the primary foundations for attracting and retaining talent in the city? Second, how prevalent is labour mobility among firms within and between sectors or clusters in the city, and what role does it play in circulating knowledge and reinforcing cross-sectoral ties and knowledge flows? In brief, the evidence from Saskatoon suggests that economic and market factors trump quality of place and that mobility between sectors is quite limited.

Primary Foundations for Attracting and Retaining Talent

Saskatoon is widely viewed to project an image to Canada and the world as a cold, remote place where nothing much happens. While many report that this image is a challenge facing the region, the prevailing local view is that once people come and experience the city, most of the top-of-mind image factors diminish. The focus shifts instead to the economic fundamentals, which, while generally positive overall, pose challenges. At least when the surveys were done, there was concern that Saskatoon employers offer lower wages than other regions and that in some sectors the labour market may be too thin to pull innovative and creative people to the community or to offer meaningful employment to spouses of immigrant workers.

One frequently cited concern is that smaller, close-knit centres may be less able to integrate migrants. This view was tested in 2008 with a survey of Saskatoon's talented individuals and their views about attitudes in Saskatoon (Phillips and Webb 2014c). Approximately one-fifth of the respondents were born and lived most, if not all, of their lives in Saskatoon; another two-fifths were born in the province and migrated to the city at some point in their life. The remaining 36 per cent came from outside the province – two-thirds from the rest of Canada and one-third from abroad. The survey targeted and included at least one significant "talent" pool – namely those with advanced training and degrees – and all were employed. A simple index of talent was developed – a straight average of the percentage of a person's life spent outside of Saskatoon (0–98 per cent), and their highest level of education (0–100 per cent, from no matriculation to PhD) – which was then correlated against measures of tolerance and other attractors in the community to determine how they may relate.

One fundamental assumption embedded in Florida's concept of creativity is that talent will be attracted to a location on the basis of its tolerance. Tolerance can relate to race, age, sexual orientation, and beliefs. No single, all-encompassing measure of tolerance could be used. When asked generally whether the community was tolerant or welcoming, the average of all responses was 7.4 (0 = not at all; 10 = totally), but it was not significantly correlated to the talent index. As a second test of tolerance, we asked the respondents of their racial or ethnic background and their experiences of discrimination. Only about 12 per cent of the sample reported they had encountered discrimination, and there was no statistical evidence that this is related to race or any other specific visible trait, and it was not correlated to talent.

Another way to measure tolerance is to determine whether the city is open to experimentation and creativity. When asked to rank the city, the average response was 6.3 out of 10 (where 10 is most tolerant), but there was no statistically significant correlation between one's talent score and one's view on the city on this measure.

The study went on to test which characteristics of living and working in Saskatoon make it an attractive place. When presented with twenty specific community features and asked to rank them on a scale from very negative to very positive, all but the tax regime generated overall positive responses, but only four features were statistically significant from zero: commute time, community environment, suitability for raising children, and work environment in the firm (see Phillips and Webb 2014c). An analysis of the links between talent and individual responses to the attractiveness of the twenty features revealed that six were correlated. Salary, cutting-edge work, and affordable living were all positively correlated to talent (at the 95 or 99 per cent confidence level), while restaurants/night life and proximity to family and friends were negatively correlated with talent (ibid.). The positive measures, all individually related and normally part of one's personal cost-benefit calculations, suggest that work in Saskatoon is a positive driver and is perceived to be appropriately compensated (both in normative and purchasing power terms). In contrast, Saskatoon is somewhat less attractive from the perspective of talented individuals (many of whom have migrated from elsewhere) because of its limited nightlife and dislocation from friends and family. This result conforms to earlier work done by Phillips and Khachatourians (2001) and Phillips (2002).

Mobility and Creativity

We also examined whether the local economy supports mobility of knowledge between jobs and sectors. A 2008 survey revealed that respondents ranked the local economy at 6.5 out of 10 (highest) in its ability to transfer knowledge between sectors, but once again there was no statistically significant correlation between this response and the talent index (Phillips and Webb 2014c).

These numbers raise a number of possibilities. One option is that Saskatoon does not tolerate creativity and innovators. To test this likelihood, we examined the effect of mobility on entrepreneurship. About 10 per cent of our respondents reported establishing a business and another 20 per cent or so reported that they had worked for a start-up firm sometime in their career. The talent index was tested against an index of entrepreneurial engagement (where 0 = never connected; 1 = employed by start-up; 2 = act as entrepreneur). A very small positive correlation between talent and entrepreneurial engagement was found (+0.06), but it was statistically insignificant.

In short, this suggests there is only weak inter-sectoral knowledge mobility and, where it does exist, it is not strongly related to entrepreneurial effort. This evidence is not strong enough to reject the talent mobility thesis, but rather does suggest that at least in Saskatoon it is not a compelling explanation for innovation and creativity.

Conclusions

Recent studies in Saskatoon offer little or no support for the hypothesis that tolerance, social, or cultural vibrancy or inter-sectoral mobility are vital to attracting, integrating, and retaining high-technology and creative workers in Saskatoon. Saskatoon is viewed as a moderately tolerant community, but those views are not significantly related to one's level of talent. The negative correlation between social vibrancy and talent suggests people who come and stay do so in spite of the local ambience. Finally, there is a perception that the community exhibits low inter-sectoral mobility and limited opportunity – rather than being attracted to the city-region by characteristics of place usually associated with creativity, the talented and creative individuals in Saskatoon appear to be essentially captured by the professional and commercial prospects of place. The fact that the city retains many high-technology workers suggests that once they become engaged in the commercial aspects of place they find value in a broader spectrum of community attributes.

Inclusive Communities and Civic Engagement

Innovative communities often generate innovative forms of governance. New opportunities require new institutions. To test this possibility, we examined two questions. First, what new governance mechanisms have emerged in the city to undertake "strategic planning" exercises or to strategically manage the urban economy? Second, how socially inclusive are these governance mechanisms, and how do they link economic, cultural, and social development agendas? The evidence is mixed. Numerous variables and indicators have been used to measure the degree of social inclusion and civic engagement. This work has focused primarily on collaborations among community-based organizations, industry associations, and the three orders of government. The collaboration among these diverse actors in the city-region in some ways constitutes a form of collaborative governance.

New Governance Mechanisms

New industries, new infrastructure, and new markets can at times facilitate or be the target of new associative forms of governance. Saskatoon in some ways has been a hotbed of institutional innovation. In the historical sense, one might argue Saskatchewan (rather than Saskatoon particularly) has been a source of many innovations of associative governance. Cooperatives occupied an early and dominant position in agriculture, finance, insurance, and wholesale and retail trade, jointly developing, owning, and controlling the majority of the marketing and supply system in the agri-food system, a plurality of the finance, insurance, and retail activity in the province, and much of the manufacturing infrastructure. Equally important from a provincial and national perspective, Saskatchewan was one of the early and most frequent users of Crown ownership of utilities and for industrial development. At one point or another, the province has been the sole operator, monopoly owner, or major shareholder in almost all of the major economic sectors in the province (including wood processing, pulp and paper manufacturing, potash, uranium, oil, gas, and farm land).

Saskatchewan, more than many jurisdictions, has found its model of governance under stress. While cooperatives and Crown corporations are fundamentally associative models of governance, they were found to be somewhat less effective when capital and labour became more mobile in recent decades. As a result, many cooperatives have been bought or converted to joint-stock enterprises, and most of the provincial industrial Crown corporations have been privatized.

In their place, the province and city have engaged in a range of "partnerships" (Phillips and Webb 2014a). As early as the 1970s the province encouraged short-line farm-machinery manufacturers to collaborate to develop their industry, providing support for an industry association (the Prairie Implement Manufacturers' Association) and a test lab at the Prairie Agricultural Machinery Institute in Humboldt. In the late 1980s the province provided the leadership and seed money to develop Ag-West Biotech (now Ag-West Bio or AWB), which became the flagship industrial organization in Saskatoon engaged in nurturing the life-sciences industry (Phillips et al. 2008). AWB, using largely government funds but directed by an arm's-length private-sector board, has provided leadership for attracting new firms to the industrial cluster, for operating a private equity pool (Procyshyn 2004), and for coordinating ad hoc teams to bid on new projects or infrastructure. AWB provided the leadership, for example, for the bid to host a National Agricultural Genomics Centre in Saskatoon; while the bid failed, the initiative pressed Ottawa into creating Genome Canada and the affiliated Genome Prairie operation, now located in Saskatoon, which provide strategic leadership for developing and managing world-scale genomics-research projects. Meanwhile, the municipality responded to this new imperative for associative governance and converted its business development office into the industry-led Saskatoon and Region Economic Development Authority (SREDA). A small group of entrepreneurs, academics, and civic leaders have used these platforms to leverage new resources into Saskatoon. The individual and collective leadership of AWB, Genome Prairie, and SREDA have been instrumental in developing proposals, lining up partners and pitching for federal support for a number of major investments in the city, including the Canadian Light Source Inc. (CLSI) and the International Vaccine Centre (InterVac).

This unconventional mix of actors has led to some interesting and innovative partnerships, as exemplified in CLSI. The driving force for this initiative being located in Saskatoon was a few intrapreneurs in the federal and provincial ministries and at the university, aided and supported by the leaders and partners in AWB and SREDA. As the project gained momentum, it became a community quest. The municipal government made an almost unprecedented investment in a national science project, contributing $2.4 million (or $10 per capita) to the capital project, members of Parliament and senators from all parties coalesced to lobby for the project in Ottawa, and the university took the lead to develop the technical aspects of the project, assigning the VP research to lead the initiative. As the project progressed, new models of management and engagement were tested. The doors were opened to let local people see the project, and the project leaders worked with community ambassadors, including taxi drivers, to educate them on the nature of the project and its impact on the city and economy. An estimated 35,000 people had toured the facility by 2009, or about 10 per cent of the regional population.

This example spawned similar ventures (albeit at a smaller scale) in innovative associative governance in pursuit of economic and social goals in the city. Leaders and partners in the synchrotron team, for instance, have fanned out and helped with recent community efforts to build indoor soccer stadiums, a new performing arts centre, and a new art gallery.

Social Inclusion

In a collaborative model of governance, the actors – civil society, industry, and government – cooperatively draw upon relevant assets within the system, whether they be knowledge, credibility, or funding, to carry out services required at the city-region level. To gauge the capacity of this governance effort, it is necessary to examine what specific services each actor provides and, more generally, what role it sees itself having within the larger community.

One theme that emerged in Saskatoon is that the community-based organizations (CBOs) have tended towards specialization; each CBO provides a specific service, to a specific group, to fulfil a specific need. This specialization of services is consciously done for a variety of reasons. CBOs, which rely almost exclusively on private and public funding, are acutely aware of resource limitations and of the value in creating and maintaining a distinct "brand." Organizations such as Habitat for Humanity (synonymous with affordable housing) are more likely to receive funding then generic, multi-purpose entities.

While specialization is valuable, there are natural limits. As funding from larger donors (especially federal and provincial governments) is often project-specific – as opposed to operational funding – organizations occasionally expand their mandate to fit grant requirements. Project-specific funding, which is perceived to deliver a greater "bang-for-the-buck" for donors, can lead to unnecessary expansion and redundancy of services. In recognition that project-specific funds can lure CBOs outside their core mandate, a majority of interviewees expressed concern that they maintain a "singularity of purpose," which both facilitates efficiencies and allows them to avoid unproductive competition with other CBOs.

One challenge for specialized CBOs is that they may have some difficulty seeing the broader "Saskatoon perspective." While all the CBOs were focused on community development, they often saw development solely from their organizational perspective. This focused, organizationally narrow perspective is understandable, as the issues that they wrestle with week-in, week-out predominate. However, the fragmented views about important development issues among the CBOs impeded development of a unified community strategy in the city-region.

Some CBOs attempt to fill this void. The United Way of Saskatoon is acknowledged by many as an "umbrella organization" able to unite numerous individuals and organizations in collective ventures. Another way this lacuna is addressed is through the Cultural Connections project initiated under Heritage Canada's Cultural Capital grant. This project looks to create an overarching governance structure for cultural organizations in Saskatoon – a structure to deliver a united voice and vision for this sector.

While Saskatoon has strong CBOs that enrich inclusiveness and enable civic engagement, there is a noticeable paucity of industry associations. Associations tend to represent members from across the entire province, and not just the city. Given that advocacy is the most common service performed by industry associations, most focus their efforts and staff in Regina, the provincial capital.

Nevertheless, industry associations do offer critical linkages. Unlike many of the CBOs, the industry associations in the city had strategies that were neither as narrow nor as specialized in scope. However, more could be done – there remain too many disparate approaches. The most obvious example of organizational silos was the large number of policies focused on labour shortages in Saskatoon. Because it is an issue that affects industries across numerous sectors, logic would presume a collaborative effort, where knowledge is shared. However, while some industry associations were aware of others examining the issue, none knew any details of those plans. While exceptions to the organizational silos of strategic planning were mentioned during the interviews – notably the Saskatoon Housing Initiatives Partnership – there was general agreement that the current model limits the effectiveness of industry associations in Saskatoon.

Governments at times attempt to engage and drive the local process, but the Saskatoon evidence points to a "policy distance" that increases as one moves from the city-region to the provincial and national levels. This change is firmly reflected in how CBOs and industry associations rated the effectiveness of government in local development. There is a common view that the city is frequently an effective integrator. The municipal government recently emerged from self-professed stagnation to steady and open growth. One driver has been the devolution of responsibility for services that were formerly the purview of the other governments (e.g., immigration settlement, affordable housing. and urban reserves). At least partly in response, the city has engaged in a range of strategic planning that has involved civic dialogue and engagement. This involvement is especially noticeable in local area planning, which has formalized the participation of specific CBOs, community associations, and the general public. However, most municipal strategies remain narrow. The unified city plan set in the late 1990s by the Saskatoon Regional Economic Development Authority was focused predominantly on economic issues. In 2010 the city delivered a strategic plan for 2013–23 to advance economic development, infrastructure investment, and quality of life. Moving to the provincial level, the ratings are mixed. With teams of people specifically responsible for strategic sector development and competitiveness in Saskatoon, the Industry and Resources Department of Saskatchewan (now Innovation Saskatchewan and the Ministry of the Economy) was viewed as particularly active and important. In an effort to reduce the natural distance in other policy areas, the provincial government developed the Saskatoon Regional Intersectoral Committee to increase intersectoral partnerships and collaboration and to reduce barriers and identify gaps. The federal government is viewed as being even more distant – generally policy and services are seen as being implemented effectively but rarely developed at the city-region level.

Against that backdrop of actors, we investigated how the collaboration works. With over fifty distinct networks and key associations involved in development in Saskatoon, the frequency of contacts, both formal and informal, between collaborators was on average rated as 8.6 on a scale of one to 10 (Phillips and Webb 2014a). During the interviews the high frequency of collaboration was attributed to regular contact and meetings between actors. Some noted that the smaller size of Saskatoon increased contact between actors – "everyone is playing in the same sandbox." Generally CBOs indicated a higher frequency of collaboration than the three levels of government or industry associations.

Despite the high frequency of collaboration between networks and associations, there appears to be limited social, cultural, or economic overlap between collaborative networks. Industry associations tend to collaborate with other industry players towards economic ends, while CBOs interact with civil society groups towards social or cultural ends. The main exceptions to these silos were the Tourism Saskatoon strategy, the Cultural Crescent project, and the Cultural Governance initiative. While all three had low barriers to entry and actively engaged large parts of the community in the formulation and implementation of policy, there were gaps – most actors expressed concern with the lack of engagement of First Nations people.

While interactions were rated as high, their effectiveness was rated only as 6.8 on a scale of 1 to 10. Two common criticisms were raised: first, while networks and organizations met regularly, few action plans were developed or implemented, and second, it was believed that the pursuit of consensus often led to ineffective and diluted policy.

The Role of Social Entrepreneurs in Creative Communities

Webb (2009) analysed social entrepreneurs in Saskatoon. Individuals who played key roles in the community were examined to determine the nature of their economic, social, and cultural interactions. These links were used to identify different types of network leadership, which were then correlated to a set of personal attributes to determine the motivations and influences on leaders. Broadly speaking, the analysis suggested that creative social entrepreneurs are not unambiguously the primary creators of social capital in the Saskatoon city-region. However, a more thorough examination of the data offered more nuanced findings. The study highlighted two broad findings.

First, it consistently indicates a strong positive relationship between high levels of professional creativity and central placement in the social system (as leaders, power brokers, and gatekeepers). Professional creatives often have large, far-flung networks; they act as connectors by bridging groups and individuals and hold positions of formal and informal structural power in their social networks. One can therefore infer that individuals who are highly educated, have a creative job, and are relatively highly inter-sectorally mobile, positively influence the creation of social capital in the city-region.

A second implication of this research is drawn directly from the result that professional creatives influence creation of social capital in Saskatoon. The literature on "creatives," especially that of Florida (2002), suggests that creative individuals are drawn to creative cities – places with vibrant and tolerant social and cultural atmospheres. The hypothesis that "creatives" are attracted to a location because of certain aspects of place is probably (at the very least anecdotally) true. However, social and cultural vibrancy are important not just in attracting and retaining creative individuals in a city. Once present in a city, creative individuals, especially professional creatives, can have a significant impact on the maintenance and growth of that vibrancy; professional creatives become involved in the community, they create or join organizations, and they bridge individuals and institutions. Members of the creative class are not just consumers of social and cultural vibrancy, they are also producers.

Conclusions

Research on Saskatoon illuminates the social dynamics of economic activity in a smaller, remote city, casting some doubt about the robustness of some core hypotheses about innovation systems and creative centres. In particular, it raises doubts about the Garreau empty-quarter thesis. His typology implies that Saskatoon should remain tied uniquely to the commodity cycle. While global markets still have potential to shift prospects, many recent investments in research and production work to diversify and decouple the economy from volatile commodity markets.

Furthermore, market dynamics appear to have a more important role in creativity in Saskatoon than the theory would suggest. Saskatoon's resource-based, knowledge-intensive economy is an ideal place to test the limits to the creativity literature. Much of the core work on creativity has focused on industries and occupations that produce disembodied outputs that can be moved at low or no cost to the intermediate or end consumer. The "creatives" generally are assumed to deliver basic, "know-why" research and the patented products derived from that knowledge (e.g., drugs and circuitry) and products of design (e.g., traditional and new media and fashion). In Saskatoon, there is extensive research and design, but it tends to get embodied into intermediate and end products, which are then produced in the Great Plains area and traded in a semi-finished or final form. While some results of local research and design might be tradable in their disembodied form, much of the knowledge is tacit and cultivated in closely knit social systems and often requires specific context for its optimal use, which limits its transferability. One tentative conclusion is that the creativity hypothesis may be more suited to specific types of creative effort and may not be universally applicable.

Similarly, tolerance may be a necessary but certainly is not a sufficient condition for explaining attraction and retention of talent in Saskatoon. The concentration of research and design in Saskatoon that generates new products, processes, technologies, organizations, and markets for the agri-food and oil, gas, and mining sector tends to sharpen the focus of individuals in the community. This may either reduce the tolerance for diversity directly or may simply be another example of the Dutch disease, where economic rents in one sector draw scarce resources (in this case, talented and creative individuals) away from lower-value-added activities into high-return areas.

Finally, innovative institutions, while important, do not appear to be sufficient to explain creativity. Institutional innovation in Saskatoon appears to be more a coincident or lagging indicator of creativity. The key innovative models – cooperatives, Crown corporations, and now public-private partnerships – all coincided with periods of intensive innovation, but there is no compelling evidence to suggest that they led the effort. More often the introduction of new technologies from elsewhere or the opening of new markets precipitated social and economic changes, which then needed new institutional support.

Notes

1 With student researchers G. Ericson, J. Karwandy, M. Kunz, T. Procyshyn, C. Ryan, and N. Zettl.

2 Spencer and Vinodrai (2006) estimate that 15 per cent of jobs in Saskatoon are in clustered sectors, compared to more than 22 per cent of Canadian jobs found in clusters.

References

Bathelt, H., A. Malmberg, and P. Maskell. 2002. "Clusters and knowledge: Local buzz, global pipelines and the process of knowledge creation." Danish Research Unit on Industrial Dynamics working paper 2002-12. Copenhagen.

Benkler, Y. 2006. *The wealth of networks: How social production transforms markets and freedom*. New Haven, CT: Yale University Press.

Florida, R. 2002. *The rise of the creative class*. New York: Basic Books.

Garreau, J. 1981. *The nine nations of North America*. Boston: Houghton Mifflin.

Niosi, J., and G. Bas. 2001. "The competencies of regions: Canada's clusters in biotechnology." *Small Business Economics* 17 (1/2): 31–42. http://dx.doi.org/10.1023/A:1011114220694.

Phillips, P. 2002. "Regional systems of innovation as a modern R&D entrepot: The case of the Saskatoon biotechnology cluster." In *Innovation, entrepreneurships, family business and economic development: A Western Canadian perspective*, ed. J. Chrisman et al., 31–58. Calgary: University of Calgary Press.

Phillips, P., and G. Khachatourians, eds. 2001. *The biotechnology revolution in global agriculture: Invention, innovation and investment in the canola sector*. Wallingford, UK: CABI Publishing. http://dx.doi.org/10.1079/9780851995137.0000.

Phillips, P., J. Parchewski, T. Procyshyn, C. Ryan, J. Karwandy, and J. Kihlberg. 2004. *Agricultural and life-science clusters in Canada: An empirical and policy analysis*. Final project report for AAFC Study of the Saskatoon Cluster, 30 March.

Phillips, P., C. Ryan, J. Karwandy, T. Procyshyn, and J. Parchewski. 2008. "The Saskatoon agricultural biotechnology cluster." In *Handbook of research on clusters: Theories, policies and case studies*, ed. C. Karlsson, 239–52. Cheltenham, UK: Edward Elgar. http://dx.doi.org/10.4337/9781848445079.00021.

Phillips, P., and G. Webb. 2008. "Talent, tolerance and community in Saskatoon." Presentation to the ISRN National Conference, Montreal, 5 May.

–. 2014a. "Cooperative and partnership governance in Saskatoon." In *Governing Urban Economies: Innovation and Inclusion in Canadian City-Regions*, ed. N. Bradford and A. Bramwell, 229–47. Toronto: University of Toronto Press.

–. 2014b. "Social dynamics, diversity and physical infrastructure in creative, innovative communities: The Saskatoon case." In *Innovating in Urban Economies: Economic Transformation in Canadian City-Regions*, ed. D. Wolfe., 269–91. Toronto: University of Toronto Press.

–. 2014c. "Talent, tolerance and community in Saskatoon." In *Seeking talent for creative cities: The social dynamics of innovation*, ISRN series vol. 2, ed. Jill L. Grant, 159–77. Toronto: University of Toronto Press.

Procyshyn, T. 2004. "The Ag Biotech cluster and the CLS." MSc thesis, University of Saskatchewan.

Ryan, C., and P. Phillips. 2004. "Knowledge management in advanced technology industries: An examination of international agricultural biotechnology clusters." *Environment and Planning. C, Government & Policy* 22 (2): 217–32. http://dx.doi.org/10.1068/c0343.

Webb, G. 2009. "Creative social entrepreneurs, social capital and collaborative governance: A Saskatoon based analysis." MSc thesis, University of Saskatchewan.

Zucker, L., M. Darby, and M. Brewer. 1998. "Intellectual human capital and the birth of U.S. biotechnology enterprises." *American Journal of Economics* 88 (1): 290–306.

12 The Social Dynamics of Economic Performance in the Public-Sector City: Kingston, Ontario

BETSY DONALD AND HEATHER HALL

The small-sized public-sector city is largely absent from the literature on urban development and innovation. This oversight is not surprising, given that the economies of public-sector cities are largely dependent on government spending and often have weak private-sector innovation systems, and their relative steady-state economies inspire little enthusiasm or analytical interest. But what we hope to show in this chapter is that public-sector cities are far from irrelevant to our understanding of the social dynamics of economic performance in Canadian city-regions. The long-term expansion in Canada of public-sector employment and programs has meant that public-sector cities are increasingly places where people live, work, and experience relative economic stability. Moreover, these public institutions construct a particular social and economic logic that can both aid and encumber innovative economic development.

Public-sector cities are perhaps most closely aligned with their "ordinary" city cousins, which Bradford (this volume) has described as those less-than-dynamic mid-size Canadian cities that lack any flagship firms or major cluster profiles to mark the local economy or have any distinguishing cultural claim. Kingston is perhaps one of Canada's best examples of a small-sized public-sector city. The city depends on several public-sector institutions including the university, the military, correctional services, and health-care services. This heavy reliance on the public sector affects the city in many profound ways and has implications for how private-sector innovation works, how labour markets operate, and how governance is shaped and plays out in the local economy. Moreover, the particular labour market – with its steady, well-paying public-sector jobs, and weaker, more precarious service-oriented ones – contributes to a spatially, socially, and politically polarized urban environment. In this chapter, we hope to show that the public-sector town, while unexceptional in many ways, is also quite distinct. Much can be learned from the public-sector city in social dynamics of economic performance.

To discuss these arguments, this chapter is divided into five sections. The first section explores the concept of the public-sector city in more detail, while the next section provides a brief socio-economic history and geography of Kingston. The remainder of this chapter is organized in terms of innovation and the formation of business clusters, the labour market, and governance arrangements.

The Public-Sector City

In his review of London, Ontario, Bradford draws on Todtling and Trippl's (2005) conceptual framework for the cognitive, organizational, and institutional gaps often found in unexceptional places. He demonstrates that the ordinary city tends to fall down in all three conceptual frames. However, he uses these shortcomings to describe and make recommendations for ordinary cities to move forward. For example, Bradford argues in this volume that some of these challenges can be addressed through strategic alliances and more collaborative and sustained forms of civic governance. However, many of these sustained forms can come about only when one or more public agencies directly engages non-state stakeholders in collective decision-making with an explicit goal of making better public policy and/or implementing effective public programs or assets (Ansell and Gash 2008). As public resources become more constrained, the benefit of sharing ideas and resources across different interests through cooperative efforts becomes more important (Bradford and Andrew 2010).[1]

Like their ordinary city cousins, small and mid-sized public-sector cities tend to perform close to the Canadian average on many social and economic indicators and maintain a reasonable standard of living and quality of life. They are not necessarily "the places to be," nor are they necessarily in dire straits. More particular to the public-sector city, however, is that they experience neither the peak of prosperous times nor the troughs of economic recession. Public-sector cities in Canada have been somewhat immune from recent recessions because of government decisions to spend on major infrastructure projects in an effort to stimulate economic growth. However, given the current era of government austerity and a lack of robust private-sector innovation to fall back on, the public-sector town could face tough times.

The results of this chapter are based on insights from a multi-year, empirical case study of Kingston, Ontario. This includes eighty-one key informant interviews focused on three themes: the social nature of innovation; talent attraction and retention; and governance. Interviews[2] were conducted with civic and business leaders as well as with knowledge, creative, and service workers.[3] Basic statistical data on the socio-economic characteristics of Kingston were also consulted. Before we report on those results, we turn to a brief overview of the city's socio-economic history and geography. This overview is important because it provides some necessary context for understanding the present challenges.

Brief Overview of Kingston, Ontario

Kingston is a small, yet stable growing city located strategically in Southeastern Ontario, along the Toronto, Montreal, Ottawa triangle. Dubbed the "Limestone City" for its many historic stone buildings and landmarks, many of these structures survive and tell the story of the formative years in the making of modern-day Canada. As Osborne and Swainson (1988) explain, Kingston was originally a Mississauga First Nations settlement named "Katarokwi" (translated into Cataraqui). French explorers settled in the area in the seventeenth century, and Kingston became an important trading post and military settlement, with the French establishing Fort Frontenac. The British captured and destroyed the fort in 1758 as part of the Seven Years War. Over the next half-century, Kingston became a heaven for United Empire Loyalists who were fleeing the American Revolution. By 1787, the British were referring to Cataraqui as "King's Town," after King George III, and the name was eventually shortened to "Kingston" in 1788. During the War of 1812, Kingston was home to the Lake Ontario Division of the Great Lakes British naval fleet, which fought the Americans for control of Lake Ontario. After the war, Britain built Fort Henry and several Martello towers to guard the entrance to the Rideau Canal, which was a major engineering feat, completed in 1832.

By 1840, Kingston had the largest population of any settlement in Upper Canada and it became Canada's first capital city in 1841. The reign was short-lived, however, as Kingston's geographic position made it vulnerable to an American attack. As a result, the capital was

Table 12.1. Major employers in Kingston, 2015

Largest employers in Kingston	# of employees
Queen's University	8,289
Canadian Forces Base Kingston	8,000
Kingston General Hospital	4,123
Limestone District School Board	3,186
Correctional Services of Canada	2,541
Providence Care	1,599
City of Kingston	1,281
Hotel Dieu Hospital	900
InvistaCanada	750
StarTek Canada	650

Source: Kingston Economic Development Corporation (2015)

moved to Montreal in 1844, then Toronto, and eventually Ottawa in 1857. Kingston's growth slowed after this and its national importance declined (Osborne and Swainson 1988).

During the late nineteenth and early twentieth centuries, Kingston became a centre for waterway shipping, shipbuilding, and railway locomotive manufacturing. It was home to the Canadian Locomotive Company (CLC), which was at one point one of Canada's largest commercial builders. The CLC closed in 1969, and since then most heavy industry has vacated the city (McQueen 2000). (It is important to note, however, that Kingston was never as industrialized as parts of Central and Western Ontario). Employment is now primarily in the institutional, military, and service-retail sectors. Today the largest employer is the the university, followed by the military, the hospitals, the school board, and correctional services (see table 12.1).

In 2007, Fort Henry, the Martello Towers, and much of the surrounding area was designated as part of the Rideau Canal UNESCO World Heritage Site, thanks in part to the perseverance of key local actors to preserve the city's unique historical character. These and other historical sites and landscapes are now popular tourist attractions, but there is always tension between development, on the one hand, and the preservation of these and other heritage sites on the other. Nevertheless, Kingston's historic character is one of its defining assets.

Table 12.2. Socio-economic Indicators

	Kingston	Canada
Population, 2006	152,350	31,612,890
% population change, 2001–6	3.8	5.4
% foreign born, 2001–6	12.5	19.8
% BA degree or higher	21.7	18.1
# employed	74,345	15,958,195
Employment growth, 2001–6	10.4	19.8
Employment rate	60.5	62.4
Unemployment rate	6.5	6.6
% "creative" occupations	37.4	33.2
% science and technology occupations	6.0	6.6
"Bohemians" per 1,000 labour force	12.7	14.2
# industrial clusters	1	255
% employment in clusters	7.5	22.1
Average FT employment income	$51,267	$51,221
% change average income 2000–5	6.6	5.5

Source: Spencer and Vinodrai (2009)

Kingston Today

Kingston has a total CMA population of 159,561 and a city population of 123,363 (Statistics Canada 2012). As seen in table 12.2, it tends to fall close to the Canadian average on many socio-economic indictors such as average full-time employment income, the unemployment rate, and employment rate. It tends to fall below the Canadian average in population growth and immigration, with a notably less ethnically diverse population than other Canadian cities. However, it appears to be slightly ahead of the curve in measurements like the percentage of the population with post-secondary education and is ranked first in per capita population with a PhD, or engineering or science degree (McKenzie 2007). By the same token, Kingston also has a higher-than-average population without high school or much formal education, and a higher percentage of low-income earners than many similar-sized Ontario cities (National Capital Resources 2008). Both these facts have helped to contribute to a marked socio-spatial geography.

In recent years, Kingston has been well placed on various quality of life indicators and noted especially for its walkable and lively heritage downtown,[4] its accessibility to the outdoors and sailing, and its excellent education and health-care systems. It also has a relatively vibrant creative arts sector for its city-size, producing well-known Canadian literary, artistic, and musical talents. In recent years, the city has been a magnet for retirees attracted to the lifestyle, small city, and quality health-care services. This has also led to a demand for senior services and a small boom in the condominium and apartment market (CMHC 2012).

Kingston's history as a military fort, a relatively stable institutional economy, and an older population is reflected in the city's federal and provincial voting patterns. Most of Eastern Ontario votes for the Conservative Party, and Kingston historically has voted Conservative. However, it has become more Liberal over the last quarter-century. With the exception of one NDP provincial representative between 1990 and 1995, Kingston has consistently voted in Liberal local mayors and Liberal candidates in federal and provincial elections, making it one of Canada's most predictable and stable political ridings. While not much has changed in Kingston's political outlook, there has been growth in the power of the left-of-centre, especially at the municipal level.

In sum, Kingston could best be described as a small, attractive, mostly liberal-conservative city with some important historical assets and a strong institutional and public-sector economy and culture. The city falls close to the national average on many socio-economic indicators, although these averages often mask a more polarized social geography between those with good jobs and those without. We now turn to a discussion of how this context in part shapes Kingston's innovation and business cluster environment, labour market, and governance.

Innovation and Business Cluster

Kingston does not have any private-sector business clusters[5] per se, although it does have a cluster of post-secondary education institutions, and the city does have some very innovative, small, knowledge-based companies in environmental technology, plant genetics, information technology, and health care. Collectively, they are estimated to employ about 700 people. Many of these companies have spun out of Queen's University, one of Canada's best research-intensive universities[6] (see table 12.3). Examples of spin-offs from Queen's University include Performance Plants, which is one of the largest plant biotechnology companies in Canada; Pathogen Detection Systems, a developer of water-borne-bacteria-detection technologies; and Qubit Systems,

Table 12.3. PARTEQ Statistics, 2009

	Total
Total patents Issued to date	390
Active technologies in portfolio	189
Start-ups formed	22 (15 active)
Other companies formed, based on PARTEQ-licensed technology	19 (16 active)
Products licensed	47
Total invested in PARTEQ-generated companies	~$910 million
Jobs created	> 700

Source: PARTEQ (2009a, 2009b)

which specializes in the design of instrumentation for research and teaching in the biological sciences. The Royal Military College also has a research-intensive arm, but many of the spin-offs or business connections are difficult to ascertain, given the confidential nature of military research and operations.[7]

With Kingston's strong education and medical sectors, one would think the city would be primed for a vibrant R&D and commercial spin-off economy, similar to places like Waterloo, Ontario. As the innovation systems literature would tell us, cities with strong "eds and meds" clusters can provide a solid research foundation for business to leverage (Morgan 1997; Leydesdorff 1995; Adams 2003; Donald 2006). Indeed, Kingston does have many of the ingredients to make this happen: an education cluster, a highly regarded university technology transfer institution (PARTEQ), and generally good inter-governmental relations in coordinated economic development policy. But for several reasons, Kingston has never really been able to "get on the map" in the dynamic, high-value-added private sector or innovation-led economic growth. The Conference Board of Canada recently rated it a "C" grade for entrepreneurship (Hendra 2013).

There are a number of reasons for this mediocre grade. First, it is important to recognize the role played by economic and institutional history, relative physical distance to other cities, and city size. Many key informants also told us that the knowledge assets of the town were disconnected from the local economy. There has never been a strong industrial tradition in Kingston, and there have never been deep linkages between academic or military research and the local private sector.

Unlike more locally embedded universities such as Waterloo, there was never a cooperative (co-op) program with local businesses or a past desire by the university to connect with local businesses or the local community. Connections between business and the university tend to be further afield. The same can be said for the Canadian Forces Base (CFB) Kingston and the Royal Military College (RMC). Despite the obvious science, engineering, information and communications technology research going on, most of it spins out in other contexts across the country and around the world.

Furthermore, inter-institutional connections tend to be weak. Kingston has a unique set of institutional actors that really have very different and incompatible objectives and local social and economic geographies. For example, Queen's University has always attracted students from other parts of Canada, and many of these students return to their hometowns once they graduate. CFB Kingston and RMC are institutions with national and global connections and constantly moving populations. Quite different still is the prison population, with its own unique set of circumstances and social challenges.

Kingston's city-size also presents challenges. Many of our key informants told us how difficult it was for firms to expand in Kingston, mainly because the city does not have the necessary suppliers, customers, deep labour market, or innovative milieu that comes with a larger, more dynamic urban centre. Several firms also spoke about their difficulties in attracting management talent to Kingston to help their firms grow and expand. Many of the talented management workers did not want to bring their families and settle in Kingston to work for one particular firm with no prospect of moving elsewhere locally if that business failed. Moreover, many of the professional spouses or partners of these prospective knowledge workers found it difficult to find employment, given Kingston's thin labour market.

With a population of only 150,000 and its relatively close proximity to other major centres, Kingston may simply not be large enough to sustain a dynamic private-sector innovation system. If a firm wants to grow, it has to relocate to larger cities. That being said, Kingston's research education cluster is still an important "spoke" in a larger hub of knowledge-intensive economic growth. Figuring out how to capitalize on it is another issue. Rather than see the "spoke" as a negative, the city's economic actors could look for ways to build on hub connections and bring them home (Gertler and Wolfe 2004).

Another factor facing the city is the government grant–dependent nature of the regional economy. While this can provide many benefits to Kingston institutions, firms, and workers, the risk is that Kingston's innovation system is more about attracting grants based on the particular government spending trends of the day. For example, one key informant told us that when government health-care sector spending is in, Kingston is the "biotechnology centre of Ontario," but when green technology is the flavour of the month, Kingston is "Canada's most sustainable city." There seems to be substantial evidence of conferences, business meetings, and one-off networking events, but as several key informants noted, there has not always been a sense of a clear, focused direction or sustained pathway for the city's longer-term economic development.

This doesn't, of course, mean that the city should not pursue whatever grant money is available. After all, inter-urban grant-based competitive economic development is typical of the kind of entrepreneurialized local economic development approach that North American cities find themselves participating in (Harvey 1989). Kingston has little choice but to play the game or lose out on job-creation and economic spin-offs. But the question is whether more can be done to leverage the knowledge assets of the town. Indeed, many of the private-sector firms, support services, and consultants could not survive without the public-sector funding that flows into this city. As the literature on innovation systems makes clear, it is increasingly difficult to separate out private-sector development from public-sector development, especially since knowledge-based economic development is highly complex and requires a host of economic actors, including a hybrid of public and private funding.

The creative arts sector is an example of a hybridized industry (Pratt and Hutton 2013). As mentioned above, Kingston has a relatively vibrant arts and culture scene (writers, theatre, art, music, crafts, creative food firms and restaurants). Many of these individuals and firms depend on the buying power of the public-sector workers and the lifestyle amenities of a public-sector, heritage town. Some creative workers told us how they could not practise their craft or risk starting their own creative business without having a spouse who was employed in the public sector (especially with the accompanying pension and health-care benefits). But these same people often spoke about their frustration with the highly managed and bureaucratic local environment, echoing Jane Jacobs's concerns about how an over-managed local environment can thwart entrepreneurial economic activity (Jacobs 1961). Our research in Kingston uncovered many stories of creative entrepreneurs who had come with big visions but felt other surrounding cities were more open to new ideas and ways of doing business.

While the job of the city, according to one entrepreneur, "is to cultivate an entrepreneur and make the environment friendly to businesses that want to come and who want to grow," much of the innovation itself must come from the entrepreneurs themselves, not the city. "We have to stop making innovation a city initiative, or a government initiative," noted Peng Sang Cau, president and CEO of Transformix Engineering Inc., who recently established a successful business in Kingston after returning to the city after her school days at Queen's University. She went on to note that entrepreneurship is "a culture, a mindset within organizations. Executives and CEOs of corporations, if they want the company to be innovative, they must be willing to take risks, they must be willing to let their employees make mistakes, must be willing to spend money on those mistakes, and … creating a culture that allows the place to be innovative" (Hendra 2013).

With so many of Kingston's organizations in the public sector and so few with private-sector business experience, it is easy to see why this entrepreneurial culture is challenging to cultivate. Despite the city's obvious distinct advantage for knowledge and skills development, the lack of business culture and private-sector innovation is the missing piece. We now turn to a discussion of the labour market and how Kingston's particular labour market and its place qualities affect talent attraction, retention, and skills development.

The Labour Market

Kingston has two major labour markets: a more flexible, less stable, private-sector market and a strong, stable, unionized public sector. The first market is more localized, and the jobs tend to be flexible, low-paying, service-oriented jobs in retail, restaurants, and other support services. Complicating matters, professional private-sector jobs are more precarious than the public-sector ones. Many knowledge-based businesses interviewed said that they had a hard time paying wages comparable to those offered in the public sector, which often made it difficult for them to attract and retain talented individuals.

The second labour market, then, tends to be stable, unionized, full-time jobs with benefits in the public sector. These latter jobs make up the majority of well-paying jobs in the Kingston economy, and many of the professional and managerial union jobs pay more than the Canadian average. As mentioned above, the largest employers in Kingston are the university (Queen's University and Royal Military College), the military (Canadian Forces Canada), the health-care sector (Kingston General Hospital and Providence Care), the school boards (e.g., The Limestone District School Board), and Correctional Services Canada. A majority of workers in these institutions are represented by large, nationally strong union organizations, such as the Public Service Alliance of Canada, the United Steelworkers, and the Canadian Union of Public Employees. As a result, these workers have been able to secure relatively stable work situations and excellent benefits. According to the Canadian Labour Congress (2015b), there are 27,300 union members working in and around Kingston in 2014 who make up about 38 per cent of the employees in the area but bring in 48 per cent of the community's weekly payroll, earning on average $8.59 more than the non-unionized workforce. Kingston also has more unionized workers who make higher wages than the Canadian average (ibid.).

The relatively generous wage and compensation packages offered to many knowledge workers in the public sector is necessary, according to one key informant, if many of Kingston's public institutions hope to attract the "best and brightest" minds to Kingston. Queen's University, for example, has always offered competitive wages and benefits to attract and retain world-class professors, health-care workers, and researchers to Kingston. This strategy in part hopes to offset the relatively thin labour market for workers' spouses, and compensate for the fewer amenities perceived by many to be found in a smaller centre. As a result, most of the academic and health-care workers interviewed for this study came for the job, not the place. These particular findings challenge the often-touted creative-class thesis that people are attracted to places rather than jobs (Florida 2002), but more accurately perhaps it confirms that the creative class is far from a coherent class or occupational sector (Storper and Scott 2008; Markusen 2006; Donald, Gertler, and Tyler 2013). While the place-over-job thesis may work for some occupational sectors in the creative class, academic workers have always been limited in their choice of location because of the narrow range of jobs available in highly specialized research areas.

What was interesting in our study was that while many of these academics interviewed came to Kingston for the job, many chose to stay because of the place. Many were attracted to the particular quality of life offered in a small city such as relatively affordable housing,[8] short commuting times, a vibrant heritage downtown, and access to natural amenities. For others, however, Kingston's place-based assets did not make up for the shortfalls. Several of the academic and professional workers interviewed found Kingston a difficult place in which to settle and put down roots. A number of our key informants worked in Kingston, but commuted from larger centres – Ottawa, Montreal, Toronto – and some even farther afield. Several reasons were cited: one is the lack of employment opportunities for their spouses or partners (see earlier discussion); another is the lack of diversity and cosmopolitan lifestyle that many knowledge-workers crave. For example, several respondents to our interviews spoke about the profound "culture of whiteness"[9] that exists in Kingston, and Eastern Ontario more generally. Others spoke about the lack of a community of diversity in Kingston compared to that in other more dynamic, multicultural cities. This lack of diversity tended to pull them closer to cities like Toronto and Montreal, with several actually leaving their jobs in Kingston to move on to bigger centres where they felt more accepted and comfortable. It is worth noting that all knowledge-workers interviewed who either commuted or had left Kingston were members of one of the designated groups under the Employment Equity Act.

Another challenge facing Kingston's labour market is that there is very little turnover in the public sector because there are so few other secure jobs in the region. Many of the full-time professional and managerial jobs are available only to older, more experienced workers. Some key informants indicated that this made the workplace environment somewhat "stale," lacking in "urgency," and sometimes leading to a "low-morale workplace." This lack of work environment "buzz" also seemed to discourage younger workers from staying in the area. Kingston has always had a difficult time attracting and retaining young graduates from the surrounding colleges and universities because there is limited upward mobility for them. According to a Queen's School of Business Monieson Centre report (2008), many young graduates indicated that they did not stay in Kingston because there were not enough good opportunities available. Given the often tense town–gown relationship, there was also a feeling that the city had not done a good enough job making students feel welcome. In more recent times, however, the city and the university have been working more closely, looking at ways of welcoming students and also encouraging students and professors to make deeper connections to the local community.

In addition to the these two main labour markets, Kingston also has a disproportionately high number of people making very low wages and/or having to draw on social assistance and other public assistance programs. Comparative city studies consistently find that Kingston has a persistently high social assistance caseload, which suggests something particular is going on in the city (National Capital Resources 2008; Bedore and Donald 2011; Bedore 2012). Many key informants spoke about the unique social challenges that come to a city with a large prison-related population. Throughout Kingston's history, many of the families of incarcerated inmates have come to live in the area, and many choose to stay on once their family member has served time. Many of these individuals and families require support of their own in the form of food assistance, childcare, health care, literacy, job training, and social and affordable housing. This demand has led to innovative health and social service programs, especially in literacy. However, these programs – especially in the current climate – are at risk of significant public spending cutbacks. The shrinking fiscal capacity of the state to fund these and other services is most noticeable when one begins to examine how all these and other social dynamics shape the city's governance.

Governance

Kingston's polarized labour market, particular historical geography, and deeply entrenched institutional economy creates a unique governance environment. At the civic municipal administration level, overall the city is well-run and managed (City of Kingston 2015). According to Standard & Poor's most recent report, Kingston is ranked AA with stable outlook. More specifically, the agency notes that "the rating on Kingston reflects our view of the city's very strong economy, exceptional liquidity, and strong financial management." The agency also notes that it is an attractive place to establish a business and there is potential for more knowledge-intensive industrial development by leveraging research at Queen's and other institutions, especially in the fields of life sciences and alternative energy research.

These are all promising signs for the region, but lurking beneath this rosy exterior is evidence of a divided city – particularly along class and party lines. Some key informants trace it back to the social divisions that are invariably reflected in the community, but other key informants said that the political divisions have become more pronounced in recent years as external agencies have become more active in local politics. According to one informant, Kingston, unlike their municipal cousins in Quebec, Manitoba, and the City of Toronto, still allows explicit corporate and union financial backing of its municipally elected candidates. In classic "growth machine style" (Molotch 1976; Logan and Molotch 1987), Kingston has always had a certain number of council representatives and mayors backed by local land developers and utility companies who have a particular land-development agenda (Glover 2012). But more recently, city council has also seen a growth in the backing of labour-friendly candidates. In 2006, the Canadian Labour Congress made an explicit policy decision to back local candidates in municipal elections by providing them with campaign funds, training, and labour-friendly policy briefing material. The union rationale, documented in their "Municipalities Matter" Action campaign, was that local communities were good places to invest in because many of their members lived and worked in cities. More importantly, the growing privatization and contracting out of essential municipal services would affect their members. Kingston in particular seemed like a good place to invest in because of the high percentage of unionized, public-sector workers in town (Canadian Labour Congress 2015a).

These actions by unions to shift priorities away from workplaces and towards external political action have resulted in a major shift in the political landscape of Canadian municipal politics. Unlike the federal and provincial levels, most municipal politics has not had a history of party politics. According to some key informants and media personalities, council has moved from a more collegial form of governance to one that is more combative and divided. Council is perceived to vote in predictable "blocks" between councillors perceived as "pro-business" and those perceived as "pro-labour." There seems to be very little middle ground (Schachter 2010; Schliesmann 2013a). The more tension-ridden politics is also evident in the workplace governance of many of the large public institutions in town. In this era of public-sector restructuring and retrenchment, management and unions battle it out over cutbacks to jobs, wage freezes, and pension reform.

Outside the more formal machines of government and behind the scenes, however, there appears to be evidence of a more collaborative type of governance. Most of these examples tend to be project-based, but nevertheless, they show that some challenges can be addressed through strategic alliances and more collaborative and sustained forms of civic governance. The following examples are recent attempts by business, community, university, and government actors to address perceived system failures in Kingston.

The first example seeks to address some of the shortcomings in leveraging the knowledge assets of the research institutions in Kingston to embed more innovative local economic activity. A network of actors from business, government, and the university have established Green Centre Canada (GCC), Canada's leading agency in reducing and/or eliminating the environmental impact of harmful compounds. The centre's aim is to commercialize and transform green-chemistry research breakthroughs (many of which originated in Queen's University) into products and technologies that will ultimately minimize environmental degradation. It was formed in 2009 and is funded and supported by a partnership between the governments of Ontario, Canada, Queen's University, and industry organizations and businesses. Kingston's research strength in green chemistry was an obvious attraction. Queen's has particular strengths in the area with the Canada Research Chair and John C. Polanyi Award–holder, Dr Philip Jessop, and the Department of National Defence Research Institute (RMC). Kingston is also home to PARTEQ Innovations, which, according to key informants, is Ontario's most experienced and successful office of technology commercialization. External funders also found Kingston an attractive place to establish this centre because of previous efforts by groups like the university, the city, and PARTEQ to open the $12 million Queen's Innovation Park. Until then, Kingston lacked the space for such research-intensive activities. The Queen's Innovation Park has provided the GCC with immediate access to state-of-the-art infrastructure and services. Although the centre is still in its infancy, it has forged strong networks with leading Canadian and international companies, including NOVA Chemical Corp., Fielding Chemical Technologies, Polycorp Ltd, Pressure Chemical Co., and Albonia Innovative Technologies Ltd. In addition to private-sector interest, the centre has received more than fifty technology disclosures from across the country and has already launched two spin-off companies (Green Centre Canada 2013; Kingston This Week 2009; GreenCentre 2009; Networks of Centres of Excellence 2009).

Organizations in Kingston have also been looking at ways to address talent attraction and retention, with particular emphasis on attracting immigrants to Kingston. Recently, Kingston secured a federal grant through the Immigrant Council Partnership program funded through Citizen and Immigration Canada. The purpose of the program is to help a community attract, welcome, include, and integrate immigrants into the community. The securing of the grant came about as a result of a working partnership between leaders in public health, literacy, and economic development. The grant has allowed English-language training programs and immigrant employment services to expand with other federally funded agencies and programs in Kingston. The Kingston Immigration Partnership has also built strong partnerships with many of the researchers at Queen's University and the province-wide Welcoming Communities Initiative (Kingston Immigrant Partnership 2013). Many of Kingston's research institutions have been actively promoting equity in the workplace and providing initiatives to effect *cultural changes* so that equity becomes everyone's concern and responsibility (Queen's University 2013). These experiences and insights also inform programs more generally throughout the city and demonstrate the benefits of government funding research programs that require action-oriented research and community outreach.

In addressing pressing social issues with economic consequences, Kingston has a long history of building social capital in the community between individuals and groups to facilitate collaboration on social projects. Kingston has a Social Planning Council that dates back to the 1930s with an explicit aim to building these kinds of collaborative networks. One such example is the "inclusive business growth plan/poverty action" reduction network (Social Planning Council Kingston and District 2013). In recent years, the United Way of Kingston, Kingston Community Health Centres, and the City of Kingston have also been working closely with other community stakeholders to develop action plans for poverty reduction in Kingston (United Way KFLA 2013). In the past, there has been concern that business interests have been disconnected from these poverty-reduction processes, but many of these more recent strategies are working to bring together stakeholders from all walks of life – land developers, labour councils, multi-faith groups, MPs, health-care workers, key businesses, and program participants. This coordinated strategy is seeking to improve quality of life while reducing the impacts of poverty by focusing on housing and homelessness, skills development and employment, community supports for education, social services, and health. These strategies are also looking for alternative sources of funding as more traditional public sources dry up.

These kinds of coordinated efforts are becoming increasingly important for Canadian cities as more senior levels of government continue to cut back on their social service spending and download many social services onto the municipal tax base and offload more responsibilities onto families and communities. In 1997 the Ontario government downloaded many of the costs of social services onto property tax. Now cities like Kingston spend a quarter of their budgets on these essential services, and with increasing pressure to hold the line on property tax increases and user fees many cities, including Kingston, will have a difficult time delivering many of these services. A recent example facing the city is the province's decision to cut back on childcare subsidies. The subsidy goes to families who need assistance paying for day care so that the parents can either hold down a minimum-wage job or return to school for more training. Now the city has to decide if it will pay for the subsidy through property tax revenues or reduce the service. One dilemma facing the city is that if it decides not to pick up the subsidies, there is a risk that many of those on the program will give up their studies or their minimum-wage jobs and end up on social assistance, placing additional demands on the city because Ontario Works (the province's social assistance program), unlike day-care subsidies, is a mandatory program for municipalities (Schliesmann 2013b).

It would appear that Kingston has a relatively active and capable civic culture for its city size. This bodes well for future governance challenges in facilitating more private-sector entrepreneurial activity, finding innovative ways to attract and retain more immigrants, and addressing pressing social issues. Having said that, this will not be easy to do. For years, upper levels of government have downloaded and offloaded service responsibilities that municipalities are increasingly incapable of handling, even during relatively good times. Now, with a prolonged period of slower growth, declining revenues, and a new round of central state austerity measures, many municipalities could face tough times ahead. While it would be ideal to see a more sustained and coordinated set of public resources flowing from the national and provincial levels for challenging municipal issues, if that is not forthcoming, it seems more important than ever that local actors share ideas and resources across different interests through increasing cooperation.

Conclusions

The research for this chapter draws attention to the idea that national and provincial institutions matter in the success or failure of Canadian cities. This point is perhaps no more obvious than in a public-sector city like Kingston. As we have seen in this chapter, Kingston is highly dependent on public institutions for its economic stability and survival. The unique institutional makeup has created a particular social and economic geography that has been challenging for private-sector innovation, the attraction and retention of immigrants and skilled workers, and the governance of the local economic and social environment.

In terms of private-sector innovation, Kingston will have to figure out ways to capitalize on its research education cluster, which is highly regarded nationally, with good international connections. Now the city's economic actors need to look for ways to build on those national and global hub connections and bring them home. The Green Centre Canada example is a good model to emulate in other sectors. Another economic focus will be to examine ways to facilitate more private-sector entrepreneurship. With so many of Kingston's organizations in the public sector and so few with private-sector business experience, it is easy to see why this entrepreneurial culture is challenging to cultivate.

The ability to facilitate a new entrepreneurial business climate may indeed be easier in a city that is open to new ways of thinking, new lifestyles, and new communities. Recent efforts by civic leaders to attract and retain new immigrants to Kingston through the federally sponsored Immigrant Partnership Program, as well as the efforts by several key organizations, to cultivate a more open, inclusive, and equitable work culture are two steps in the right direction. Both initiatives demonstrate the benefits of public funding programs that require action-oriented research results and community outreach.

In terms of social challenges, Kingston can come across as a very divisive and socially divided community. Some social analysts have argued that many of the most innovative and creative cities are also the most polarized and segregated (Hulchanski 2010). It seems, however, that the kind of policy innovation needed in a small city is harder to achieve if that city is also divided along class and party lines. Unlike a big city with both strong and weak ties, the amount of small-city social capital is limited, and burnout is a very real possibility. In the few examples presented, we show how collaborative efforts that seek to forge trust and build learning networks seem to be moving the city in the right direction. But these networks are still very fragile and dependent on sustained funding sources, particularly those that come from public agencies. Indeed, without those sustained funding sources from public agencies, the city could face difficult times ahead – not only in building successful decision-making models, but also more fundamentally in delivering essential services, retaining jobs, and maintaining economic stability.

Notes

1 We are grateful to Melanie Bedore for bringing these ideas to our attention.

2 The authors would like to acknowledge the assistance of many excellent research assistants who conducted in-depth interviews and analysis for this study, including Jacinthe Beyea, Dustin Murray, Melanie Bedore, Austin Hracs, Heather Hall, Nathaniel Lewis, and Janina Balfour-Fisher.

3 It was part of the multi-year, multi-city Major Collaborative Research Initiative (MCRI) SSHRC research project designed and led by D.A. Wolfe and M. Gertler on the social dynamics of economic performance in Canadian city-regions.

4 Interviewees consistently rated Kingston's relatively vibrant, walkable heritage downtown as one of the city's key quality-of-life assets. Kingston still has some independent retail shops and services, entertainment options, and a viable downtown infrastructure including family neighbourhoods, a mix of housing options, parks and recreation, and good local schools. Over the last decade, the downtown has managed to survive in the face of the usual threats: increased car-oriented development, increased big-box retail square footage in the suburbs, and increased Internet shopping. More recently, however, the downtown has experienced major blows. It is no longer a full-service downtown: it has lost two department stores, a major book retailer, and the only first-run movie theatre. Moreover, the only and oldest publicly funded downtown high school is slated to close in 2018–19. While there was a groundswell of local support for keeping the high school open, the school was caught in the middle of a funding deficit due to declining enrolment and provincial incentives to consolidate school populations and build new schools on larger tracts of affordable land further away. No doubt the loss of an attractive city high school will be a major setback to the viability of downtown. These market- and policy-induced forces in conjunction with the City of Kingston's tax rebates for commercial vacancies in the downtown do not bode well for the very asset that sets Kingston apart from its competitors.

5 See Spencer and Vinodrai (2009) for definitions and cluster profiles in Canadian city-regions.

6 Queen's University consistently ranks in the top five of Canadian universities in the medical and doctoral category, and the Queen's School of Business School is one of the top in the country.

7 Canadian Forces Kingston is home to an advanced military communications system and the highly regarded Canadian Forces School of Communications and Electronics (CFSCE) and Canadian Military and Communications Museum, which tells the story of Canada's innovation in military communications.

8 *Relative* is the key term here, as compared to many of the larger Canadian city-regions, Kingston's housing market is relatively affordable – especially for those making a good public-sector wage. However, for many people who work in more precarious, low-paying service jobs, housing is very unaffordable. There is also a very tight rental market in Kingston's downtown largely because of the university and college student demand for affordable rental accommodations close to the universities and colleges.

9 "Culture of whiteness" is defined as something that is created, a cultural and ideological question (Kobayashi and Peake 2000).

References

Adams, C. 2003. "The meds and eds in urban economic development." *Journal of Urban Affairs* 25 (5): 571–88. http://dx.doi.org/10.1111/j.1467-9906.2003.00003.x.

Ansell, C., and A. Gash. 2008. "Collaborative governance in theory and practice." *Journal of Public Administration: Research and Theory* 18 (4): 543–71. http://dx.doi.org/10.1093/jopart/mum032.

Bedore, M. 2012. "Geographies of capital formation and rescaling: A historical-geographical approach to the food desert problem." *Canadian Geographer / Le Géographe canadien* 57 (2): 133–53. doi:10.1111/j.1541-0064.2012.00454.x.

Bedore, M., and B. Donald. 2011. "Revisiting the politics of class in urban development: Evidence from the study of the social dynamics of economic performance." *Journal of Urban Affairs Review* 47 (2): 183–217. http://dx.doi.org/10.1177/1078087410390304.

Bradford, N., and C. Andrew. 2010. "Local immigrant partnership councils: A promising Canadian Innovation. Prepared for Citizenship and Immigration Canada.

Canada Mortgage and Housing Corporation (CMHC). 2012. *Housing now: Kingston*, 4th quarter. Ottawa: Canadian Mortgage and Housing Corporation.

Canadian Labour Congress. 2015a. "Municipalities matter." http://convention2014.canadianlabour.ca/national/news/municipalities-do-matter.

–. 2015b. "The union advantage." http://canadianlabour.ca/why-unions/breakdown-community/kingston.

City of Kingston. 2015. "City maintains 'AA' Standard & Poor's credit rating." https://www.cityofkingston.ca/-/city-maintains-aa-standard-poor-s-credit-rati-1?redirect=https%3A%2F%2Fwww.cityofkingston.ca%2Fcity-hall%2Fbudgets%3Fp_p_id%3D101_INSTANCE_Ec7wKPssxQXU%26p_p_lifecycle%3D0%26p_p_state%3Dnormal%26p_p_mode%3Dview%26p_p_col_id%3D_118_INSTANCE_mIrojY3TeRAO__column-2%26p_p_col_pos%3D3%26p_p_col_count%3D5.

Donald, B. 2006. "From growth machine to ideas machine: The new politics of local economic development in the knowledge-intensive city." In *The competitive city in the new economy*, ed. Diane-Gabrielle Tremblay and Rémy Tremblay, 269–84. Montreal: University of Quebec Press, Political Economy Collection.

Donald, B., M.S. Gertler, and P. Tyler. 2013. "Creatives after the crash." *Cambridge Journal of Regions, Economy and Society* 6 (1): 3–21. http://dx.doi.org/10.1093/cjres/rss023.

Florida, R. 2002. *The rise of the creative class*. New York: Basic Books.

Gertler, M.S., and D.A. Wolfe. 2004. "Local social knowledge management: Community actors, institutions and multilevel governance in regional foresight exercises." *Futures* 36 (1): 45–65. http://dx.doi.org/10.1016/S0016-3287(03)00139-3.

Glover, B. 2012. "Party politics at city hall." *Kingston Whig Standard*, 23 July. http://www.thewhig.com/2012/07/23/party-politics-at-city-hall.

GreenCentre. 2009. "The ideal location for the Green Chemistry Commercialization Centre." Email correspondence.

Green Centre Canada. 2013. Homepage. http://www.greencentrecanada.com.

Harvey, D. 1989. "From managerialism to entrepreneurialism: The transformation in urban governance in late capitalism." *Geografiska Annaler. Series B, Human Geography* 71 (1): 3–17. http://dx.doi.org/10.2307/490503.

Hendra, P. 2013. "Entrepreneurship is more important than innovation." *Kingston Whig Standard*, 16 January 16. http://www.thewhig.com/2013/01/16/entrepreneurship-more-important-than-innovation.

Hulchanski, D. 2010. *The three cities within Toronto*. Toronto: Cities Centre, University of Toronto.

Jacobs, J. 1961. *The death and life of great American cities*. New York: Random House.

Kingston Economic Development Corporation. 2015. "Major employers." http://business.kingstoncanada.com/en/statistics/majoremployers.asp.

Kingston Immigrant Partnership. 2013. http://kipcouncil.ca.
Kingston This Week. 2009. "Ontario provides $13.6 M for Green Centre Canada." *Kingston This Week,* 30 September. http://www.kingstonthisweek.com/2009/09/24/ontario-provides-136-m-for-green-centre-canada.
Kobayashi, A., and L. Peake. 2000. "Racism out of place: Thoughts on whiteness and an antiracist geography in the new millennium." *Annals of the Association of American Geographers* 90 (2): 392–403. http://dx.doi.org/10.1111/0004-5608.00202.
Leydesdorff, L. 1995. "The triple helix: University-industry-government relations: A laboratory for knowledge-based economic development." *EASST Review* 14 (1): 14–19.
Logan, W., and H. Molotch. 1987. *Urban fortunes: The political economy of place.* Berkeley: University of California Press.
Markusen, A. 2006. "Urban development and the politics of a creative class: Evidence from a study of artists." *Environment & Planning A* 38 (10): 1921–40. http://dx.doi.org/10.1068/a38179.
McKenzie, M. 2007. "Where are the scientists and engineers?" Ottawa: Statistics Canada, Science, Innovation and Electronic Information Division.
McQueen, D.R. 2000. *Constructed in Kingston: A history of the Canadian locomotive companies 1854 to 1968.* Kingston: Kingston Division, Canadian Railroad Historical Association.
Molotch, H.L. 1976. "The city as a growth machine: Toward a political economy of place." *American Journal of Sociology* 82 (2): 309–32. http://dx.doi.org/10.1086/226311.
Monieson Centre. 2008. *Creative economy challenges: Retention of Queen's graduates in the Greater Kingston Area. A KEDCO/Queen's University collaborative study.* Kingston: Monieson Centre, Queen's School of Business.
Morgan, K. 1997. "The learning region: Institutions, innovation and regional renewal." *Regional Studies* 31 (5): 491–503. http://dx.doi.org/10.1080/00343409750132289.
National Capital Resources. 2008. "A socio-economic profile of Kingston, Ontario." http://business.kingstoncanada.com/en/about-us/resources/Reports_and_Studies/KEDCO-NCR-SocioeconomicProfileOct2208.pdf.
Networks of Centres of Excellence. 2009. "Government of Canada announces new green chemistry commercialization centre in Kingston." Government of Canada. http://www.nce-rce.gc.ca/Media-Medias/news-communiques/News-Communique_eng.asp?ID=24.
Osborne, B., and D. Swainson. 1988. *Kingston: Building on the past.* Westport, ON: Butternut.

PARTEQ. 2009a. "PARTEQ Innovations receives $9.1 M to establish National Centre of Excellence in Green Chemistry." http://www.parteqinnovations.com/news-archive/parteq-innovations-receives-91-m-establish-national-centre-excellence-green-chemistry.

–. 2009b. "PARTEQ Innovation statistics for 2009." Email correspondence.

Pratt, A.C., and T. Hutton. 2013. "Reconceptualising the relationship between the creative economy and the recession: Learning from the financial crisis." *Cities* 33: 86–95. doi:10.1016/j.cities.2012.05.008.

Queen's University. 2013. "The Equity Office." http://www.queensu.ca/equity/home

Schachter, Harvey. 2010. "Feature 1 – Eight key votes: The debate behind key council decisions." kingstonlife, September/October. http://www.kingstonlife.ca/sitepages/?aid=2306&cn=Feature%201&an=FEATURE%201%20%97%20Eight%20Key%20Votes.

Schliesmann, Paul. 2013a. "City braces for child care cuts." thewhig.com, 21 January. http://www.thewhig.com/2013/01/21/city-braces-for-child-care-cut.

–. 2013b. "No middle ground for council." thewhig.com, 10 January. http://www.thewhig.com/2013/01/10/politics-no-middle-ground-for-council.

Social Planning Council Kingston and District. 2013. Homepage. http://spckingston.ca/index.html.

Spencer, G., and T. Vinodrai. 2009. "Innovation systems research city-region profile: Kingston." In *Program on globalization and regional innovation systems*. Toronto: University of Toronto, Munk School of Global Affairs.

Statistics Canada. 2012. *Focus on Geography Series, 2011 Census*. Statistics Canada catalogue no. 98-310-XWE2011004. Ottawa: Statistics Canada. Last updated 24 October.

Storper, M., and A.J. Scott. 2008. "Rethinking human capital, creativity and urban growth." *Journal of Economic Geography* 9 (2): 147–67. http://dx.doi.org/10.1093/jeg/lbn052.

Todtling, F., and M. Trippl. 2005. "One size fits all? Towards a differentiated regional innovation policy approach." *Research Policy* 34: 1203–19.

United Way KFLA. 2013. *Poverty reduction plan: Kingston newsletter,* 16 January. http://www.unitedwaykfla.ca/wp-content/uploads/2012/05/Newsletter-Issue-1-Jan2013.pdf.

13 Moncton: Innovative or Resilient City?

YVES BOURGEOIS

Introduction

The Greater Moncton economy has weathered significant turbulence in its history, most recently in the 1980s and 1990s, to become Canada's fifth-fastest-growing city-region and the fastest east of the prairies. Such demographic and economic growth for a city-region of 150,000 is unusual in Canada and warranted further investigation. Previous work found no conclusive evidence that the city-region had built formidable creative (Bourgeois 2014b) or innovative capacity (Bourgeois 2014a) commensurate with the scale of its growth. This chapter finds more promising interpretations of rapid small-city growth from the emerging literature on economic resilience in cities, which focuses on the ability of cities to recover and grow following exogenous recessionary or restructuring shocks. Economic resilience is attributed either to *actor agency-led* factors (e.g., local champions, entrepreneurship, inclusive governance) or *economic structure and amenity-based* factors (e.g., labour markets, industry mix, culture, infrastructure). This chapter draws upon more than eighty in-depth interviews conducted with Greater Moncton government, economic development, business, and not-for-profit leaders, as well as individual workers. It finds that city resilience provides a more fruitful conceptual framework to understand Greater Moncton's success than the literature on *innovative milieux* and *creative cities*. While structural assets like location, a bilingual workforce, and financial services were building blocks upon which the regional economy was restructured in the 1990s, success would have been questionable were it not for the role of local champions, new entrepreneurs, and new governance mechanisms in overcoming historical linguistic cleavages and forging new growth trajectories for the region. The findings support the literature that suggests hyper-specialization into innovative niches may be difficult, even dangerous, in small cities. It may undermine their ability to build resiliency. Local efforts matter, provided they connect with outside networks, decisions, and capital.

Resilience

Resilient cities and *regions* have made a recent appearance in urban and regional scholarship to explain the varying ability of city-regions to overcome exogenous shocks. City-regions confronting shocks is nothing new. For millennia, wars, natural disasters, technological revolutions, and changing global trade patterns relegated some cities to obscurity and created a sense of destiny for others. What is new is a focus on the urban phoenix: attempts to uncover, measure, and plan city-regions' regenerative capacity in light of external shocks. This stems from a conflation of factors that have become particularly salient in the new millennium:

1. a seeming increase in the frequency and intensity of climate change–induced natural disasters that have led to massive loss of life, damage, and population relocations (earthquakes, tsunamis, hurricanes);
2. transnational terrorist attacks on civilian built environment;
3. the 2008–9 global economic recession; and
4. the ongoing global industrial restructuring in traditional manufacturing regions coupled with a new, globalizing digital economy.

As a result of these four far-ranging millennial currents, *resilient cities* have come to reflect *resilience to* very different things, engendering at least three popular sub-strands of scholarship, and moved urban and regional planners to contemplate new areas of planning (Eraydin and Tasan-Kok 2013): *resilience to* climate-change natural disasters (Vale and Campanella 2005; Chernick 2005), *resilience to* physical and electronic attacks to the built environment (Zhao et al. 2013; Cartalis 2014), and *economic resilience to* recessions (Hervas-Oliver, Jackson, and Tomlinson 2011; Davies 2011; Martin 2012; Fingleton, Garretsen, and Martin 2012; Martin and Sunley 2015) and economic restructuring (Cowell 2013; Evans and Karecha 2014; Williams and Vorley 2014).

The relative novelty of resilience begs for sounder theoretical underpinnings (Bristow and Healy 2014a; Martin and Sunley 2015). While there is no orthodoxy in which to situate Moncton as a resilient city, resilience as the ability to overcome economic shocks certainly applies to the Moncton case and provides an opportunity to expound upon the literature on a small city-region. Resiliency planning has been added to the purview of economic development planning, increasingly called upon to build shock-resilient regional economies (Cowell 2013; Martin and Sunley 2015). Where to focus policy attention runs the gamut. One way to dissect the emerging literature on economic resilience is by dividing it into two different perspectives: those that focus on *agency*-based resilience factors and those that focus on *structure*-based resilience factors. They are not mutually exclusive; however, to some extent one can be seen as the instrument of the other.

In *agency-based regional economic resilience,* economic structures and trajectories are very mutable to the efforts of local and regional actors. What exact role they have, how local agents are organized, and how they operate within complex regional systems will vary significantly by region and presents us with an important empirical challenge (Bristow and Healy 2014b). Invariably, strong local business leaders are linchpins to resilience (Hill 2012), particularly in capacity-building and economic diversification (Williams and Vorley 2014). How they coordinate and hence build intra-regional governance mechanisms between private, public, and civic sectors, as well as between levels of governments, are also seen as key to shaping the trajectories attainable for the city-region. And so, while Evans and Karecha (2014) argue location factors and agglomeration effects are structural factors that worked favourably to Munich's advantage, they ascribe more value to agency and Munich's effective regional governance and intelligent urban planning. Regions where small business and local ownership thrive will invest more in the workforce and achieve more inclusive growth (Dudley 2013) and resilience, provided decision-making and capital are decentralized (Cowell 2013). In contrast, regions with "absentee landlords" where decision-making and investments are centralized outside the region will be slower to adapt to shocks.

In *structure-based regional economic resilience,* it is the global, national, and regional structures that shape the trajectories available to regional and local actors. Structures include key infrastructure and assets, location with respect to markets, culture, labour force, and industrial specialization that may see economies specialized in resource, manufacturing, and lower-order or higher-order services. For example, Rose and Wei (2013) focus on infrastructure, specifically Texas seaports Beaumont and Port Arthur and the accompanying petrochemical manufacturing complex, attempting to estimate the restorative effect of resiliency in attenuating the negative economic effects of port shutdowns. Crespo, Suire, and Vicente (2014) argue that structure and hierarchy are key to understanding how regional specializations and knowledge clusters can evolve successfully. In differentiating between cities that merely survive shocks (resilience A cities) and those that grow following shocks (resilience B cities), Polèse (2015) identifies key factors to resiliency, including an educated workforce, a strong orientation towards growing markets, a diversified economy with higher-order services, and a better climate than other national centres. For Sensier and Artis (2014), housing and manufacturing-sector employment were the best predictors of Welsh regional resiliency. Slowly evolving local cultures can also be key determinants of resiliency, which can either be helpful or harmful (Vanolo 2015).

Conceptualizing these emergent debates on regional economic resilience in this way presents us with four more sets of challenges. The first is empirical, and leads us to focus on resilience determinants and to link them with long-term growth (Martin and Sunley 2015). By which measure, degree and time period of restructuring can we determine a resilient outcome to exogenous shocks? How do we distinguish resilient outcomes between regions (Lin 2012; Cellini and Torrisi 2014)?

The second challenge is fitting resiliency into the *object of regional economic planning*. If they are planning for economic resiliency, should regional planners look to channel local economies into growing sub-industries and clusters or rather to help diversify the local economy? On the one hand, there may be innovation-related advantages to greater specialization for smaller regions (Beaudry and Schiffauerova 2009), such as specialized skills, services, and infrastructure. Kemeny and Storper (2014), however, question whether regional wage advantages to specialization accrue in small cities or whether only in larger cities that achieve a critical mass of workers and firms. On the other hand, building stronger globally oriented competitive advantages and faster regional growth trajectories may run counter to improving regional resiliency. Lin's (2012) index posits that smaller urban size, lower educational levels, and less industrial diversity undermine regional economic resilience. Polèse (2015) suggests that specialization can be linked to technological lock-in. When an industry carries more relative weight in a city-region, the more a surrounding industrial culture may set in and resist change, and the more major employers reaping local agglomeration benefits ("rentiers") may block the entry of new firms that could otherwise drive diversification. In terms of resiliency, *which* specialization may matter more than *whether* a region specializes or not. Polèse expresses particular concern with resource-dependent economies. Psycharis, Kallioras, and Pantazis (2014) report that in the Greek context manufacturing regions suffered more from the global recession, while tourism-dependent islands were more resilient. With respect to small cities, it could be generalized that smart specialization and innovation strategies present great rewards but also great risks, whereas diversity improves resilience. This is easier said than implemented.

The third challenge is fitting resiliency into the *process of regional economic planning*. Whether we think structure or agency matters more to a region's resiliency, it will shape the policy tools used to build conditions of resiliency. Diversifying the structure and the skills base of the local economy is a long-term endeavour and not a recipe for the rapid mobilization of efforts against shocks. It is arguable whether regions can do much to change structural factors like the degree of market connectivity in light of a disadvantageous physical location. In all cases, the resiliency challenge is about providing the region not only with the ability to weather shocks, but also the long-term ability to establish future growth trajectories (Boschma 2014), particularly in developing wider networking opportunities within and especially outside the region (Hervas-Oliver, Jackson, and Tomlinson 2011). As van Oort (2015, 269) writes, "There needs to be increased attention on facilitating specific local needs, promoting positions in networks rather than branding places per se, and determining 'smart specializations' in relation to the positions of other regions and cities in networks."

This leads us to the fourth challenge in conceptualizing resilient cities, the role of urban hierarchy. Do regions get to diversify and build conditions of resilience irrespective of city size, and irrespective of how they connect to other cities in the urban system? Dijkstra, Garcilazo, and McCann (2013) argue that second-rank cities have been outperforming first-rank cities since the Great Recession, leading

Parkinson, Meegan, and Karecha (2015) to argue that national governments should decentralize resources and powers to second-tier cities to ensure larger national aggregated benefits. Camagni, Capello, and Caragliu (2015) evoke city-network theory to suggest that the scale economies that individual cities cannot achieve internally to the region may be achieved through cooperation networks with other cities. This raises the question of whether Moncton's positive economic performance and resiliency is due to its role as an adaptive, diversifying regional hub, more than the innovative potential derived from the specialization and related variety it can achieve by *borrowing size* through greater cooperation through the New Brunswick urban system or up Canada's urban hierarchy.

To summarize the relevance of this discussion for the Moncton case: we need to understand why some city-regions succeed in managing the treacherous waters of recessions and economic restructuring, while others struggle. We need to unpack the factors of resiliency, to assess and compare them. There is a particular dearth of studies on smaller cities. Is *resiliency* a low-risk, low-return economic-development strategy choice for regions, as opposed to higher-risk "smart specialization" strategies that promote growth from innovation and targeted sectors, of which smaller cities may be more vulnerable? Finally, is resiliency a function of the role of the city-region in the urban hierarchy – higher resiliency being achieved the less it is specialized, or locked in, within a polycentric or functional urban system? As we shall see, Moncton provides a great case in which to examine small-city regional economic resilience.

This chapter poses three questions:

1. What were the factors of resilience that helped Moncton navigate a tumultuous 1980s decade, and are they there now?
2. Are they agency- or structure-based resiliency factors?
3. Does resilience or innovation better explain Greater Moncton's success?

The study is based on eighty in-depth interviews conducted in 2008–9 with leaders from all three levels of government, municipal and economic development, business, not-for-profits including poverty and immigrant services–based organizations, as well as individual workers and immigrants. The research is intended to explain how the city-region overcame recent economic challenges in order to sustain growth, and to specify how the city and key economic sectors have aligned themselves with technological changes and globalizing production networks to meet the challenges ahead. It also raises some questions, by putting recent growth and local efforts in a broader context of urban hierarchies and urbanization in New Brunswick and Canada.

Resurgo

Few cities have resilience built in their motto the way Moncton does: *Resurgo*, or "I rise again." The motto dates back to the late nineteenth century, as the city re-incorporated following the demise of its main industry – wooden shipbuilding – and the loss of its city charter. As documented by Savoie and Bourgeois (1994), the city negotiated several crises over the following century that repeatedly threatened job loss and depopulation, but none as great as the implosion of its shipbuilding industry in 1858 and the subsequent loss of its charter in 1862, as well as the rapid succession of downsizings and the ultimate closure of the CN rail repair shops in 1988. In that year CN relocated 5,000 high-paying jobs to Central and Western Canada. This represented more than 9 per cent of the city's and 6.5 per cent of the economic region's total workforce (Statistics Canada 2011a, 2011b), and managed to relegate Moncton's identity as a railway town to the realm of nostalgia. The fact that the city-region rapidly made the transition away from its bread-and-butter industry, and that it quickly regained lost jobs and continued growing at a strong pace, provides evidence of the degree of resilience that some writers have dubbed the "Moncton miracle" (Farnsworth 1994).

First, the point should not be overlooked that what the city-region achieved was successful diversification away from industries it could no longer sustain: wooden shipbuilding in the nineteenth century, then railway services in the twentieth. It does not suggest that shipbuilding or railways were dead-end industries, only that the region could no longer provide a competitive home for the industries. Second, a successful transition away from these industries does not tell us what trajectories the Moncton economy has forged today. Hence Moncton presents itself as a fascinating case through which to examine resilience in smaller city-regions.

Growth

Not only did the Moncton city-region survive the economic turmoil of the 1980s, its population continued to grow, including a 9.7 per cent increase between 2006 and 2011, from 126,424 to 138,644. Greater

Moncton was the fifth-fastest-growing Census metropolitan areas (CMAs) in Canada, the fastest of any CMA east of Saskatoon. This is all the more remarkable in light of New Brunswick's demographic performance, which as a province grew by 2.9 per cent in the same period. Were it not for Moncton and Saint John, as well as New Brunswick soon-to-be third CMA Fredericton, the province would have lost population as all other Census areas (CAs) and rural areas experienced population loss. It is not coincidental that New Brunswick's and Atlantic Canada's largest cities are growing concurrently to adjacent rural depopulation.

During interviews, it was common for Greater Moncton economic boosters to extrapolate current growth rates indefinitely. Extrapolations and projections are quite different, even if they are sometimes used equivalently in promoting residential, commercial, and infrastructure developments. It is crucial to reflect upon the sources of population and its underlying economic growth in order to map future growth trajectories and strategic public investments. While Greater Moncton's recent demographic growth has been considerable, a closer examination of the composition of its population growth suggests the future pace of growth should diminish. When looking at mobility, immigration, and diversity indicators, Moncton becomes more typical of small Canadian city-regions of similar size (100,000 to 200,000). Focusing on mobility to understand the source of Greater Moncton's population growth, table 13.1 reveals that recent *international* migration (2.0 per cent) is similar to that of other small-sized cities (1.7 per cent) – that is, much lower than the rate for Canadian CMAs as a whole (5.1 per cent). International migrants are barely a tenth of recent migration into Greater Moncton (19.1 per cent), whereas they represent approximately one-third of migrants into other CMAs combined.

Interestingly, as with other Atlantic Canadian CMAs (6.6 per cent), Greater Moncton has relied a lot more on recent *interprovincial* migration (6.4 per cent) than for CMAs as a whole (2.5 per cent) and for CMAs of similar size (2.7 per cent). The most important source of migration for all CMAs is interprovincial, and here Greater Moncton's rate (10.7 per cent) is on a par with other CMAs combined and with those of similar size. Three-quarters (74.1 per cent) of Greater Moncton's population was born within the province, which is consistent with small cities (78.9 per cent) across Canada, including those in Atlantic Canada (74.7 per cent). In common with Atlantic Canadian cities but less true for small cities across Canada, a much higher

Table 13.1. Key population characteristics, Moncton, and aggregated city sizes, 2011

Characteristics	Moncton CMA	Census metropolitan agglomerations						Census agglomerations	
		All sizes	1M +	500k–1M	200–500k	100–200k	ATL	Canada	NB
Population (2011)	138,644	23,123,441	15,331,645	2,216,677	3,225,652	2,349,367	853,699	4,311,534	195,612
2006–11 growth (%)	9.7	7.4	8.6	5.2	4.6	5.4	6.3	4.2	3.3[a]
Non-immigrants (%)	4.4	27.1	33.6	16.0	16.6	9.2	5.8	7.4	4.3
Born in province (%)	74.1	60.7	53.9	76.0	69.6	78.9	74.7	75.6	77.8
Born outside province (%)	21.1	10.8	10.8	7.3	12.8	11.4	18.7	16.5	17.3
Immigrants (%)	4.4	27.1	33.6	16.0	16.6	9.2	5.8	7.4	4.3
Visible minority (%)	3.4	26.4	34.5	12.2	12.1	6.1	5.9	4.0	2.9
Intraprovincial migrants (%)	10.7	10.2	10.1	8.7	10.2	11.7	7.2	12.2	8.7
Interprovincial migrants (%)	6.4	2.5	2.4	1.6	3.2	2.7	6.6	4.0	5.4
External migrants (%)	2.0	5.1	6.2	3.6	3.1	1.7	2.5	1.7	1.5

[a] Includes Fredericton. As Fredericton may soon reach CMA status, Census areas in New Brunswick would have lost 1.8% of their population between 2006 and 2011.

Statistics Canada (2013), author's compilations and aggregations percentage of Monctonians (21.1 per cent) were born outside the province, approximately twice the rate for any size CMA. However, a very small percentage of Monctonians (4.4 per cent) are immigrants, when compared to the CMA average of 27.1 per cent or even CMAs of similar size (6.1 per cent). Visible minorities are also much less present in Greater Moncton (3.4 per cent), half that of similar-sized CMAs (5.9 per cent) and eight times fewer than all CMAs (26.4 per cent). In sum, if Moncton is to continue to enjoy strong population growth, it will have to maintain its success at interprovincial in-migration and increase international migration significantly.

Part of Greater Moncton's economic growth is due to its demographic growth. Non-exporting, population growth–dependent sectors such as education and health care (8.5 per cent) were two of Greater Moncton's four leading employment generators between 1999 and 2004, and public administration (10.9 per cent) and construction (10.2 per cent) were two of the three leading job creators between 2004 and 2009 (Bourgeois 2014a). Growing populations require more schools, hospitals, public services, and housing.

If population growth can buttress some economic growth, it remains a challenge to explain why New Brunswickers chose to settle in Greater Moncton and to a lesser extent Saint John. First, as discussed in the rest of the chapter, this is the result of considerable efforts deployed by growth coalitions during the 1980s and 1990s, aligning provincial and local efforts along the way. By the time the CN shops closed for good in 1988, the mood had already begun to lift, as employment in southeastern New Brunswick had started growing again in 1987 and has consistently surpassed the national average. Leaders helped diversify the local economy, first by compensating for the closure of Canadian National railcar maintenance shops and transitioning to broader road-transportation, logistics, warehousing, and retail activities, thus modernizing the city's advantage as a regional transportation and commercial hub. Second, regional development concentrated on small but globally competitive information-and-communication technology (ICT) manufacturers, nationally focused insurance and business-support services, such as call centres, and establishment of the city-region as a regional hub for other professional services. Professional and business services were the two other leading Greater Moncton job creators between 1999 and 2004, and finance, insurance, and real estate was the second-fastest-growing sector between 2004 and 2009.

Whether Greater Moncton's maintains its competitive advantage as a lower-cost locale for business and professional services as well as ICT manufacturing and services is not assured. The globalization of ICT and professional services industries suggests Moncton's cost advantages nationally may prove disadvantageous globally. Advanced telecommunications networks and relatively low wages among an educated workforce were resiliency factors in the 1980s but may stand out less now in an economy that has since globalized significantly.

Innovation and Knowledge Flows in Greater Moncton: Supply Chain Linkages Matter More Than Research Facilities

Whether innovation is the key explanation to Moncton's success or not, it remains a crucial imperative to sustaining Greater Moncton's economic growth. How are Greater Moncton firms innovating to stay competitive, and from where are knowledge and technologies coming? Our interviews reveal that supply chain firms were by far the most important sources of knowledge: clients, suppliers, and competitors. Greater Moncton's role as a distribution and retail centre made proximity to customers an advantage for those serving Atlantic Canadian markets. For exporters, proximity to customers was seen as a major disadvantage, and their ability to harness knowledge was more limited. For most, distance to suppliers, competitors, and consultants was a major obstacle in their attempts to innovate.

In Greater Moncton, R&D collaborations with universities and governments were rather weak. While IT and advanced manufacturing sectors cited technical and scientific R&D as very important to their competitiveness, few were actively engaged in collaborative arrangements, at least not with Moncton institutions and labs. An IT technical director pondered that they "probably should [collaborate with Université de Moncton and NRC IT researchers], but never get around to it."

These weak collaborations are the result, in part, of the limited research capabilities of local universities. Newly created Crandall University, Université de Moncton, and nearby Mount Allison University are primarily teaching-based institutions. There are some graduate degree programs and research laboratories, including science and engineering and NRC IT research facilities, but their outreach remained limited, according to IT firms interviewed. Two advanced manufacturing CEOs and one IT firm director did mention R&D collaborations with the University of New Brunswick in Fredericton because of its reputation, specialized resources, business-mindedness, and relative proximity. "It's important to be within two hours' drive with researchers, as we like to see what they're doing, and they need to see what we're doing ... Fredericton is close enough," one manufacturer admitted.

Post-secondary institutions, particularly Université de Moncton, played a pivotal role in training bilingual workers and entrepreneurs who facilitated the transition away from railway service to call centres and increased employment in the insurance sector in the 1980s and 1990s. A growing number of post-secondary institutions will likely ensure resilience in continuing to train workers and entrepreneurs, although rising youth unemployment is driving young graduates out of the province, and the business community provides numerous examples of SMEs struggling to integrate a large number of international graduates into the local workforce. Post-secondary institutions will also need to do a better job of connecting with the business community in co-producing R&D and innovations.

How Knowledge Flows into the Region: Owner Must Travel

For Moncton IT, knowledge-intensive business services (KIBS), and manufacturing firms, knowledge generally does not flow into the region through local research infrastructure, whether universities, federal labs, or private R&D facilities. While there was evidence of learning by interacting with customers and suppliers, much of it was either endogenous learning or knowledge circulation among local actors. Instead, knowledge flowed primarily through worker mobility, and to a lesser extent via electronic communications.

The mobility of workers that mattered most was that of owners and managers. The stewards of Moncton's innovative businesses travel frequently outside the region. Trade shows, national conventions, and networking events in larger urban centres were often cited as providing venues for learning new ideas, competitor moves, and market trends. Those interviewed suggested that more important than fortuitous encounters during temporary knowledge clusters in the form of international trade shows (Schuldt and Bathelt 2011) were scheduled out-of-town meetings and site visits with customers and suppliers alike. For those exporting goods or services outside the province, face-to-face relationships with supply chain partners mattered most. The Internet was used more for competitive intelligence.

IT, KIBS, and advanced-manufacturing owners and managers not only valued travel, but they also treasured outside talent, as both a source of new ideas and a means to bridge skills gaps. In smaller metro areas like Moncton, the labour market for specific skills is thin. For advanced manufacturing firms, this shortage of qualified labour impels them to automate production, sometimes more than they would like, because as one advanced manufacturing owner reported, "It is easier to import machines than to find the right workers." This situation not only curtails company growth, but it also hinders spin-offs when potential local workers are substituted with imported technology.

Lowest-Hanging Fruit: Local Markets and Global Technologies

Export markets are often portrayed as a threshold of success, and there is often a presumed higher value of global connectedness and knowledge (Weterings and Ponds 2009). For several firms interviewed, their choice of serving local markets was strategic: their intimate knowledge of local markets was precisely their main asset, and investments in training and new technologies were pre-emptive strategies to stave off the entry of outside firms promising shinier products or tools. As one IT custom-solutions provider described it, "We make no bones about picking the lowest-lying fruit. It's just as tasty." The need to understand the local market well and customize IT and business solutions accordingly shelters medium-sized markets from large-scale producers and leave "lower-lying" fruit to smaller, local firms.

Innovations, in these cases, tend to be first to local market. KIBS and IT services firms import global technologies, many of which are Internet-accessible, to customize solutions for local clients. Those clients, however, may be global exporters, and so technologies and services need to be state-of-the-art, which in strategic communications have been made easier with social media and small-scale, high-quality video production.

If KIBS firms were focused predominantly on local markets, IT firms were polarized in their choices between global and local markets, which affected how knowledge entered and circulated within the region. For off-the-shelf (OTS) software producers, both market and technical knowledge were global. Customers remained crucial in refining the product and developing subsequent versions, but they did not need to be local, and interactions were not face-to-face. Customer feedback was crucial to improving their product, but this feedback could be gleaned electronically. When customers encounter bugs or crashes, they can provide feedback by email, and the software itself automatically generates and sends error codes to the manufacturer. For custom software and IT solutions providers, face-to-face interactions were indispensable. One ICT manufacturer noted that, ironically, while their remote and wireless technologies helped clients bypass the need for human workers to travel and collect data, the key to their success was developing an intimate knowledge of local customer needs, which required frequent face-to-face interactions. Global competitors could not rival them in this knowledge of local markets, which he called "lower-lying fruits."

To all IT firms interviewed, technical knowledge was global, such as open-source codes and online technical references. While economic development officials spoke of an IT cluster, there was little evidence of clustering, of local formal or informal knowledge exchanges to resolve bottlenecks, to share resources, or to plan strategically. In fact, there was displeasure that social activities organized by a newly created IT association were used by some firms to poach workers from others. There appeared to be little collaboration between firms or anything that anchored globally exporting IT firms in Moncton, beyond being owned by people having grown up locally or having started their company there. The region's two largest IT firms were bought in recent years by multinational firms – one flourishes while the other has downsized considerably. As Giblin (2011) found in Ireland, large anchoring firms alone are not a sufficient condition to sustain clustering effects.

Manufacturers saw face-to-face exchanges with business partners – suppliers in particular – as their main source for innovative products and processes, highlighting the importance of meetings and international trade fairs as temporary knowledge clusters (Ramírez-Pasillas 2010; Schuldt and Bathelt 2011). As these partners were mostly outside the region, poor connections from the local airport were deplored as a major obstacle to innovation. Unlike KIBS firms, manufacturers could not build competitive advantages from an intimate knowledge of local markets, and there were few local competitors with whom they could interact and learn. Unlike off-the-shelf software producers, manufacturers could not interact with customers or suppliers electronically in meaningful ways. Neither face-to-face exchanges nor ICTs helped Moncton manufacturers overcome isolation as a barrier to innovation.

In sum, meaningful knowledge exchanges were weak on a local level, posing a challenge to fostering innovation. There are successful innovative entrepreneurs and products, but collectively there was little evidence of a Greater Moncton culture of innovation. Generating a critical mass of expertise within regional networks is a challenge because of Moncton's small scale. However, Moncton business leaders seemed more successful at building active networks with outside supply chain partners. Many of the company owners and operators interviewed were well travelled and globally connected, knowledge-pipeline builders to the outside world (Bathelt, Malmberg, and Maskell 2004). Global knowledge flows were fairly lubricated, for manufacturers and many IT firms. Fitjar and Rodríguez-Pose (2011) suggest that in some peripheral regions, economic success can owe more to connectedness with larger, world cities than proximity and exchanges among local firms. Hervas-Oliver, Jackson, and Tomlinson (2011) and van Oort (2015) have suggested these were key features of regional resilience as well, and they appeared to apply in Moncton.

Smaller Cities License Creative Freedom, but Lack Creative Mass

While the Internet and other technologies are helping Greater Moncton firms overcome some isolation challenges, there remain important constraints to innovation resulting from limited opportunities to collaborate with distant customers and suppliers. This section argues that worker mobility offers an important opportunity to substitute weak customer-supplier-competitor interactions as a source of knowledge, enabling Greater Moncton firms to innovate and sustain economic growth once New Brunswick urbanization rates subside. First, it is important to understand how worker mobility works in the region.

Talented workers come to Greater Moncton for job opportunities. Most outside *talent* admitted knowing nothing about Moncton's cultural amenities or leisure opportunities upon moving to the area. They came to take up jobs, sometimes in related creative fields, sometimes not. Cultural and leisure opportunities did have an impact on their decision to stay, however, perhaps more than employment opportunities, given the shallow labour market for specialized workers.

Large institutional employers played a key role in attracting creative workers in a small metropolitan area. For those working in TV and film production, some came to Université de Moncton to study as the means to establish their foothold in the region. Société Radio-Canada

(SRC) was seen as an even more pivotal player in TV/film, where many in the industry had cut their teeth. Large institutional employers like the universities and SRC train and employ the creative class, but more importantly they employ the *consumptive class*. The success of Greater Moncton's arts and culture community is buoyed by the presence of such institutional employers – including three universities, two hospitals, two large insurance companies, and several federal government departments – and the thousands of well-educated, well-salaried workers who disproportionately attend cultural events and buy cultural products.

Greater Moncton ranks low on cost-of-living indices, and this was cited as an advantage by many artists and cultural groups. Time needed working to pay the bills is shorter, leaving artists with more time to work on their creations. However, repressed real estate prices and property taxes have been increasing rapidly with the city's recent growth. Neighbourhoods, such as that surrounding the Aberdeen cultural centre on St George Street, are blossoming with creative events and venues, including new galleries, restaurants, and coffee houses. Its Victorian architecture attracts business and medical professionals to establish residence and practice, increasing housing demand and prices, pushing struggling artists and Monctonians on fixed incomes to the city's edges. Ever-sprawling development has made alternative means of transportation difficult, so many lower-income Monctonians spend more of their budget on cars than in other cities.

Small scale was construed as a mixed advantage. A smaller metropolitan area afforded fewer specialization opportunities for young professionals, but made for a good career incubator: "[Small-town law firms] make you practise every kind of law there is," while big city law firms can require undesirable hyper-specialization in a particular field. Culinary artists were drawn by job vacancies and the presence of a growing population as an opportunity to establish their own restaurant, but lack of curiosity in the overall population was an obstacle to "pushing the boundaries" as they would in other regions. "It's harder to experiment because of this conservatism," said one chef. Another quipped, "I keep having to explain why peppered steak is not on the menu." Regional "frugality" was another problem: "People here have a hard time spending 200 dollars on a meal." "Local cultivated folks (with more disposable income or on company travel budgets) wait for trips to 'the big city' to spend money on fine dining," while fewer Montrealers, Ottawans, and Torontonians come to Moncton for business or fun.

Both anglophones and francophones singled out the "French presence" as a cultural advantage. Moncton Acadians have learned to bridge both linguistic cultures. Bolstered by the music and drama departments at Université de Moncton, the francophone cultural scene has become buoyant. Once an abandoned school used by artist squatters, the Aberdeen cultural centre is now bursting at the seams with artists, studios, and production companies. A stage artist, a poet, and a television writer echoed a common sentiment, in suggesting shared cultural identity was more evident among francophone artists. For francophones, the *other* against which identity was carved was Moncton's English-language majority and the risk of assimilation. For anglophones, the *other* was a more distant Central Canadian and American mass culture. As a result, networks, cultural conscience, and political organization became much stronger among francophone artists in Greater Moncton.

Decades of struggles for equality have swung the pendulum towards success and strength for the francophone minority. However, francophone and anglophone artists alike suggest a siege mentality lingers, some referring to the Université de Moncton as the "fortress on the hill." "The university has isolated itself and given the impression that it is off limits to the broader community," worried one francophone writer. The sentiment extended beyond the artistic realm and onto the business world, where some anglophone business leaders steered away from linking with the French university because of a perception that instruction and research would be conducted only in French.

While it is often implied that the greater diversity of cultures in larger cities affects creativity more, smaller cities can be more conducive to creativity. Many creatives in smaller urban centres like Moncton found the freedom to create, sheltered from the rigid artistic hierarchies of larger metropolitan areas. "It's easier to take chances, easier to experiment," lauded one performance artist. In major cities, where many Moncton artists toil periodically, it is often customary to work in the shadows of giants, pay tribute, and slowly earn one's stripes along the way, to get the chance perhaps one day to see one's play, music, or choreography performed. In smaller centres, there were fewer hierarchies to climb, easier for upstarts to get their break.

This freedom to create comes at a price. Many artists had established in Moncton after successful training and careers in global cultural centres. However, once in Moncton they found it difficult to maintain and upgrade their skills, partly from a lack of institutions, but mostly from limited interactions with other professionals in their fields. They found it difficult gleaning inspiration and discipline from the work of others. "The lack of artistic base in the region makes it easier to make a contribution [than in larger cities], but it is also harder to get inspired." Proximity to New York, Montreal, and Toronto, where creatives rejuvenate themselves, was cited as indispensable to staying in Moncton.

The city's small stature was a challenge to artists and young professionals. "There's little competition in our field – it keeps the bar low. We have to catch up by reading and travelling frequently, collaborate with outsiders to round out our experiences and skills." Creatives cited not only the lack of disciplinary effect from few competitors, but also from a population that "is content with too little" or "may not appreciate avant-garde. I look forward to doing these performances in Montreal."

No single narrative explains the choice of Moncton by talented professionals. In fact, many of the city's strong suits identified by some were viewed as major weaknesses by others. While some cherished the "countryside city" with open spaces and "very few high-rises to obstruct the view of the horizon," others lamented the car-dominated sprawl into "Dieppenamese suburbia," northern Moncton, and the Northumberland Strait coastline. Sprawl was seen to undermine opportunities to create a denser core, with a critical mass and sense of buzz that could sustain more diverse cultural activities, a better mass transit system, and other amenities friendly to artists and to workers of more limited means found in more densely populated cities.

In larger cities, artists have a greater chance to make a full-time living practising their art and are not always impelled to collaborate with artists outside their immediate realm. With few artists in any one field, smaller cities almost require artists to collaborate with others outside their discipline, accelerating the cross-fertilization of ideas. Several Monctonian writers considered indispensable the cross-sector collaborations among authors, musicians, and visual artists. Creatives in other fields, such as in dance and culinary arts, recognized the advantages of collaboration, but egos remained difficult to overcome, by their own admission.

This provides two insights about the flow of knowledge into and across smaller cities like Moncton. First, it highlights how creative migrant workers are a major source of knowledge gleaned from larger metropolitan areas. From new lighting and cinematography techniques to genre development and business opportunities, creative migrant workers are constantly upgrading the local knowledge base by working elsewhere, importing new ideas and techniques on one hand, and exporting local cultural products on the other. Second, even the most established artists in Moncton's cultural sectors work part-time or full-time gigs in other local industries, and this enhances the flow of knowledge from one cultural sector to the next, and throughout the broader economy.

This section has surveyed some general mobility patterns by key creative knowledge workers in the local economy. Business professionals travel frequently to larger cities to meet colleagues, clients, and suppliers and to attend trade events. The travel patterns of creative workers depend on the artistic field, but even at different frequencies they all travel to replenish creative juices, and by doing so they become exposed to new trends, techniques, and business opportunities. Through this acute mobility, business professionals and artists become Greater Moncton's key knowledge brokers, the region's privileged point of access to new ideas and markets. While there was evidence of knowledge-sharing and spillovers between artistic fields, there was much less evidence of knowledge spillovers between artistic fields and the broader local economy, or between professional services firms. On the whole, the dynamism of cultural workers and their need to travel and to moonlight provide important connections to outside networks and in circulating knowledge, ideas, and opportunities within the local economy.

Shocks Induce Stronger Regional Governance; Prosperity Induces Parochialism

Difficult times impel people to work together. In Greater Moncton, the 1980s brought linguistic communities to lower drawbridges, to plan and work together to overcome the major economic challenges. Urban employment growth in a province of economic stagnation and depleting rural communities propelled mass urbanization into the Greater Moncton CMA. What some called the "Moncton miracle" (Farnsworth 1994) was really a broad, concerted effort by Greater Moncton leaders to put the economy back on its feet. "The only true miracles are the ones you build," quipped an economic development official. Throughout the 1990s and 2000s the Greater Moncton economy increased employment in financial and business services sectors, securing call centres and back offices de-located by national head offices. These were not the highest-paying jobs or easiest to sustain in the long term in a globalizing world, but they had an immediate palliative effect: they kept workers in Greater Moncton and attracted others at a time when employment rates were shrinking across the province. "You need the kindling to build the fire," summarized one elected official.

While direct linguistic cleavages dissipated in the 1980s and 1990s, indirectly they transposed themselves onto municipal boundaries. The catalyst for this outcome was the provincial plan to amalgamate Greater Moncton's three municipalities of Moncton, Dieppe, and Riverview in 1993, which raised fears among many residents of the mostly French-speaking city of Dieppe that French-language services would be diluted if shared with English-speaking majorities in Moncton and Riverview. Plans for amalgamation were shelved in favour of greater regionalization of municipal services between 1994 and 1999, but Dieppe leaders remained concerned that enhanced regional planning and service delivery would prove a slippery slope towards future amalgamation.

Relative prosperity attenuates the urgency to plan. If population growth rates subside, the construction and retail boom will slow as well. The growth of the health and education sectors may also slow as the province seeks to reign in a now-spiralling deficit. Greater Moncton faces several major challenges that will affect its ability to implement the broader regional planning strategies it will need to support future economic growth.

Herding Cats: Planning as One

The rebranded 3+, formerly Enterprise Greater Moncton, is the economic development agency for the entire city-region, created by the province but largely funded by the three municipalities, to develop economic strategy and programs for the Moncton CMA. While EGM oversees the city-region's economic development strategy, individual municipalities in the Greater Moncton CMA have created their own municipal economic-development agencies and strategies since the 2000s. The City of Dieppe created its economic development corporation in 2004, prompting the City of Moncton and most recently the Town of Riverview to follow suit. Priorities are sometimes aligned with the regional strategy, and sometimes not. Overall, while officials from all economic development agencies reported positive relationships with other agencies and informally recognized the need for greater regional planning, the regional capital amassed during the difficult 1980s seems to have depreciated. "Don't forget," reminded a municipal economic development official, "our mission is to increase our municipal tax bases ... which means business attraction and expansion within our municipal limits." Municipal revenues are based first on local, not regional success.

Evans and Karecha (2014) suggest that economic resilience depends on strong regional governance. Inter-community and inter-governmental cooperation was perhaps the most important factor that helped the Moncton economy transition through the difficult 1980s. Elected officials and economic development officials concurred that region-minded planning had become more dormant in recent years, and that local decision-makers seemed relatively more concerned with municipal-level growth. Nevertheless, goodwill and the mechanisms for greater collaboration remain and could be reactivated if called upon by new shocks.

Listening to Silent Voices

Immigrants and immigration settlement officials believed multiculturalism in Moncton was only "crawling forward," largely because so few natives of Moncton had the experience of living abroad and hence a proper understanding of the challenges of settling into a new environment.

Many immigrants "convince themselves of just being in the 'wrong city'" and leave for larger metropolitan areas and other provinces, lamented one advocate for new Canadians. Several argued Moncton has become a bicultural but not yet multicultural city-region. Local skills shortages could be bridged by greater efforts to integrate immigrant and low-income earners. However, immigrant and poverty-group officials lamented there were few attempts to collaborate and to coordinate efforts at a local or regional level. There seemed to be a mismatch of efforts between immigration settlement groups and local economic-development agencies. Economic development agencies were leading immigration recruitment abroad, and municipalities organize policy forums to get people working together, while immigrant settlement groups were having difficulty meeting the daily needs of immigrants already in Moncton – immigrants having newly arrived and international students having recently graduated. The tri-cities of Greater Moncton are now working to implement an immigration strategy adopted in 2014.

If immigrant settlement groups believed municipal and regional efforts were misaligned, poverty groups suspected there were scant efforts at all to address the employability of poor Monctonians. As regional incomes rise for the average Monctonian, the plight of the working poor and difficulties accessing economic opportunities are often forgotten. Affordable housing and day care, post-secondary education accessible to children of poor families, mental illness, and addictions were all singled out as important obstacles that prevented many Monctonians from greater economic participation. One hurdle that seemed particularly restrictive in Moncton was the inability to access affordable transportation to access work and services. New Brunswickers and Monctonians are among the most car-dependent travellers in Canada, with 88.3 per cent of workers commuting by car in 2011, an increase from 2006 (Bourgeois and Folster 2014). This translates into inadequate active and shared transportation alternatives, which immigrants and low-income workers rely upon disproportionately. Provincial siting decisions and Moncton's own property-development decisions reinforce this car dependence with sprawl and downtown reserved for parking. One economic development official highlighted that "40 per cent of downtown physical space is parking lot."

If low-income earners cannot move easily into and within the city, if accessing jobs, college, or other enabling institutions is predicated on car ownership because of sprawl and limited mass transit, then businesses miss opportunities to bridge labour shortages. If immigrants cannot put valuable skills to work because of lack of credential recognition, better integration programs, or open-mindedness by employers, then the region squanders important knowledge and human capital that increase regional competitiveness. Economic development efforts that ignore the barriers to economic integration faced by immigrants and the poor risk widening income gaps between haves and have-nots, and risk limiting the city-region's economic growth by not fully using its human capital.

Greater inclusiveness and transparency in new governance mechanisms can threaten longstanding networks that benefit from older forms of local social and political organization. As Safford (2009) has shown in comparing Allentown's successful transition to Youngtown's demise, there is a downside to social capital and network density, and that civic relationships can facilitate collective action sometimes and impede it at others. Sceptics about the effectiveness of new governance initiatives alluded to a concentric-ring model of governance, with several layers of decision-making. The outside layer envisions inclusive and consultative mechanisms to glean citizen and stakeholder input. In the middle layer, decisions remain in the purview of elected officials on municipal governments and boards, with more limited public consultation. At the centre, however, there remains a small core group of influential leaders who can "get the job done" after a few speed dial calls. Informal decision-making mechanisms that centred on strong local leaders worked well to transition the local economy out of the 1980s. However, these same tight networks may stand in the way of more inclusive governance mechanisms. Only future shocks will show which governance mechanisms will prove more useful to Moncton's regional economic resilience.

Conclusion

Three questions were raised in the introduction: Were the source of the region's economic resilience factors of the 1980s present today? Were they agency- or structure-based? And does resilience or innovation better explain Greater Moncton's success?

Answering the last question first, it seems resilience carries more weight in explaining Greater Moncton's success than innovation. Certainly there were many dramatic examples of small-scale successfully innovative companies, as well as larger insurance companies adopting digital technologies that allowed them to scale from regional to national markets. However, linkages were essentially weak within the innovation ecosystems, whether between firms or with knowledge institutions. There was little attention focused on increasing productivity and value added through technology and training investments. Instead, several business leaders were more comfortable championing the region as cheaper cost alternatives, even if less sustainable in the long term in a globalizing world. While geographic isolation from central markets limited opportunities for Greater Moncton firms to innovate through customer-supplier-competitor interactions, there remains an untapped potential to use the mobility patterns of business professionals and creative workers to the benefit of the broader local economy.

By creating jobs at the same time that the city-region was losing its main private-sector employer in the mid 1980s, Greater Moncton kept many of its workers in the region. Regional economic resilience was not only facilitated by the growth of private-sector insurance companies, call centres, and retail, but it was also abetted by the presence of anchoring public institutions, including federal departments like Fisheries and Oceans (DFO) and the Atlantic Canada Opportunities Agency (ACOA), and federally funded agencies such as the Canadian Broadcasting Corporation and Société Radio-Canada.

At first glance, it may seem that anchoring institutions provided a structure-based explanation for the region's economic resilience. Other structural factors like Greater Moncton's physical location as a transportation hub helped the city-region shore up its position as a regional centre for health, education, transportation, and retail.

However, it became evident during the research that strong local networks of business and political leaders, new regional governance mechanisms and initiatives that cut across traditional cleavages based on language and municipal borders, and a new generation of entrepreneurs were instrumental in weathering the economic shocks of the 1980s. In fact, strong local leadership and networks are also cited as key in fighting to keep the anchoring institutions mentioned above, DFO, ACOA, and SRC being in constant threat of downsizing by decisions made in Central Canada. These resiliency factors have become more dormant today as a result of relative regional success. Mechanisms and relationships have largely endured. It remains to be seen how they may become reactivated when future shocks occur.

There were no clear future growth trajectories being articulated or planned. There were certainly a number of tech-based initiatives as one expects in any region. The city has recently (2015) invested in new dark-fibre capabilities, although how infrastructure investments will translate into job creation has not been explained. There were no initiatives that connect technological changes to traditional strengths such as transportation and retail.

Predicting future shocks is a tall order. Certainly the region can expect a slowing of its population growth and provincial spending. Difficulties in retaining and integrating immigrants into the labour market will exacerbate difficulties in hiring both higher- and lower-skilled workers. Reasons range from accreditation, to the dearth of headquarters with internationally experienced human resource departments, to the lack of affordable transportation and efforts from the business community to link with educational institutions. The slowing of the demographic growth rate will also affect construction, education, health-care, and retail sectors. Retail is healthy as the region seems to increase its catchment area, although there are signs this growth is also slowing and may be jeopardized by consumers migrating to online purchases, with few locally headquartered retail operations looking to online markets outside the region. Aggressive greenhouse gas–reduction targets in other industrialized regions could spell hardship for Moncton's trucking industry if it falters in transitioning to greener supply chain management and logistics sooner than later. Trucking is among the region's few large-scale employers that have headquarters in the city, in turn supporting a number of professional service agencies.

Moncton may not be the most innovative city, but its remarkable resilience may provide a better set of tools for continued growth in a sea of drowning small-size, peripheral city-regions.

Acknowledgments

I am indebted to the Social Sciences and Humanities Research Council for its generous funding, as well as Robert MacKinnon and Tracy Chiasson of UNBSJ, and Rodrigue Landry and Hélène Gallant of CIRLM. I thank Daniel Bourque for research support, and of course to eighty interviewees who volunteered their precious time. I am grateful to David Wolfe and Meric Gertler for their admirable stewardship of this comparative project and doubly to David for comments on this chapter.

References

Bathelt, Harald, Anders Malmberg, and Peter Maskell. 2004. "Clusters and knowledge: Local buzz, global pipelines and the process of knowledge creation." *Progress in Human Geography* 28 (1): 31–56. http://dx.doi.org/10.1191/0309132504ph469oa.

Beaudry, Catherine, and Andrea Schiffauerova. 2009. "Who's right, Marshall or Jacobs? The localization versus urbanization debate." *Research Policy* 38 (2): 318–37. http://dx.doi.org/10.1016/j.respol.2008.11.010.

Boschma, Ron. 2014. "Towards an evolutionary perspective on regional resilience." *Regional Studies* 49 (5): 733–51.

Bourgeois, Yves. 2014a. "How ICTs and F2F mediate knowledge flows in and within Moncton." In *Innovating in urban economies: Economic transformation in Canadian city-regions*, ed. David Wolfe, 292–317. Toronto: University of Toronto Press.

–. 2014b. "Small cities and talent accelerators: Talent mobility and knowledge flows in Moncton." In *Seeking talent for creative cities: The social dynamics of innovation*, ed. Jill Grant, 219–39. Toronto: University of Toronto Press.

Bourgeois, Yves, and Natalie Folster. 2014. *Road worriers: The costs of car dependence in New Brunswick*. Saint John: UNB Urban and Community Studies Institute.

Bristow, Gillian, and Adrian Healy. 2014a. "Building resilient regions: Complex adaptive systems and the role of policy intervention." *Raumforschung und Raumordnung* 72 (2): 93–102. http://dx.doi.org/10.1007/s13147-014-0280-0.

–. 2014b. "Regional resilience: An agency perspective." *Regional Studies* 48 (5): 923–35. http://dx.doi.org/10.1080/00343404.2013.854879.

Camagni, Roberto, Roberta Capello, and Andrea Caragliu. 2015. "The rise of second-rank cities: What role for agglomeration economies?" *European Planning Studies* 23 (6): 1069–89. http://dx.doi.org/10.1080/09654313.2014.904999.

Cartalis, Constantinos. 2014. "Toward resilient cities: A review of definitions, challenges, and prospects." *Advances in Building Energy Research* 8 (2): 259–66.

Cellini, R., and G. Torrisi. 2014. "Regional resilience in Italy: A very long-run analysis." *Regional Studies* 48 (11): 1779–96. http://dx.doi.org/10.1080/00343404.2013.861058.

Chernick, Howard. 2005. *The resilient city*. New York: Russel Sage Foundation.

Cowell, Margaret. 2013. "Bounce back or move on: Regional resilience and economic development planning." *Cities* 30: 212–22. http://dx.doi.org/10.1016/j.cities.2012.04.001.

Crespo, J., Raphael Suire, and Jerome Vicente. 2014. "Lock-in or lock-out? How structural properties of knowledge networks affect regional resilience." *Journal of Economic Geography* 14 (1): 199–219. http://dx.doi.org/10.1093/jeg/lbt006.

Davies, Sara. 2011. "Regional resilience in the 2008–2010 downturn: Comparative evidence from European countries." *Cambridge Journal of Regions, Economy and Society* 4 (3): 369–82. http://dx.doi.org/10.1093/cjres/rsr019.

Dijkstra, Lewis, E. Garcilazo, and Philip McCann. 2013. "The economic performance of European cities and city regions: Myths and realities." *European Planning Studies* 21 (3): 334–54. http://dx.doi.org/10.1080/09654313.2012.716245.

Dudley, Michael, ed. 2013. *Public libraries and resilient cities*. Chicago: American Library Association.

Eraydin, Ayda, and Tuna Tasan-Kok, eds. 2013. *Resilience thinking in urban planning*. Dordrecht: Springer.

Evans, Richard, and Jay Karecha. 2014. "Staying on top: Why is Munich so resilient and successful?" *European Planning Studies* 22 (6): 1259–79. http://dx.doi.org/10.1080/09654313.2013.778958.

Farnsworth, Clyde. 1994. "The 'Moncton miracle': Bilingual phone chat." *New York Times*, 17 July.

Fingleton, Bernard, Harry Garretsen, and Ron Martin. 2012. "Recessionary shocks and regional employment: Evidence on the resilience of UK regions." *Journal of Regional Science* 52 (1): 109–33. http://dx.doi.org/10.1111/j.1467-9787.2011.00755.x.

Fitjar, Dahl Rune, and Andrés Rodríguez-Pose. 2011. "Innovating in the periphery: Firms, values and innovation in southwest Norway." *European Planning Studies* 19 (4): 555–74. http://dx.doi.org/10.1080/09654313.2011.548467.

Giblin, Majella. 2011. "Managing the global-local dimensions of clusters and the role of 'lead' organizations: The contrasting cases of the software and medical technology clusters in the west of Ireland." *European Planning Studies* 19 (1): 23–42. http://dx.doi.org/10.1080/09654313.2011.530529.

Hervas-Oliver, Jose-Luis, Ian Jackson, and Philip Tomlinson. 2011. "'May the ovens never grow cold': Regional resilience and industrial policy in the North Staffordshire ceramics industrial district – with lessons from Sassoulo and Castellon." *Policy Studies* 32 (4): 377–95. http://dx.doi.org/10.1080/01442872.2011.571855.

Hill, Edward. 2012. "Economic shocks and regional economic resilience." In *Building resilient regions: Urban and regional policy and its effects*, vol. 4, ed. Nancy Pindus, Margaret Weir, Howard Wial, and Harold Wolman, 193–274. Washington: Brookings Institution.

Kemeny, Thomas, and Michael Storper. 2014. "Is specialization good for regional economic development? *Regional Studies Online.* http://dx.doi.org/10.1080/00343404.2014.899691.

Lin, Jeffrey. 2012. "Regional resilience." Federal Reserve Bank of Philadelphia. Working paper 13-1. http://dx.doi.org/10.2139/ssrn.2191653.

Martin, Ron. 2012. "Regional economic resilience, hysteresis and recessionary shocks." *Journal of Economic Geography* 12 (1): 1–32. http://dx.doi.org/10.1093/jeg/lbr019.

Martin, Ron, and Peter Sunley. 2015. "On the notion of regional economic resilience: Conceptualization and explanation." *Journal of Economic Geography* 15 (1): 1–42. http://dx.doi.org/10.1093/jeg/lbu015.

Parkinson, Michael, Richard Meegan, and Jay Karecha. 2015. "City size and economic performance: Is bigger better, small more beautiful or middling marvellous?" *European Planning Studies* 23 (6): 1054–68. http://dx.doi.org/10.1080/09654313.2014.904998.

Polèse, Mario. 2015. "The resilient city: On the determinants of successful urban economies." In *Cities and economic change*, ed. Ronan Paddison and Tom Hutton, 145–61. London: Sage.

Psycharis, Yannis, Dimitris Kallioras, and Panagiotis Pantazis. 2014. "Economic crisis and regional resilience: Detecting the 'geographical footprint' of economic crisis in Greece." *Regional Science Policy and Practice* 6 (2): 121–41. http://dx.doi.org/10.1111/rsp3.12032.

Ramírez-Pasillas, Marcela. 2010. "International trade fairs as amplifiers of permanent and temporary proximities in clusters." *Entrepreneurship and Regional Development* 22 (2): 155–87. http://dx.doi.org/10.1080/08985620902815106.

Rose, A., and D. Wei. 2013. "Estimating the economic consequences of a port shutdown: The special role of resilience." *Economic Systems Research* 25 (2): 212–32. http://dx.doi.org/10.1080/09535314.2012.731379.

Safford, Sean. 2009. *Why the garden club couldn't save Youngstown: The transformation of the rust belt*. Cambridge, MA: Harvard University Press.

Savoie, Donald, and Yves Bourgeois. 1994. "Moncton making the transition: Myth or reality." In *Shock waves: The Maritime urban system in the new economy*, ed. George De Benedetti and Rodolphe Lamarche, 231–48. Moncton: Canadian Institute for Research on Regional Development.

Schuldt, Nina, and Harald Bathelt. 2011. "International trade fairs and global buzz. Part II: Practices of global buzz." *European Planning Studies* 19 (1): 1–22. http://dx.doi.org/10.1080/09654313.2011.530390.

Sensier, M., and M. Artis. 2014. "The resilience of employment in Wales: Through recession and into recovery." *Regional Studies Online*. http://dx.doi.org/10.1080/00343404.2014.920083.

Statistics Canada. 2011a. "Table 282-0054: Labour force survey estimates (LFS), by provinces and economic regions." CANSIM (database), Using E-STAT (distributor).

–. 2011b. "Table 282-0061: Labour force survey estimates (LFS), employment by economic region and North American industry classification system (NAICS), annual (persons), CANSIM (database)."

–. 2013. "NHS profile." Statistics Canada catalogue no. 99-004-XWE. Ottawa: Statistics Canada. http://www12.statcan.gc.ca/nhs-enm/2011/dp-pd/prof/index.cfm?Lang=E.

Vale, Lawrence, and Thomas Campanella. 2005. *The resilient city: How modern cities recover from disaster*. Oxford: Oxford University Press.

Vanolo, Alberto. 2015. "The Fordist city and the creative city: Evolution and resilience in Turin, Italy." *City, Culture and Society* 6 (3): 69–74. http://dx.doi.org/10.1016/j.ccs.2015.01.003.

van Oort, Frank. 2015. "Unity in variety? Agglomeration economics beyond the specialization-diversity controversy." In *Handbook of research methods and applications in economic geography*, ed. Charlie Karlsson, Martin Andersson, and Therese Norman, 259–71. Cheltenham, UK: Edward Elgar. http://dx.doi.org/10.4337/9780857932679.00019.

Weterings, Anet, and Roderik Ponds. 2009. "Do regional and non-regional knowledge flows differ? An empirical study on clustered firms in the Dutch life sciences and computing services industry." *Industry and Innovation* 16 (1): 11–31. http://dx.doi.org/10.1080/13662710902728035.

Williams, Nick, and Tim Vorley. 2014. "Economic resilience and entrepreneurship: Lessons from the Sheffield city region." *Entrepreneurship & Regional*

Development 26 (3–4): 257–81. http://dx.doi.org/10.1080/08985626.2014.894129.

Zhao, Pengjun, Ralph Chapman, Edward Randal, and Philippa Howden-Chapman. 2013. "Understanding resilient urban futures: A systemic modelling approach." *Sustainability* 5 (7): 3202–23. http://dx.doi.org/10.3390/su5073202.

14 The Social Dynamics of Economic Performance in St John's: A Metropolis on the Margins

ROB GREENWOOD AND HEATHER HALL

Introduction

Innovation and creative capacity are now widely perceived as paramount for economic growth and prosperity in the contemporary economy. Despite prophecies that "distance is dead" (Cairncross 1997) or that the "world is flat" (Friedman 2005), there is burgeoning research that depicts city-regions as the critical sites in which innovation and creativity thrive (see Gertler 2001; Wolfe and Bramwell 2008; Wolfe 2009; Florida 2002; 2005; 2008). This work emphasizes the underlying social dynamics present in city-regions that play a significant role in shaping economic performance. For example, localized knowledge and collaboration between individuals, firms, and institutions are fostered by proximity, while urban amenities, openness, and tolerance are widely perceived as preconditions for attracting talented individuals (Florida 2002, 2005, 2008; Wolfe and Bramwell 2008; Wolfe 2009).

Within this research, size matters. Large city-regions offer diversity and dense concentrations of people, firms, and institutions with global reaches. Not surprisingly, much of the research on innovation and creativity is focused on large city-regions. However, there is a growing movement to "look beyond the metropolis" (Petrov 2007) and unpack the social dynamics of innovation and creative capacity in smaller cities on the periphery (Sands and Reese 2008; Doloreux and Dionne 2008; Hall and Donald 2009).

St John's, Newfoundland and Labrador, provides a unique setting to explore the social dynamics of innovation, talent attraction and retention, and governance. As Lepawsky, Phan, and Greenwood (2010) argue, St John's is a "metropolis on the margins" with a dual character.

As the provincial capital and largest city in Newfoundland and Labrador (NL), it has many of the common features expected in large city-regions. However, its size and relative location in comparison to other Canadian city-regions and its economic reliance on natural resources also reveals a number of peripheral realities (Hall and Donald 2009). This chapter thus explores the impacts of size and relative location on the social dynamics of economic performance in a small city-region on the periphery.

This chapter is divided into four parts. We begin with a discussion of innovation and creativity on the periphery, which situates St John's as a metropolis on the margins. This is followed by a discussion of the social dynamics of innovation in St John's highlighting collaboration in the ocean technology cluster and the challenges of knowledge flows and innovation. We then turn to the third section that explores talent attraction and retention in St John's, emphasizing the dual character of the city-region and the importance of "home." The final section examines the twin nature of governance in the St John's region between weak local governance – particularly regionally – and the thriving social sector.

Innovation and Creativity on the Periphery: Situating St John's

Peripheral cities are often perceived as "inauspicious" spaces for the dynamic and innovative preconditions of the contemporary economy (Johnstone and Haddow 2003; Hayter 2005; Virkkala 2007; Hall and Donald 2009). One argument is that peripheral cities lack the necessary diversity and density of firms, actors, and institutions to support an environment capable of stimulating innovation (Doloreux and Dionne 2008). Smaller peripheral cities also often have less diversified economies that are dependent on commodity fortunes largely determined outside their control, making them more vulnerable to external economic shocks. As Wolfe (2009) explains, "The industrial structure of such cities increases the risk that they will be locked into declining sectors or obsolete technologies that may be supplanted by newer ones" (29).

However, as Polèse et al. (2002) argue, the overwhelming number of innovations that are produced in large metropolitan areas "sometimes leads to the assumption that almost all innovation occurs in large cities ... but this can blind us to the innovations occurring outside these regions" (133). Moreover, examples of innovation in the periphery are often overlooked because they occur within traditional sectors like mining or forestry rather than sectors at the forefront of technological developments (Polèse et al. 2002; Rutherford and Holmes 2007; Doloreux and Dionne 2008). For example, Polèse et al. (2002) provide a detailed study of innovative activities in Quebec and Atlantic Canada where entrepreneurs are creating innovative products, processes, and solutions in new mining techniques, technology, and consulting; new cutting techniques for wood products; and environmental engineering and aquaculture techniques. In Northern Ontario, Hall and Donald (2009) discovered companies and institutions within a mining supply and services cluster that are producing new technologies or methods to improve the efficiency, safety, and sustainability of the mining industry. They also found a number of companies involved in forestry that are creating or adapting processes for pest management, reforestation, and carbon sequestering.

In terms of the social dynamics of innovation in peripheral cities, Doloreux and Dionne (2008) discovered a number of important attributes in their study of La Pocatière, Quebec, which included strong institutional actors with the capacity to respond to economic and technological change over time; community entrepreneurs who mobilized around initiatives emerging from public institutions; and knowledge exchange and collaboration between institutions, between firms, and between firms and institutions. Their work highlights the importance of public institutions for innovation in smaller peripheral cities. Their case study also demonstrates how small size actually facilitates trust and collaboration. Doloreux and Dionne (2008) do, however, note difficulties with attracting highly skilled workers, especially when taking into account the professional integration of a partner.

Likewise, Hall and Donald (2009, 2012) discovered a number of "peripheral realities" in their research on Northern Ontario, including geographic isolation, which is exacerbated by high transportation costs, limited transportation options, and infrastructure constraints. Many smaller cities in peripheral locations also have challenges associated with attracting and retaining talented individuals due to limited education and economic opportunities. They also described the difficulties entrepreneurs encounter with access to capital and to institutions promoting innovation. These lending and innovation institutions are often located in large city-regions and can be biased against supporting entrepreneurs in peripheral cities. Their work further explained how innovations often become "locked in" in the region, supplying local and regional markets but failing to connect to national or global markets.

Over the last decade, the work of Richard Florida on the creative economy has attracted the attention of policymakers and stimulated vibrant debate in academic research. The heart of his argument is that economic growth is now dependent on the talent of a "creative class" who innovate and create new ideas, new technologies, and/or creative output (Florida 2002). In the creative economy literature, Florida and his contemporaries argue that the creative class are attracted to places that offer tolerance, openness, and a wide range of natural, cultural, and recreational amenities (Florida 2002, 2005, 2008; Gertler et al. 2002). This has translated into economic development strategies aimed at attracting highly skilled workers and promoting quality of place. Urban design features like streetscaping, along with vibrant downtowns and an arts-and-culture scene are argued to be crucial in attracting and retaining these talented individuals.

The creative economy literature has traditionally been fixated on large cities in core regions. There is, however, an emerging body of research looking at the creative economy in rural communities (see Hall 2011 for an overview), and smaller, peripheral cities that highlight different variables for attracting highly skilled workers (Sands and Reese 2008; Lewis and Donald 2010; Hall and Donald 2009, 2012). For example, in their work on American rural counties, McGranahan and Wojan (2007) note that the rural creative class is older and more likely to be married. Thus, economic development strategies geared at improving the quality of local schools may be more critical in rural areas rather than creating trendy downtowns with an arts-and-culture scene, while Hall and Donald (2009, 2012) found that affordability, proximity to family, and natural amenities often mattered more in Northern Ontario cities.

This discussion on innovation and creative capacity in peripheral cities sets the context for our case study of St John's, NL. The province has long been considered a have-not in the Canadian political economy. However, the province is enjoying newfound status as a "have" province. The St John's city-region, in particular, was experiencing unprecedented prosperity from oil and gas development off the province's east coast. As the provincial capital and largest city in NL, the city-region offers many of the common features expected in large city-regions. However, St John's is small and isolated compared to national and international urban systems. For example, on the basis of population size, St John's ranks twentieth out of thirty-three CMAs in Canada

Table 14.1. St John's profile

Socio-economic Indicators	St John's	NL	Canada
Population, 2006	181,115	505,470	31,612,890
Population change, 2001–6	4.7	−1.5	5.4
% foreign-born	2.9	1.7	19.8
% BA degree or higher	18.8	11.3	18.1
# employed	87,890	202,060	15,958,195
Employment growth	17.3	9.6	19.8
Employment rate	58.7	47.9	62.4
Unemployment rate	10.0	18.6	6.6
% "creative" occupations	38.6	29.2	33.2
% science & technology occupations	8.0	5.7	6.6
"Bohemians" per 1,000 labour force	11.3	7.0	14.2
# industrial clusters	5	n/a	255
% employment in clusters	19.9	n/a	22.1
Average FT employment income	$48,392	$45,223	$51,221
% change average income 2000–5	7.4	6.4	5.5

Source: Spencer and Vinodrai (2012)

(Statistics Canada 2006). This presents a number of contrasting peripheral realities.

As seen in table 14.1, the population of the St John's city-region in 2006 was 181,115, representing a 4.7 per cent increase from the previous census period. The city has a higher percentage of creative and science and technology occupations when compared to Canada. The percentage of foreign-born is, however, significantly lower than the Canadian average, but progress is being made with the number of immigrants moving to the St John's CMA almost doubled from the previous census period (CCDA 2008). Newfoundland also enjoys a high rate of return migration of "been-aways"[1] who have left for work or education elsewhere in Canada and return "home" when labour market conditions improve.

St John's is home to five industrial clusters, including oil and gas; maritime; ITC services; business services; and higher education. The labour market dominance of St John's extends beyond the province's Avalon Peninsula. Close to half of the province's population now resides in communities within the St John's commuting area. In the wake of the fisheries closures and restructuring, the closure of two paper mills, and the ongoing rural-to-urban and urban-adjacent shift, the St John's city-region dominates the provincial economy more than ever. Significant wealth is still generated from fisheries, and mining continues to be a major source of wealth-creation on the Island and in Labrador. The provincial economy, however, is now dominated by oil production. Ironically, oil and gas fields have been found primarily on the Grand Banks closest to St John's. Thus, the province's political, educational, and service centre is now also home to the largest resource sector.

The results of this chapter are based on seventy-six interviews across the ISRN themes of inquiry: the social nature of innovation; talent attraction and retention; and governance and inclusion.[2] Interviews were conducted with creative workers, businesses and research organizations in leading clusters and sectors of the economy, NGOs, and various levels of government. We turn now to a discussion of the major findings from these interviews.

Innovation and Knowledge Flows in St John's

In a globalizing knowledge-economy, innovative capacity is a significant contributor to economic performance. This innovative capacity is facilitated through collaboration and knowledge flows and many argue that city-regions provide the necessary social dynamics for this "flow of ideas" (Gertler 2001; Wolfe and Bramwell 2008; Wolfe 2009). As Wolfe and Bramwell (2008, 171) explain, "The interactive and social nature of innovation makes city-regions the ideal space in which social learning processes can unfold." This research on innovation highlights the importance of collaboration between firms and institutions within a cluster as well as between diverse sectors within a city-region (Jacobs 1969; Porter 2000; Wolfe and Bramwell 2008; Wolfe 2009). In St John's we discovered that its dual character as a "metropolis on the margins" both helps and hinders innovation and knowledge flows. As we discuss below, local jealousies related to the city's small size negatively affect knowledge flows, while the city's reliance on the oil-and-gas sector reveals a number of peripheral realities. However, the ocean technology cluster exhibits substantial collaboration and investments in knowledge and research infrastructure like those found in larger cities. We turn now to a discussion of innovation and knowledge flows in St John's.

In St John's, some small- and-medium-sized enterprise interviewees cited concerns about competition from similar businesses and thus were reluctant to share knowledge and collaborate. They were worried about the protection of intellectual property and feared that prosperity would encourage local jealousies. For example, one interviewee noted, "[We have] a lot of trade secrets, we don't publish everything, we don't publish a lot about the company," while another stated, "No one shares information here." However, several interviewees observed that this trend is changing towards more collaborative competition. As one interviewee described it, "I've got competitors that we're friendly competitors with. We go head-to-head on work, but I can still call him up and ask him a question," while another noted, "I just want to say, there's times when you collaborate and there's other times when you want to keep it close to the vest." We also discovered little evidence of knowledge flows between sectors in the St John's city-region. Interviewees highlighted the challenges with creating these connections, including the time and effort required to engage in these partnerships and a great deal of trust. As noted, these local jealousies deter collaboration within and between some sectors.

Within the ocean technology cluster, however, interviewees discussed the advantages of being in a city with a concentration of similar businesses. For example, one oil-and-gas interviewee described the "synergy opportunities" in St John's. They stated that their company is located in St John's because "obviously you want to be in the region where the resource is." However, they also described how St John's has a critical mass of companies, which results in lower costs for some products and services, opportunities for sharing best practices (especially around safety), and a collective voice when needed. More importantly, they highlighted how these opportunities are facilitated through face-to-face interactions within the sector. As they explained, "Clearly it's very important to be located close enough so you can have ongoing meetings and communication other than just email and phone calls."

In fact, a recent study of the ocean technology cluster discovered that there is substantial collaboration between firms and other organizations within the cluster and that there is clear evidence of labour flows between firms and organizations (Lepawsky 2009). As one oil-and-gas interviewee explained, "When you're more open with your innovations and collaborate with various partners, we believe that the innovation becomes stronger, and we ... it's just a ... philosophy or a culture that we have adhered to."

The ocean technology study also detailed the importance of Memorial University of Newfoundland as a collaborator, buyer, and supplier within the cluster. As one oil-and-gas interviewee described it, "MUN is by far either equal or better than any other university in Atlantic Canada, and from a petroleum perspective, at being engaged with industry ... I guarantee you that MUN is doing a better-than-average job in the Atlantic Canadian context of being at outreach and being involved with the oil-and-gas industry."

The post-secondary institutions were often discussed in relation to knowledge creation and sharing. In general, businesses have access to a pool of talented graduates; researchers undertake local research and share findings; the post-secondary institutions and research centres often build relationships with local businesses; and these institutions and research centres have global connections that local businesses can access for outside knowledge (Greenwood, Pike, and Kearley 2011).

For example, Memorial University and the College of the North Atlantic work-term students and recent graduates are hired to work with the oil-and-gas companies. In 2005, 2006, and 2007 the industry provided work terms for over 300 students from Memorial's Faculty of Engineering and Applied Science. In 2006, 223 students from petroleum-related programs at the college received work-terms (Stantec 2009). These young knowledge workers have been assigned to Norway, the United Kingdom, the United States, Calgary, and elsewhere. While some move away for employment, many return, bringing with them insider knowledge of R&D and corporate processes that enhance knowledge capacity in local firms and local branches of foreign-based firms.

Interviewees in several sectors, however, indicated that the post-secondary institutions are not as closely networked or connected with local businesses, organizations, and governance structures as they could be. As one interviewee explained, "I think that there's regularly dissatisfaction with the university." They continued on to explain that small oil-and-gas supply companies are disappointed because researchers at Memorial are "not sitting there waiting to do an exact specific scope of work and deliver against that scope of work for a company who told them so." However, another interviewee discussed the challenge of balancing applied research with education, noting, "I think they forget sometimes why they're here in the first place, you know? I think Memorial forgets that it's here to educate students."

This oil-and-gas interviewee also argued, "Research performance is badly done in engineering schools ... One professor with three graduate students focusing on one project for $15,000 of an NSERC grant, they're going to solve nothing." On the other hand, this interviewee explained that their organization "will get $100,000 to do a two-month research contract that addresses real market needs in a timely fashion." Interviewees also raised concerns about the rules around intellectual property in universities and colleges and the difficult business relationship they create. As one interviewee stated, "We find dealing with the university and the Research Council, they are so caught up on IP that it's just not worth dealing with them on it." These comments highlight the struggle of Memorial University in a metropolis on the margins. Universities in smaller cities are often more focused on undergraduate education, while universities in larger cities are more often research intensive (Maclean's 2012; Jarvey and Usher 2012; Berkowitz 2012). Memorial thus shares a dual character with the city of St John's. As the only university in the province and the largest university in Atlantic Canada (based on student enrolment), it is building on a traditional emphasis on undergraduate education with a growing focus on research and public engagement.

Interviewees in our study also frequently mentioned the importance of industry associations in providing the formal means of bringing firms together. These include industry associations like the Newfoundland Ocean Industries Association (NOIA), the main association for the oil-and-gas sector; the Newfoundland Alliance of Technical Industries (NATI), which represents the IT sector as well as other technical industries; and the Newfoundland Environmental Industries Association (NEIA). These industry associations allow firms to share sector-specific knowledge, share and learn best practices, and discover potential new markets. For example, one oil-and-gas interviewee provided an in-depth explanation of the benefits of being involved with NOIA:

> Being associated with NOIA, they provide a forum in which we get to know the industry and maintain our relationships with the industry at a local level. NOIA also ... represents the supply community, service and supply community, so when we're doing business we tend to link into the membership to do business, and they are a great method of distribution of information for us to go out looking for contracts, to distribute information about what we're doing here locally. In return, we show great respect and keep them up to date on what we're doing ... The other thing that we do with NOIA is that we provide speakers when they're doing seminars and they're trying to help raise the level of awareness in the service/supply community ... we will provide speakers and information and intelligence on best practices that we use internationally.

As noted, industry associations also benefit through the expertise of their membership.

In the ocean technology cluster there is also a strong institutional presence facilitated through organizations like OceansAdvance Inc., a membership-based cluster organization that includes fifty-one firms as well as a number of research units at Memorial University and the College of the North Atlantic. In 2009, it led an extensive strategic planning process entitled "Outward Bound 2015: Accelerating the Growth of the Ocean Technology Cluster Sector in Newfoundland and Labrador." The goal is to achieve a billion dollars in annual revenue over the next five to ten years by developing, attracting, and retaining expertise; expanding and directing research in areas of competency; and ensuring effective governance (OceansAdvance 2009). Supported by the federal and provincial governments and the National Research Council, OceansAdvance provides the forum for the private-public-community-R&D sectors to work together.

The federal and provincial governments have also played a key role in developing this "institutional thickness" (Amin and Thrift 1994, 1995) through significant investments in marine-related infrastructure, including Memorial's engineering faculty, the Marine Institute, various chairs and programs, and the National Research Council's Institute of Ocean Technology, which is located on Memorial's campus. In fact, a number of interviewees emphasized how infrastructure investments made by the provincial and federal governments are a competitive advantage for St John's. In addition, there have been a number of federal-provincial funding agreements and provincial and federal programs that have supported industry, education, and R&D development related to ocean technology (Colbourne 2006).

For example, in 2009 the Government of NL established a not-for-profit Research and Development Corporation (RDC), with a focus on ocean technology and energy, to act as a catalyst and funder of R&D projects in academia and industry initiatives with long-term economic benefit for the province (RDC 2011; Memorial University of Newfoundland 2010). The RDC has a number of business-led programs available for small and medium-sized business to improve access to researchers, facilities, and equipment as well as reduce the technical and financial risk of pre-commercial R&D. The RDC also has a number of academic-led programs that focus on strengthening R&D capacity by investing in the development of highly qualified researchers; aligning R&D activities with business needs, competitive advantages, and development opportunities; and investing in R&D infrastructure (RDC 2011).

More importantly, under development regulations set by the federal-provincial offshore petroleum board, oil-and-gas producers are required to spend a certain percentage of their revenues on research and development and education and training in Newfoundland and Labrador.[3] When oil and gas was first discovered off the coast of NL in the 1970s, the provincial government was determined to reverse a history of exporting resource revenue to other countries, provinces, and companies beyond its borders. The Atlantic Accord was the result of much legal and political wrangling, but it ultimately gave NL the same powers over its offshore oil-and-gas development as if it were on land.

To help meet this requirement the Petroleum Research Atlantic Canada (PRAC), a partnership of oil-and-gas producers, academia, and the Newfoundland and Nova Scotia governments, was created. In 2011, it was restructured into the Petroleum Research Newfoundland and Labrador to focus on offshore oil and gas and industry-based R&D in the province. It is a member-based organization that funds and facilitates collaborative R&D on behalf of the offshore oil-and-gas industry (Petroleum Research 2012). The multinational character of the oil-and-gas industry would likely lead to innovations occurring closer to head offices in large cities. But by requiring the oil-and-gas producers to spend revenue on R&D and education and training investments, the province is encouraging innovation to remain in NL.

In St John's, we did discover a number of challenges to innovation and knowledge flows related to the industrial structure and the size of the city. For example, a lack of capital was noted by a number of interviewees. As one explained, "There's no lack of innovative ideas, there's no lack of innovative will, there's no lack of expertise. Our lack is in being able to finance it to a large extent." Added another, "Lack of capital for growth is certainly an issue … you're not on Bay Street … you can't go down and knock together a few investors … I don't think you'll find one private company around here that won't tell you that's a chronic problem in this part of the world."

The study on the ocean technology cluster also found that the cluster is outwardly organized to other firms or organizations outside the region with regards to buyers and suppliers. This outward orientation combined with a reliance on relatively few firms within the cluster suggests that the cluster is vulnerable to external economic shocks

(Lepawsky 2009). As one key informant explained, "By and large, [the local offshore industry] has been set up as 'Stick pipes in the ground, suck the oil out, put it in tankers, and ship it away.'" The connection to natural resources also causes this sector to be highly susceptible to external economic conditions.

In sum, the St John's case highlights the importance of collaboration among firms, local research and development institutions, government, and industry associations in leveraging the ocean technology sector. These relationships are, however, still in their infancy, especially with regards to oil-and-gas producers who, as noted earlier, are required to spend a portion of their revenues on research and development and education and training in Newfoundland and Labrador. As one research facilitator explained, it takes time to establish relationships and roles: "I think the single biggest challenge facing this community of associations is the lack of maturity. The fact that this is all new – there's a huge amount of churn from the oil and gas companies right down to the individual professors, you know, and researchers ... People are still figuring out the rules, including the regulator – the regulator who made up this requirement which constitutes a paragraph in the guidelines."

Moreover, as Wolfe (2009) explains, the economic outlook for smaller cities is often tied to the specific sectors in which they are specialized. The economic prospects of St John's are thus intimately tied to the oil-and-gas sector. However, reinvesting resource wealth in innovation-related activities and education will help strengthen the city's economic assets and institutional capacity.

"There's No Place Like Home" for the Talented in NL

Inspired by the work of Richard Florida (2002; Florida, Mellander, and Stolarick 2008; Gertler et al. 2002), quality-of-place attributes like diversity, tolerance, and a wide array of natural, cultural, and recreational amenities are seen to be paramount to the economic performance of city-regions. In St John's we discovered that a key factor in shaping the attraction and retention of talented and highly educated workers to the city-region had to do with its relative size and location with respect to provincial, national, and international urban systems (Lepawsky, Phan, and Greenwood 2010). This "metropolis on the margins" exhibits "large city" quality-of-place attributes because of its size and functional role relative to the provincial urban system. But the small size and isolation of St John's, relative to national and international urban systems, affects its ability to attract and retain talented individuals.

As the largest city in NL and the provincial capital, St John's offers a more diverse economy and job opportunities as well as a number of amenities, including a large arts-and-culture scene, restaurants and nightlife, health-care services, shopping, and post-secondary educational institutions. For example, in 2006 the city-region was home to 66 per cent of the province's professional, scientific, and technical service businesses; 59 per cent of all mining and oil-and-gas extraction businesses (although most mining occurs elsewhere in the province); 67 per cent of all head offices; and 58 per cent of all information and cultural industries (CCDA 2008). St John's also attracts a significant number of people from smaller communities in the province. Residents are thus able to take advantage of these "large" city attributes but remain in the province.

The small size and isolation of St John's do, however, affect its ability to attract and retain talented individuals. As one interviewee noted, "We've struggled to get high-quality people, engineers, and that for our R&D work." Another major issue cited by many interviewees is the lack of affordable and convenient transportation options. As one SME interviewee explained, "We have a disadvantage to some extent because of the transportation system that we have ... You used to be able to get on a plane and fly directly to London and you can't do it anymore. Quite often now to fly to Europe, I've got to fly three hours west to Toronto and get on a plane to fly to Frankfurt or to Munich or somewhere, and that's ... an expensive issue for us to do business." This is a lesser issue in other major Canadian cities like Toronto and Vancouver, highlighting St John's peripherality in the Canadian urban system.

One interviewee in arts and culture also explained how they often have to combat negative perceptions for being located away from Toronto. "There is a perception that if you're away from Toronto you are ... you know, not going to do as well." They also explained how in some economic sectors, whether you're located in Toronto or St John's matters little on the international scene. They argued, "Whether you're from St John's, Toronto, Vancouver, or Hamilton, you're still a hillbilly. You know, it's the great equalizer. It's phenomenal. They do not care. The whole St John's, Halifax, Toronto, Montreal construct is completely Canadian."

Interviewees also indicated that St John's and the province as a whole lacked diversity. While St John's is home to the majority of immigrants attracted to NL (CCDA 2008), it is less diverse in ethnicity and birth locations than other Canadian cites. The interviews highlighted high barriers to entry, including a divide between native Newfoundlanders and Labradorians and "CFAs" (come-from-aways). As one interviewee in St John's explained, "We're still very much an insular community ... Although we're very friendly, we're also very ... I don't want to say suspicious, but whenever I sit down with anyone, I still get the 'Who's your father?' 'Where were you born?' Right? It's very important to find out how you're connected to Newfoundland. And I think that can be a real barrier."

Many migrants and immigrants are, however, combatting the CFA label by saying they are "NBCs" (Newfoundlanders-by-choice). As one interviewee argued, "I live here by choice. You know, there's no court order keeping me here."

Small size, location, isolation, and quality of place were also a cited as positive qualities. Interviewees attributed the dense social networks and culture of mutual support in the city to its small size and isolation. For example, interviewees working in arts and culture explained how they benefited from this dense social support, especially during downturns, which often resulted in helping them find alternative employment. They further valued the unique Newfoundland identity and the creativity of the local arts scene in St John's. We also discovered that interviewees saw St John's as a staging ground to prepare for opportunities in larger centres like Toronto, Montreal, and Halifax (see Lepawsky, Phan, and Greenwood 2010).

In terms of quality of place, a number of interviewees cited affordability, the Newfoundland culture, and natural amenities. For example, one interviewee explained, "We're selling a lifestyle that's not caught up in just the work environment and commuting back and forth. We're selling an opportunity to get involved in the outdoors, we're selling an opportunity to breathe clean air, have physical activity. There are attractions there, and I think we've undersold those over the years."

Interviewees were keenly aware that not everyone wants to live in St John's, but not everyone wants to live in Toronto or Vancouver either. In fact, one oil-and-gas interviewee explained how workers brought in from Europe "embrace this culture with a fervour that I've never seen before. They love it."

The debate on talent attraction and retention has focused largely on whether people move to cities where they can maximize their access to job opportunities or for the natural and cultural amenities, tolerance, and diversity (see Florida 2002, 2005; Markusen 2006; Storper and

Manville 2006; Sands and Reese 2008; Pratt 2008). This debate, however, fails to take into account the importance of "home" – broadly defined to include family, geography, and culture – as a key factor in determining where people decide to live (Greenwood, Pike, and Kearley 2011). We discovered that many interviewees located in St John's because it is "home." They emphasized proximity to family as well as the familiar culture, landscape, and lifestyle. In addition, many firm representatives interviewed indicated that they were located in St John's because it was home versus being located close to their markets. For example, one interviewee explained that they would probably be more successful in a place like Boston or Silicon Valley but were more content working at "home." Another firm also emphasized the importance of being in St John's because it is "home," despite their industry counterparts being located in other cities around the world.

Our study of St John's also discovered that a number of firms use "home" to their advantage by focusing on attracting highly educated and skilled Newfoundlanders back to the province. More importantly they are proud that they can bring people back home because, as one interviewee explained, "Newfoundlanders, by and large, would love to stay at home, but they have not had that luxury." One interviewee described their company as having "the ultimate goal of keeping kids home – you know, keeping them in Atlantic Canada and not having them have to leave to do cool stuff." Employers also often use the dense social networks of current workers trying to help friends and family find jobs "back home": "We try to get good people versus cheap people, and a lot of these people just really want to come back, and we get them through other people. Most of it comes through referrals, not an ad in the paper ... we brought back somebody from Texas, and now we have two of that person's friends working with us as well, that are also from here that were in Texas."

In Northern Ontario, Hall and Donald (2009, 2012) found a similar trend of people moving back "home" in their thirties for the affordability and lifestyle. These "been-aways" return with skills and contacts, contribute new ideas and knowledge, and represent a hidden diversity. This is important, because regional and local development policies are often focused on preventing youth out-migration. However, there is value in policies that focus on attracting people back home. One final point to consider is that despite the significance of "home," interviewees for the St John's study emphasized the importance of jobs in attracting and retaining talented people in NL.

Governance in St John's: Dysfunctional and Collaborative

There is growing recognition that collaborative, inclusive, and flexible governance mechanisms are critical to the economic performance of city-regions. As Wolfe (2009) argues, "Recent experience suggests that in order to formulate strategies to improve their prospects for economic development, city-regions require the presence of strong, responsive relationships between the economy and community that give both firms and the community a sustained advantage. These relationships are mediated by civic entrepreneurs and by collaborative organizations that bring the respective economic, social, and civic interests together to cooperate on strategies for the community" (126).

Bradford (2003) also highlights the importance of local champions, adequate financial and technical resources, and institutional intermediaries for community-based innovation processes. In St John's, the ocean technology cluster and a dynamic network of social-sector non-governmental organizations (NGOs) provide positive examples in associative governance and the strategic management of the urban economy. However, we also discovered extremely poor collaborative municipal and regional economic governance that hampers more inclusive regional development between St John's and its neighbours (see Greenwood 2014).

Dysfunctional Municipal and Regional Economic Governance

Canada has the weakest local government in the OECD, and NL has the weakest local government in Canada. Municipalities across the country are "creatures of the provinces"; however, municipalities in NL have fewer responsibilities and insufficient resources when compared to their counterparts in other Canadian provinces (OECD 2002; Felt 2009; Greenwood 2009, 2014). This creates an environment where municipalities are forced to turn to the provincial government for decision-making and fiscal resources. Many of the community and municipal representatives interviewed discussed frustration over the lack of capacity at the local level. More importantly, this provincially centralized decision-making prevents more collaborative forms of governance. Indeed, several people interviewed expressed fear about speaking out, for risk of being excluded from provincial government contracts or program funding.

Interviews in St John's were also conducted during a period of intense federal-provincial conflict between Premier Williams and Prime Minister Harper over a number of issues including resource revenue. This prompted a number of interviewees to discuss the negative impact these political battles had on collaborative governance between the three levels of government. As one interviewee explained, "The one thing I find is a barrier is the federal-provincial squabbling in recent times, because what happens is that it impacts the partnership, in that sometimes it gets to the point that if they're involved and they're going to bring money to the table, you realize that we're not going to do it," while another stated, "My impression is that the relationship of all three levels of government could be improved dramatically and we could get a lot more accomplished if all three had better, stronger, and more successful relationships."

Interviewees also argued that the province "fails to recognize the importance of cities," as rural communities often band together to voice their concerns. As one interviewee explained,

> I think the province could have more respect for the municipal level in the sense of the importance of a city the size of St John's as an economic driver and as a leader at the municipal level. They don't want to do anything for St John's that they can't do for the whole province ... you can't have a one-size-fits-all solution to it ... I would like to see better linkages, formal linkages, between the provincial government and the city government, and with the federal government ... treating municipalities in the way they do constitutionally tends to, I think ... I use the word *denigrate* ... it fails to recognize the real importance of cities.

Lack of cooperation was also a source of contention between St John's and its neighbouring municipalities due in large part to the threat by St John's of amalgamation (see Greenwood 2014 for a detailed discussion).

The Regional Economic Development Board (REDB)[4] in the St John's region also had difficultly in overcoming the contentious relationship between St John's and its neighbours. As one interviewee noted, the REDB was seen as "competition" by various industry associations that have provincial offices in St John's, which challenges more collaborative regional economic governance. The REDBs also had narrow mandates focused entirely on economic development and no money for implementation. As one key informant explained, "We were set up as planners, facilitators, but not implementers. We were provided with a core budget from the feds and the province on a 75/25 split, but no money for implementation." Although the St John's city-region is highly dysfunctional in municipal and regional economic governance, it is thriving with innovative governance approaches with its emerging ocean technology cluster and the social-sector NGOs.

Collaborative Ocean Technology Cluster and Social Sector NGOs

The St John's ocean technology cluster, as discussed earlier in this chapter, provides one example of exceptional coordination and collaboration among federal, provincial, and municipal governments, industry, and the post-secondary educational institutions in the city-region. More recently, the provincial government has harnessed resource riches to advance a significant poverty-reduction strategy. As we have described elsewhere (Greenwood 2014), this strategy has unleashed a thriving NGO sector that many argue is leading the country in associative governance.

During the 2003 election campaign, the Progressive Conservative Party promised it would transform Newfoundland and Labrador within ten years from the province with the most poverty to the one with the least (Progressive Conservative Party of NL 2003). After a consultation process in 2005, the province proposed "a comprehensive approach with a mix of policy options...to have a significant impact on poverty." It continued on to explain that such a comprehensive strategy "requires input from all orders of government, community-based groups, business, labour, and individuals about the best approaches and policy mix to reduce poverty in the province" (Government of Newfoundland and Labrador 2005, preface). In 2006, *Reducing Poverty: An Action Plan for Newfoundland and Labrador* was released, and it focused on providing a stronger social safety net, improved earned incomes, early childhood development, and a better-educated population. In the 2006–7 provincial budget, over $30 million was committed for twenty initiatives under the poverty-reduction strategy. By the 2010–11 provincial budget, $134 million was committed to more than eighty initiatives (Government of Newfoundland and Labrador 2010).

A number of compelling results emerged from the interviews, including the importance of collaboration, access to funding, and leadership. Interviewees emphasized the close relationship between the province and the NGOs. For example, one senior provincial official explained how government departments worked closely with grassroots organizations in implementing the strategy. Interviewees from leading social-sector NGOs also discussed this close relationship with the province. As one social-sector interviewee explained, their access to provincial government officials is excellent and he can regularly count on meetings, while another reported being able to "make one phone call" to solve an issue for a client. As one senior government official noted, "We finally figured out that government is better served by engaging in equal partnerships, where not only do you learn stuff from other people but you're better at executing it and recognizing it." They also argued that the level and professionalism of this collaboration was a unique strength in NL compared to other provinces.

We also discovered that this level of collaboration and cooperation is evident between NGOs in St John's. For example, one interviewee noted, ten years ago the NGOs would not work together because they saw themselves as competitors. However, "today they're sitting on each other's boards," and if one organization applies for funding, it gets letters of support from other organizations. As one NGO leader explained, "People are starting to understand that sharing information is not giving it away."

The success of the social-sector NGOs and collaborative policy environment is strongly tied with access to funding. One NGO interviewee described how they started with a grant of $20,000 to organize a conference and "ended up having a $180,000 conference ... with people here from all over Canada." Several NGO leaders also highlighted the City of St John's for its support. For example, one NGO received a land donation worth $50,000 from the city. That organization owns its own building, "mortgage free," and rents office space to another NGO and twenty provincial staff. The private sector was also mentioned by social-sector NGOs for their contributions, including companies in the energy (oil and gas), mining, and banking sectors.

The ocean technology cluster and the social-sector NGOs in the St John's city-region attribute much of their success to the efforts of their leaders. As one interviewee observed, developing partnerships with organizations, businesses, and governments in the community takes a good deal of time and effort, but these partnerships are cultivated by strong leaders who often use their skills to find ways of leveraging funding to keep their organizations in operation. In the social-sector NGOs, these extremely dynamic and effective leaders are often paid staff and can dedicate their time to the organization versus busy volunteer leaders who stretch their time to the limit. We discovered that

NGO leaders repeatedly referenced each other as trusted collaborators who share information, partner on projects, and foster innovation in social programming. As one NGO leader explained, these relationships are vital for program delivery: "The only tool in the toolbox I have is a decent relationship … the breadth of relationships and partnerships you develop … You've got to know your stuff. You've got to have your evidence, you've got to be competent, you've got to be capable … it's about having decent relationships backed up by 'these guys can do the work.'"

The small size of St John's was also seen as a positive attribute in bringing people together. The St John's ocean technology cluster and the social-sector NGOs thus provide a compelling contrast to the weak and dysfunctional municipal and regional economic governance. These examples demonstrate an attempt to make the most of NL's newfound prosperity by developing the ocean technology cluster and advancing a significant poverty-reduction strategy to extend these fiscal gains.

The fact that the ocean-technology cluster development and the poverty-reduction strategy have very clear desired outcomes helps forge collaboration and foster a common purpose. Municipal and regional economic governance, on the other hand, are broader, multifaceted, ongoing exercises. Conflicts can arise in any multi-actor initiative, especially one that lacks a singularity of purpose that can enable focus. In NL, these are all complex processes, but in the absence of this common focus, combined with provincial reluctance to recognize local governance, the barriers to associative governance between the Northeast Avalon municipalities and the REDBs are daunting.

One interviewee suggested a stronger role for the university to act as a facilitator, to create an "association of associations." Universities and colleges are increasingly establishing programs, strategies, and units to support regional engagement. As we noted elsewhere (Greenwood 2014), one major difference between the non-collaborative Northeast Avalon municipalities and REDBs and the thriving ocean technology cluster and social-sector NGOs is money. There are no financial incentives to increase or induce collaboration. There is also a lack of leadership in encouraging the communities to work together on a regional basis. Federal and provincial recognition, including financial support, would go a long way to enhance the chances of success. However, in the current Canadian and provincial political context in NL, that prospect is not on the radar.

Conclusions

The St John's city-region provides a compelling case to study the social dynamics of economic performance. As a "metropolis on the margins" it has a dual character as the largest city and provincial capital of Newfoundland. However, its size, relative location, and economic reliance on natural resources also exposes a number of peripheral realities. For example, innovation, attracting and retaining skilled workers, accessing knowledge and research capacity from universities are often significant challenges for smaller city-regions. The ocean technology cluster in St John's, however, is proof that a small city-region can build a cutting-edge, globally competitive, and innovative cluster. In understanding the social dynamics of innovation, the ocean technology cluster study revealed the importance of collaboration among firms, local research and development institutions, government, and industry associations. It also emphasized the significance of strategic thinking by government to ensure that a percentage of the revenue from the oil-and-gas industry is invested in research and development and education and training in Newfoundland and Labrador. However, one major challenge is the cluster's vulnerability to world markets and external economic shocks.

As the "metropolis on the margins," St John's offers a number of "big-city" amenities – like a diverse economy, a large arts-and-culture scene, restaurants and nightlife, health-care services, shopping, and post-secondary educational institutions – which were valued by interviewees. However, almost without exception, interviewees emphasized the importance of home and belonging as a key factor in deciding where to live. As noted, "home" has been overlooked in the debates on talent attraction and retention. Some, however, noted that this sense of belonging could be hard to break into as a "CFA." Moreover, despite the significance of "home," interviewees underlined the importance of jobs in attracting and retaining talented people in Newfoundland.

The biggest weakness confronting the social dynamics of economic performance in Newfoundland is weak and dysfunctional governance, especially for municipalities and regional economic development. Almost all those interviewed on governance in St John's recognized that greater local capacity was needed to succeed. However, the oceans technology cluster and social-sector NGOs offer promising examples of more innovative governance. As noted, the importance of collaboration, access to funding, and leadership are paramount to the success of the social-sector NGOs. As Greenwood (2014) argues, municipalities and REDBs are overly reliant on their federal and provincial superiors and have yet to gain sufficient capacity or legitimacy. Like city-regions across the country, regardless of size, municipalities in NL are insisting on a greater role in decision-making and fostering the conditions that drive the local economy.

Notes

1 "Been-aways," coined by Greg Spencer, is an extension of the term "come-from-aways" or "CFAs" – a label sometimes placed on newcomers to the close-knit society of the province. It was coined during the Newfoundland and Labrador ISRN Team workshop on 18 and 19 February 2010 (see Hall 2010 for more detail).

2 The ISRN NL project was led by Rob Greenwood, director of the Leslie Harris Centre of Regional Policy and Development at Memorial University. Ann-Marie Vaughan, director of distance education, learning and teaching support at Memorial University led the investigation into theme I; Josh Lepawsky, Department of Geography at Memorial University led theme II; while Rob Greenwood led theme III. This chapter is based on results already published in Lepawsky (2009); Lepawsky, Phan, and Greenwood (2010); Greenwood, Pike, and Kearley (2011); and Greenwood (2014).

3 This contribution is based on price and production volumes. As noted elsewhere (Greenwood 2014) two companies are contesting the amount, with a NAFTA challenge. However, others have begun to determine how to invest their required amounts. Already the accumulated amounts are in the hundreds of millions of dollars (Locke 2009).

4 In the mid-1990s a federal-provincial task force recommended the establishment of twenty economic zones across NL. Each zone included a Regional Economic Development Board (REDB) composed of representatives of municipalities, business, labour, community development organizations, education and training institutions, and others representatives from the region (Task Force on Community Economic Development 1995).

References

Amin, A., and N. Thrift, N. 1994. "Living in the global." In *Globalization, institutions, and regional development in Europe*, ed. A. Amin and N. Thrift, 1–22. Oxford: Oxford University Press.

–. 1995. "Institutional issues for the European regions: From markets and plans to socioeconomics and powers of association." *Economy and Society* 24 (1): 41–66.

Berkowitz, P. 2012. "U-15 begins to formalize its organization." University Affairs, 30 May. http://www.universityaffairs.ca/news/news-article/u-15-begins-to-formalize-its-organization/.

Bradford, N. 2003. "Cities and communities that work: Innovative practices, enabling practices." Discussion paper F | 32. Canadian Policy Research Networks. http://www.cprn.org/documents/20506_en.pdf.

Cairncross, F. 1997. *The death of distance: How the communications revolution will change our lives*. Boston: Harvard Business School Press.

Capital Coast Development Alliance (CCDA). 2008. "Strategic plan December 2008." Newfoundland and Labrador Regional Economic Development Association.

Colbourne, Bruce. 2006 "St. John's ocean technology cluster: Can government make it so?" *Canadian Public Administration* 49 (1): 46–59. http://dx.doi.org/10.1111/j.1754-7121.2006.tb02017.x.

Doloreux, D., and S. Dionne. 2008. "Is regional innovation system development possible in peripheral regions? Some evidence from the case of La Pocatière, Canada." *Entrepreneurship & Regional Development* 20 (3): 259–83. http://dx.doi.org/10.1080/08985620701795525.

Felt, Larry. 2009. "A tale of two towns: Municipal agency and socio-economic development in Akureyri, Iceland, and Corner Brook, Newfoundland." In *Remote control: Governance lessons for and from small, insular, and remote regions*, ed. G. Baldacchino, R. Greenwood, and L. Felt, 148–69. St John's: ISER Books.

Florida, R. 2002. *The rise of the creative class*. New York: Basic Books.

–. 2005. *Cities and the creative class*. New York: Routledge.

–. 2008. *Who's your city*. Toronto: Random House Canada.

Florida, R., C. Mellander, and K. Stolarick. 2008. "Inside the black box of regional development: Human capital, the creative class and tolerance." *Journal of Economic Geography* 8 (5): 615–49. http://dx.doi.org/10.1093/jeg/lbn023.

Friedman, T.L. 2005. *The world is flat: A brief history of the 21st century*. Waterville: Thorndike Press.

Gertler, M. 2001. "Urban economy and society in Canada: Flows of people, capital and ideas." *Isuma: Canadian Journal of Policy Research* 2 (3): 119–30.

Gertler, M.S., R. Florida, G. Gates, and T. Vinodrai. 2002. *Competing on creativity: Placing Ontario's cities in North American context*. Toronto: Ontario Ministry of Enterprise, Opportunity and Innovation and the Institute for Competitiveness and Prosperity.

Government of Newfoundland and Labrador. 2005. "Reducing poverty in Newfoundland and Labrador: Working towards a solution background report and workbook." St John's: Government of Newfoundland and Labrador. http://www.gov.nl.ca/publicat/povertydiscussion-final.pdf.

–. 2010. "Newfoundland and Labrador's poverty reduction strategy: Consultation guide 2010." St John's: Government of Newfoundland and Labrador. http://www.swsd.gov.nl.ca/publications/pdf/prs/2010_PRS_Consultation_Guide.pdf.

Greenwood, G., and C. Pike, with W. Kearley. 2011. *A commitment to place: The social foundations of innovation in Newfoundland and Labrador*. St John's: Harris Centre. https://www.mun.ca/harriscentre/reports/research/2011/CommitmenttoPlace_Harris_Sept2011Web.pdf.

Greenwood, Rob. 2009. "Doing governance for development: The way forward for Newfoundland and Labrador." In *Remote control: Governance lessons for and from small, insular, and remote regions*, ed. G. Baldacchino, R. Greenwood, and L. Felt, 280–94. St John's: ISER Books.

–. 2014. "Embarrassment and riches: Good governance and bad governance in the St John's city region." In *Governing urban economies: Innovation and inclusion in Canadian city regions*, ed. N. Bradford and A. Bramwell, 161–83. Toronto: University of Toronto Press.

Hall, H.M. 2010. "The social dynamics of economic performance: Innovation and creativity in city-regions – Newfoundland and Labrador project preliminary findings – St John's, Clarenville, Corner Brook, & West Labrador." Workshop report prepared for the Harris Centre at Memorial University, St John's, Newfoundland and Labrador.

–. 2011. *Harvesting the rural creative economy: Knowledge synthesis prepared for the Monieson Centre*. Kingston: Queen's School of Business.

Hall, H.M., and B. Donald. 2009. "Innovation and creativity on the periphery: Challenges and opportunities in Northern Ontario." Working paper series: Ontario in the Creative Age. REF. 2009-WPONT-002.

–. 2012. "Clarifying culture and creativity in a small city on the Canadian periphery: Challenges and opportunities in Greater Sudbury." In *The cultural political economy of small cities*, ed. A. Lorentzen and B. van Heur, 80–94. New York: Routledge.

Hayter, R. 2005. "Regions as institutions, inter-regional firms and new economic spaces." In *New economic spaces: New economic geographies*, ed. R. Le Heron and J.W. Harrington, 192–205. Burlington UK: Ashgate Publishing.

Jacobs, J. 1969. *The economy of cities*. New York: Random House.

Jarvey, P., and A. Usher. 2012. *Measuring academic research in Canada: Field-normalized university rankings 2012*. Toronto: Higher Education Strategy Associates.

Johnstone, H., and R. Haddow. 2003. "Industrial decline and high technology renewal in Cape Breton: Exploring the limits of the possible." In *Clusters old and new: The transition to a knowledge economy in Canada's regions*, ed. D.A. Wolfe, 187–212. Montreal and Kingston: McGill-Queen's University Press.

Lepawsky, J. 2009. "The organization and dynamics of clustering and innovation in the ocean technology sector in Newfoundland and Labrador and the St John's city-region." St John's: Harris Centre, 30 September.

Lepawsky, J., C. Phan, and R. Greenwood. 2010. "Metropolis on the margins: Talent attraction and retention to the St John's city-region." *Canadian Geographer / Le Géographe canadien* 54 (3): 324–46. http://dx.doi.org/10.1111/j.1541-0064.2010.00315.x.

Lewis, N.M., and B. Donald. 2010. "A new rubric for 'creative city' potential in Canada's smaller cities." *Urban Studies* 47 (1): 29–54. http://dx.doi.org/10.1177/0042098009346867.

Locke, Wade. 2009. "Presentation to Newfoundland Ocean Industries Association, June 18," cited in Memorial University, "Background Report to the Development of the Memorial University Research Plan," February 2010, 18.

Maclean's. 2012. "2013 primarily undergraduate university rankings." http://www.macleans.ca/education/2012/11/01/2013-primarily-undergraduate/.

Markusen, A. 2006. "Urban development and the politics of a creative class: Evidence from a study of artists." *Environment & Planning A* 38 (10): 1921–40. http://dx.doi.org/10.1068/a38179.

McGranahan, D., and T. Wojan. 2007. "Recasting the creative class to examine growth processes in rural and urban counties." *Regional Studies* 41 (2): 197–216. http://dx.doi.org/10.1080/00343400600928285.

Memorial University of Newfoundland. 2010. Background report to the development of the Memorial University research plan. http://www.mun.ca/research/plan/Background_Report_web.pdf.

OceansAdvance. 2009. "Outward Bound 2015: A strategic agenda for accelerating growth of the ocean technology sector in Newfoundland and Labrador." St John's: Oceans Advance.

OECD. 2002. *Territorial review of Canada*. Paris: OECD, Territorial Reviews and Governance Division.

Petroleum Research. 2012. "About Petroleum Research." http://www.pr-ac.ca/index.php?id=2.

Petrov, A.N. 2007. "A look beyond metropolis: Exploring creative class in the Canadian periphery." *Canadian Journal of Regional Science* 30 (3): 452–74.

Polèse, M., R. Shearmur, P.M. Desjardins, and M. Johnson. 2002. *The periphery in the knowledge economy: The spatial dynamics of the Canadian economy and the future of non-metropolitan regions in Quebec and the Atlantic Provinces*. Montreal and Moncton: Institut national de la recherche scientifique and the Canadian Institute for Research on Regional Development.

Porter, M.E. 2000. "Location, competition, and economic development: Local clusters in a global economy." *Economic Development Quarterly* 14 (1): 15–34. http://dx.doi.org/10.1177/089124240001400105.

Pratt, A. 2008. "Creative cities: The cultural industries and the creative class." *Geografiska Annaler. Series B, Human Geography* 90 (2): 107–17. http://dx.doi.org/10.1111/j.1468-0467.2008.00281.x.

Progressive Conservative Party of NL. 2003. *Real leadership, the new approach: Our blueprint for the future (Blue Book)*. St John's: Progressive Conservative Party of NL.

RDC. 2011. "Who we are." http://www.rdc.org/connect/who-we-are/.

Rutherford, T.D., and J. Holmes. 2007. "Entrepreneurship, knowledge and learning in cluster formation and evolution: The Windsor, Ontario, tool, die and mould cluster." *International Journal of Entrepreneurship and Innovation Management* 7 (2–5): 320–44. http://dx.doi.org/10.1504/IJEIM.2007.012887.

Sands, G., and L.A. Reese. 2008. "Cultivating the creative class: And what about Nanaimo?" *Economic Development Quarterly* 22 (1): 8–23. http://dx.doi.org/10.1177/0891242407309822.

Spencer, G., and T. Vinodrai. 2012. Innovation systems research network city region profile: Newfoundland and Labrador Profile. Toronto: Program on Globalization and Regional Innovation Systems, Munk School of Global Affairs, University of Toronto.

Stantec. 2009. "Socio-economic benefits from petroleum industry activity in Newfoundland and Labrador, 2005–2007." Prepared for the Petroleum Research Atlantic Canada. File no. 1039339, 13 February. http://www.pr-ac.ca/files/files/MP08-01_NL_BenefitsUpdate.pdf.

Statistics Canada. 2006. "Census of population. Table 3: Population of census metropropolitan areas in 2006." http://www12.statcan.ca/census-recensement/2006/as-sa/97-550/table/t3-eng.cfm.

Storper, M., and M. Manville. 2006. "Behaviour, preferences and cities: Urban theory and urban resurgence." *Urban Studies* 43 (8): 1247–74. http://dx.doi.org/10.1080/00420980600775642.

Task Force on Community Economic Development in Newfoundland and Labrador. 1995. *Community matters: The new regional economic development*. St John's: Atlantic Canada Opportunities Agency.

Virkkala, S. 2007. "Innovation and networking in peripheral areas: A case study of emergence and change in rural manufacturing." *European Planning Studies* 15 (4): 511–29. http://dx.doi.org/10.1080/09654310601133948.

Wolfe, D.A. 2009. *21st century cities in Canada: The geography of innovation*. 2009 CIBC Scholar-in-Residence Lecture. Ottawa: Conference Board of Canada.

Wolfe, D.A., and A. Bramwell. 2008. "Innovation, creativity and governance: Social dynamics of economic performance in city-regions." *Innovation: Management, Policy & Practice* 10: 170–82.

Appendix A
City-Region Profiles

Toronto

Socio-economic indicators	Toronto CMA	Canada
Population	5,583,064	33,476,690
Population change 2006–11	9.2%	5.9%
Foreign born	47.9%	22.0%
% BA or higher	29.9%	20.9%
PhDs per 1,000	9.1	7.6
Employment growth 2006–11	5.8%	3.6%
Unemployment rate	8.6%	7.8%
In creative occupations	37.1%	32.0%
Science tech occupations	8.7%	7.2%
Bohemians per 1,000	20.7	13.9
Number of clusters	12	214
Employment in clusters	55.4%	15.8%
Average full-time employment income	$65,903	$58,129
Change in Income 2006–11	8.5%	13.5%

Leading clusters	Location quotient 2011	Growth 2006–2011
Textiles and apparel	1.3	0.4%
Automotive	1.3	–9.2%
Biomedical	1.6	–6.5%
Business services	1.3	–1.7%
Creative and cultural	1.6	0.6%
Finance	1.7	2.1%
Food	1.2	9.6%
Higher education	1.0	–0.9%
ICT manufacturing	1.8	–0.5%
ICT services	1.3	–2.4%
Logistics	1.5	–1.5%
Plastics and rubber	1.4	–8.7%

Montreal

Socio-economic indicators	Montreal CMA	Canada
Population	2,313,328	33,476,690
Population change 2006–11	9.3%	5.9%
Foreign born	40.0%	22.0%
BA or higher	21.0%	20.9%
PhDs per 1,000	11.7	7.6
Employment growth 2006–11	3.4%	3.6%
Unemployment rate	7.7%	7.8%
In creative occupations	32.8%	32.0%
Science tech occupations	8.1%	7.2%
Bohemians per 1,000	16.8	13.9
Number of clusters	10	214
Employment in clusters	44.1%	15.8%
Average full-time employment income	$53,817	$58,129
Change in income 2006–11	14.9%	13.5%
Leading clusters	**Location quotient 2011**	**Growth 2006–2011**
Textiles and apparel	2.7	8.3%
Biomedical	1.6	2.8%
Business services	1.2	–2.5%
Creative and cultural	1.4	0.5%
Finance	1.1	3.6%
Food	1.1	–4.1%
ICT manufacturing	1.2	11.5%
ICT services	1.4	–0.8%
Logistics	1.3	2.1%
Plastics and rubber	1.3	–1.2%

Vancouver

Socio-economic indicators	Vancouver CMA	Canada
Population	2,313,328	33,476,690
Population change 2006–11	9.3%	5.9%
Foreign-born	40.0%	22.0%
BA or higher	24.1%	20.9%
PhDs per 1,000	12.6	7.6
Employment growth 2006–11	7.0%	3.6%
Unemployment rate	5.1%	7.8%
In creative occupations	33.6%	32.0%
Science tech occupations	7.7%	7.2%
Bohemians per 1,000	20.7	13.9
Number of clusters	10	214
Employment in clusters	51.1%	15.8%
Average full-time employment income	$61,416	$58,129
Change in Income 2006–11	17.0%	13.5%
Leading clusters	**Location quotient 2011**	**Growth 2006–2011**
Biomedical	1.0	5.5%
Business services	1.3	0.8%
Construction	1.3	2.0%
Creative and cultural	1.6	8.0%
Finance	1.2	2.6%
Food	1.2	–12.1%
Higher education	1.5	–0.1%
ICT services	1.3	4.9%
Logistics	1.3	9.1%
Maritime	1.5	–7.5%

Ottawa

Socio-economic indicators	Ottawa-Gatineau CMA	Canada
Population	1,236,324	33,476,690
Population change 2006–11	9.1%	5.9%
Foreign-born	19.4%	22.0%
BA or higher	25.0%	20.9%
PhDs per 1,000	18.5	7.6
Employment growth 2006–11	8.8%	3.6%
Unemployment rate	4.7%	7.8%
In creative occupations	40.7%	32.0%
Science tech occupations	11.3%	7.2%
Bohemians per 1,000	13.5	13.9
Number of clusters	5	214
Employment in clusters	26.5%	15.8%
Average full-time employment income	$65,684	$58,129
Change in Income 2006–11	16.5%	13.5%
Leading clusters	**Location quotient 2011**	**Growth 2006–2011**
Business services	1.2	−14.2%
Creative and cultural	1.0	−6.2%
Higher education	1.4	−7.3%
ICT manufacturing	1.9	−6.8%
ICT services	1.4	−10.0%

Calgary

Socio-economic indicators	Calgary CMA	Canada
Population	1,214,839	33,476,690
Population change 2006–11	12.6%	5.9%
Foreign-born	26.2%	22.0%
BA or higher	24.9%	20.9%
PhDs per 1,000	10.1	7.6
Employment growth 2006–11	8.1%	3.6%
Unemployment rate	4.5%	7.8%
In creative occupations	35.7%	32.0%
Science tech occupations	11.8%	7.2%
Bohemians per 1,000	12.4	13.9
Number of clusters	8	214
Employment in clusters	44.1%	15.8%
Average full-time employment income	$77,710	$58,129
Change in income 2006–11	40.5%	13.5%
Leading clusters	**Location quotient 2011**	**Growth 2006–2011**
Business services	1.5	3.2%
Construction	1.9	16.0%
Higher education	1.1	10.9%
ICT manufacturing	1.0	–2.4%
Logistics	1.2	–2.1%
Mining	1.5	–14.5%
Oil and gas	5.0	–0.1%
Steel	1.1	14.5%

Hamilton

Socio-economic indicators	Hamilton CMA	Canada
Population	721,053	33,476,690
Population change 2006–11	4.1%	5.9%
Foreign-born	23.5%	22.0%
BA or higher	18.8%	20.9%
PhDs per 1,000	9.8	7.6
Employment growth 2006–11	0.4%	3.6%
Unemployment rate	5.6%	7.8%
In creative occupations	29.5%	32.0%
Science tech occupations	6.3%	7.2%
Bohemians per 1,000	11.7	13.9
Number of clusters	8	214
Employment in clusters	27.9%	15.8%
Average full-time employment income	$62,323	$58,129
Change in income 2006–11	17.8%	13.5%
Leading clusters	**Location quotient 2011**	**Growth 2006–2011**
Automotive	1.5	3.0%
Biomedical	1.2	9.2%
Finance	1.1	2.6%
Food	1.2	–0.7%
Higher education	1.1	2.2%
Logistics	1.2	–0.7%
Plastics and rubber	1.0	4.6%
Steel	1.9	–28.2%

Kitchener

Socio-economic indicators	Kitchener CMA	Canada
Population	477,160	33,476,690
Population change 2006–11	5.7%	5.9%
Foreign-born	23.1%	22.0%
BA or higher	18.5%	20.9%
PhDs per 1,000	11.9	7.6
Employment growth 2006–11	2.0%	3.6%
Unemployment rate	5.1%	7.8%
In creative occupations	28.7%	32.0%
Science tech occupations	8.7%	7.2%
Bohemians per 1,000	12.4	13.9
Number of clusters	8	214
Employment in clusters	26.0%	15.8%
Average full time-employment income	$59,238	$58,129
Change in income 2006–11	17.5%	13.5%
Leading clusters	**Location quotient 2011**	**Growth 2006–2011**
Textile and apparel	1.1	−11.7%
Agriculture	1.0	6.6%
Automotive	3.4	5.8%
Biomedical	1.0	−16.7%
ICT manufacturing	4.2	57.1%
Logistics	1.0	−1.5%
Plastics and rubber	1.5	−17.4%
Steel	1.2	−17.3%

London

Socio-economic indicators	London CMA	Canada
Population	260,600	33,476,690
Population change 2006–11	11.4%	5.9%
Foreign-born	10.7%	22.0%
BA or higher	17.7%	20.9%
PhDs per 1,000	12.3	7.6
Employment growth 2006–11	−1.6%	3.6%
Unemployment rate	5.9%	7.8%
In creative occupations	27.7%	32.0%
Science tech occupations	5.7%	7.2%
Bohemians per 1,000	11.3	13.9
Number of clusters	3	214
Employment in clusters	14.5%	15.8%
Average full-time employment income	$56,869	$58,129
% change in income 2006–11	15.6%	13.5%
Leading clusters	**Location quotient 2011**	**Growth 2006–2011**
Automotive	2.4	−5.6%
Finance	1.2	2.9%
Food	1.1	3.9%

Halifax

Socio-economic indicators	Halifax CMA	Canada
Population	390,328	33,476,690
Population change 2006–11	4.7%	5.9%
Foreign-born	8.1%	22.0%
BA or higher	23.1%	20.9%
PhDs per 1,000	12.2	7.6
Employment growth 2006–11	4.4%	3.6%
Unemployment rate	5.8%	7.8%
In creative occupations	33.1%	32.0%
Science tech occupations	7.9%	7.2%
Bohemians per 1,000	12.2	13.9
Number of clusters	2	214
Employment in clusters	13.9%	15.8%
Average full-time employment income	$53,796	$58,129
Change in income 2006–11	15.6%	13.5%
Leading clusters	**Location quotient 2011**	**Growth 2006–2011**
Business services	1.3	–0.9%
Maritime	2.1	3.8%

Saskatoon

Socio-Economic Indicators	Saskatoon CMA	Canada
Population	474,786	33,476,690
Population change 2006–11	3.7%	5.9%
Foreign born	18.8%	22.0%
BA or higher	19.5%	20.9%
PhDs per 1,000	15.4	7.6
Employment growth 2006–11	14.2%	3.6%
Unemployment rate	4.5%	7.8%
In creative occupations	29.1%	32.0%
Science tech occupations	6.7%	7.2%
Bohemians per 1,000	9.7	13.9
Number of clusters	4	214
Employment in clusters	28.4%	15.8%
Average full-time employment income	$60,071	$58,129
Change in income 2006–11	35.8%	13.5%

Leading clusters	Location quotient 2011	Growth 2006–2011
Agriculture	1.4	–9.6%
Business services	1.3	5.7%
Construction	1.3	35.4%
Higher education	2.1	9.0%

Kingston

Socio-economic indicators	Kingston CMA	Canada
Population	159,561	33,476,690
Population change 2006–11	4.7%	5.9%
Foreign-born	11.8%	22.0%
BA or higher	16.9%	20.9%
PhDs per 1,000	26.2	7.6
Employment growth 2006–11	3.8%	3.6%
Unemployment rate	6.3%	7.8%
In creative occupations	30.8%	32.0%
Science tech occupations	5.9%	7.2%
Bohemians per 1,000	11.4	13.9
Number of clusters	1	214
Employment in clusters	9.5%	15.8%
Average full-time employment income	$56,103	$58,129
Change in income 2006–11	16.7%	13.5%

Leading clusters	Location quotient 2011	Growth 2006–2011
Higher education	3.2	26.1%

Moncton

Socio-economic indicators	Moncton CMA	Canada
Population	138,644	33,476,690
Population change 2006–11	9.7%	5.9%
Foreign-born	4.4%	22.0%
BA or higher	18.2%	20.9%
PhDs per 1,000	7.3	7.6
Employment growth 2006–11	9.9%	3.6%
Unemployment rate	6.3%	7.8%
In creative occupations	29.9%	32.0%
Science tech occupations	6.2%	7.2%
Bohemians per 1,000	9.5	13.9
Number of clusters	2	214
Employment in clusters	8.9%	15.8%
Average full-time employment income	$49,208	$58,129
Change in income 2006–11	20.2%	13.5%

Leading clusters	Location quotient 2011	Growth 2006–2011
Food	1.5	13.0%
ICT services	1.2	10.7%

St John's

Socio-economic indicators	St John's CMA	Canada
Population	127,761	33,476,690
Population change 2006–11	4.4%	5.9%
Foreign-born	4.3%	22.0%
BA or higher	18.6%	20.9%
PhDs per 1,000	11.9	7.6
Employment growth 2006–11	14.6%	3.6%
Unemployment rate	6.1%	7.8%
In creative occupations	33.7%	32.0%
Science tech occupations	9.2%	7.2%
Bohemians per 1,000	11.1	13.9
Number of clusters	3	214
Employment in clusters	16.9%	15.8%
Average full-time employment income	$58,319	$58,129
Change in income 2006–11	29.4%	13.5%
Leading clusters	**Location quotient 2011**	**Growth 2006–2011**
Business services	1.4	10.8%
Food	1.1	32.9%
Maritime	2.4	61.8%

Appendix B
Maps

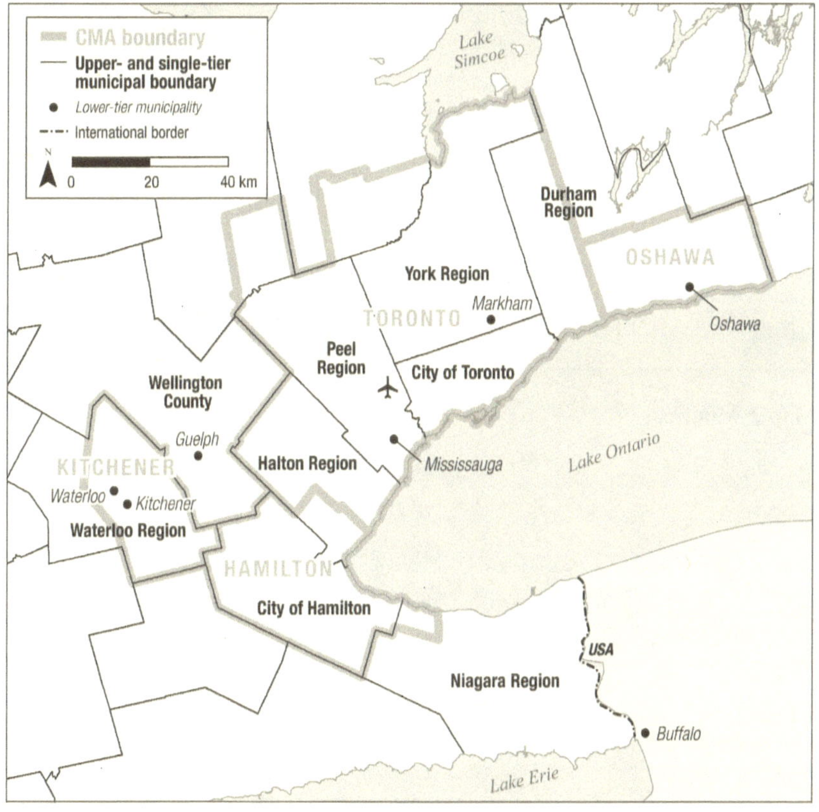

Map 1 Toronto

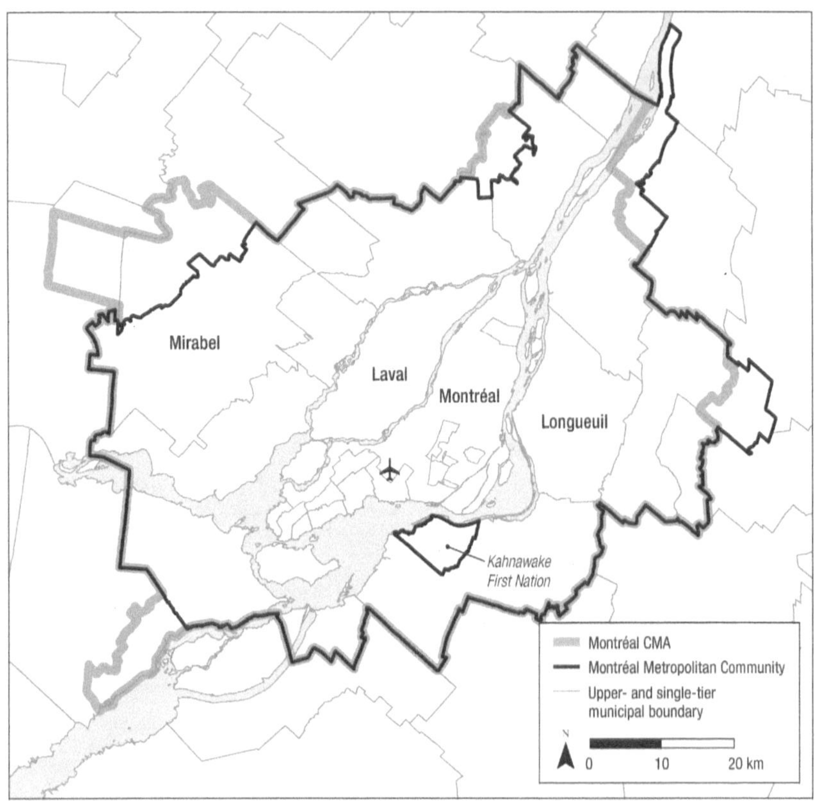

Map 2 Montreal

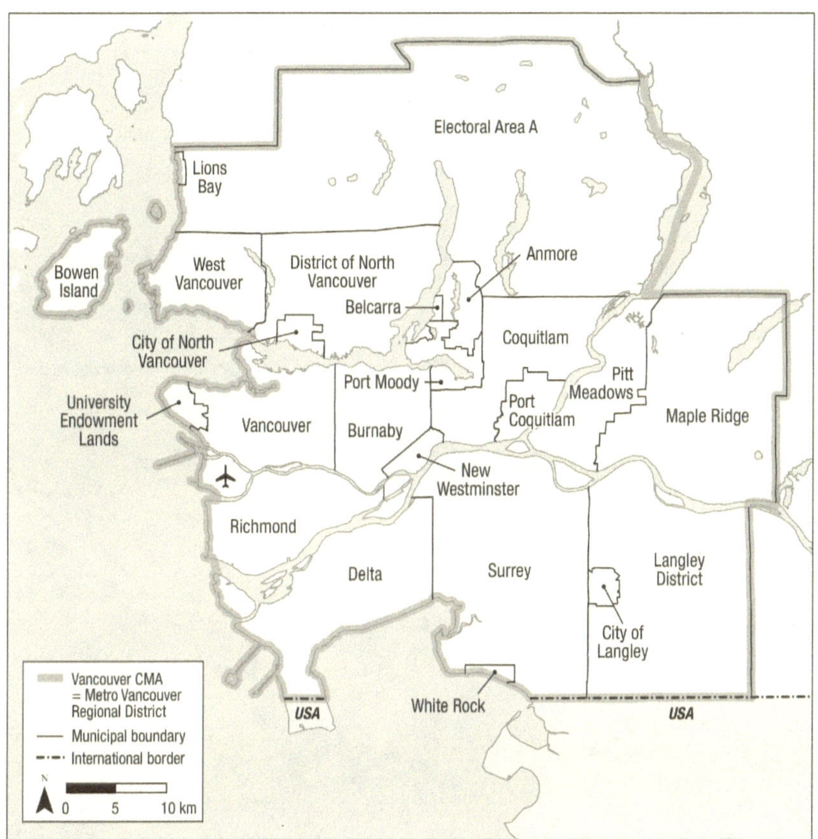

Map 3 Vancouver

CMA boundary
Upper- and single-tier municipal boundary
Lower-tier municipality
0
15
30 km
Antoine-Labelle
Papineau
La Vallée-de-la-Gatineau
GATINEAU
Pontiac
Les Collines-de-l'Outaouais
Prescott and Russell
Gatineau
Quebec
Ontario
Ottawa
Renfrew
OTTAWA
Stormont, Dundas and Glengarry
Lanark
Leeds and Grenville

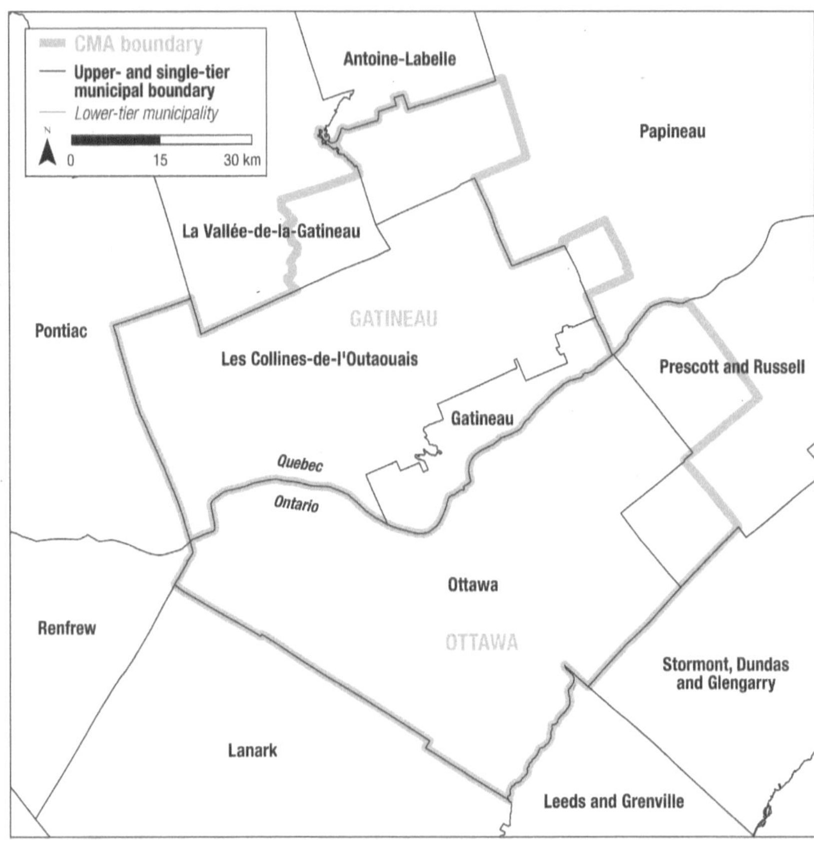

Map 4 Ottawa

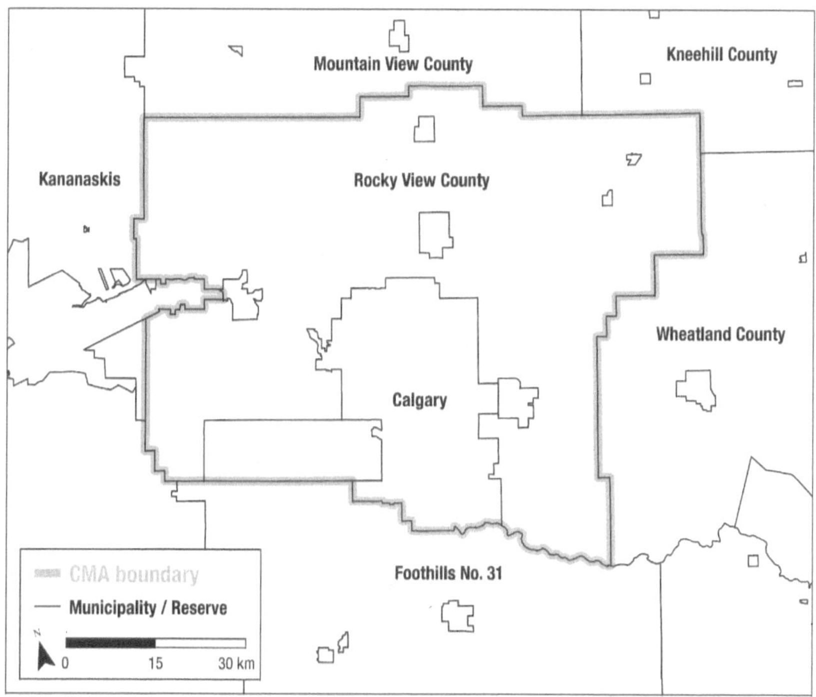

Map 5 Calgary

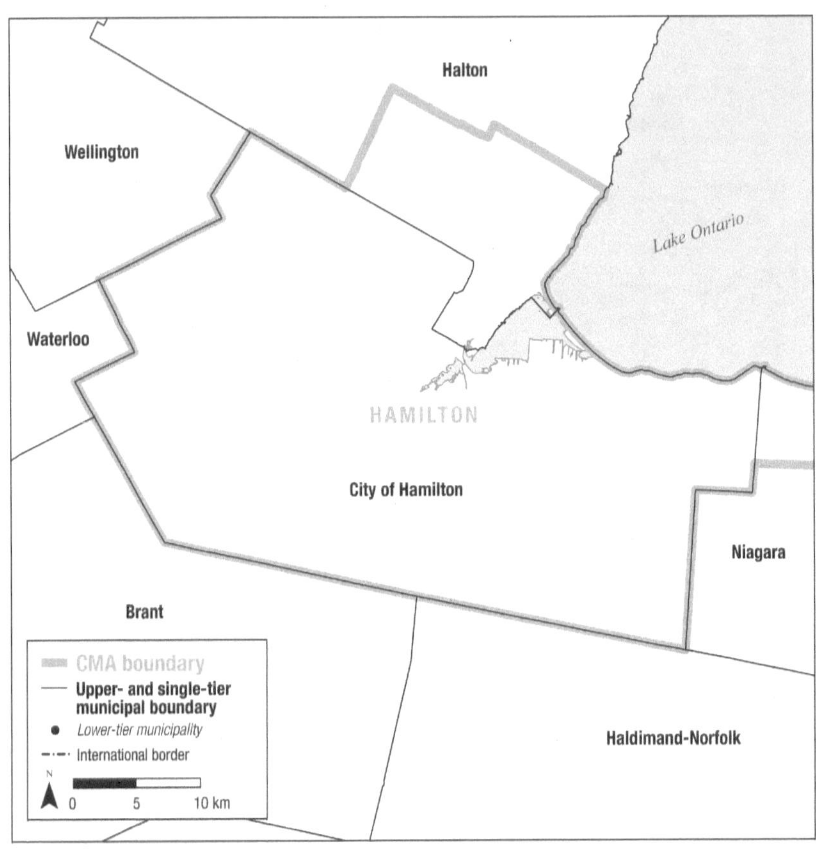

Map 6 Hamilton

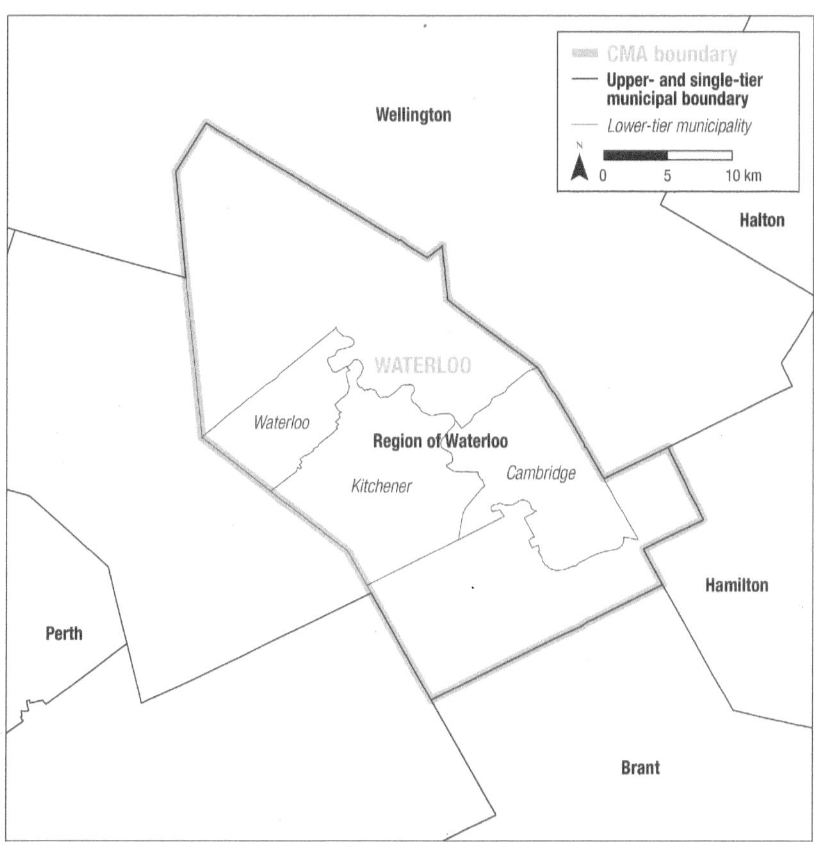

Map 7 Kitchener

Huron
Perth
Oxford
Middlesex
London
Lambton
Elgin
Lake Ontario
CMA boundary
Upper- and single-tier municipal boundary
Lower-tier municipality
N
0
10
20 km

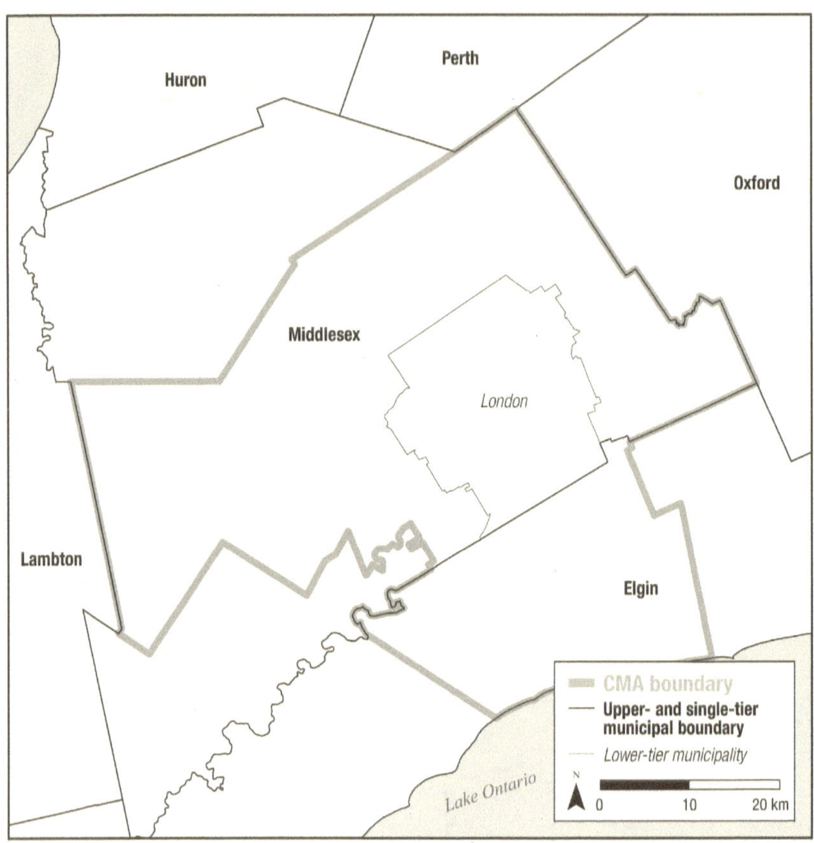

Map 8 London

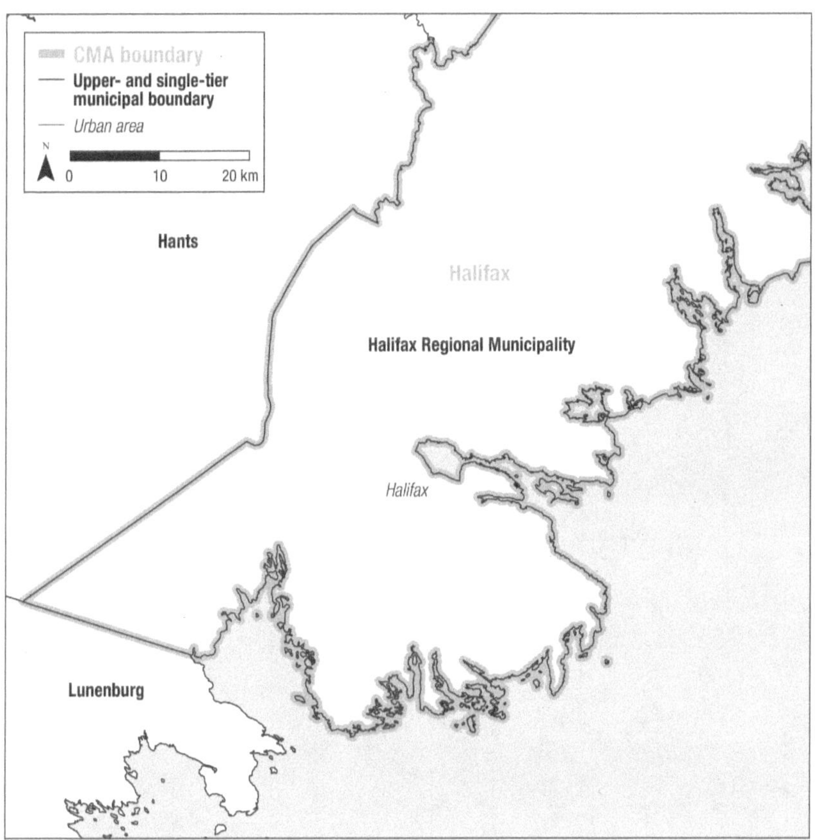

Map 9 Halifax

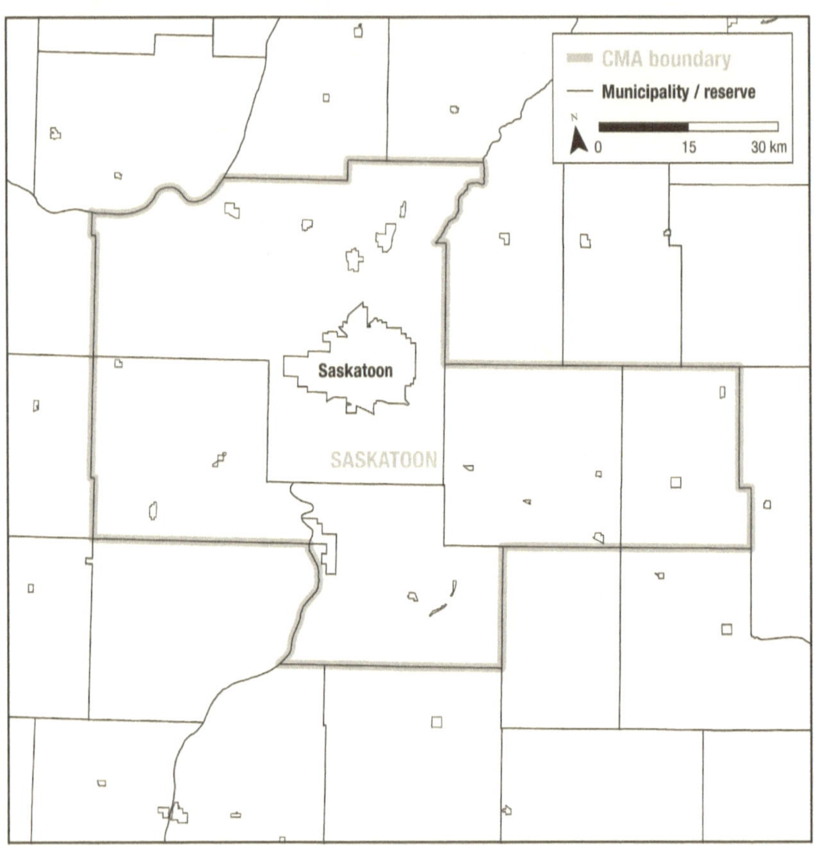

Map 10 Saskatoon

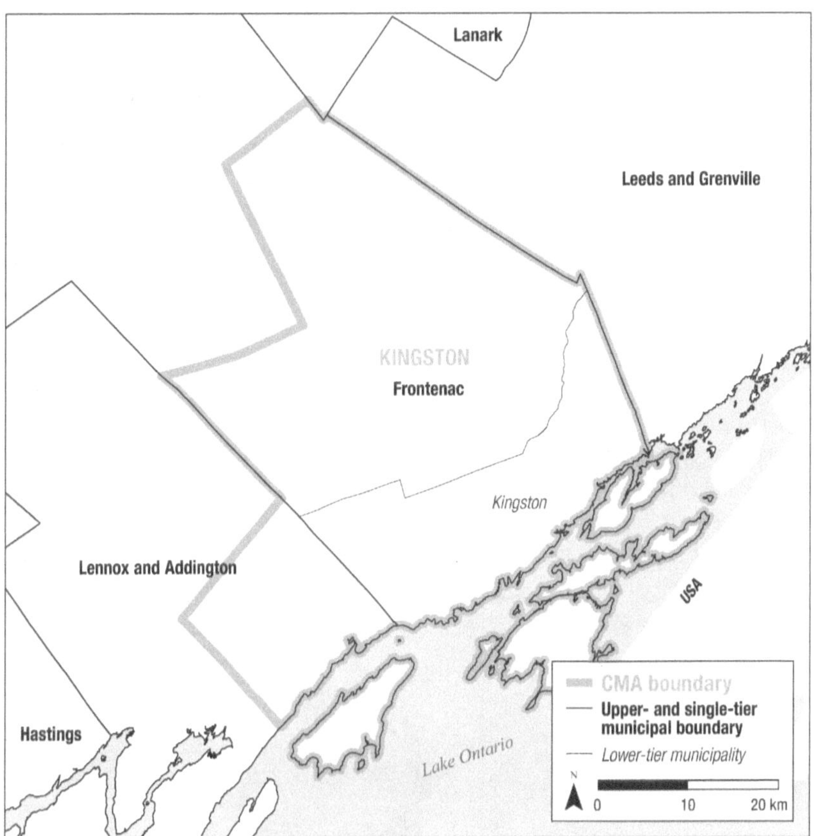

Map 11 Kingston

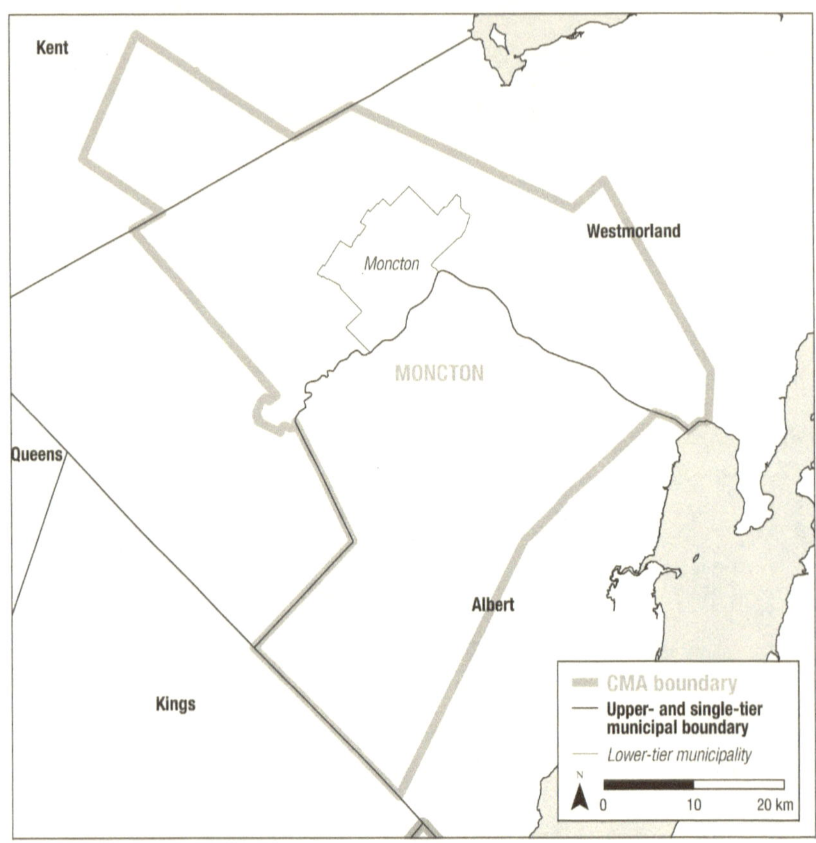

Map 12 Moncton

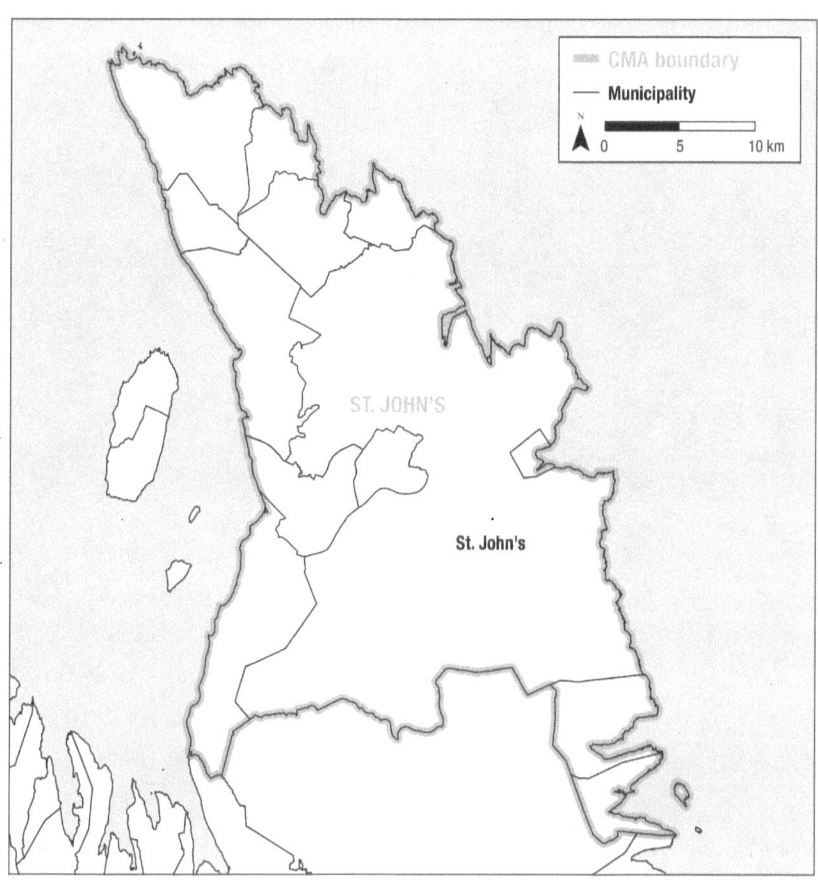

Map 13 St John's

Contributors

Caroline Andrew is the director of the Centre on Governance at the University of Ottawa. Her research interests focus on the analysis of local government policies of equity and diversity and include an evaluation of the implementation of the Equity and Inclusion lens by the City of Ottawa, and studying the Ottawa partnership behind the Youth Futures program.

Trevor Barnes is professor and distinguished university scholar in the Department of Geography, University of British Columbia. His research interests include Vancouver's new economy and its effects on the city, the history of American geography from the Second World War through the Cold War, and a continuing interest in forest economies, primarily BC's, but also those in the Antipodes.

Yves Bourgeois is director of the Urban and Community Studies Institute at the University of New Brunswick. A graduate of UCLA (PhD), Edinburgh, Oxford, and Moncton universities, he writes on the linkages between the city and cultural identity, innovation, and growth.

Neil Bradford teaches political science at Huron University College, Western University. His research interests include place-based public policy, urban and community economic development, and multi-level governance.

Allison Bramwell is assistant professor of political science at University of North Carolina Greensboro. She specializes in urban politics, governance, and political economy, while her research interests include urban policy networks and local state-society relations, cross-sector development in complex policy areas, and the politics of workforce development.

David Doloreux is a professor in the Department of International Business at the HEC Montréal. His research interests include innovation in manufacturing and service industries and the factors that influence innovation at the regional and national levels.

Betsy Donald is an associate professor of geography at Queen's University in Kingston, Ontario. She teaches and does research on the cultural economy, cities and regional development, and sustainable food systems.

Meric S. Gertler is president of the University of Toronto. Prior to that he was dean of arts and science at the University of Toronto. He served as co-director of the ISRN's two major collaborative research initiatives from 2001 to 2011.

Jill L. Grant is professor of planning at Dalhousie University in Halifax, Nova Scotia. Her research interests include development trends in Canadian suburbs, health and the built environment, and the factors that attract musicians and artists to Halifax. She is the author or editor of four books and dozens of articles.

Rob Greenwood is executive director of public management at the Leslie Harris Centre of Regional Policy and Development at Memorial University of Newfoundland in St John's.

Heather Hall is a postdoctoral fellow in the International Centre for Northern Governance and Development, University of Saskatchewan in Saskatoon. Her research interests include the politics of regional development as well as planning and economic development in peripheral cities and regions.

Tom Hutton is professor in the Centre for Human Settlements and School of Community & Regional Planning, University of British Columbia, and an associate of the Peter Wall Institute for Advanced Studies, UBC. Dr Hutton's research is concerned with the cultural economy of the city, with recent work including articles on creative industries and labour, the influence of space and built environment on the shaping of new industry formation, and the role of the inner city in cultural development.

Juan-Luis Klein is head of the Center for Research on Social Innovations (Centre de recherche sur les innovations sociales, CRISES) and professor in the Department of Geography at the Université du Québec à Montréal. He is in charge of the Geographie contemporaine Series published by the Presses de l'Université du Québec and has authored or co-authored several books and articles on the topic of regional development, local initiatives, and social innovation.

Cooper H. Langford is faculty professor in communication and culture at the University of Calgary. His previous appointments include vice president for research, University of Calgary, and director of Physical and Mathematical Sciences at NSERC. His research focuses on innovation and knowledge flows.

Ben Li has diverse interests as a member of the University of Calgary InnoLab, as a policy and communication analyst at the Legislative Assembly of Alberta, and as a social media consultant, holding degrees in biology, political science, and open-source innovation.

Peter W.B. Phillips, an international political economist, is professor of public policy in the Johnson Shoyama Graduate School of Public Policy at the University of Saskatchewan. He undertakes research on governing transformative innovation, including biotechnology regulation and policy, innovation systems, intellectual property, supply chain management, and trade policy.

Norma M. Rantisi is a professor in the Department of Geography at Concordia University. Her research interests are centred on urban economic development, and her research focuses on socio-spatial organization of the contemporary circus arts and apparel industries. She is examining how contemporary economic development policy and practice are shaping the evolution of these industries, as well as how neoliberal governance approaches are altering the nature and forms of work, in addition to the prospects for more equitable forms of development.

Camille D. Ryan is a former post-doctoral fellow with the University of Calgary and is now a professional research associate with the

Department of Bioresource Policy, Business and Economics, College of Agriculture and Bioresources at the University of Saskatchewan.

Diane-Gabrielle Tremblay is Canada Research Chair on the Socio-Organizational Challenges of the Knowledge Economy (www.teluq.ca/chaireecosavoir), professor of labour economics and human resources management at the Télé-université of University of Québec, and director of the Community-University Research Alliance (www.teluq.ca/aruc-gats) on Work-Life Articulation over the Lifecourse.

Tara Vinodrai is associate professor at the University of Waterloo. Her research addresses innovation, creativity, labour markets, and economic development in urban economies. Her current projects examine design-led innovation in Canada and Denmark, and urban-rural linkages and governance models in sustainability and creativity-oriented regional economic development initiatives.

Peter Warrian is senior research fellow at the Munk School of Global Affairs, University of Toronto. He is Canada's leading academic expert on the steel industry. His research is on knowledge networks, supply chains, and engineering labour markets.

Graeme Webb is a PhD candidate in the School of Communications at Simon Fraser University.

David A. Wolfe is professor of political science at the University of Toronto Mississauga and co-director of the Innovation Policy Lab at the Munk School of Global Affairs. He was the national coordinator of the Innovation Systems Research Network from its inception until 2011 and the principal investigator on its two major collaborative research projects.

www.ingramcontent.com/pod-product-compliance
Lightning Source LLC
LaVergne TN
LVHW090759070826
844660LV00022B/1035
9781442629448